PROFESSIONAL
Vegetarian Cooking

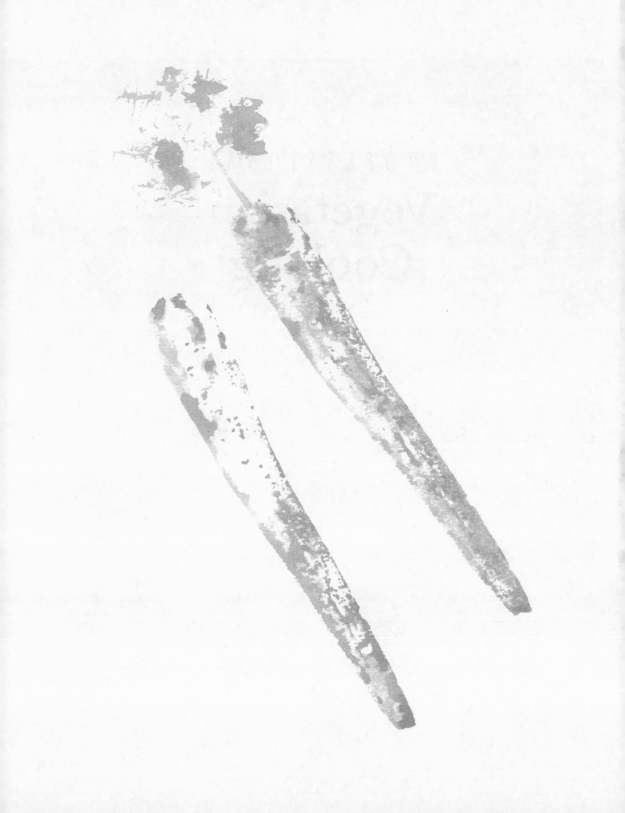

PROFESSIONAL

Vegetarian Cooking

KEN BERGERON

JOHN WILEY & SONS, INC.

New York • Chichester • Weinheim • Brisbane • Singapore • Toronto

Library of Congress Cataloging-in-Publication Data
Bergeron, Ken.
    Professional vegetarian cooking / Ken Bergeron.
        p.   cm.
    Includes bibliographical references and index.
    ISBN 0-471-29235-4 (alk. paper)
    1. Vegetarian cookery.   I. Title.
  TX837.B475   1999
  641.5′636--dc21   98-47051

Printed in the United States of America

10   9   8   7   6   5   4   3   2   1

To my wife Heidi for her ongoing support
and to my children Mariel and Will for their patience
while I worked on the manuscript.

Acknowledgments

Thanks first to my parents who provided both inspiration and encouragement for my chosen profession. Many of my earliest memories are of watching my mother cook for our large family. In between her basic duties, she also managed to bake delicious cakes and pastries. She left me with my love for cooking and serving food. Thanks to my father, who along with my mother, enthusiastically supported my decision to become a chef and who continues to be one of my best promoters. Gratitude to my brothers and my extended family who have always been willing to try whatever new food or recipe I came up with.

Thanks to my editor Pam Chirls and her editorial assistant Andrea Johnson whose skillful guidance kept the manuscript on track and on time.

For providing the introductions that led to the publishing of this book, special thanks go to Ed Quinn, of the Innerworks Company and the Path to Mastery Program, who provided the contact with Chef Wayne Umberger of the Wood Company, who facilitated my introduction to Andy Schloss, Director of Culinary Quality, also of the Wood Company, who recommended me to my original editor Amy B. Shipper.

I am especially grateful to those who tested recipes for me including Karen and Willie Althammer, Bruce Applegate, Susan Block, Margaret Chaffee, Jim Crossin and Dave Sales, Lisa Dyer, Susan Fair, Norma Fine, Barbara Frankl, Leslie Gorden, Bill Mudd, Gladys Seymour, Bonni Price, Ely Pugh, Rob Smith, Dawn Soldate, Sally Wipple, and Daniella Zandsberg.

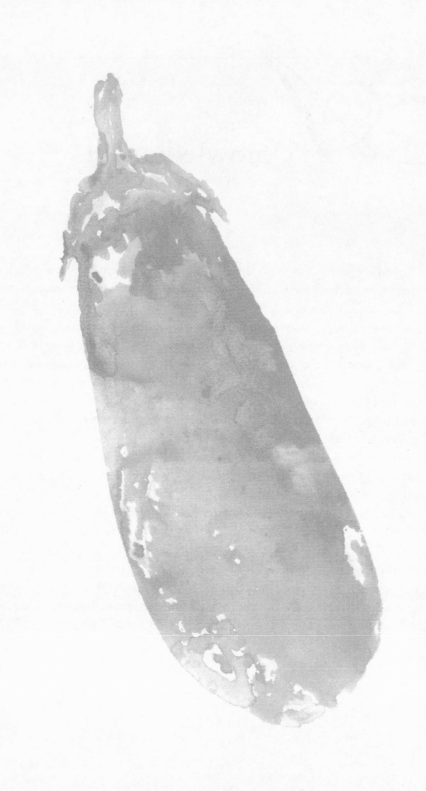

ontents

$\mathcal{R}$ecipe Contents

CHAPTER ONE

Why Serve Vegetarian Dishes?

One of the most exciting areas of cooking today focuses on elegant and delicious vegetable-based creations. Spurred on by an increasing client demand for meatless dining options, cutting-edge chefs across the country and around the world are seeking new avenues of culinary expression.

Foods from the vegetable kingdom offer more flavors than one can imagine, a full spectrum of colors and a vast variety of textures. They can provide chefs from the entire range of foodservice positions with the raw materials to fill meatless meal requests.

For several years now there have been many indicators showing the move toward a plant-based diet as being a viable dining choice. Vegetarian titles for the home cook continue to be a strong area for publishers, and many of the classic vegetarian cookbooks of the past have been revised and updated to provide better nutrition and better recipe organization. Cooking magazines regularly feature articles that focus on grains, vegetables and beans, and well-known chefs have begun to offer special vegetarian tasting menus and to write books about vegetable-based cooking.

Supermarket produce sections continue to grow in size and scope, with many offering tofu, tempeh, vegetarian-style burgers and meatless hotdogs. In the frozen food department of many supermarkets one can find frozen breakfast "meat" alternatives, meatless burgers, dairy-free sorbets and tofu-based frozen desserts. Natural foods grocery stores have an even wider variety of these and many other types of foods in recognition of this growing consumer market share. These opportunities are available to all in professional food service as well, with those who are first and/or best at providing these options most likely to enjoy success.

The public interest in health has also been an important factor in the demand for meatless menu options. The value of vegetables has been established in the effort to help keep the body free from many of the illnesses of modern times.

There are now new food pyramids that offer an all-vegetarian version and a modern interpretation of the four food groups; grains, fruits, vegetables and beans comprise the new model. Both plans endorse diets composed of plant-based foods.

College and university campuses have shown tremendous growth in meatless dining. My personal experience in this area has shown me that at some schools, if the vegetarian option is appealing enough, the percentage of students choosing a vegetarian meal could be as high as 40%. With a percentage such as this, the meals could be planned to accommodate these diners as part of the daily workload and not as an extra part of the menu for just a few. To assist those serving large numbers, several companies now make meatless meals in large- and institutional-size packaging.

The college-age group requesting meatless menu options is being referred to as Generation V—for vegetarian. Upon graduation they take their place in the dining mainstream, where those who serve food to the public will want to attract their patronage.

The youth are not the only market for this style of eating. Personal experience has shown me that there is interest in every age group and that senior citizens can be as keen about vegetarianism as younger consumers. Older diners' concern for maintaining health is often the catalyst for this trend.

Meeting the Demands and Opportunities of the Market

To begin serving this increased demand for meatless menu options, it is critical to understand the vegetarian diet and some of the most common versions being followed. This knowledge will allow you to offer dishes that your clients can order without the fear they may contain hidden meat products. Another helpful way of building your guests' trust is to understand the reasons why some people choose this style of eating, such as for health or religious beliefs. This is covered in Reasons People Choose a Vegetarian Diet (page 7). Appendix B contains a Guide for Waitstaff and Kitchen Personnel with questions to ask guests about their personal eating program in order to better serve them. These steps lay the groundwork for placing vegetarian items on the menu that will satisfy your guests and keep them coming back.

Unless indicated otherwise by specific dietary proscriptions, the flavor and seasoning of vegetarian cuisine should appeal to the mainstream palate. While some vegetarians want simply seasoned dishes, my experience shows that the majority prefer full-flavored food.

Once the dietary guidelines are understood, a simple first step to offering plant-based dishes is to scan existing menus for appropriate ingredients that can be combined for a new vegetarian option. Since most foodservice operations have vegetable components in many of the items they offer, this approach allows you to start serving vegetarian dishes without having to rewrite the menu or order special new ingredients. This way of entering the market can ease the transition to feature more meatless menu options. New ingredients can be brought in gradually, allowing the staff time to learn how they are cooked and presented. At the same time you have a chance to sample the new dishes, letting your guests help choose those to include on the permanent menu.

When dining in a restaurant without any listed vegetarian options, I often examine the menu for some of my favorite foods and see if the chef is willing to assemble a special dish for me. One such meal, for instance, drew oyster mushrooms, broccoli, garlic and linguine from separate locations on the menu. The chef used a little extra virgin olive oil and some red pepper flakes. He created a meal that was not only delicious, but because he was willing to go out of his way, he also left me with a wonderful memory as a bonus. Incidentally, the five other members of my dinner party also opted for the same dish, which meant that the chef could prepare one dish instead of possibly six, making his job a little easier. This is an example of how existing menu items can be combined and offered as a new meatless special. A dish such as this can be added to a special insert or menu board, making the ordering process simpler and letting your guests know that your vegetarian program has begun.

Pizza, pasta, salads, baked potatoes, rice and vegetable side dishes now form parts of most menus, and can be served as is or tailored to the tastes of the clients by removing or replacing any meat or meat stock that may be in the recipe. Because these are familiar choices to many vegetarians, you might consider how to make your renditions stand out from the rest. One way is to garnish them with select items such as specialty mushrooms, sundried tomatoes, flavored oils or interesting vinaigrettes.

After my own change to a vegetarian diet I began working at a natural foods store and found myself faced with an enormous number of new and unfamiliar ingredients. This situation provided me with a great culinary challenge. Having reached a respectable level of mainstream cooking knowledge and skill, I was eager to attain that same level with vegetarian cooking. Also faced with preparing new versions of meatless diets at that time, I experienced the anxiety one feels when serving meatless meals to clients when it is not one's regular business. A great resource has been the many chefs and cooks who shared their knowledge, saving me years of trial and error. While this applies to special ingredients and techniques, there are many classical recipes that fit the parameters of vegetarian menu items or that need only a slight modification to do so.

As we begin to serve vegetarian items we avail ourselves of the benefit of increased business from these guests. Another benefit comes from the additional business that vegetarian clients generate when they return with family or friends. Consider that those seeking plant-based dining choices dine out with co-workers and business associates, and that these parties seek out an establishment where there is something on the menu for everyone. Therefore, a group of four or six people, with one following a vegetarian diet, could provide a restaurant with a much larger increase in business due to the availability of meatless menu items.

There are also opportunities to increase sales by catering special events such as weddings and birthdays. These events can represent considerable income when one becomes known for these services. For example, one of the largest catered events is the North American Vegetarian Society's annual "Vegetarian Summerfest." The Summerfest, held at a different college campus each year, brings together nationally and internationally known speakers on many aspects of vegetarianism, along with many of the best vegetarian chefs in the country. Each day features related workshops, cooking demonstrations and activities. The dining staff may provide from 4,000 to 9,000 totally meatless meals in the course of a week's time.

Many other events held throughout the country by local vegetarian societies range from large regional conferences that may attract a couple thousand people for a one-day event, to small monthly meetings at an area restaurant.

In addition to the invaluable good will and "word of mouth" advertising from your new loyal customers, your creativity and willingness to provide vegetarian meals may be of interest to area newspaper and magazine food editors who can provide another priceless link to potential business. Others interested in your offerings may include your local heart association, area colleges and of course any local vegetarian societies or chapters of EarthSave, who will applaud and support your endeavors.

My membership in the Connecticut Chefs Association, the local chapter of the American Culinary Federation (ACF), and taking part in ACF and international culinary competitions has been of great benefit as far as publicity, business contacts and continued culinary education are concerned. Any way that you can make people aware of your new meatless menu options including in-house signs, menu inserts, table tents or the personal touch of having your waitstaff describe them will further improve your success.

Another reason why serving meatless meals makes good business sense is that it can be done with a relatively low food cost, especially when the dishes are based on grains, beans and legumes, or pasta. For many dishes the more expensive vegetables, nuts or specialty mushrooms can play a supporting role as a garnish. And even these types of ingredients can be selected to balance the overall menu cost or be chosen to fit with the average cost of other menu offerings. For example, a high-end restaurant may use wild mushrooms and macadamia nuts, while an establishment serving moderate- to low-priced foods could use white mushrooms and sunflower seeds in place of the high-cost items to achieve similar tastes and textures. See a note on less expensive substitutions in the Ingredients Chapter.

In the last decade, several restaurants in New York City, a number in California and a sprinkling across the country have found a niche serving complete vegetarian menus. The restaurant business is notoriously difficult to succeed in, yet these businesses have shown that a sound menu, good service and an attractive setting can make meatless cuisine work.

Redefining the "Center of the Plate" with Elegant Vegetable-Based Dishes

The term "center of the plate" refers to the main ingredient or focal point of a dish. In the past this has usually referred to an animal source of protein accompanied by one or two vegetables and a starch such as potatoes or rice. This way of viewing a dish can be accomplished using plant-based components by shifting the focus to different types of vegetable, grain, pasta, bean and alternative protein-based entrees, pairing them with a distinguished vegetable side dish or salad and presenting them in an elegant way.

Contemporary presentation has provided new ways to display cuisine. A nod to classical plating sees assembling the components in separate mounds, placed as if they were at different time on the face of a clock. To add a modern approach, large plates are used and the foods are arranged closer to each other at the plates' center to maintain heat. Departures from this way of serving food include creations that use the center of the plate as a hub from which extends portions of the main course underlined by a base of either cooked or salad greens, with other ingredients interspersed with the main course for color and textural variety. Progressing from this type of display, one sees dishes presented in even more layers, sometimes hiding taste surprises in their midst. The gradual ascent of foods upwards from the plate is culminated by those masters of architectural cuisine whose food seems to hover over the dish. The many styles of culinary artists are also played out with sauces and herbs that are spooned, squirted, piped and strewn onto their creations.

Some examples are to serve White Bean Chili with Caramelized Onions along with Ruby Grapefruit, Pomegranate and Assorted Greens, Tofu Pecan Cutlets stacked against Gingered Butternut Squash on a base of Brazilian-Style Greens sauced with Thai Coconut Sauce, Vegetable Bouillabaisse with Black Olive Crostini, Oyster Fried Mushrooms served over Winter Vegetable Pancakes with Watermelon Catsup, and Hazelnut Squash Ravioli with Wild Mushroom Sauce on a bed of Red Swiss Chard Sauté with Garlic.

Getting enough protein and other nutrients when following a vegetarian diet is simply a matter of eating a variety of foods that supply the necessary protein, building amino acids along with the required amounts of carbohydrates, minerals, vitamins and other nutrients. Beans and/or grains can be eaten throughout the course of a day instead of having to be present at every meal. The value of fiber and the special health-maintaining qualities of many vegetables are recognized as an important part of the overall diet.

While healthy foods may be an important consideration to a restaurateur or caterer, the issue of serving balanced meals is critical to those serving the same clients for more than one meal per day. These chefs have the opportunity to spread out the nutritional needs through the course of a day's menu, and may wish to consult with a dietitian to insure that a sound diet is provided.

Reasons People Choose a Vegetarian Diet

There are many reasons why people choose a vegetarian diet, and these reasons can influence the type of diet they follow. The major reasons are health, religious proscription, cultural practice and moral or ecological concerns.

HEALTH REASONS FOR A VEGETARIAN DIET

When health is the reason for adopting a meatless eating plan, there can be many underlying causes. Some people follow this diet as part of a heart disease reversal program. Some do so to gain more energy or to slow the effects of aging. Both the government and the healthcare establishment in recent years have recognized the benefits of a plant-based diet. Many studies have observed that this way of eating is a natural diet for people in other parts of the world, and that it not only sustains life, but it can actually aid people in avoiding many of the most common western illnesses.

RELIGIOUS REASONS FOR A VEGETARIAN DIET

Religion plays a part in the reason many choose not to consume flesh foods. The major religious groups that prescribe a meatless diet include the Buddhists, the Taoists, Hindus and Jains. Certain sects of Judaism, Islam and Christianity do so as as well. Worldwide, these groups account for hundreds of millions of people. Their traditions of preparing food often include great recipes and are a wonderful resource for vegetarian dishes. One of the main reasons that these cuisines are so well developed is that often they have existed for hundreds to thousands of years.

The vegetarian cuisine of India has entire books chronicling the recipes of its repertoire and it abounds with the flavor of its regional spices. Indian restaurants in the U.S. offer many vegetarian menu choices, with some devoting the entire menu to Indian vegetarian cuisine. Such dining experiences are a great source of inspiration for chefs interested in developing their meatless recipe file.

Specialized vegetarian cooking also has emerged from temples of China and Japan to offer the first vegetarian cuisine to mimic the tastes and textures of flesh foods by using soy bean curd (tofu). From Japan comes a 600-year-old tradition of cooking that originated in the Zen Temples called Shojin Ryori, which the March/April 1996 issue of *Yoga Journal* hailed as "...now the hottest rage in Japanese haute cuisine." This style of cuisine aims to assist the practitioner in spiritual progress, which is how its Japanese name, Shojin Ryori, translates. Shojin cooking like any great cuisine seeks to offer satisfying meals composed of a variety of tastes and textures. Rice cooked with chestnuts might be served with braised shiitake mushrooms, deep fried sweet potatoes and nori squares, sake braised asparagus in broth and a portion of pickled daikon radish. While some may consider this style of cooking to be austere, it evolved to enable those in the religious centers to dine with enjoyment and in appreciation of the seasons, also of great importance to this cuisine's heritage. We see the integrity of these ideas reflected in our cuisine today with attention to organic farming, cooking by the seasons and trying to preserve the true flavors of the best produce available.

Another style of cookery to rise from this same lineage is called Kaiseki, which was originally reserved for the royalty of Japan. Kaiseki's trademark is the plating of foods in small beautiful, almost gem-like settings which, incidentally, influenced Nouvelle Cuisine.

Moral Reasons for a Vegetarian Diet

Many people forgo meat for moral reasons. They are usually as particular about not wanting to consume any animal products as those who have religious reasons. Many chefs are familiar with the concept of Kosher cooking or cooking for people with certain food allergies. Perhaps when viewed from this perspective the vegetarian diet can be better understood. With these ideas in mind we can see that it is very important to those to whom we serve vegetarian meals that their wishes be respected.

Environmental Reasons for a Vegetarian Diet

Concern for the environment motivates still others to adopt a plant-based eating program. Such people observe that fewer natural resources are used when people choose to follow a meatless diet. They are also concerned with doing the least amount of harm to the earth when raising their food. Through organic farming, sustainable agriculture and trying to maintain an unpolluted ecosystem, their goal is to be able to pass on to future generations a planet that still functions.

The concept of organic farming is certainly not new to the many chefs throughout the country already supporting local organic farmers. These farmers in turn provide the chefs with otherwise unavailable types of quality produce. At my restaurant we bought from several local organic farmers. They brought items such as More Gold Pumpkins—a delicious sweet variety that I never had heard of—yellow tomatoes, various chiles, wild edible plants like lamb's quarters that grew on their property, wonderful sundried tomatoes and the season's best berries, including yellow raspberries. These are just a few of the more unusual items they delivered, along with many other herbs, vegetables and even edible flowers. We purchased most of their crop when the season was at its peak for production and prices were reasonable.

Different Types of Vegetarian Diets

The word vegetarian refers to a way of eating that employs plant-based menu items and may also be characterized as a meatless diet. According to the North American Vegetarian Society, in the U.S. over 12 million people prefer a diet entirely free from meat or meat byproducts. Also, many people today do not follow a vegetarian diet full-time but choose to eat meatless meals on a regular basis. At my former restaurant I estimate that 75 percent or more of the people who dined there did not follow a completely vegetarian diet.

There are many different types of diets within the scope of vegetarianism. Some of those main types are: Vegan, Ovo-Vegetarian, Lacto-Vegetarian, Ovo-Lacto-Vegetarian, Natural Hygiene, Raw Foods and Macrobiotic.

VEGAN (ALSO STRICT OR PURE VEGETARIAN)

A vegan diet excludes meat, poultry and fish and their byproducts such as gelatin, stocks and bases. In addition, the vegan diet excludes eggs and dairy products and their byproducts such as lactose, casein and dried egg whites or yolks used in baking. Many people who follow a vegan diet also avoid white cane sugar, as it is often filtered through charred animal bones. Others exclude honey from their vegan diets as it is an animal product; some also forgo yeast. Many food products that sound like they would be appropriate for the vegan diet such as soy cheese may contain some dairy byproducts such as casein or whey. Chefs also need to be aware and make their staff aware that sauces that contain butter or cream should not be added to a vegan menu item. Chef colleagues have recounted stories of preparing a vegan dish that they then passed on to a line cook, who doused it with an inappropriate sauce or stock, thus canceling out their work. When planning menu additions, vegan dishes serve the widest variety of vegetarian diets. It is also easier for the serving staff because they can recommend these items to those following ovo-vegetarian, lacto-vegetarian, and ovo-lacto-vegetarian diets.

OVO-VEGETARIAN DIET

Ovo refers to eggs; therefore an ovo-vegetarian diet includes eggs. The use of eggs, but not milk, in the diet is characteristic of the vegetarian cooking styles of China, Japan, and their surrounding countries. For some people the use of eggs in a vegetarian diet may only mean eggs that are from free-range hens that are organically fed.

LACTO-VEGETARIAN DIET

Lacto refers to milk and dairy products; therefore a lacto-vegetarian diet includes milk and dairy products. For some people the use of milk or dairy products in a vegetarian diet is restricted to those products from certified organic farms employing humane farming practices. Owing to religious reasons the use of milk in the diet but not eggs is particular to some of the vegetarian cooking styles of India.

LACTO-OVO-VEGETARIAN DIET

Lacto-ovo is a vegetarian diet that includes both dairy products and eggs. This type of diet may be followed in the same way as those vegetarian diets that include only dairy products or eggs. Having taken into account some of the reasons and rules for including these items in a vegetarian diet, most chefs know to cook with these items and would be able to accommodate guests following this way of eating.

NATURAL HYGIENE

Natural Hygiene is a vegetarian diet system that stresses combining certain foods to promote digestion and absorption of nutrients. Fruit is usually eaten first thing in the morning and not combined with any other food. At lunch and dinner either high-protein foods such as tofu or beans are combined with vegetables or high-carbohydrate foods such as rice or barley are taken together with vegetables, but carbohydrate-rich and protein-rich foods are not combined. Raw foods are stressed, as are foods of organic origin.

RAW FOODS

Practitioners of this vegetarian diet have a style of cuisine that is entirely made up of raw fruits, vegetables and sprouts, using some of the principals of Natural Hygiene. Many interesting and tasty recipes from soups to desserts have been devised by raw food chefs.

The types of vegetarian diets mentioned so far include general guidelines to give a better understanding of the vegetarian way of eating. Some people also follow one of these diets with additional adjustments due to allergies or other personal reasons for avoiding certain foods. Whatever reason a guest has for following a vegetarian diet, I have found that when they are treated with integrity and presented with a tasty meal that conforms to their specific needs they become loyal customers.

MACROBIOTICS

Many people have heard of this type of diet and while the cooking does not employ strong spices it is not just brown rice either. While at first this diet may seem full of challenges it is also full of opportunity to serve more clients and learn some great cooking ideas.

What is macrobiotics? The philosophy of macrobiotics studies the correlation of diet and lifestyle to health and well-being. While not a strict vegetarian program, a macrobiotic diet can be completely vegetarian and is for the most part a diet composed of plant-based menu items. Macrobiotics maintains that by observing the natural whole foods diets of traditional cultures we can find clues that show us how to eat in a balanced way and maintain or regain health and well-being.

A complete meal is often referred to in restaurants as the macro-platter, and it is made up of about 50% whole grain such as organic brown rice, millet, barley and/or other whole grains. In addition there is usually a protein source such as beans, tofu or tempeh, with root vegetables like carrots or parsnips, sea vegetables such as nori, arame, or kombu/kelp, and a leafy green vegetable like kale or collards. To round out the meal are some miso soup, a little pickle to aid digestion and a sprinkle of a condiment such as gomasio, made of toasted sesame seed and sea salt. Bancha tea made from twigs is a preferred beverage. Organic ingredients are preferred and pressure cooking the method of choice for beans and grains. The traditional foods of many cultures from around the world are included, with a strong Japanese influence.

At my former restaurant, we made a sincere effort to serve the macrobiotic meals and were rewarded with their steady patronage and increased culinary knowledge. I was able to learn about new ingredients, like sea vegetables, along with new cooking methods and techniques which have become part of my repertoire.

CHAPTER TWO

Ingredients

Vegetarian cuisine has some fairly unique

elements, such as the protein alternative style

dishes that have been developed. It also reflects

mainstream cuisine, combing the world for new

tastes and techniques, and exploring kitchen

traditions from around the world for unique flavor

profiles and potential for cross-cultural seasonings.

This culinary approach might study the cuisine of France, Italy, China, India and Japan, as well as South American and Middle Eastern nations, and then feature accurate portrayals of historic recipes and or intertwine ingredients and techniques from different backgrounds for new gustatory sensations.

Ethnic kitchens provide many vegetable-based dining possibilities. From these sources have come many staple vegetarian ingredients. Some examples of Asian origin would be protein-rich tofu, silken tofu, miso and tempeh. While foods like these offer menu diversity they are not always needed to provide fine plant-based dining.

Another important development has chefs forming partnerships with local organic farmers. The farmers deliver great-tasting and sometimes unique produce when the growing season is at its peak, and the chefs get wonderful produce when prices are generally at their best. There are also many ecological reasons for forming these alliances and they can be accessed from the Committee for Sustainable Agriculture, P. O. Box 1300, Colfax, CA 95713. A key word to look for in the future when purchasing ingredients for vegetarian meals is *Veganics,* which is organic farming without the use of any animal byproducts such as bone meal or manure throughout the entire process.

USE OF INGREDIENTS

A recipe is a set of guidelines for us to prepare a certain dish. For the recipe to come out as intended the ingredients should be as close as possible to those used by the author. With many ingredients the flavor, texture, and the way they respond to the cooking or baking process changes from batch to batch and season to season. This is especially true of less processed natural foods.

Ingredients

PURE WATER

In the process of cooking, water is often a major ingredient. Whether used to blanch, boil or steam foods or as the body for stocks or soups, much of cooking depends upon water. It is important, therefore, to use water from a pure and good-tasting source.

Some kitchens have good-tasting well water which, when regularly tested and free from contamination, represents the ideal situation. Bottled spring water probably would be a good solution for those kitchens that do a small volume of cooking and where expense is not a major concern.

Municipally treated tap water is monitored for contamination, but while it is important to chlorinate water to make it safe for consumption, the residual chlorine may add a bleach taste to food. Also, some areas have tap water with a noticeable sulfur smell.

At my former restaurant and in my home I use a solid carbon, point-of-use water filter. It is an effective and affordable method to purify and remove flavors from tap water used for drinking or cooking.

VEGETABLES

In general, vegetables are best when they are picked and used in their peak season. It is important to be aware that produce can change in flavor and texture from batch to batch and season to season, and to "season to taste" accordingly.

Avocados

The small, dark-green-when-ripe Haas avocados seem to have the best flavor. Split in half lengthwise and tap the pit with the base of a chef's knife so it just sticks, then twist and remove. Peel and slice or scoop out the avocado as called for in the recipe.

Root vegetables

Root vegetables can be purchased and used in their peak season. They also hold well when kept in cool, dark, dry, ventilated storage. Their firm solid texture and sweet earthy flavor make root vegetables great candidates for sautéing or roasting, which takes advantage of their high sugar content and brings out their natural sweetness. Drawing up flavor and minerals from the earth makes root vegetables a valuable addition that differs nutritionally from other vegetables.

Carrots have perhaps the broadest range in western-style cooking. They may be juiced for beverages and reduction sauces, oven roasted or grilled, sautéed in mirepoix for soups, or grated raw for salads, pancakes and cake batter. Joining carrots in their potential for many of these menu possibilities are parsnips, rutabaga and turnips, with special use for burdock, a long root that is usually less than 1 inch/2.5 centimeters in diameter with a strong earthy taste.

Potatoes

While not truly roots, the tubers, potatoes, sweet potatoes and yams, can be explored for their varied tastes, colors and textures. According to a friend from Peru—the native land of the potato—there are over 200 varieties there alone, with many other hybrids through out the world. Among the many popular varieties available in our markets are the waxy types such as yellow Finn or Yukon gold, Red bliss and other red-skinned potatoes, purple Peruvian, great for potato salads or gnocchi and the drier starchy white russet type that is the standard baking potato. Other varieties of small or baby potatoes such as the banana fingerling are popular with cutting-edge chefs.

Another product made with potatoes that I thought was gone from my panty forever is instant flakes, which work well as a thickener in potato-based soups or in place of wheat flour when needed.

Sweet potatoes and yams, both of the same family, appear in markets as Red Garnet, Red Jewel, and Ruby Red yams, with yellow types sometimes available, all excellent to use in the recipes.

Leafy greens

These are greens that are generally cooked including kale, collards, mustard greens, turnip greens, beet greens, spinach, green and red Swiss chard, broccoli and broccoli rabe, Chinese cabbage, bok choi and napa. Cook quickly to keep color and maintain vitamins. If using lemon or other citrus juice or vinegar for seasoning, add them at the end of cooking to keep the acid from tarnishing the color. Greens make a great base for grains, roasted vegetables, and to serve an entrée in a "stacked" fashion.

Onion family

Onion family members should be firm to the touch and free from bruises and deterioration. When the bulb begins to sprout, it is an indication of deterioration. Once the sprout appears the bulb will deteriorate. Store bulb onions such as white, red, Spanish, very sweet Vidalia types, and garlic bulbs and shallots in a cool, dry, dark place. Scallions and leeks can be stored in the refrigerator. If the storage area becomes very warm in summer months, store in the refrigerator during this period. Keep onions away from potatoes in storage as potatoes give off gases that hasten the decaying process of the onions.

Garlic This potent member of the onion family is more popular than ever. I use caution when adding raw garlic to pesto, hummus and other formulas that won't be cooked for several reasons. The first is that garlic in the raw state can carry harmful (potentially fatal) botulism bacteria that thrives in an anaerobic environment, which is created when minced garlic is stored in oil and then allowed to stay in the unsafe temperature zone of 40° to 140°F (4.4° to 60°C). Other concerns are that raw garlic can easily overpower the other flavors in a dish and some people have trouble digesting large doses. On the plus side is garlic's inimitable big flavor. Used in cooked dishes minced, diced or sliced, it is generally sautéed to tame its pungent flavor and take advantage of its wonderful aroma.

Choose garlic bulbs that are firm to the touch and do not show any signs of green sprouts coming from the top or pointed end of the bulb. The sprouts change the flavor to a bitter "green" taste. If green sprouts show at the tips of the individual cloves, split them lengthwise and remove the entire shoot.

To separate the cloves, press the bulb's pointed end firmly down on a cutting board and they will all come apart. To peel, whack the cloves with the side of a chef's knife, loosening the papery skin, which will then slide off.

To chop large amounts of garlic, put peeled cloves into a food processor and chop. Garlic can be covered with oil and keep refrigerated if the precautions for raw garlic listed above are heeded. As a further precaution, remove only the amount needed in a recipe. Chopped garlic is now available commercially, with water and citric acid added to preserve it.

Roasted whole in bulbs, garlic cloves can be squeezed from their papery cover onto bread and served with extra virgin olive oil or used in other recipes.

Leeks   The flavor of leeks has been long appreciated in France and the British Isles. Menus today feature leeks in their traditional role in soups and as wrappers in terrines, and for modern plate presentations leeks are julienne, fried and piled in haystack fashion as a garnish. Leeks tend to be sandy and need to be cleaned well between the layers.

Red onions   Great for their color and flavor, red onions are especially good when added raw to salads like Avocado Orange and Red Onion Salad (page 173) and more substantial entrée-type salads such as tabouli (page 306), sautéed and added to Salad Rouge with Glazed Red Onions and Walnuts (page 179). Red onions can be tamed a little by marinating them in red wine vinegar, as in Orange Sesame Udon Noodles (page 276).

Scallions or green onions   These are used in cooked dishes, added all at once or with the white part added early in the recipe as for onion and the green part added toward the end like a fresh herb. Also, scallions can be thinly sliced and added as a garnish, especially to grain and bean dishes.

Shallots   Shallots boast a subtle and unique onion flavor that has long been a favorite in French cuisine, especially for sauces.

Vidalia   The Vidalia from Georgia is one example of a super-sweet onion variety. Other sweet varieties include the Walla Walla from Washington state and the Maui from Hawaii.

Salad Greens

Salad greens may be various shades of green, red or white. Romaine, Boston and red-and green-leaf lettuce have been joined by raddiccio, Belgium endive, oak leaf, arugala, frisée, mizuna, peacock kale, baby beet and red Swiss chard leaves. Many others are available for salads individually or in a mixture called mesclun or Spring Mix.

Squash

There are many varieties of squash available, falling into two basic categories. Summer squash are best eaten young and small while their skins and seeds are still tender and their interior is still firm, soft and juicy. This group includes the various types of green and golden zucchini, yellow crookneck and yellow summer squash. Delicata and patty pan are other varieties that are best consumed when young and soft-skinned. Spaghetti squash, with its noodle-like edible interior, has a longer shelf life, but is often available before the winter squash makes its debut and has a long growing season. Summer squash varieties, lacking the long-term keeping qualities of their winter cousins, are usually best for taste and price when consumed in season. A bonus of the summer growing season are edible squash blossoms, which can be fried with or without a stuffing.

The hard-skinned winter squash types require a longer growing time to be mature enough to eat. Their skins, when still tender, may be consumed, but are usually removed either before or after cooking. Their seeds, which are also generally discarded, can be roasted for a snack or used as a garnish. This selection includes butternut, green and golden acorn, hubbard and buttercup squashes, along with the small dense sugar pumpkins of New England. Especially good are the More Gold and the kabocha-type pumpkins of Japan, including the Hokkaido. Large jack-o-lantern pumpkins are not grown for eating but for display. The winter squash flavor and sugar content change season to season, so sometimes the cook needs to make adjustments to get the same flavor when they "season to taste."

If a cool, dark storage space is available, and a particularly good crop is ready, one may be able to buy several months' supply of winter squash at a good price. This type of arrangement helps both local organic farmers and chefs.

Cute tender miniature or 'baby' squash of both the winter and summer types provide another option especially for an elegant occasion. They can be cooked whole, halved, fanned or stuffed.

FRUIT

One of the main concerns when purchasing fruit is its degree of ripeness. Ripe fruit is at the point of fullest flavor and sweetness. It is important to use ripe fruit quickly, since once it ripens it begins to deteriorate.

Some fruit are picked ripe. When purchasing, the amount of time before the fruit is used in your recipe must be considered. If you have several days before you need the fruit for a recipe, then for certain fruit you may have time to ripen it.

Apples

There are many kinds of apples with regional varieties that only appear locally. A good place to start getting to know apples is to visit local orchards. By tasting their fruit and noting the characteristics of each type such as sweetness, tartness, the perception of other fruit flavors and texture that may be crisp, soft, dry or juicy, one can begin to understand how the apples will work in recipes. Apples are generally divided into two main groups: those good for eating out of hand or in salads, and those good for cooking and baking into pies, cakes and pastries, with subcategories for applesauce and cider. Some orchards provide charts that indicate an apple's best use.

If your supply is limited to just a few varieties, sometimes cooking time and the size of the apple pieces cut for a recipe can allow you to use varieties on hand. Also, when very ripe, most apples tend to lose their crispness.

Fall is the prime season for apples in North America, however, they are kept throughout the year in atmospherically controlled cold storage rooms. Some varieties I use from Connecticut and New England are Braeburn, Red and Green Delicious, Fuji, Macoun, Macintosh, Ida Red, Granny Smith, Mutsu and Rome.

Berries

Blueberries can be washed ahead of time in a bowl of cool water, removing stems and any other debris. They're great for cakes, pies and cobblers.

Raspberries need gentle handling. If possible wash just before use. Great taste and color are available in yellow and other varieties.

Strawberries should be uniform in color with no white shoulders. Wash with hulls on to prevent them from becoming waterlogged. Look for Alpine and other heirloom varieties for full flavor.

Mangoes

This fruit should be orange to red when ripe, soft to the touch and aromatic. Mangoes are great as a sliced garnish or as a puree for desserts.

Pears

Pears are generally picked before they are ripe in order to ship with a minimum of bruising. They ripen well; ripe fruit can be determined by a fragrant aroma and a slightly soft stem end. Left out at room temperature, they will usually ripen in three to four days. They can be coaxed to ripen a little faster by placing them in a bag or covering them to trap their natural gases, which hastens the process. Some common pear varieties are: Anjou, Bartlett, Bosc, Comice and Seckel.

Watermelon

The seedless varieties make this delicious fruit easy to use in recipes. Thump for a hollow sound as a ripeness check.

SEA VEGETABLES/EDIBLE SEAWEED

Sea vegetables are one of the most exciting discoveries I've made since starting to cook exclusively vegetarian cuisine. They may be used as vegetables and also as "new" herbs with the ability to impart the taste of seafood to vegetarian cuisine. I prefer calling these edible ocean plants sea vegetables because people are sometimes put off by the name seaweed.

From 80 main varieties come over 250 different types of edible sea vegetables found in the oceans throughout the world. Traditionally these highly nutritious and low-calorie underwater vegetables have been consumed only by those people living in proximity to the sea. With the emergence of East-West cuisine, the popularity of the sushi bar and the search for a new and clean food supply, more of these sea-dwelling delicacies are coming to market.

In the U.S., especially from the coast of Maine, come examples such as dulse and kelp, which are smoked as well as sundried, along with other varieties known to native peoples. From Japan and the South Pacific, where most of the world's edible sea vegetables come from, some crop-leading varieties are kombu, hijiki and nori. Nori is used to make the popular sheets for wrapping around rice to make sushi.

Agar or agar agar

Called kanten in Japanese, this is a sea vegetable-derived gelatin that comes in sticks, flakes and powder. It is used to make gelatin dishes, to thicken puddings and pie fillings, and as a thickener in savory presentations. The flakes or sticks need to be simmered to dissolve, and are best for dessert; the stronger flavored powder is best used in savory presentations.

Ao nori, green nori, sea cress

These flakes have a mild seafood flavor great for soups, sauces and coated with bread crumbs for a fried seafood effect. They are very firm in texture and benefit from being ground finer in a spice grinder or in a blender.

Arame

This dark sea vegetable comes in shredded lengths about the size of angel hair pasta. The savory flavor runs from mild to strong, and some brands may need to be soaked and drained before using. Arame works well with soy, ginger and sesame oil as a vegetable side, added to pancakes, or tossed with salad or sautéed greens.

Dulse

This native to the northern coast of Maine up into Canada has a briny, distinct flavor that is great for soups, tomato sauce, and breading to create a shrimp flavor. Pan-fried or toasted, it can be sprinkled on grain or boiled potatoes or used on a dulse, lettuce and tomato sandwich. Also available is a smoked variety that imparts the taste of smoked salmon to a dish.

Hijiki

This black sea vegetable has a somewhat metallic taste that is tamed by soaking and draining the soak water. (Pour discarded water onto potted herbs, plants or onto a garden.) Cook as a side vegetable with onions, carrots, ginger, soy sauce, a little sweetener, and sesame oil; serve as is or tossed with salad or sautéed greens.

Kelp or kombu

There are many varieties in the kelp family—called kombu in Japanese—consisting of dried dark green strips in various widths depending on the variety. Kelp adds a seafood flavor to dishes. In small amounts kelp will be undetectable in taste yet provide a natural flavor-enhancing quality; however, in large quantities it can overwhelm the flavor of a dish. This dried mineral-rich plant is used in cooking after it has been re-hydrated by soaking in water or by being added to boiling water and then removed once it has been cut into serving size pieces. Slippery when wet, knives can bounce off its rubbery texture. Cook beans with a small piece of kelp, because its natural mineral makeup will soften beans, making them easier to digest. Smoked kelp is available from Maine.

Nori, asakusa-nori

This is the nori used as a rolling mat in sushi and because of this use it is the most popular sea vegetable with over seven billion sheets consumed annually. Toasting brings out the flavor and can be done by quickly and cautiously fanning the sheets over a heated burner until they are fragrant and a golden green. The toasted sheets can be cut into fancy shapes and used to garnish miso and other soups, salads and grain dishes.

There are many other varieties of sea vegetables, with great flavors like wakame, or colors like tosakanori, which is a stunning red algae. Check Japanese, macrobiotic and natural foods cookbooks and suppliers.

Sea vegetables to add a seafood/flavor of the sea

Sea vegetable	Flavor	Use
arame	seafood	side vegetable, salads, pancakes
dulse	seafood, shrimp	chowder, sauces, breading
hijiki	seafood	side vegetable, ravioli filling
kelp	seafood	flavor enhancer, softens beans, side dish
nori sheets	oyster	wrapper for grains, cut as a garnish
nori flakes	oyster	chowders, sauces, breading
ao nori	oyster	chowders, sauces, breading, firm texture
smoked dulse	salmon	creme soup, tofu boursin style

MUSHROOMS

Mushrooms offer great tastes and textures to plant-based cuisine unlike any others from the vegetable kingdom. The cultivated varieties were for many years almost exclusively the white, agaric types sold in different sizes from button to stuffing grades. Other members of the agaric family now offered include the cremini, portobello and baby bella as well. Former wild varieties, sometimes called "exotic" to distinguish them from truly wild specimens, such as shiitake, enoki and oyster mushrooms, also are readily available.

Tips for handling mushrooms

When slicing mushrooms before cooking, cut them on the thick side to maximize flavor. Portobellos can be sliced paper-thin after cooking for a carpaccio-like effect. Button mushrooms can be cooked whole or halved.

Signs of freshness for the agaric varieties including white mushrooms in all sizes, cremini and baby bellas, are caps that are closed tightly around the stem, and if starting to open, a tan color inside. When fresh, the portobello mushroom's cap will be pulled away from the stem, the edge of the cap will be turned under and the gills will be a light cocoa color.

For all mushrooms, avoid those that are bruised or discolored, have black wet gills, those that are slimy on the outside or give off any unpleasant (sometimes ammonia-like) odors. As the mushroom matures, the gills will appear darker with the release of the spores. This will give a stronger flavor and darken the recipe's color, which may be or may not be pleasant depending how old the mushrooms are. Cook a couple to check the flavor and color.

Mushrooms will spoil faster if wrapped in airtight containers. Store mushrooms in brown paper bags or in the perforated bulk cardboard boxes that they arrive in to allow air circulation without being exposed to the drying air inside a refrigerator.

Because washing mushrooms can hasten deterioration, wash them as close to cooking time as possible. If this is not practical, try to remove as much moisture from them after washing by toweling them off. Oyster mushrooms are especially delicate and benefit the most from washing just prior to use. The truly wild varieties should always be cooked before serving. This includes the dried varieties such as the porcini or cepe.

Mushroom types and techniques for cooking

White mushrooms

For all sizes sauté, braise, duxelle; the largest ones are good for stuffing. *Sauté Method 1:* Quickly sauté in a hot pan that won't cool when mushrooms are added, browning the outside and sealing in the juices. *Sauté Method 2:* Mushrooms are allowed to exude their juices while cooking and are cooked to the point at which all the juices evaporate and the flavor is concentrated. This is the method used in duxelles.

Oyster

This pearl of a mushroom comes in gray, pink, yellow and shades of brown. It can be sautéed, deep fried or braised.

Portobello

This mushroom can be sautéed, braised, grilled or broiled. The stems can be used for soup and stock.

Foods that enhance the flavor of mushrooms

onions, shallot, garlic, scallions, leeks
red and green bell peppers, chiles
soy sauce, tamari, miso paste
salt, fresh ground black pepper
Wine, especially Sherry, Marsala, Madeira
fresh herbs, especially parsley, rosemary and thyme
extra virgin olive oil, soy margarine, toasted sesame oil
Maple syrup and other sweeteners in a very tiny amount
Vinegar including Sherry, balsamic and apple cider varieties
Sea vegetables, especially chopped dulse or nori
cashew creme and cashew and hazelnut butters

Dried mushrooms

Agaric or common white and shiitake are two readily available types of dried mushrooms. Many of the edible wild varieties also can be purchased dried. The value of dried mushrooms is their intense flavor. This is due to the fact that they are as much as nine times heavier before dehydration.

Dried mushrooms pulverized in a blender or spice grinder and added toward the end of cooking are a great way to intensify the mushroom flavor of a dish.

ETHNIC INGREDIENTS

Achar

Salty, spicy, intensely aromatic East Indian pickles made from lemons, limes, chiles, green mango and assorted other vegetables. Traditionally served as a condiment, achar can be chopped or crushed and added to a recipe for some zip.

Fillo

This super-thin, versatile pastry, traditionally used in Greek and Middle Eastern cuisine, can be used for savory and sweet preparations that are formed into many different shapes as rolled wrappers, tulip-shaped containers and garnishes.

The delicate nature of the pastry sheets can at times be challenging; however, with a few tips and a little experience, they make a great addition to your culinary repertoire.

Specifically, whole wheat fillo is well worth the effort to acquire. It has great texture and is usually easier to work with because it is a little thicker than all-white fillo. Depending on the desired flavor profile, herbs and spices for savory dishes, or cinnamon and sweetener for desserts can be sprinkled between the layers of filo sheets.

Fillo sheets become quickly brittle and unusable when exposed to air. If a fillo sheet tears, simply place a piece of fillo over the tear and use a little oil or margarine to seal it. When making large quantities of fillo-wrapped pastries, have all components ready and use a long work table. First, prepare all the pastry wrappers, then add the filling. The number of items that can be worked on at one time depends on how fast the task can be done without the filo dough drying out and starting to break. The number of people doing the job also affects the output.

Mustard

Mustard seeds can be dry-roasted until they pop for curry-style dishes and others that need a flavor boost. Prepared mustard works well as a flavor booster in many

Quick guide to working with fillo

While working with a sheet of the fillo, always keep the unused stack covered with a dry towel or cover with plastic wrap to keep it from drying out and shattering when you return to use it.

Work quickly, brushing the fillo with oil or an oil margarine combination, which will keep it from drying as you work and cause it to be flaky when it bakes.

If the filling you are using is wet it can cause the pastry to break apart, spilling the contents. As appropriate to the recipe, drain off or squeeze out moisture from filling ingredients or dry them by cooking off the moisture. Sometimes a recipe will need a thickening agent such as bread crumbs, cornstarch, flour or arrowroot added to hold the moisture in place.

Fillo-filled pastries can be made into shapes such as triangles, rolls, cigar or tube shapes, flowers and cups. For a dessert container dip edges in melted chocolate and nuts. Unfilled sheets can be cut, brushed with a savory or sweet shortening and baked into triangle or other shapes for a garnish. Traditionally, fillo lines and layers a casserole with a filling to make a type of pie.

recipes. There are many types of prepared mustards. If a recipe states simply prepared mustard, it is your choice as the mustard acts as a secondary source of flavor enhancement. When specific types of mustard are called for such as Dijon-style, coarse brown or yellow mustard, they play a more distinct role in the recipe. Beans especially respond to the flavor of mustard.

Tahini, or sesame seed butter

The toasted variety is preferred, as the un-toasted tahini is a little bitter. Both are thick and sticky. Tahini works well when mixed or blended with other ingredients to make dressings, sauces, dips, and as a flavoring agent in a dish. The oil often rises to the top and needs to be mixed with the bottom sediment. Warming the tahini can make this job easier. Place the bucket, tin or jar in a warm place or over hot water. A small amount can be softened in a microwave. High heat can cause the tahini to separate, giving it a curdled appearance.

Japanese-style miso varieties

Miso paste

Available from Korea as well as Japan, most of the miso on the market is a Japanese-style savory fermented paste traditionally used in soups and sauces. Miso is made from soy, salt, water, and aspergillus oryzae—a starter culture—and may include grains such as barley or rice. It is also made from chickpeas under the name chick peaso. Several varieties form the basic lineup and depending on their recipe ingredients and the amount of time they have been aged, they range from mild in flavor and light in color to very intense-tasting and dark. By taking into account the depth of flavor of the type of miso you are working with you can use miso paste as a flavoring agent in the same way that base or bouillon is used.

White or mellow white miso

Usually a tan color aged the shortest amount of time, white miso is one of the mildest forms and is often the type used in miso soup. I use it in recipes to give a cheese-like flavor to savory dishes such as Pesto (page 141) and sweet preparations such as Icing (page 398).

Chick peaso

Made from chickpeas, this is similar in flavor and color to white miso.

Red miso

Longer aged, darker, and more robust in flavor, this is saltier than the lighter misos.

Hatcho miso

This miso, made with barley, is a very dark paste with an intense and unique flavor.

Add miso to soup by either holding a strainer into the soup and pressing it through the strainer to disperse it, or by removing some of the miso stock to a small container and dissolving the paste in it, then stirring it into the soup.

Ume boshi, ume vinegar: Japanese pickled plums, available whole with pit intact, or in a pink-colored paste. The brine is converted into ume vinegar, with a unique aromatic, salty, sour flavor.

Wasabi

This is a potent Japanese condiment similar to horseradish. It is available as a powder which is mixed with a little water to form a paste; wasabi is also available premixed; traditionally served with sushi.

ALTERNATIVE SWEETENERS

Syrups

When measuring syrups, lightly oil the measuring cup or spoon, or measure oil first if included in the recipe to help ease handling and removal from the measure.

Refrigerate after opening as they can form mold or start to ferment; the simple sugar-eating enzymes present in the fermenting process can counteract the effect of a thickener and cause recipes to fail. If there is slight fermenting in a product without a full-blown yeast taste present, it may be possible to boil the syrups to stabilize them. For instance, in the pudding recipes boiling is recommended before a thickener is added.

Maple syrup and sugar

My favorite sweeteners are pure maple sugar and syrup. The high price is due to the fact that it takes about 40 gallons of sap to produce one gallon of syrup by evaporation, which requires a lot of fuel and equipment. The weather also plays an important part in the quantity and quality or grade of the syrup that will be produced each year. The major maple syrup producing countries are the U.S. and Canada.

The grades of maple syrup are:

Extra fancy
Grade A medium amber
Grade A dark amber
Grade B (very dark)

The best grades of syrup are usually reserved for pouring on to pancakes, waffles or other foods, where the wonderful flavor can be truly appreciated. Experience has taught me that color does not always indicate the flavor and that sampling is the only way to evaluate the syrups available in one's area. Also, the Kosher symbol on maple syrup ensures that no animal fat was added as an anti-foaming agent during evaporation.

Brown rice syrup

This is a thick, mildly sweet syrup often used in macrobiotic cooking and for those who wish to keep down the amount of sugar in their diets. It works fairly well when exchanged with maple syrup in recipes, however, the maple is much sweeter.

Barley malt syrup

This is another mildly sweet syrup with its own unique flavor and similar properties as brown rice syrup.

Fruit juices

Fruit juice is used in the recipes as a base for certain sauces and flavoring agents in baked goods and desserts. They are used as body and flavor for some salad dressing and reduced to syrups for some of the other dressings. Many flavors of juices are available through natural foods purveyors and stores. Some of these flavors are apple blends like apple strawberry, apple raspberry, apple blackberry and apple cranberry. Other fruit juices include peach, pear, mango and pina colada.

Dry sweeteners

Date sugar

These large granules of sugar made from dates are mildly sweet and have a distinctive flavor; however, they are hard to dissolve by just mixing them into a batter or recipe.

Maple sugar

Pure maple sugar is allowed to reach the candy stage, then cooled and granulated to make this New England specialty. It has great flavor but the price may make this product too expensive for many food service operations.

Florida crystals

This dark tan to pale-colored dry sweetener is made from less processed sugar cane juice and is natural foods' answer to white sugar.

Succanat

The name stands for *sugar cane nat*ural, evaporated cane juice granulated with a strong molasses flavor. It can replace white sugar by volume in a recipe but the flavor needs to be taken into consideration.

VINEGAR

There are many different types and grades of vinegar, ranging in price from inexpensive to quite costly. And as with any product, it is worth tasting the available examples to determine which suit you best. As with other products, such as wine, in some instances less expensive labels are equal to the higher priced ones.

Apple cider vinegar

Made from fermented apple cider, this vinegar works in many different applications from salad dressings to sweet and sour sauce. The organic examples offer a more complex flavor, but they may carry some sediment.

Balsamic vinegar

Balsamic vinegar is a dark, sweet and sour specialty of the Modena region of Italy. Juice from the Trebbiano grape, which is boiled and reduced to half its volume, creates its characteristic sweetness. The higher grades of barrel-aged product may cost from $15 up to $100 a bottle. Commercial grades start at around $4 a bottle. There is now a white balsamic vinegar available that is less intense than the dark, but great for recipes in which the dusky color of the *tradizionale* would overwhelm a plate presentation. Balsamic vinegar is great on salad greens or roasted vegetables and can be used to enhance flavor in many dishes.

Herb and fruit vinegar

There are many herb- and fruit-flavored types of vinegar made by boiling the vinegar, then adding fresh herbs, spices, garlic, hot peppers or fresh fruit. A slower method is to just steep the ingredients for several days until the flavor is to your taste.

Red wine and white wine vinegar

With the characteristics of the wines they are made from, the more intense red wine vinegar delivers a hardy flavor and the less assertive white wine vinegar provides a clean, light and fruity tang.

Rice vinegar

The large-production examples exhibit a taste reminiscent of a light apple cider vinegar. The smaller batch fermented organic brown rice samples have a more developed flavor that to me shares some of the characteristics of sherry vinegar.

Shanxi vinegar

New to the market, this product made from sorghum barley and peas has been around for thousands of years in northern China and bears the name of its native province. It can be used to enhance flavor in much the same way as balsamic vinegar.

Sherry vinegar

An upscale product with the wonderful nutty flavor that Sherry is known for, it combines well with walnut oil to accentuate that quality.

Ume vinegar

Made from the ume boshi or Japanese pickled plum, it showcases the unique aromatic and salty flavor in a wonderful pink liquid format.

BEANS AND GRAINS

There are nine essential amino acids that need to be present to allow the assimilation of what is referred to as complete protein. Grains possess certain amino acids required to form proteins needed by the human body. Nuts and seeds contain similar amino acids to grains. Beans have amino acids in their makeup that, when combined with those from nuts, seeds or grains, make complete protein. Modern thinking on this subject says that these amino acids as in bean-grain, bean-nut combinations can be accomplished by more than one meal and do not always have to be present together as long as they are represented in the diet during the course of a day's menus. Interesting to note are the many traditional dishes that have these combinations intact, such as the beans and seeds present in hummus, pasta and beans soups of Italy, rice and bean dishes from Latin American cuisine, Cajun cooking and in recipes of India.

Rice, the world's most popular grain, comes in over 200 strains, such as wahani, black japonica, arborio, basmati, and jasmine to name a few popular types. Brown rice comes in short, medium and long grains. Wheat has relatives such as spelt and kamut, which were once popular and are now becoming known again. Other ancient grains such as quinoa from Peru have been used in their native countries until present and are now being discovered by the rest of the world.

Rice
Barley, brown hulled barley and pearled barley

For pearled barley use 3 parts water to 1 part barley, boil, then simmer for 45 minutes plus. For brown hulled barley, use 4 parts water to 1 part grain, and boil then simmer for an hour plus. Brown hulled barley has more protein and vitamins which are lost in the removal of the outer layers of the grain from pearled barley.

Basmati rice

This delicious, aromatic rice is a staple in the cuisine of India and surrounding countries such as Afghanistan and Pakistan. It's available in brown and white varieties, both imported and domestic.

Brown rice

Brown rice comes in short, medium and long grains and takes about 50 minutes to cook. There is quick-cooking (ten minutes, precooked and dehydrated) brown rice available for times when regular rice will not be ready in time.

Corn

Use dried whole and ground corn as a grain or cooked fresh on the cob as a vegetable.

Cous cous

There are now several varieties of cous cous on the market. Some cous cous is made from the polished hearts of semolina wheat, while other types are made from a pasta-like dough which is cut or formed into various sizes.

Wheat berries

Wheat berries can be cooked like brown rice or together with short-grain brown rice. They take a little more time to cook than the rice, but this can be evened out by rinsing the wheat berries and soaking them overnight. Then cook them alone or along with the short-grain brown rice.

Wild rice

Gourmet grain of slender aquatic grass, considered by some to be a cousin to domestic rice varieties, these delicately roasted kernels can be featured in any course of a meal.

Beans

Beans provide robust taste and texture, and an important vegetable-based protein source. Beans are cost-friendly and easy to prepare.

All dried beans need to be sorted through for small stones or other debris. I prefer to do this by spreading the beans out in a stainless steel pan and pushing them a few at a time, back and forth three times. The shiny surface of the stainless steel pan helps to show any foreign matter in the beans. Be especially vigilant as a small pebble could chip a guest's tooth. Continue looking for unwanted particles during the next step, washing the beans.

Dried beans ususally double in size when cooked. They may be boiled, pressure cooked or braised. Macrobiotic cooking recommends that a piece of kelp, also called by the Japanese name kombu, be added to the beans while they cook. The natural chemical components of kelp help soften the foods it is cooked with and enhance their flavor.

Boiling most beans requires three parts water to one part beans, with some of the longer-cooking varieties like chickpeas using four or more parts to one part beans. While cooking beans, add hot water as needed to keep beans covered and stir for more even cooking.

When considering dried beans for the menu, available cooking time plays an important role in the choice of bean. I like to think of beans in categories by how fast they will cook and whether or not soaking is required. Those beans that need to be soaked require advance planning. They can be soaked overnight to be ready for the next day.

For a quick-soak method when overnight is not an option, clean and rinse beans, then cover them with water, bring to a boil for five minutes then remove from heat. Cover and let set for 45 minutes to an hour. Drain and proceed.

There are hundreds of varieties of beans grown throughout the world. When substituting, use beans of similar size and shape. They all seem to provide flavor and a hearty richness when cooked, and usually taste great with the traditional seasoning.

Adzuki

Adzuki beans are small mahogany-colored beans popular in Japanese and macrobiotic cooking. They are also made into a sweet paste used as filling for steamed buns and other Asian pastries. Season with ginger, garlic, sesame oil or soy sauce; use scallions as garnish. Adzuki beans can also be used for Mexican dishes.

Black beans

Sometimes called turtle beans, black beans are great in soups. A wonderful side dish can be created by seasoning with cumin, lime, lemon, tomato, (hot) habanero peppers, cilantro and garlic.

Black-eyed peas

Also called cow-peas, black-eyed peas are a favorite in the southern United States and lend themselves to bean salads. They are available fresh and frozen. Black-eyed peas can be seasoned with black pepper, scallions, garlic, vinegar and soy sauce.

Cannellini

This is a large white bean and is shaped like a kidney bean. These beans can be purchased in cooked form and used in dishes seasoned with garlic, onions, tomatoes, parsley, basil and oregano.

Chickpeas, also called garbanzos

These round tan-colored beans are the base for such dishes as hummus and falafel. Chickpeas are good in soups and pasta dishes as well. They can be seasoned with garlic, tomatoes, Italian-style herb seasoning, tahini, lemon juice, ume paste and soy sauce.

Kidney beans

These large red kidney-shaped beans are popular in southwestern and Mexican dishes and are used in other cuisine as well. They can be seasoned with cumin, onions, garlic, tomatoes and ancho or other southwestern chiles.

Lentils

The khaki-colored flat variety of lentil beans stay intact until well cooked. Lentils are great for soups and salads, and can be served with roasted vegetables. The red and yellow varieties of lentil beans can be used for soups. They can be seasoned with garlic, curry spices, Italian spices, soy sauce and mustard.

Peas, green and yellow split

The yellow variety of peas has a rich color, but they can be interchanged in recipes with the green split peas, which have a slight edge in flavor. These fast-cooking peas are primarily used in soups. There are now smoked green split peas on the market from Canada that are great for pea soup or adding smoke flavor to other soups. Season with mirepoix, bay leaf, soy sauce and black pepper.

Pinto beans

Pinto beans are especially good for soup and other long-cooking recipes. They can be seasoned with cumin, onions, garlic, tomatoes and ancho or other southwestern chiles.

Soybeans, white

Protein-rich soybeans are processed in various ways and used in many different preparations. Using techniques developed in ancient China and Japan, they are made into soy milk, which is available in plain and flavored varieties or curdled and turned into tofu, also known as bean curd. Soybeans also form the base for soy sauce and miso, a paste made from cultured and salted soybeans with some recipes including grains such as barley or rice. They are inoculated with a culture to produce the Indonesian specialty tempeh, which is a type of whole soybean cake that may include other beans or grains in the recipe. Using western technology, soybeans undergo a metamorphosis as they are formed into many types of meat analogs, such as burger patties, breakfast sausages and crumbled meat replacer. Silken tofu is small-curd tofu that has not been pressed to remove water, and is very smooth in texture, making it great for desserts and sauces. See Alternative Proteins (page 319).

Soybeans, black fermented

Chinese-style black fermented soybeans are a salty condiment used to impart a unique flavor. They should be rinsed, minced or mashed, and then sautéd with ginger and garlic.

White beans

There are many varieties of white beans, including navy, great northern and small white pea beans. Traditionally they are featured in recipes for baked beans and hardy soups. They can be seasoned with mirepoix, garlic, black pepper, liquid smoke, mustard, bay leaf and thyme.

Frozen peas, lima beans and cooked canned beans of many varieties can be used in the recipes by adjusting in the cooking times and using less liquid. Dried flaked beans are also available and cook quickly, making them useful for soups and sauces.

Nuts and seeds

In most cases I prefer the flavor of nuts and seeds that have been toasted. In a few instances such as for cashew, sunflower or pumpkin seed creme, the raw stage provides a creamy texture without the assertiveness of toasted nuts or seeds. Even for these applications, sometimes the raw or toasted nut creme may be interchangeable, as for the Mushroom Cashew Creme Soup (page 112).

Nut butters such as hazelnut, almond, cashew and sesame tahini can be used to flavor recipes, and thicken sauces and soups. They are darker in color than the nut cremes made with nuts and seeds that are not toasted.

ALTERNATIVE PROTEIN SOURCES

Soy foods are more popular than ever in the west due in part to the many scientific reports touting their health-related benefits. With an increased understanding of how to cook and flavor these traditional preparations, protein alternatives such as tofu and tempeh will continue to grow in popularity.

Soy milk and tofu

To make tofu, also called bean curd, one needs to first make soy milk. The process requires that the soybeans, usually a high-protein-yielding variety grown especially for that purpose, be soaked overnight in well or purified water. The beans are then drained, ground and added to a large steam kettle, where they are again covered with purified water and brought to a boil. The soy milk is strained to remove the bean pulp, which still contains a certain amount of protein.

The soy milk is returned to the cauldron and simmered for about 10 minutes. Then a curdling agent such as the sea water derivative nigari (magnesium chloride), also known as bittern—a traditional Japanese coagulant—or calcium chloride is stirred into the simmered soy milk. The curds form and are then strained from the whey and pressed into a form to give the tofu its shape.

The pressing time and removal of whey determine the type of tofu. As the whey is removed the tofu becomes soft, medium, firm and extra firm. Silken tofu is made by not draining the whey, and is often done with a special process right inside the package. This process results in a tofu that has the consistency of flan or custard. Silken tofu is available in densities from soft to extra firm, but I use the firm or extra firm in both the full and low-fat varieties.

The recipes generally suggest some type of treatment for the tofu before it is used in a dish. These instructions are for flavoring or cooking the tofu, which also has the advantage of keeping the tofu from becoming scrambled when it is combined with other ingredients. Traditional ways to accomplish this textural change are deep-frying and pan-frying. As an alternative, using an oven will reduce the need for oil and free up the stove top burners.

We can get protein into our diets from members of this group and especially the essential complimentary amino acids that are lacking in the grain and nut food groups. While it was once thought that all of the essential amino acids must be present at one meal to provide quality-complete protein, today's viewpoint allows the proteins from beans or bean-based protein alternatives such as soy milk, tofu, tempeh and textured vegetable (soy) protein to join with the proteins available from grains, seeds and nuts as long as they are present at some point in a day's meals—not necessarily always together at the same meal. If you are providing all the meals your guests consume then check with your dietitian when planning your menu cycles.

Some interesting vegetarian protein alternatives are referred to as "meat" analogs. This category contains many products aimed at the market group that grew up with certain tastes and textures and would still like to have meatless versions of those products. Soy- or grain-style burgers, vegetarian hot dogs, meatless breakfast sausage, ham, luncheon meats, ground beef replacement and other items have been created to satisfy this demand.

Soy milk

Also called soy beverage, soy milk is made in its simplest form by boiling soybeans. The market brands usually contain sweeteners and flavor such as vanilla, chocolate or carob. There are new rich and smooth silky varieties of soy milk, as well as rich, shake-like beverages and coffee creamer.

Tempeh

A high protein and vitamin B-12-rich cultured soy food native to Indonesia, tempeh was made originally with all soybeans, but is now available in the U.S. in many different combinations of soy plus other grains, beans, vegetables and sea vegetables.

Three-grain tempeh with millet, rice and barley added to the soy, and also a three-bean, three-grain, fermented variety formed into cakes.

Tempeh benefits from marinating or seasoning much the same as tofu. While tempeh has more texture than tofu, it still gains from cooking, which crisps and firms it further. Tempeh is the most popular soy food of Indonesia, where it originated in Java prior to 1750. Tempeh is a cultured food that is prepared somewhat in the same way as cultured cheeses or yogurt. To make tempeh, the original method calls for cooked soybeans to be mixed with a rhizopus culture, wrapped in banana leaves and then set aside while the culture spreads its filaments to form a network of mycelium threads visible in a slab of tempeh. The process breaks down the beans making it more digestible, and gives a solid form to the beans, adding to the flavor as well.

The flavor of tempeh varies from one producer to another. Also, the recipe ingredients play a part in the flavor profile. To my taste the all-soy products are strong in flavor and take more of an acquired taste. I prefer the flavor of the multi-grain tempeh, which has soy along with brown rice, millet and barley.

TVP texturized vegetable (soy) protein

Texturized vegetable (soy) protein is available dry in small granules and in large chunks of various sizes. It is used for its meat-like texture. TVP needs to be rehydrated when added to recipes, and can be seasoned at that time or can be added dry to a recipe that has more liquid added to compensate.

FLAVORINGS, HERBS, SPICES, AND SEASONINGS

Black sesame seeds

Black sesame seeds are great for their dramatic visual effect as a garnish. Toasting brings out their flavor. White sesame seeds can be used as an alternative for flavor.

Cilantro

This herb comes from the pungent leaves of the coriander plant. Cilantro is used in Asian and South American cuisines. Cilantro is usually added at the end of cooking.

Ginger root

Fresh ginger root, with its unmistakable piquant flavor and fragrance, has come from the kitchens of Asia to be a staple in the west. Traditionally in Chinese cuisine, ginger is used in tandem with garlic, delivering a delicious double strike to the palate. The freshest ginger has skin that is smooth and almost translucent.

Ginger is available as a powdered or ground dry spice. It has a much different taste than fresh and is used in baking to provide the familiar flavor of gingerbread or ginger snaps. Two other ginger preparations available are thinly sliced and sweetened pickled sushi ginger and crystallized ginger candied in sugar syrup.

Lemon zest
There are several ways to remove lemon or orange zest. It's best to use unsprayed organic fruit, which can be grated on a plastic-wrap covered box grater, so the zest is removed and then can be scraped easily from the plastic wrap. A special zester tool can also be used.

Salt
Sea salt is preferred for its flavor and trace elements. Other salty condiments include tamari, shoyu, soy sauce, miso, ume plum paste and Indian achar pickle.

Sambal
This is a chile paste used in Thai and Southeast Asian cooking.

Sumac
Sumac is a middle Eastern spice used for its lemony astringent flavor and burgundy color.

Soy sauce
Soy sauce is a generic term for a salty, fermented liquid, soy-based cooking condiment used through Southeast Asia. Specifically referred to in Japanese cooking as tamari, wheat-free Japanese-style soy sauce, and shoyu, Chinese- and Japanese-style soy sauce differ, so tasting is the best way to get to know those available to you.

Tamari
This is a name for a style of Japanese soy sauce that is brewed in smaller batches. It differs from generic soy sauce in the way that micro-brewed beer compares to large-vat, volume brewed beer—rich in flavor and sometimes a little thicker in body. Tamari is a great flavor booster for the underlying flavor that non-vegetarian bases play in mainstream cooking.

Vanilla extract and vanilla bean
Vanilla is the seed pod of a tropical orchid. The fermented and dried beans are used by cutting them lengthwise and scraping out the seed paste, which show up as dark specs in a recipe. If the vanilla beans are heated in some of the recipe's liquid, it

will release some flavor and make them easier to work with. Pure vanilla extract, which is called for in the recipes, is made by steeping the pods in alcohol to extract the essence. To make your own extract place 3 or 4 vanilla beans into a pint bottle and fill it with rum or vodka.

Wines

The type of wine called for in some recipes is either by grape type such as cabernet sauvignon or by the generic color reference, such as red or white wine. When wine is not available or when cooking for guests who wish to avoid these beverages, substitute apple juice combined with apple cider vinegar. Put 1 table-spoon/15 milliliters vinegar into a 1 cup/240 milliliter measure, then fill it with apple juice.

FATS AND OILS

With so many studies pointing to the reduced role of fat in our diets, we cannot ignore this subject. As a chef, I must take into consideration the taste of the food I prepare, what happens when I choose to change a recipe's basic structure and how fat carries flavor and texture. As a vegan chef I also concern myself with the source of the ingredients to be added to or subtracted from a recipe such as "Will dairy butter be replaced by oil, margarine, fruit puree or a combination?"

Because the type and the amount of fat used in a recipe can affect many aspects of taste and texture, I have found that reducing the amount of fat needs to be a recipe-by-recipe procedure. For many of the cooking recipes, the amount of fat I formerly would have included has been reduced by 75% or more. In the baking recipes it proved to be more difficult to make such large reductions, and often required some type of substitute such as apple butter or prune puree.

I also prefer to take into consideration the amount of fat in an entire meal rather than to isolate each dish. This allows for a course that may be deep-fried or a rich dessert to be included. Serving size is important here, as is the source of the fat, the amount of fiber in the meal, the amount of sweeteners and the overall caloric makeup.

The occasion also plays a determining factor. A special-occasion meal would generally be made up of richer foods than an everyday meal. Whether one's guests are having all or most of their meals in your dining room or just a weekly or special occasion meal may also determine the richness of the cuisine served.

The types of fat depend on the recipes. For some recipes, ethnic origin may call for a certain type of fat or oil such as olive oil in Mediterranean and Italian cooking, or toasted sesame oil for Asian-style cuisine. The role that fat plays as cooking medium that transfers heat—as in frying or sautéing—or its contribution to texture—as for a tart crust—is also important in considering its reduction or replacement. Using nonstick pans and brushing on the oil can help reduce the amount of fat needed.

Canola oil

Canola is a neutral-tasting, all-purpose oil used in this book for cooking and baking. For baking it's used sometimes in combination with soybean margarine to lower the amount of saturated fat.

Corn oil

A preferred oil for macrobiotic cooking is unrefined corn oil, available through natural foods distributors.

Flavored oils

There are now many flavored oils available, including olive oil infused with basil, curry spices, sweet red pepper, hot red pepper, lemon and others. These may be used to drizzle on a dish just before serving for an added flavor boost and to add color to the plate design.

Hazelnut oil

This oil I've used as a bonus byproduct of hazelnut butter, also called filbert butter, which, when purchased, has oil floating on the top. I like to pour off this oil and use it for Silken Creme dessert sauces where the hazelnut butter would darken the finished product.

Nasoyaise® or Vegenaise®

These are two registered brand names for vegan mayonnaise-type dressing.

Olive oil

Extra virgin and virgin olive oils come from the first pressing of the olives and are the most flavorful and the most expensive. However, not all brands of extra virgin olive oil taste the same, nor can the flavor be determined by the color, which can be golden to dark green. To find which brands suit you best, sample those available and let your taste buds decide.

Generally extra virgin olive oil is best drizzled on a dish at the point of service or added to a dish when the heat has been reduced either by lowering the heat source or adding liquid to the pan. Heat, especially high temperatures, breaks down the flavor and evaporates aroma from these delicious oils.

For all-around cooking and to start dishes that will later be flavored with extra virgin olive oil, use oil that is called 100% olive oil. Avoid the cheapest olive oil, sometimes called pomace oil, as it is the dregs of the olive-oil-making process, treated with chemical solvents to remove any remaining oil.

Peanut oil

The clear refined variety is great for deep frying if the budget allows. Because peanut oil can take higher temperatures than other oils without burning, it may be worth the extra money in the long run because it can last longer. There is also an unrefined cold pressed dark peanut oil available through natural foods stores and distributors that has similar flavor qualities as toasted sesame oil but cannot be used to deep-fry.

Safflower oil

This is another oil with a high smoke point that I really like for deep frying. It produces a delicious, delicate flavor.

Soy margarine

The soybean margarine on the market available from natural foods distributors has a better flavor than the commercial varieties and doesn't contain all the additives. It is a hydrogenated oil, which makes it more of a health risk, so I use it for those recipes that truly need its particular qualities, especially in baking and pastry-making. A small amount added to savory recipes at the end of cooking is also an option.

Toasted sesame oil

Toasted sesame oil is used in Asian-style cuisine and also to impart smoke flavor in recipes. In this book, the recipes call for the toasted variety.

Walnut oil

This specialty oil is great for salads and its flavor combines especially well with sherry vinegar.

About Taste and Flavor

When guests evaluate food served to them, the order in which they do so is by appearance, aroma, and then taste, which showcases texture and temperature at the same time.

The way one cooks reflects one's background, and the same applies to the way people bring their own experience of tastes, personal likes and dislikes, and expectations to the table. Their set of taste memories has been formed by their experiences of family meals, restaurant encounters, where they grew up, travel, ethnic background and so forth.

Age plays a factor too as the taste buds on the tongue disappear from about 250 sensors in a young adult to 90 or so for an advanced senior. However, the older diner may have more access to food memories and have developed a keener sense of taste than the younger guest.

Like most of the population, those who follow a vegetarian diet want well-flavored food, and some like their food spicier than others.

"Season to taste" at the end of a recipe is the point when we can make our final statement of flavor. It is at this juncture that a flat-tasting recipe can be made flavorful and an already tasty dish can be made to approach the sublime.

Often salt, pepper, soy sauce or a little lemon juice will suffice to perk up a dish but because the flavor of ingredients changes from batch to batch, season to season, we have the task of "correcting the seasoning" by using our incredible faculty of taste. Our taste buds and memory of foods we have tasted can tell us how close we've come in duplicating the flavor of a recipe that we have created or tasted in the past, or whether or not we enjoy the present item being sampled. The process of making a recipe more savory is done by heightening the sensations of taste as picked up by our various taste buds. For instance, by first accessing our memory for its ideal taste of Winter Squash Hazelnut Bisque (page 97) we can begin to compare the degrees of salt, sweet, sour, bitter and acid present and add a little bit of an ingredient according to the missing part of our taste observation. Lack of acid taste could be corrected with lemon juice or apple cider vinegar. Also, when one supporting flavor dominates, we need a strategy; balance sometimes needs to be restored. When a recipe tastes too salty add something sweet. Salty-flavored ingredients such as tamari, ume plum paste and Indian achar could be used when more than salt is needed. For a sweet flavor addition, use maple and other sweeteners. Dill pickle brine, lemon or lime juice, different types of vinegar can also perk up a dish.

The size of a recipe batch changes the amount of flavor-boosting needed. It's good to first start by adding more of the seasoning ingredients called for in the particular recipe, such as lemon, herbs, spices, soy sauce, salt and pepper, then depart from there.

SEASONING AT A GLANCE

All of the following ingredients can be added in small quantities in order to heighten the flavor without making their presence obvious.

Sweet: maple syrup, barley malt syrup, rice syrup, succanat, Florida crystals, other dry sweeteners of choice, dried fruit, fruit juice

Sour: lemon juice, lime juice, tamarind paste

Acid: lemon juice, vinegar. An abundance of fresh parsley, as in tabouli, can have an acid affect on the tongue.

Salty: sea salt, sea vegetables, miso paste, tamari or other soy sauces, vegetable bouillon or base; Ume boshi plums, ume boshi plum paste, ume boshi plum vinegar

Spicy Hot: ginger, chiles, green, ground black or white peppercorns, Thai green chili paste, and hot aromatics: horseradish, mustard and wasabi

Aroma: To heighten the aroma: fresh herbs, toasted spices, lemon and other citrus zest

Smoked flavor: toasted sesame oil, liquid smoke, smoked dulse, tempeh bacon, smoked peas

Deep base tones: molasses, instant grain beverage (coffee substitute), chocolate chips, caramelized vegetables and root vegetables, soy sauce, tamari, miso

SUBSTITUTIONS

Depending on the budget and the prevailing food cost percentage in effect, certain ingredients may be too expensive to use for every kitchen. In order to still take advantage of a recipe some adjustments may be needed using less expensive varieties of the item called for. Some examples would be using domestic white mushrooms in place of wild or exotic varieties, or using all brown rice in a recipe that called for more expensive rice varieties such as wild rice. The reverse of this idea would be for those with higher menu pricing to use the high-cost ingredients to increase value and add distinction to their offerings. Some general examples would be:

Ingredient	
Lower Cost	**Higher Cost**
fresh white mushrooms	fresh oyster, portobello, shiitake
dried white mushrooms	dried shiitake, cepes, porcini
white or brown rice, basmati	wild, wehani, Arborio
peanuts, sunflower seeds	cashews, almonds, pecans, walnuts, pine nuts
red onions	shallots
domestic black ripe or green olives	imported calamata, Niçoise, large green Italian, and other olives

SERVING AND PLATING THE VARIOUS COURSES

The following criteria are judging guidelines for culinary shows. In the cold foods categories plating is the key way to show one's skills to the judges. These rules are for plate and platters presented in an elegant way, when their basis is understood they can be carried over to less formal hot or cold line service, where the components that would form an individual plate are now placed side by side in chafing dishes or platters and bowls.

1. color: The color of food can either attract or repel a guest depending on the dish. Well-cooked ingredients in a stew or caramelized onions or roasted vegetables present the impression of a full-flavored savory fare. In contrast, overcooked vegetables as a side dish may appear lifeless. Brightly sautéed or steamed provide examples of bright tones.
2. variety of textures
3. variety of cooking methods
4. proper cooking technique
5. portion size, proper vessel/plate
6. ingredient variety (onion, scallion, shallot, etc.)
7. craftsmanship
8. practicality
9. creativity
10. overall appearance

When offering a new dish think about the appearance, aroma and taste when it will be plated or presented.

NOTE ON MEASUREMENT CONVERSION TO METRIC

For the recipes I based conversion to metric on the following equations: 1 ounce dry U. S. to equal 28 grams. The number of dry weight ounces $\times$ 28 grams so that 13 ounces = 364 grams. (They are written in the manuscript with cup measure as well as 1 cup/4 ounces/112 grams). For liquid measure most conversions are the same as water which equal 1 cup/8 fluid ounces/ 240 milliliters.

For pan size 1 inch = 2.5 centimeters.

For temperature 300°F (Fahrenheit) = 150°C (Celsius) so that the text may read:

Preheat oven to 375°F/190°C.

CHAPTER THREE

Appetizers

Appetizers bridge the gap between a hungry guest and one whose taste buds have been stimulated for the meal to follow. They give the guest an opportunity to try more items from your repertoire and help business by improving the overall check average.

Appetizers can go by many names, including Middle Eastern *mezze* like the Toasted Spice Hummus (page 51); Spanish tapas, which could include Fried Breaded Zucchini (page 74); Italian *primi* like Polenta with Spinach Pesto (page 72); and the French *hors d'oeuvre* or *canapé,* which could feature Vegetable Walnut and Pecan Pâté (page 52).

Another French term for an opening course is *bouche amuse,* which means to amuse the mouth. Sometimes these small offerings are referred to as "teasers" and are presented as a welcoming gift of the house. They may only be a bite or two, such as a couple of Dates Stuffed with Almonds (page 77), but they're a gesture usually much appreciated by hungry guests.

At the other end of the spectrum are somewhat larger portions of highly flavored food such as Sautéed Oyster Mushrooms over Herb Scones (page 60). Many of the main course pasta dishes work well as appetizers when served in smaller portions. An item too expensive to fit the format of an entree makes a special treat as a preliminary course, such as the Chilebella Mushrooms (page 59), Crostini with Sundried Tomato Pesto (page 56) or the Black Olive Pesto (page 57) when made with imported olives.

Experience has taught me that guests, in anticipation of a special meal, will arrive at a restaurant famished and as soon as they've had a bite to eat their sense of well-being is remarkably improved. At my former restaurant we provided our own baked bread along with a vegetable spread as soon as anyone was seated. Sometimes we served a tiny gratis appetizer to show our appreciation for their patronage.

Many restaurants offer a selection of small plates to satisfy the dining public's craving for new types of foods and allow them to sample more of a chef's particular style of cooking.

Carrot Hazelnut Spread

YIELD 10–12 SERVINGS

$\frac{1}{4}$ CUP/60 MILLILITERS

*This spread provides a tasty, low fat and nutritious alternative to
serving butter with bread.*

carrots, large dice	$2\frac{1}{2}$ cups	340 grams
corn oil	1 teaspoon	5 milliliters
onions, medium dice	1 cup	112 grams
water	$\frac{1}{4}$ cup	60 milliliters
hazelnut butter	1 tablespoon	15 grams
white miso	1 tablespoon	15 grams
salt and pepper	as desired	as desired

GARNISH

onion, scallion, or chives, minced	as needed	as needed

Sauté the carrots in oil over medium-high heat for 2 to 3 minutes. Add the onion, lower heat to medium-low and sauté for 5 minutes. Add the water, cover and cook 5 minutes longer, or until the carrots are very tender. Allow the carrots and onions to cool in the pan for a few minutes.

Put the sautéed vegetables, hazelnut butter, white miso, and salt and pepper into a food processor and process until smooth, scraping down the spread from the sides of the bowl as needed. Season to taste. Chill before serving.

GARNISH: Spread can be served in one bowl family-style or in individual servings. Garnish with minced onions, scallions, or chives.

VARIATION: Replace all or some of the carrots with butternut squash, parsnips or sweet potatoes. A teaspoon of minced ginger could be added at the same time as the onions. Other nut butters could be used in place of the hazelnut butter, such as almond butter or peanut butter. Toasted hazelnuts could be used in place of the hazelnut butter by placing them in the food processor first to grind them and then adding the other ingredients.

SERVE WITH: Sesame, Sunflower and Poppy Seed Bread (page 356), India-Style Flatbread (page 353) or other breads.

Adzuki Bean Ancho Pâté

YIELD 10 SERVINGS

$\frac{1}{4}$ CUP/56 GRAMS

Adzuki or aduki beans are common in Japanese cooking. In this recipe they are combined with flavors from Mexico, particularly the ground dried version of the fresh poblano chile called ancho molido.

adzuki beans, sorted, rinsed and soaked	$\frac{3}{4}$ cup	112 grams
onions, fine dice	1 cup	112 grams
ginger root, minced	1 tablespoon	7 grams
garlic, minced	1 tablespoon	7 grams
ancho molido	1 tablespoon	6 grams
whole cumin seeds	1 teaspoon	2.33 grams
water	3 cups	720 milliliters
salt	$\frac{1}{2}$ teaspoon	3 grams
soy sauce	1 tablespoon	15 milliliters
kelp (optional)	1 inch piece	2.5 centimeter piece
ground black pepper	pinch	pinch
salsa, prepared	$\frac{1}{4}$ cup	60 milliliters
cilantro, minced	1 tablespoon	7 grams
lime juice	1 teaspoon	5 milliliters

Clean and soak the adzuki beans several hours or overnight. In a pot large enough to cook the beans, sauté the onions, ginger and garlic over medium heat for 3 to 4 minutes. Add the ancho molido and cumin seeds to the pot and sauté for 1 minute. Stir in the water, adzuki beans, salt, soy sauce, kelp and black pepper. Bring to a boil, then simmer slowly uncovered for about 30 minutes. Cover the pan, reduce heat further and simmer for 30 minutes longer or until the beans are tender and almost all of the liquid is evaporated. Allow the mixture to cool before processing.

Turn the cooked beans into a food processor and add salsa, cilantro and lime juice. Process until smooth. Season to taste.

GARNISH: Garnish with chopped fresh cilantro and cilantro leaves.

VARIATION: Other red beans such as kidney beans or black beans could be used; however, their cooking time will be longer and they may require a little more water. Chili powder can be substituted for the ancho molido.

SERVE WITH: Corn chips or toasted tortilla wedges.

Toasted Spice Hummus

YIELD 10 SERVINGS
$\frac{1}{2}$ CUP / 112 GRAMS

The flavor of this Middle Eastern chickpea spread is heightened with the addition of the toasted spices. Because of the pungency of raw garlic, I start with a small amount and then increase it to taste.

TOASTED SPICES

coriander seeds	$2\frac{1}{2}$ teaspoons	7 grams
cumin seeds	$2\frac{1}{2}$ teaspoons	7 grams
sesame seeds	$2\frac{1}{2}$ teaspoons	7 grams
salt	$\frac{1}{2}$ teaspoon	3 grams
ground black pepper	pinch	pinch

HUMMUS INGREDIENTS

chickpeas, cooked	$3\frac{1}{3}$ cups	630 grams
chickpea cooking juice	10 tablespoons	150 milliliters
tahini (sesame spread)	5 tablespoons	75 milliliters
garlic, crushed	1 teaspoon	5 grams
lemon juice	5 tablespoons	75 milliliters
extra virgin olive oil	$2\frac{1}{2}$ teaspoons	12.5 milliliters
hot sauce	a few drops	a few drops

GARNISH

fresh parsley, minced	$\frac{1}{4}$ cup	28 grams
extra virgin olive oil	to drizzle on	to drizzle on

In a heavy bottomed sauté or frying pan, toast the spice seeds until fragrant. Add salt and pepper. Immediately remove from the pan to either a mortar and pestle or an electric spice grinder and grind, leaving the mixture somewhat coarse. Set the mixture aside. Place all the hummus ingredients in a food processor with half of the toasted spice mixture and process until smooth. Season to taste.

GARNISH: Spread hummus on individual plates or a platter, drizzle with extra virgin olive oil and sprinkle on the reserved spice mixture and chopped parsley.

SERVE WITH: India-Style Flat Bread (page 353), pita bread, and/or raw vegetables for dipping. It also can be used as a sandwich spread.

Vegetable Walnut and Pecan Pâté

YIELD 10 SERVINGS

ABOUT $\frac{1}{4}$ CUP/56 GRAMS

This rich vegetable nut pâté has a lightly smoked flavor achieved by adding a few drops of liquid smoke.

onions, medium dice	$\frac{1}{2}$ cup	56 grams
carrots, medium dice	$\frac{1}{2}$ cup	63 grams
celery, medium dice	$\frac{1}{2}$ cup	56 grams
olive oil	1 tablespoon	15 milliliters
ginger root, minced	1 tablespoon	7 grams
garlic, minced	1 teaspoon	3.5 grams
scallions, small dice	$\frac{1}{2}$ cup	14 grams
red wine vinegar	2 teaspoons	10 milliliters
soy sauce	1 tablespoon	15 milliliters
Dijon-style prepared mustard	1 tablespoon	15 milliliters
salt	$\frac{1}{4}$ teaspoon	1.5 grams
ground black pepper	pinch	pinch
liquid smoke, hickory flavor	8 to 10 drops	8 to 10 drops
toasted sesame oil	$\frac{1}{2}$ teaspoon	2.5 milliliters
soy margarine	2 tablespoons	28 grams
walnuts, toasted	$\frac{2}{3}$ cup	63 grams
pecans, toasted	$\frac{2}{3}$ cup	63 grams
vegetable stock	$\frac{1}{4}$ cup	60 milliliters

Sauté the onions, carrots and celery in olive oil over medium heat for 5 minutes. Add the ginger, garlic and scallions and sauté for 5 minutes. Turn the heat to low and add all remaining ingredients except the stock to the pan and sauté 5 minutes.

Turn ingredients into a food processor. Deglaze the pan with vegetable stock and pour into the food processor. Process the mixture to a smooth pâté. Chill the pâté before serving.

Toast pecans on a sheet pan in a 350°F/180°C oven for 4 to 5 minutes, stir and check after 3 minutes to keep nuts at the edges from burning. Toast walnuts the same way.

VARIATION: Omit the scallions and replace with half the volume of diced onion.

SERVE WITH: Bread or crackers, India–Style Flat Bread (page 353), Fresh Pear Chutney (page 131), crudité, and one or more of the following: chopped onion, chopped dill pickles or cornichons (pickled baby cucumbers).

Note: A key to making a smooth pâté is to process the mixture in a food processor with a very sharp blade. Liquid smoke comes in hickory and mesquite flavor.

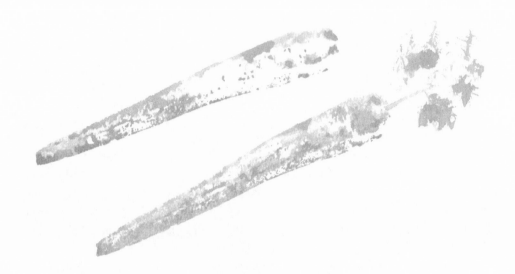

Vegetable Walnut and Pecan Terrine

YIELD 10 SERVINGS

$\frac{1}{4}$ CUP/56 GRAMS

To prepare a terrine using the Vegetable Walnut and Pecan Pâté recipe, leave the pâté mixture in the food processor and proceed from that point.

Vegetable Walnut and Pecan Paté (page 52)	$2\frac{1}{2}$ cups	560 grams
cornstarch	2 tablespoons	16 grams
apricot jam, warmed	1 tablespoon	17 grams
fresh parsley, minced	2 tablespoons	7 grams
crushed black peppercorns	$\frac{1}{2}$ teaspoon	1 gram
toasted black sesame seeds	1 tablespoon	6 grams

Process the cornstarch into the pâté mixture.

To form into a small terrine, line a 2-cup/480 milliliters terrine or demi-loaf pan with enough aluminum foil so that it hangs over the sides and can be folded over to cover the pâté completely as it cooks. Repeat with a layer of plastic wrap, which will separate the foil from the pâté. Add the pâté mixture to the pan, and fold over plastic and foil to seal. Bake in a water bath at 350°F/180°C for about 1 hour. Chill thoroughly.

Turn out terrine from the mold and remove wrappers. Brush on the apricot jam. Mix the chopped parsley, crushed peppercorns and black sesame seeds, and use them to coat the outside of the terrine.

SERVE WITH: Slice terrine and serve with India-Style Flat Bread (page 353), Pear Chutney (page 131). Drizzle on a little Carrot Juice Cinnamon Reduction Sauce (page 153) or Walnut Sherry Vinaigrette (page 182).

Crostini

YIELD 10 SERVINGS

3 CROSTINI PER PERSON

*When spread with one of the following pesto recipes, these savory toasts make
great appetizers or they can be served as a garnish for salad or soup.
There are recipes for pesto in the sauce chapter.*

FOR THE CROSTINI

French baguette, in thin diagonal slices	30	30
extra virgin olive oil	about $\frac{1}{4}$ cup	about 60 milliliters
salt	as desired	as desired
ground black pepper	as desired	as desired

Preheat the oven to 375°F/190°C.

Brush both sides of the baguette slices lightly with olive oil. Place them on a sheet
pan, sprinkle with salt and pepper if desired, and bake them for 5 minutes. Turn over
the crostini and bake for another couple of minutes.

VARIATION: Add 1 teaspoon/2.5 grams crushed garlic to the oil to make Garlic
Crostini.

Sundried Tomato Pesto

YIELD 1 CUP/280 GRAMS

ABOUT 25 CROSTINI

The intense tang of the tomatoes sets the taste buds in motion. A little of this pesto could be swirled into a soup such as the Tomato Sunflower Creme (page 94) for an additional flavor charge.

sundried tomatoes	$1\frac{1}{3}$ cup	84 grams
orange juice	$\frac{1}{4}$ cup	60 milliliters
water	$\frac{3}{4}$ cup	180 milliliters
garlic	1 teaspoon	5 grams
extra virgin olive oil	2 tablespoons	30 milliliters
fresh rosemary leaves	1 teaspoon	2 grams
hot pepper flakes	pinch	pinch
balsamic vinegar	1 tablespoon	15 milliliters
salt	$\frac{1}{4}$ teaspoon	1.5 grams
pepper	pinch	pinch
capers	1 tablespoon	7 grams
GARNISH		
toasted pine nuts	2 tablespoons	14 grams
fresh oregano, minced	2 tablespoons	7 grams

Put all ingredients except the garnish in a pan and bring to a boil. Cover the pan and remove from heat, allowing tomatoes to soften for 20 minutes. Stir several times to distribute the moisture. Put all ingredients except garnish in a food processor and grind to a chunky paste.

GARNISH AND PRESENTATION: Lightly coat crostini with pesto and garnish with pine nuts and fresh oregano.

Olive Pesto

YIELD 1 CUP/250 GRAMS

MAKES ABOUT 25 CROSTINI

Olives have such a range of flavor, from the mild taste of domestic ripe black olives to the intense mouth-puckering power of certain green or black Mediterranean examples. A medley of olives may be used in this recipe to achieve the desired level of tang.

ripe black olives, pitted	1 cup	140 grams
imported olives, pitted	$\frac{1}{2}$ cup	84 grams
capers	2 tablespoons	28 grams
garlic	$\frac{1}{2}$ teaspoon	1.25 grams
extra virgin olive oil	2 teaspoons	10 milliliters
balsamic or red wine vinegar	2 teaspoons	10 milliliters

Combine all ingredients in a food processor and process to a coarse paste.

SERVE WITH: Crostini (page 55), French bread or crackers.

VARIATION: Other crostini toppings Exotic Mushroom Duxelle (page 265), Toasted Spice Hummus (page 51), Oyster Mushroom Sauté (page 60), Artichoke Filling (page 64), Spinach Pecan Pesto (page 140).

Roast Vegetable Spread

YIELD 10 TO 12 SERVINGS
$\frac{1}{4}$ CUP/60 MILLILITERS

*Flavor development is accomplished by roasting the vegetables for this spread. Serve it with bread
as an alternative to butter, margarine or olive oil.*

butternut squash, large dice	3 cups	378 grams
onions, large dice	1 cup	112 grams
carrots, large dice	1 cup	112 grams
olive oil	2 teaspoons	10 milliliters
salt	$\frac{1}{4}$ teaspoon	1.5 grams
pepper	pinch	pinch
sliced almonds	$\frac{1}{3}$ cup	28 grams
water	$\frac{1}{4}$ cup	60 milliliters

Preheat oven to 400°F/200°C. Put the squash, onions and carrots on a baking sheet.
Toss with olive oil, salt and pepper. Roast for 25 to 30 minutes or until the carrots
and squash are tender. Stir the mixture once or twice during cooking time. Add the
almonds to pan for the last 3 minutes to toast them. Remove the pan from the oven
and deglaze the pan with water. Allow the mixture to cool, then process in a food
processor until smooth. Season to taste.

SERVE WITH: India-Style Flatbread (page 353), Crostini (page 55), toast points or
bread of choice.

Note: Roasting the vegetables at a lower temperature may result in a longer cooking time,
less caramelization, and cause them to dry out, reducing the yield.

Note: See page 207 for Garlic and Herb Spread.

Chilebella Mushrooms

Ground ancho chile peppers, referred to as ancho molido, along with the cumin and other seasonings, give the portobello mushroom caps a southwestern flavor.

portobello mushroom caps	10 caps	900 grams
olive oil	5 teaspoons	25 milliliters
orange juice	$1\frac{1}{2}$ cups	360 milliliters
lime juice	2 tablespoons	30 milliliters
soy sauce	3 tablespoons	45 milliliters
garlic, minced	1 tablespoon	15 grams
ginger root, minced	1 tablespoon	15 grams
ancho molido	$2\frac{1}{2}$ teaspoons	5 grams
cumin, ground	$1\frac{1}{4}$ teaspoons	2.5 grams

Clean the mushroom caps with a damp towel or under running water. Dry the caps of any residual water. Brush each cap top with olive oil. In a large skillet, sauté the portobello caps until golden brown on top, remove from the pan and continue until all caps are browned.

Add the mushrooms back to pan with all remaining ingredients, including any mushroom juices. Cover and simmer for 5 minutes or until tender.

VARIATION: Add a few drops mesquite-flavored liquid smoke.

SERVE WITH: Make red corn polenta using the recipe Polenta with Spinach Pesto (page 72).

Note: Mushroom weight is for caps without stems at about 3 ounces/84 grams each. If purchased whole, save stems for soup or soup stock. Chili powder can be used in place of the ancho molido and cumin.

Sautéed Oyster Mushrooms over Herb Scones

YIELD 10 SERVINGS

Oyster mushrooms are very delicate and must be handled gently. As they are generally clean when purchased, you may need only to cut away any residual soil left on the stems and give them a quick rinse just before using.

garlic, minced	2 tablespoons	14 grams
olive oil	2 tablespoons	30 milliliters
oyster mushrooms	2 pounds	450 grams
fresh rosemary, minced	1 teaspoon	2.3 grams
soy margarine (optional)	1 tablespoon	14 grams
salt	pinch	pinch
pepper	pinch	pinch
flour	$\frac{1}{4}$ cup	35 grams
sherry	1 tablespoon	15 milliliters
apple juice	$\frac{1}{4}$ cup	60 milliliters
vegetable stock, hot	$3\frac{1}{4}$ cup	780 milliliters
Oatmeal Herb Scones, small size, (page 355)	$\frac{1}{2}$ recipe (12)	$\frac{1}{2}$ recipe (12)

GARNISH

watercress	1 bunch	1 bunch

Sauté the garlic in olive oil over medium–high heat for about 10 seconds, then add the mushrooms to the pan and sauté for 3 minutes longer. Add the rosemary, margarine, salt, pepper and flour. Stir and cook for about 1 minute. Add the sherry wine, apple juice and slowly stir in the vegetable stock. Simmer for about 6 minutes longer or until the oyster mushrooms are tender and the sauce is slightly thickened. Season to taste.

Serve the oyster mushrooms and sauce over small Oatmeal Herb Scones that have been split in half.

GARNISH: Use watercress to garnish the plates. Toss the watercress with a little oil and sherry vinegar or Walnut Sherry Vinaigrette (page 182).

Note: Since oyster mushrooms can vary in size, they may need to be cut to a uniform size before cooking.

Guacamole in Nasturtium Blossoms

YIELD 10 SERVINGS

3 BLOSSOMS EACH

This great serving idea was presented by Martha Paul of Martha's Herbary in Pomfret,
Connecticut, during one of her classes on edible flowers.

GUACAMOLE

avocados, peeled and pitted	1 cup	168 grams
lime juice	1 tablespoon	15 milliliters
plum tomato, seeded, chopped	1 cup	140 grams
scallions, minced	1 tablespoon	3.5 grams
fresh cilantro, minced	1 tablespoon	3.5 grams
salt	pinch	pinch
pepper	pinch	pinch
hot sauce	$\frac{1}{4}$ teaspoon	1.25 milliliters
garlic, crushed	$\frac{1}{4}$ teaspoon	1.25 grams

GARNISH

nasturtium blossoms	30	30
black sesame seeds, lightly toasted	1 tablespoon	7 grams
round corn chips	30	30

Mash all the guacamole ingredients together with a fork. Season to taste. Spoon some guacamole into each blossom and sprinkle with black sesame seeds. To secure the nasturtiums, place a dab of guacamole on each corn chip and top with a filled blossom.

Fried Zucchini Blossoms

YIELD 10 SERVINGS
3 BLOSSOMS EACH

A great summer appetizer when zucchini blossoms are abundant.

zucchini blossoms	30	30
flour	1½ cups	140 grams
garlic powder	½ teaspoon	½ teaspoon
salt	½ teaspoon	3 grams
ground black pepper	pinch	pinch
water	1½ cups	360 milliliters
bread crumbs	2 cups	168 grams
fresh basil, minced	2 tablespoons	7 grams
safflower oil	for frying	for frying
GARNISH		
lime wedges	30	30
basil leaves	10	10

Rinse the blossoms gently and examine for insects. Dry thoroughly with paper towels, cover and refrigerate until ready to use.

Combine the flour with the garlic powder, salt and pepper. Place two-thirds of the flour mixture in a bowl. Place remaining one-third of the flour mixture in another bowl and gradually whisk in the water. In another bowl, combine the bread crumbs with the basil.

To bread the zucchini blossoms, dip them first into the dry flour mixture, then into the wet flour mixture, then into the bread crumbs.

Heat the oil to 350°F/180°C. Fry blossoms for a few minutes until golden, turning them over once during cooking. Drain on absorbent paper. Season with salt and pepper if desired.

GARNISH: Place zucchini blossoms on a platter or individual plates and garnish with lime wedges and basil leaves.

SERVE WITH: Sea Czar Salad in place of or along with Blackened Tofu, (page 175) or serve with Fusion Tartar Sauce (page 155).

Note: Be aware that bees sometimes get trapped inside blossoms when they close up for the night.

Stuffed Zucchini Blossoms

YIELD 10 SERVINGS
3 BLOSSOMS EACH

For a more substantial first course the zucchini blossoms are stuffed before frying.

Fried Zucchini Blossoms, (page 62)	1 recipe	1 recipe
STUFFING		
vegetarian sausage, cooked and crumbled	2 cups	182 grams
soy sauce	1 tablespoon	15 milliliters
Vegenaise	3 tablespoons	45 milliliters
ground black pepper	pinch	pinch
fresh basil, minced	2 tablespoons	7 grams

Combine all ingredients for stuffing. Place a heaping tablespoon of stuffing in each blossom and fold over the top to enclose filling. Follow breading procedure as for Fried Zucchini Blossoms (page 62).

Stuffed blossoms can be deep-fried, sandwiched between 2 fryer baskets to help keep stuffing intact. Alternately, fry stuffed blossoms in a large sauté pan or skillet, about 2 minutes per side.

GARNISH: See Fried Zucchini Blossoms (page 62).

SERVE WITH: Fusion Tartar Sauce (page 155), Watermelon Catsup, (page 135).

Artichoke Hearts in Fillo

YIELD 10 SERVINGS
1 CUP FILLING MIXTURE
2 SMALL FILLO TRIANGLES EACH

Most often fillo dough is purchased frozen. By slowly defrosting it in the refrigerator for several hours or overnight, it is easier to separate and handle.

ARTICHOKE FILLING

marinated artichoke hearts	1 cup	335 grams
Veganaise	$\frac{1}{4}$ cup	60 milliliters
white miso	1 tablespoon	14 grams
parsley, minced	1 tablespoon	3.5 grams
ground black pepper	pinch	pinch

WRAPPER

fillo sheets	10	10
soy margarine, melted	4 tablespoons	56 grams

GARNISH

lemon wedges	10	10

Preheat oven to 375°F/190°C.

Drain the artichoke hearts and feel for any hard leaves which need to be cut or pulled off and discarded. Put the artichokes and all other filling ingredients into a food processor and process to a chunky paste.

Cut fillo sheets in half widthwise. Brush each half sheet with some of the melted soy margarine. Fold fillo into thirds, lengthwise. Place a heaping tablespoon of filling at the end of the fillo strip and fold it up into a triangle. Place the triangle on a baking sheet and brush the top with soy margarine. Continue to make triangles until filling and fillo sheets are used up.

Bake the triangles for 13 to 15 minutes.

Serve warm to hot with lemon wedges, 2 per plate, or all on a platter. For a special presentation, serve individual servings on a bed of dressed lettuce greens.

VARIATION: The artichoke filling can be served hot as a dip with chips or flatbread. Mint or cilantro can be used in place of the parsley.

Note: Keep fillo sheets covered with a dry towel as they dry out and become unusable quickly. Handle fillo sheets gently as they tear easily. If they do tear, simply overlap at the tear using a little oil or margarine to seal. When making large quantities of fillo-wrapped pastries, have all the components ready and use a long work table. First, prepare all the pastry wrappers, then add the filling and roll up. The number of items that can be worked on at one time depends on how fast the task can be done without the fillo dough drying out and starting to break. The number of people doing the job also affects the output.

Olive, corn, canola or other oil could be used in place of the soy margarine.

Peach and Tomato Salsa

YIELD 10 SERVINGS
$\frac{1}{2}$ CUP/120 MILLILITERS

This and the following salsa recipes all combine tomato — technically a fruit — with other fruits. They can be made with all tomato or all fruit, and the possibilities are only limited by imagination. Other variations follow these 3 recipes.

peaches, peeled and pitted, small dice	$2\frac{1}{2}$ cups	350 grams
tomatoes, seeded, small dice	$2\frac{1}{2}$ cups	350 grams
cilantro, chopped	$\frac{1}{4}$ cup	7 grams
lime juice	2 teaspoons	10 milliliters
garlic, crushed	$\frac{1}{2}$ teaspoon	1.25 grams
balsamic vinegar	2 teaspoons	10 milliliters
salt	$\frac{1}{4}$ teaspoon	1.25 grams
ground black pepper	pinch	pinch
cayenne pepper	pinch	pinch

Combine all ingredients, cover and allow flavors to marry for at least 1 hour. Season to taste before serving.

SERVE WITH: Serve with corn chips as an appetizer and also as a sauce for savory pancakes.

Pineapple and Tomato Salsa

YIELD 10 SERVINGS
$\frac{1}{2}$ CUP/120 MILLILITERS

Today salsas may be used as dips, sauces over pasta, for grilled, sautéed, or fried foods, and added to other dishes to enhance the flavor.

pineapple, peeled and cored, small dice	$2\frac{1}{2}$ cups	350 grams
tomatoes, seeded, small dice	$2\frac{1}{2}$ cups	350 grams
cilantro, chopped	$\frac{1}{4}$ cup	14 grams
lime juice	2 teaspoons	10 milliliters
red onion, minced	1 tablespoon	7 grams
white balsamic vinegar	2 teaspoons	10 milliliters
salt	$\frac{1}{4}$ teaspoon	1.25 grams
ground black pepper	pinch	pinch
cayenne pepper	pinch	pinch

Combine all ingredients, cover and allow flavors to marry for at least 1 hour. Season to taste before serving.

SERVE WITH: Serve with corn chips as an appetizer and also as a sauce for pancakes.

Plum and Tomato Salsa

YIELD 10 SERVINGS
$\frac{1}{2}$ CUP/120 MILLILITERS

Plums are used raw, combined with tomato for this salsa, and in the sauce chapter they are used as a substitute for tomato in a cooked sauce intended for pasta.

plums, peeled and pitted, small dice	$2\frac{1}{2}$ cups	350 grams
tomatoes, seeded, small dice	$2\frac{1}{2}$ cups	350 grams
cilantro, chopped	$\frac{1}{4}$ cup	14 grams
lime juice	2 teaspoons	10 milliliters
scallion, minced	1 tablespoon	7 grams
white balsamic vinegar	2 teaspoons	10 milliliters
salt	$\frac{1}{4}$ teaspoon	1.25 grams
ground black pepper	pinch	pinch
cayenne pepper	pinch	pinch

Combine all ingredients, cover and allow flavors to marry for at least 1 hour. Season to taste before serving.

SERVE WITH: Serve with corn chips as an appetizer and also as a sauce for Savory Pancakes (pages 71, 250, 251).

SALSA VARIATIONS: These additions will take the salsa recipes in different taste directions. Hot peppers such as jalapeño or habanero may be added for flavor and spice. By adding a tiny bit at a time one can control the heat. Other fruits, vegetables and spices that can be added to or substituted in the salsa recipes include mango, oranges, cucumbers, ginger, basil and mint. Rice vinegar or sherry vinegar might also be used.

Spinach in Fillo

YIELD 10 SERVINGS
2 PASTRIES EACH
2 CUPS/560 GRAMS FILLING

By squeezing out the excess moisture after cooking the spinach you will keep the fillo pastry bottoms from getting soggy during backing.

onions, fine dice	$1\frac{1}{2}$ cups	168 grams
olive oil	4 tablespoons	60 milliliters
garlic, crushed	1 tablespoon	7 grams
salt	$\frac{1}{2}$ teaspoon	3 grams
ground fennel	1 teaspoon	2.33 grams
ground nutmeg	$\frac{1}{3}$ teaspoon	.75 grams
ground black pepper	pinch	pinch
chopped cooked spinach	$1\frac{3}{4}$ cups	392 grams
fillo sheets	10	10
olive oil	1 tablespoon	15 milliliters
soy margarine	2 tablespoons	28 grams

GARNISH

lemon wedges	10	10

Preheat oven to 375°F/190°C.

Sauté the onions in 1 tablespoon/15 milliliters olive oil over medium heat for about 5 minutes or until soft and starting to brown. Stir in the garlic, salt, fennel, nutmeg and pepper. Sauté for another 2 to 3 minutes. Stir in the spinach and sauté for 1 minute. If there is liquid present, increase the heat and allow it to evaporate as excess moisture can weaken the bottom of the pastries. Season to taste.

In a small pan heat the remaining olive oil with soy margarine until the margarine is melted.

Prepare fillo sheets as for Artichoke Hearts in Fillo (page 64) and make triangles or use whole sheets of fillo and roll up 10 cylinder shapes.

Cut spinach cylinders in half diagonally and place on a platter with lemon wedges, or serve individual servings with dressed lettuce greens.

Note: To use fresh spinach, blanch 2 pounds/900 grams spinach in a large pot of boiling water, drain, cool with cold water, then squeeze out excess moisture. Chop the spinach coarsely and set aside. A little white miso could be added to flavor the spinach mixture.

Korean-Style Cucumbers with Spicy Miso Sauce

YIELD 10 SERVINGS
ABOUT 1 TABLESPOON/15 MILLILITERS SAUCE
WITH 4 CUCUMBER SPEARS

Travelers returning from Korea have reported that the warming effect of spicy food is popular to offset the intensely cold winters and augment the uncertain fuel supply.

pickling cucumbers, peeled	5	1.3 kilograms (5 × 224 grams)

SPICY MISO SAUCE

red miso	$\frac{1}{2}$ cup	168 grams
maple syrup	2 tablespoons	30 milliliters
rice wine vinegar	1 tablespoon	15 milliliters
ginger root, minced	2 teaspoons	4.6 grams
water	2 tablespoons	30 milliliters
cayenne pepper	pinch	pinch
toasted sesame oil	$\frac{1}{4}$ teaspoon	1.25 milliliters

GARNISH

toasted sesame seeds	1 tablespoon	7 grams
chopped scallions or chives	2 tablespoons	7 grams

Cut the cucumbers lengthwise into 8 spears each. In a small bowl combine all ingredients except garnish until well mixed.

GARNISH AND PRESENTATION: Serve 4 spears of cucumber with a dollop of sauce per person. Sprinkle with sesame seeds and chopped scallions.

Note: Choose pickling cucumbers that are about 5 inches/13 centimeters long.

Corn and Arame Pancakes

YIELD 10 SERVINGS

2 PANCAKES, $2\frac{1}{2}$ INCHES/6 CENTIMETERS EACH

For these and other pancakes, a stick-free griddle allows them to be cooked with a minimal amount of oil.

arame (sea vegetable), dry	1 cup	21 grams
water	3 cups	720 milliliters
soy sauce	2 tablespoons	30 milliliters
toasted sesame oil	1 teaspoon	5 milliliters
ginger root, minced	1 teaspoon	2.3 grams
rice vinegar	2 teaspoons	10 milliliters
all-purpose flour	$\frac{3}{4}$ cup	105 grams
whole wheat pastry flour	$\frac{3}{4}$ cup	105 grams
salt	$\frac{1}{4}$ teaspoon	1.5 grams
baking powder	$1\frac{1}{2}$ teaspoons	8 grams
carrots, grated	$\frac{1}{2}$ cup	56 grams
scallions, thin diagonal slices	$\frac{1}{2}$ cup	28 grams
corn kernels, frozen	1 cup	140 grams

Soak the arame in 1 cup of water for 5 minutes and drain. Put the softened arame, remaining water, soy sauce, sesame oil, ginger and rice vinegar into a pan. Bring to a boil, then simmer for 6 to 8 minutes or until the arame is tender. Drain liquid from the arame into a measuring cup, and add enough water to make $1\frac{3}{4}$ cups. Set the arame and liquid aside.

In a bowl, combine the flours, salt and baking powder. Add the carrots, scallions and corn to the flour mixture, combine well and push to one side of the bowl. Add the arame and liquid to the other side of the bowl and gently fold together.

Lightly oil and preheat a griddle over medium heat. Spoon the pancake batter onto the griddle and spread to make thin pancakes about $2\frac{1}{2}$ inches/6 centimeters. Turn when bubbles form across the top of each pancake and the edges are starting to brown. Cook for about a minute longer on the second side. Keep the pancakes warm until batter is used up.

SERVE WITH: Simple Dipping Sauce (page 143), or maple syrup mixed with a little horseradish or wasabi.

Note: The water used to soak arame can be used to water plants.

Soft Polenta with Spinach Pesto

YIELD 10 SERVINGS
ABOUT $\frac{1}{3}$ CUP/80 MILLILITER INCLUDING PESTO

For dishes like polenta a heat diffuser or "flame tamer" can give a little extra protection if one is called away from the stove for a few minutes. A steam jacket kettle can also provide the same sort of safety from burning.

water	3 cups	720 milliliters
white miso	1 tablespoon	14 grams
salt	pinch	pinch
pepper	pinch	pinch
yellow cornmeal	1 cup	168 grams
soy margarine	1 tablespoon	14 grams

GARNISH

toasted pecans, chopped	$\frac{1}{3}$ cup	35 grams
spinach leaves	20	20
Spinach Pecan Pesto (page 140), $\frac{1}{2}$ recipe	2 cups	480 milliliters

Bring the water, miso, salt and pepper to a boil. Using a wire whip, gradually stir in cornmeal. Reduce the heat and simmer the polenta, stirring constantly for 10 to 15 minutes. A longer cooking time will produce a creamier texture. Stir in the soy margarine and season to taste.

Polenta may be served soft-style right from the pot.

GARNISH WITH: Serve polenta in small bowls or on small plates garnished with toasted pecans, spinach leaves and Spinach Pecan Pesto (page 140).

VARIATION: Polenta can also be served in several other ways. For firm polenta, spread the cooked polenta onto a flat surface or into a small sheet pan, level it to about $\frac{1}{2}$ inch/1.25 centimeters then allow it to cool and firm. It may then be cut into triangles or punched out with cutters to make rounds or other shapes. Top polenta with a pesto of choice, place on a lightly oiled sheet pan, cover and heat in the oven until warmed through.

A traditional way of shaping polenta is to put it into a loaf pan, allow it to cool and become firm, then turn it out and slice it. The polenta may then be sautéed until golden on each side. Serve with sauce or serve for breakfast with maple syrup.

SERVE WITH: Sundried Tomato Pesto (page 56), Olive Pesto (page 57) or a combination including the Spinach Pecan Pesto (page 140), Pizziola Sauce (page 213).

Note: Try making red, white or blue cornmeal polenta. Yellow corn grits are ground a little coarser and cook up with a pleasant grainy texture.

Fried Breaded Zucchini

YIELD 10 SERVINGS

4 TO 5 STICKS EACH

For this recipe both the flavor and texture of small zucchini work best.

zucchini, 7 inches/ 18 centimeters	3	3
FLOUR MIXTURE		
flour	$\frac{1}{2}$ cup	70 grams
garlic powder	$\frac{1}{2}$ teaspoon	1 gram
salt	$\frac{1}{2}$ teaspoon	3 grams
ground black pepper	2 pinches	2 pinches
orange juice	$\frac{1}{2}$ cup	120 milliliters
BREAD CRUMB MIXTURE		
bread crumbs	1 cup	84 grams
fresh parsley, minced	2 tablespoons	7 grams
fennel seeds, crushed	1 teaspoon	2.33 grams
orange zest, minced	1 teaspoon	3.5 grams
safflower oil	for frying	for frying
GARNISH		
fresh parsley, coarsely chopped	$\frac{1}{4}$ cup	14 grams
lime wedges	10	10

Cut the zucchini in half lengthwise, then cut each half into 4 lengths. Cut strips in half to make 48 sticks.

In a bowl combine the flour, half the garlic powder, half the salt, and a pinch of pepper. Reserve the orange juice. In another bowl, combine the remaining salt, garlic powder and pepper. Combine all ingredients for the bread crumb mixture.

Toss the zucchini sticks with the flour mixture, then shake off excess flour back into the bowl. Gradually add the orange juice to the flour mixture to make a batter. Dip floured zucchini sticks into the batter, then coat with the seasoned bread crumb mixture. Shake off loose crumbs.

Heat oil to 350°F/180°C. Fry the zucchini about 2 minutes or until golden brown. Drain on absorbent paper and serve hot.

GARNISH: Garnish with chopped parsley and lime wedges.

SERVE WITH: Watermelon Catsup (page 135) or Fusion Tartar Sauce (page 155).

Roasted Whole Garlic Bulbs

10 SERVINGS
$\frac{1}{2}$ BULB EACH

Roasted garlic is now popular served as a spread for bread along with extra virgin olive oil. It can also be used as a flavor-boosting ingredient in other dishes.

whole garlic bulbs	5	5
olive oil	1 tablespoon	15 milliliters
salt	pinch	pinch
ground black pepper	pinch	pinch
rosemary leaves	pinch	pinch

Preheat oven to 400°F/200°C.

Gently peel away outer paper-like skin of the garlic, keeping the bulbs intact. Cut the sprout or pointed end of garlic bulb flat. Drizzle bulbs with olive oil and sprinkle with salt, pepper and rosemary. Place in a covered baking dish or wrap loosely with foil and bake bulbs for 30 minutes. Uncover the garlic and continue to bake for 10 minutes longer or until garlic is tender. Serve warm, squeezing the cloves onto bread.

SERVE WITH: Serve with extra virgin olive oil and French or Italian bread. Chopped fresh herbs, salt and freshly ground black pepper may be sprinkled into small bowls or plates of olive oil.

Serving a selection of extra virgin olive oils from different producers or different countries provides both hosts and guests with the opportunity to discover the wide range of flavors that premium olive oils offer and which style suits their taste.

Note: Bulbs of garlic vary in size. The smaller ones will cook faster.

Vegetable Tempura

YIELD 10 SERVINGS
ABOUT 2½ OUNCES/70 GRAMS,
A FEW SLICES OF EACH VEGETABLE

The use of cornstarch in the batters helps create the signature crunchiness of tempura fried foods. To appreciate its crisp texture, tempura should be served as quickly as possible after frying.

VEGETABLES FOR TEMPURA

zucchini, thin diagonal slices	$1\frac{1}{2}$ cups	168 grams
green beans, whole	$1\frac{1}{2}$ cups	168 grams
onion rings	$1\frac{1}{2}$ cups	168 grams
red pepper, thin strips	$1\frac{1}{2}$ cups	168 grams
sweet potato, peeled	2 cups	224 grams

TEMPURA BATTER

all purpose flour	$\frac{1}{3}$ cup	46 grams
cornstarch	$\frac{2}{3}$ cup	93 grams
ice-cold water	$\frac{3}{4}$ cup	180 milliliters
salt	pinch	pinch
pepper	pinch	pinch
oil	for frying	for frying

Prepare and slice the vegetables with sweet potato just peeled to maintain color. Slice sweet potato just before using. Cover and place the vegetables in refrigerator while preparing the batter and heating oil for frying. Prepare the batter and heat oil to about 360°F/185°C.

Using tongs or chopsticks, dip each vegetable piece into tempura batter. Fry for a minute or so on each side. You can fry one type of vegetable at a time or several, taking into consideration that the thicker, harder vegetables will take longer to cook. Drain on absorbent paper, then serve a selection of vegetables.

SERVE WITH: Simple Dipping Sauce (page 143).

Dates with Almonds

The stuffed dates can be made without the vegetarian ham, but it is really worth the effort to acquire it. See Source Guide in the Appendix.

40 whole almonds	3 ounces	84 grams
soy sauce	2 teaspoons	10 milliliters
liquid smoke, hickory-flavored	4 drops	4 drops
dried, pitted dates	40	450 grams
vegetarian ham	20 slices	20 slices

Toast the almonds. While still hot, toss the toasted almonds with 1 teaspoon/5 milliliters soy sauce. Add liquid smoke to remaining soy sauce. Stuff the dates with almonds, then toss the stuffed dates with the remaining soy sauce. Cut the vegetarian ham slices in half. Wrap each stuffed date with a half-slice of the vegetarian ham. Bake in the oven for a couple of minutes or until heated through. Serve warm.

Note: Be sure your guests know that the dates are filled with almonds not date pits! Tempeh bacon, also called smoked tempeh strips, can be used in place of vegetarian ham.

CHAPTER FOUR

Soups

Soups can be long-simmering affairs that

perfume the air and kindle appetites with the

promise of tastes to come. They also can be

achieved almost instantly by blending chilled

ingredients to yield the bright colors and flavors

of cool summer purées.

As a seasoned broth, a silken vegetable crème, or a hardy bean concoction, soups wear many guises. Served hot or cold, with a simple garnish or an elaborate design, soup can set the stage for the meal to come or take center stage as the main course itself.

One of the recent trends to re-emerge in soup presentation is that of serving from a tureen at tableside. A modern twist that adds to service and the enjoyment of the course is the delivery of the soup in two stages. First, the bowl is presented with the garnish artistically arranged at the bowl's bottom, then the broth or liquid portion of the dish is carefully poured into the serving vessel. Mushroom Cashew Crème Soup (page 112) and the Mushroom Barley Soup (page 111) with sautéed mushrooms, and the Black Bean Soup with Cumin and Garlic (page 102) with the full garnish treatment could be served in this way.

Most of the soups, especially the hardy bean soups, could be the main course of a light meal when paired with salad and bread, or featured as a main course served over a mound of garnished rice or other grain.

Making Stock

Stock provides the foundation for soups and sauces. The French term for stock is "fond de cuisine," which means the "base of cooking." It refers to the role that stock plays in providing the underlying structure to these preparations. The liquid that is used to braise a dish may also be referred to as stock.

After blanching vegetables for other dishes, use the resulting "fortified" water as the liquid for stock or in place of stock in recipes. Use fortified water that complements the soup being prepared. For instance, water used to blanch broccoli would be good in a cabbage soup, but may be too strong for other types of soups.

Deglaze pans from roasting vegetables by adding some stock, fortified water, plain water, wine or diluted vegetable juice to the pan, then scraping up any caramelization sticking to the pan. Use this liquid in a stock recipe. If the roasting pan has burned spots, avoid loosening them as they will make your stock bitter.

Be aware that too much of any one vegetable or peelings from a vegetable will dominate the flavor of a stock and will show up in the finished dish. Take into consideration what the flavor of the finished soup or sauce will be and use complementary flavored vegetables in the stock.

When using the peelings from vegetables, do not include more than two or three cups for the amount of water in the basic stock recipe. When adding other fresh herbs, use up to one cup total with stems included. The stems from mushrooms, especially woody ones like some portobello or shiitake, also add flavor, especially when mushrooms are incorporated into the final preparation.

When making vegetable stock, 40 to 45 minutes is adequate to extract the flavor from most vegetables. Longer cooking may result in a bitter-tasting stock. Strain the stock when it is done as the vegetables will continue to cook if left in, and again may impart a bitter flavor to the stock.

Further Building the Foundation

MIREPOIX

To create underlying flavor for many of the stocks and soups, I start with a mirepoix, traditionally a mixture of diced and sautéed onions, carrots and celery. For some soups or dishes, other vegetables are added to this basic mixture. The mirepoix is sautéed in a little olive or canola oil to bring out the natural sugars, create carmelization and add a rich flavor to the recipe.

Other vegetables can be used in place of or in addition to the basic onion, carrot, and celery:

Add to mirepoix	Herbs or spices to complement them
leeks, scallions	parsley, tarragon, chervil, dill, bay leaf
scallions	ginger, garlic, star anise, cumin
shallots	tarragon, chervil, thyme, bay leaf
garlic	basil, oregano, bay leaf
	ginger, cumin, corriander
fresh anise or bulb fennel	garlic, basil
bell peppers	scallions, garlic, bay leaf, basil, oregano, thyme, ginger, cumin, corriander
parsnips, rutabagas, turnips	parsley, dill, thyme

Sauté the vegetables in a little olive or canola oil for 10 to 15 minutes over medium heat or until they start to brown, then add water and proceed with recipe.

Vegetables for stock can also be over-roasted first. Both of these methods yield a brown-tinted stock, which should be used in soups or sauces in which that color is desired.

Dried herbs are great for stock and long-simmering soups to build foundation flavor. Fresh herbs will maintain their characteristic bright tang when added at the end of cooking time, allowing long enough for the taste and aroma to be extracted but not so long that they are diminished. Use your nose and taste buds to help in timing.

When adding stock to any flour-thickened soup or sauce, it is best to have the stock hot so that it will mix easily with the roux. Roux is a mixture of flour and a fat that may also contain mirepoix. The oil and flour are cooked to remove some of the starch flavor of the flour and the combination also helps prevent lumps from forming when mixed with stock. Cold stock added to hot roux can create little balls of flour which, once formed, usually won't mix together with the stock. If this occurs in a soup, the only solution may be to purée the entire batch in a blender. The same solution may work for a sauce or it may be passed through a fine sieve and recovered.

Bean Soup Basics

Beans are a great source of vegetable protein and lend themselves wonderfully to be made into soup. Their hardy flavors and terrific textures complement their many varieties.

For the large, longer-cooking beans, starting with precooked beans will hasten the preparation time. Lentils, split peas and other quick-cooking beans can be cooked quickly right in the soup.

In the past I have often used a pressure cooker to prepare the longer-cooking types and sautéed the mirepoix as they cook. By sautéing a mirepoix, then adding the seasonings, cooked beans with their cooking liquid (if available) and vegetable stock, a delicious bean soup can be prepared in a relatively short time. The recipe on page 99 for Pinto Bean Soup follows the basic format for quantities.

To complement most bean soups

garlic	dry herbs and seasonings
prepared mustard	smoked dried green split peas
dill pickle brine	grated raw onion
lemon juice	chopped scallions to sprinkle on top
lime juice	balsamic vinegar
bay leaf	red wine vinegar
tomato	apple cider vineger
liquid hickory or mesquite smoke flavor	

Basic Light Vegetable Stock

YIELD ABOUT 9 CUPS/2.16 LITERS

*Great for adding a subtle flavored liquid to a recipe, the taste of this all-purpose stock
won't overpower the flavor focal point of a dish. The herbs are a combination
often used in French kitchens.*

onions, coarsely chopped	$1\frac{1}{2}$ cups	168 grams
carrots, coarsely chopped	$1\frac{1}{2}$ cups	189 grams
celery, coarsely chopped	$1\frac{1}{2}$ cups	168 grams
sprig of thyme	1	1
bay leaf	1	1
salt	1 teaspoon	6 grams
black peppercorns	2	2
vegetable peelings	1 cup each	42 grams
parsley stems	$\frac{1}{4}$ cup	14 grams
whole garlic cloves, bruised	2	2
water	12 cups	2.88 liters

Place all ingredients in water and bring to a boil. Reduce the heat and simmer for 30
to 40 minutes. Vegetables should be well cooked. Strain and discard boiled vegetables
and other solids.

Eastern European dishes or stock can be further flavored with dill stems, a few
dried mushrooms, parsley, garlic, scallions, mustard, tomato, celery, bay leaf, onion,
carrot, parsnips, peppercorns and salt.

The following ingredients can also be added to enhance most vegetable stocks:

prepared mustard
dill pickle brine
lemon juice
lime juice
fresh parsley, and other herbs as fit
the soup

bay leaf
tomato
soy sauce
liquid smoke, hickory or mesquite
flavor

To add body to stock, add a handful of red or green lentils or some yellow split
peas, or use the liquid that beans have been cooked in. This will add a slight thickness
to the stock. The red lentils and yellow split peas can add a gelatinous texture and
work well when combined with the herbs associated with stuffing—parsley, sage,
rosemary and thyme. Fresh or canned tomato can also be used in stocks when they
appear in the final recipe.

Basic Enriched Vegetable Stock

YIELD ABOUT 9 CUPS/2.16 LITERS

Sautéing the mirepoix in a little oil develops caramelization, which, along with a dash of soy sauce, yields an enriched stock.

onions, coarsely chopped	$1\frac{1}{2}$ cups	168 grams
carrots, coarsely chopped	$1\frac{1}{2}$ cups	189 grams
celery, coarsely chopped	$1\frac{1}{2}$ cups	168 grams
whole garlic cloves, bruised	2	2
olive oil	1 teaspoon	5 milliliters
spring of thyme	1	1
bay leaves	2	2
salt	1 teaspoon	6 grams
black peppercorns	2	2
vegetable peelings	1 cup each	42 grams
parsley stems	$\frac{1}{4}$ cup	14 grams
water	12 cups	2.88 liters
soy sauce	1 tablespoon	15 milliliters

Sauté the onions, carrots, celery and garlic in olive oil over medium heat for about 10 minutes or until browned. Add the remaining ingredients to the pot and bring to a boil. Reduce heat and simmer for 40 minutes. Vegetables should be well cooked. Strain and discard boiled vegetables and other solids.

Note: To bruise garlic cloves (leave skins on and lightly crush them with the side of a chef's knife).

Mediterranean Stock

To avoid a bitter flavor when using basil leaves, be sure to remove any flowering tops,
which look like a tall column of tiny leaves with or without the blossoms showing.
Leaves may be left on tender stalks of basil as well as oregano, which can be
used along with the basil or in its place.

onions, coarsely chopped	$1\frac{1}{2}$ cups	168 grams
carrots, coarsely chopped	$1\frac{1}{2}$ cups	189 grams
celery, coarsely chopped	$1\frac{1}{2}$ cups	168 grams
whole garlic cloves, bruised	2	2
olive oil	1 teaspoon	5 milliliters
bay leaves	2	2
salt	1 teaspoon	6 grams
black peppercorns	2	2
fennel seeds	1 teaspoon	2.33 grams
orange zest	1 tablespoon	9 grams
parsley stems	$\frac{1}{4}$ cup	14 grams
tomato, coarsely chopped	1 cup	140 grams
water	12 cups	2.88 liters
basil leaves	$\frac{1}{2}$ cup	28 grams

In the bottom of a stock pot, sauté the onions, carrots, celery and garlic in olive oil over medium heat for 10 minutes. Add all remaining ingredients except basil and bring to a boil. Reduce heat and simmer for 40 minutes. Add the basil to the pot and simmer 10 more minutes. Vegetables should be well cooked. Strain and discard boiled vegetables and other solids.

Note: Fennel flavor can be extracted from herb fennel or fennel bulb.

Asian Stock

YIELD ABOUT 9 CUPS/2.16 LITERS

This stock is seasoned with Chinese-style spices and can be adapted to the cuisine of other Southeast Asian nations by some of the suggestions below.

onions, coarsely chopped	1½ cups	168 grams
carrots, coarsely chopped	1½ cups	189 grams
scallions, coarsely chopped	1½ cups	168 grams
whole garlic cloves, bruised	2	2
ginger root, coarsely chopped	1 tablespoon	14 grams
peanut oil	1 teaspoon	5 milliliters
toasted sesame oil	1 teaspoon	5 milliliters
star anise	1 star	1 star
cilantro stems	¼ cup	14 grams
dry shiitake	½ cup	14 grams
salt	½ teaspoon	3 grams
black peppercorns	2	2
water	12 cups	2.88 liters
soy sauce	3 tablespoons	45 milliliters

In the bottom of a stock pot, sauté the onions, carrots, scallions, garlic and ginger in the peanut oil over medium high heat for 10 minutes. Put all remaining ingredients into pot and bring to a boil. Reduce heat and simmer for 40 minutes. Vegetables should be well cooked. Strain and discard boiled vegetables and other solids.

VARIATION: To make Southeast Asian Stock, prepare the recipe for Asian Stock. After the vegetables have been sautéed, add 2 stalks of bruised lemongrass. During the last 10 minutes of simmering, add ½ cup/28 grams basil leaves.

Note: Two slices of lemon could be used in place of the lemongrass along with a little lemon juice.

Chinese Five-Spice Cooking Stock

YIELD ABOUT $1\frac{1}{2}$ CUPS

This intensely flavored broth is infused with the spices that are traditionally ground together to make five-spice powder, a seasoning staple of Chinese cuisine.

scallions, coarsely chopped	3	3
garlic cloves, bruised	3	3
star anise	2 stars	2 stars
cinnamon stick	1 inch piece	2.5 centimeter piece
whole cloves	3	3
fennel seeds	large pinch	large pinch
black peppercorns	3	3
salt	pinch	pinch
water	3 cups	720 millileters

Put all ingredients into a small pan and simmer for 20 minutes. Strain and return to the pan. Reduce to $1\frac{1}{2}$ cups.

Note: A pinch of Szechuan peppercorns can be used in the stock in place of peppercorns. A tea ball or cheesecloth sachet bag can be used to contain the spices for the stock. Five-Spice Cooking Stock can be made in advance.

Enriched Mushroom Vegetable Stock

YIELD ABOUT 9 CUPS/2.16 LITERS

Dried mushrooms are used here to provide the designated flavor and could be mild dried white domestic mushrooms or more intensely flavored dried cèpe type or dried shiitake.

onions, coarsely chopped	$1\frac{1}{2}$ cups	168 grams
carrots, coarsely chopped	$1\frac{1}{2}$ cups	189 grams
celery, coarsely chopped	$1\frac{1}{2}$ cups	168 grams
olive oil	1 teaspoon	5 milliliters
dried mushrooms	1 cup	56 grams
soy sauce	2 tablespoons	30 milliliters
white wine	$\frac{1}{4}$ cup	60 milliliters
thyme	1 sprig	1 sprig
bay leaves	2	2
salt	1 teaspoon	6 grams
black peppercorns	2	2
parsley stems	$\frac{1}{4}$ cup	14 grams
whole garlic cloves, bruised	2	2
water	12 cups	2.88 liters

Sauté the onions, carrots and celery in olive oil over medium high heat for about 10 minutes or until browned. Add the remaining ingredients to the pot and bring to a boil. Reduce heat and simmer for 40 minutes. Vegetables should be well cooked. Strain and discard boiled vegetables and other solids.

Eastern European Stock

ABOUT 9 CUPS/2.16 LITERS

Other vegetables such as cabbage, kale or collard trimmings could be added to this stock when they are featured in a soup, such as Potato and Cabbage Soup with Dill (page 90).

onions, coarsely chopped	$1\frac{1}{2}$ cups	168 grams
carrots, coarsely chopped	$1\frac{1}{2}$ cups	189 grams
celery, coarsely chopped	$1\frac{1}{2}$ cups	168 grams
whole garlic cloves, bruised	2	2
olive oil	1 teaspoon	5 milliliters
bay leaves	2	2
dried mushrooms	$\frac{1}{4}$ cup	14 grams
salt	1 teaspoon	6 grams
black peppercorns	2	2
dill stems	$\frac{1}{4}$ cup	14 grams
liquid smoke	4 drops	4 drops
water	12 cups	2.88 liters

Sauté the onions, carrots, celery and garlic in olive oil over medium-high heat for about 10 minutes or until browned. Add the remaining ingredients to pot and bring to a boil. Reduce heat and simmer for 40 minutes. Vegetables should be well cooked. Strain and discard boiled vegetables and other solids.

Potato and Cabbage Soup with Dill

YIELD 10 SERVINGS
1 CUP/240 MILLILITERS

The brine from dill pickles enhances this Eastern European-style soup. In lesser amounts the brine can provide underlying flavor for other types of soups. The dry potato flakes called for in this recipe are a great substitute for flour as a thickener.

onions, small dice	$1\frac{1}{2}$ cups	168 grams
celery, small dice	$1\frac{1}{2}$ cups	168 grams
carrots, small dice	$1\frac{1}{2}$ cups	189 grams
canola oil	4 teaspoons	20 milliliters
garlic, minced	1 tablespoon	15 grams
green cabbage, large dice	4 cups	180 grams
salt	1 teaspoon	6 grams
ground black pepper	pinch	pinch
vegetable stock	6 cups	1.44 liters
bay leaves	2	2
thyme	2 4-inch sprigs	2 10-centimeter sprigs
dill pickles, small dice	$\frac{1}{2}$ cup	56 grams
dill pickle brine	$\frac{1}{2}$ cup	120 milliliters
prepared mustard	1 tablespoon	15 milliliters
fresh dill weed, minced	2 tablespoons	7 grams
parsley, minced	$\frac{1}{4}$ cup	14 grams
celery leaf, minced	$\frac{1}{4}$ cup	14 grams
potatoes, $\frac{1}{2}$-inch dice	2 cups	280 grams
water	2 cups	480 milliliters
dry potato flakes	$\frac{1}{2}$ cup	28 grams

Sauté the onions, celery and carrots in canola oil over medium heat for 10 minutes. Add the garlic, cabbage, salt and pepper and continue to sauté for another 10 minutes over medium-low heat. Add the vegetable stock, 1 bay leaf, 1 sprig of thyme, dill pickles, brine and prepared mustard. Bring to a boil and then simmer for 20 minutes. While the soup is simmering put fresh dill weed, the remaining bay leaf and thyme, parsley, celery leaf, potatoes and water into a small pot and bring to a boil, then simmer until potatoes are tender. Add them to the soup. Remove the soup from heat. Remove 3 cups of soup solids and 2 cups of broth to a blender. Allow the ingredients to cool a bit, then purée and return to the soup. Bring the soup back to a simmer and stir in the dry potato flakes to thicken the soup. Season to taste.

Note: Use caution when blending any hot foods as the steam pressure builds and can blow the top off the blender.

GARNISH AND PRESENTATION: Sprinkle the bowls of soup with chopped parsley or fresh dill. For a special presentation season some mashed potatoes with chopped fresh dill and put them into a pastry bag with a large star tip. Pipe a mound of potatoes into shallow soup bowls, then ladle the soup around the mound. Garnish with a dill sprig stuck into the top of the potatoes and some chopped fresh dill.

VARIATION: If the soup is served as part of a multi-course meal, purée the entire soup. This treatment will make the soup seem lighter and bring together all the flavors, allowing them to be tasted simultaneously as they coat the palate. In a meal of fewer courses and when soup will play a feature role, the more substantial chunky version is appropriate.

SERVE WITH: Red Swiss Chard Sauté with Garlic (page 194), Savory Winter Pancakes (page 251), Hungarian Style Braised Mushrooms (page 247).

Note: Soups and long-cooked dishes allow the concentrated flavor of dried herbs to be extracted and exploited. For this soup garnish with fresh dill weed and/or add it to the soup only for the last few minutes of cooking to maintain its aroma.

Broccoli Tahini Soup

YIELD 10 SERVINGS
1 CUP/240 MILLILITERS

Tahini, ground sesame seed paste, is available in 2 styles. One style is made from raw seeds and the other is prepared with toasted sesame seeds. For seeds and nuts in general, the toasting process provides a deep, rich flavor. For this soup I prefer the more developed flavor of the toasted sesame version. The tahini also adds a creamy texture to the soup.

onions, small dice	$1\frac{1}{2}$ cups	168 grams
carrots, small dice	$1\frac{1}{2}$ cups	189 grams
celery, small dice	$1\frac{1}{2}$ cups	168 grams
olive oil	1 tablespoon	15 milliliters
garlic, minced	1 teaspoon	5 grams
all-purpose white flour	$\frac{1}{2}$ cup	70 grams
vegetable stock, hot	6 cups	1.44 liters
bay leaf	1 or 2	1 or 2
oregano, dry	$\frac{1}{2}$ teaspoon	2.5 milliliters
basil, dry	$\frac{1}{2}$ teaspoon	2.5 milliliters
prepared mustard	1 teaspoon	5 milliliters
lemon juice	2 teaspoons	10 milliliters
salt	1 teaspoon	5 milliliters
ground black pepper	pinch	pinch
broccoli, finely chopped	6 cups	434 grams
parsley, chopped	$\frac{1}{2}$ cup	120 milliliters
toasted sesame tahini	$\frac{3}{4}$ cup	180 milliliters
toasted black sesame seeds	1 tablespoon	15 milliliters

Sauté the onions, carrots and celery in olive oil over medium heat for 10 minutes. Add the garlic and sauté 5 minutes. Stir in the flour thoroughly, then slowly stir in the hot vegetable stock. Add the bay leaf, oregano, basil, mustard, lemon juice, salt and pepper. Bring to a boil and then simmer for 10 minutes. Add the broccoli and all but one tablespoon of parsley. Simmer for a few minutes longer until the broccoli is tender yet still green. Turn off the heat and stir in the tahini. Season to taste. Do not boil again as this may cause tahini to separate.

GARNISH: Garnish soup with toasted black sesame seeds and reserved parsley.

SERVE WITH: Orange Braised Butternut Squash with Ginger and Garlic (page 199), Golden Potato Salad with Olives and Apricots (page 176).

Note: To increase sesame flavor, add up to $\frac{1}{4}$ cup/60 milliliters tahini. Broccoli stems and peels may be cooked for a short time in the vegetable stock for this soup. Cooking them for a long time can make the stock bitter.

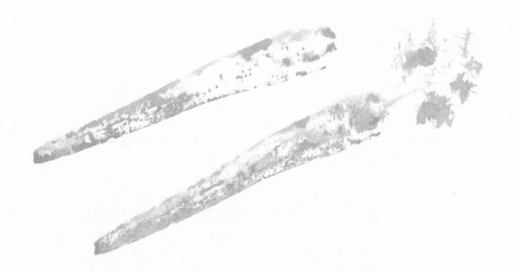

Tomato Sunflower Crème

YIELD 10 SERVINGS
1 CUP/240 MILLILITERS

The nostalgic flavor of this soup is enhanced by the creamy texture of blended sunflower seeds. When puréed with water in a blender, sunflower seeds provide a plant-based crème that can be used much like dairy cream to give a silky, light feeling in the mouth.

onions, small dice	$1\frac{1}{2}$ cups	168 grams
carrots, small dice	$1\frac{1}{2}$ cups	189 grams
celery, small dice	$1\frac{1}{2}$ cups	168 grams
olive oil	1 tablespoon	15 milliliters
garlic, minced	1 teaspoon	5 grams
all-purpose white flour	$\frac{1}{2}$ cup	70 grams
vegetable stock, hot	7 cups	1.68 liters
salt	1 teaspoon	6 grams
ground black pepper	pinch	pinch
oregano, dry	2 teaspoons	4 grams
bay leaf	2	2
balsamic vinegar	2 teaspoons	10 milliliters
tomato purée	$1\frac{1}{2}$ cups	360 milliliters
fresh parsley, minced	$\frac{1}{4}$ cup	28 grams
fresh celery leaf, minced	2 tablespoons	7 grams
Sunflower Crème (page 158)	1 cup	240 milliliters

Sauté the onions, carrots and celery in olive oil over medium heat for 10 minutes. Stir in the garlic and sauté 5 minutes longer. Add the flour and stir well to distribute. Slowly stir in the hot vegetable stock. Add the salt, pepper, oregano, bay leaf and balsamic vinegar. Reserve 3 tablespoons/45 milliliters tomato purée and add the remainder to the soup. Bring the soup to a boil, then simmer slowly for 15 minutes.

Strain $\frac{1}{3}$ cup of sunflower crème through a fine strainer and reserve for garnish. Add the remaining sunflower crème and any strained particles to the soup along with the celery leaf and half of the parsley. Remove the soup from the heat and remove the bay leaves. Season to taste.

GARNISH AND PRESENTATION: Garnish the soup by streaking some of the reserved Sunflower Crème and tomato sauce across the surface, then sprinkle with some of the reserved parsley. For a special presentation, float a large crouton topped with Spinach Pecan Pesto (page 140) or Basil Pine Nut Pesto (page 141) on top of the soup along with the other garnish.

SERVE WITH: Savory Tofu Salad (page 324), Tangy Tempeh Salad (page 335).

Green Pea and Watercress Soup with Mint

YIELD 10 SERVINGS

1 CUP/240 MILLILITERS

To maintain the beautiful color of this soup do not keep in a steam table; rather, heat to order and serve.

watercress	3 cups	168 grams
onions, thinly sliced	$1\frac{1}{2}$ cups	168 grams
salt	1 teaspoon	6 grams
water	6 cups	1.44 liters
green peas, frozen	6 cups	840 grams
fresh ground black pepper	pinch	pinch
fresh mint leaves	$\frac{1}{4}$ cup	14 grams
fresh mint sprigs	10	10
Cashew Crème (page 157)	$\frac{1}{4}$ cup	60 milliliters
black sesame seeds	1 tablespoon	7 grams

Blanch the watercress in boiling water for 2 to 3 minutes. Drain, discard liquid and cool under running water. Place the onions and salt in measured water and bring to a boil. Simmer for 5 minutes, then add the peas, mint leaves and black pepper. This cooks the soup ingredients and creates its own stock. Simmer for another 5 minutes, then strain the stock and reserve. Place the peas and watercress in a blender with enough of the reserved stock to blend to a very smooth texture. Combine the purée with the remaining stock, return to the heat and bring to a simmer. Season to taste. Serve immediately.

GARNISH: Garnish with a drizzle of the cashew crème, a sprinkle of toasted black sesame seeds and a sprig of mint. For an elegant presentation, float a small crouton topped by an edible flower blossom on the soup along with the above garnish.

SERVE WITH: Asparagus with Strawberry Dressing (page 164), Savory Summer Pancakes (page 250), Coconut Curry Biscuits (page 360).

Carrot Ginger Almond Bisque

YIELD 10 SERVINGS
1 CUP/240 MILLILITERS

As the sweetness of carrots changes from batch to batch you may wish to add a little maple syrup or other sweetener to the finished soup to round out the flavor.

carrots, large dice	6 cups	756 grams
onions, small dice	1 cup	112 grams
celery, small dice	1 cup	112 grams
gingerroot, minced	5 teaspoons	23 grams
salt	1 teaspoon	6 grams
ground cinnamon	$\frac{1}{2}$ teaspoon	2.5 milliliters
water	$7\frac{1}{2}$ cups	1.8 liters
almond butter	$\frac{1}{3}$ cup	80 milliliters
soy sauce	3 tablespoons	45 milliliters
black pepper	pinch	pinch

GARNISH
toasted almonds, chopped	3 tablespoons	17 grams
parsley, finely chopped	1 tablespoon	315 grams

Place the carrots, onions, celery, ginger, salt and cinnamon into water and bring to a boil. Simmer for 20 minutes or until carrots are tender. Cool to room temperature and blend together with almond butter, soy sauce and black pepper. Reheat, season to taste and serve garnished with toasted almonds and chopped parsley.

VARIATION: Vegetables and ginger may be sautéed first in 1 tablespoon of canola oil; then proceed as above. Add a little juice and or zest from citrus such as lemon, orange or lime. Carrot juice can be added to the soup to intensify the flavor.

Winter Squash Hazelnut Bisque

YIELD 10 SERVINGS
1 CUP/240 MILLILITERS

Any winter squash such as butternut, hubbard, Japanese Hokaido or
sugar pumpkins may be used in this soup.

onions, medium dice	1 cup	112 grams
carrots, medium dice	1 cup	126 grams
celery, medium dice	1 cup	112 grams
ginger root, minced	2 tablespoons	28 grams
canola oil	1 tablespoon	15 milliliters
winter squash, peeled, large cubes	6 cups	840 grams
water or light vegetable stock	$7\frac{1}{2}$ cups	1.80 liter
salt	1 teaspoon	6 grams
ground cinnamon	$\frac{1}{2}$ teaspoon	1 gram
ground nutmeg	$\frac{1}{8}$ teaspoon	.25 gram
soy sauce	2 tablespoons	30 milliliters
hazelnut (filbert) butter	$\frac{1}{3}$ cup	80 milliliters
maple syrup	1 tablespoon	15 milliliters
black pepper	pinch	pinch

GARNISH

hazelnuts, chopped and toasted	2 tablespoons	14 grams
chopped chives or parsley	2 tablespoons	7 grams

Sauté the onions, carrots, celery, and ginger in oil over medium heat for 10 minutes. Add the squash and sauté for 5 minutes longer. Add water or stock, salt, cinnamon, nutmeg and soy sauce. Bring to a boil and simmer for 10 minutes or until the squash is tender. Remove the soup from the heat and stir in the hazelnut butter, maple syrup and black pepper. Cool the soup to room temperature, then place it in a blender and puree until smooth. Season to taste. Garnish with toasted chopped hazelnuts and chopped parsley or chives.

Note: Depending on how sweet each batch of squash is, more or less maple syrup may be added. Add a little juice and or zest of lemon, orange or lime. Fresh sage, rosemary, and parsley as well as other herbs could be used for a slight undercurrent of flavor.

Sweet Potato Peanut Bisque

YIELD 10 SERVINGS
1 CUP/240 MILLILITERS

Any winter squash such as butternut, hubbard, Japanese Hokaido or
sugar pumpkins may be used in this soup.

onions, medium dice	1 cup	112 grams
carrots, medium dice	1 cup	126 grams
celery, medium dice	1 cup	112 grams
gingerroot, minced	2 tablespoons	28 grams
canola oil	1 tablespoon	15 milliliters
sweet potatoes, peeled, large cubes	6 cups	840 grams
vegetable stock	$7\frac{1}{2}$ cups	1.80 liter
salt	1 teaspoon	6 grams
cinnamon, ground	$\frac{1}{2}$ teaspoon	1 gram
allspice, ground	$\frac{1}{8}$ teaspoon	.25 gram
soy sauce	2 tablespoons	30 milliliters
peanut butter	$\frac{1}{3}$ cup	80 milliliters
maple syrup	1 tablespoon	15 milliliters
black pepper	pinch	pinch

GARNISH
peanuts, chopped and toasted	2 tablespoons	14 grams
chopped chives	2 tablespoons	7 grams

Sauté the onions, carrots, celery and ginger in oil over medium heat for 10 minutes. Add the sweet potatoes and sauté for 5 minutes longer. Add the stock, salt, cinnamon, allspice and soy sauce. Bring to a boil and simmer for 10 minutes or until the sweet potatoes are tender. Remove the soup from the heat and stir in the peanut butter. Cool the soup to room temperature and then place in blender and purée until smooth. Season to taste.

GARNISH: Garnish with toasted chopped peanuts and chives.

VARIATION: Add a little juice and/or zest of lemon, orange or lime. Fresh sage, rosemary and parsley as well as other herbs could be used for a slight undercurrent of flavor.

Note: Depending on how sweet each batch of sweet potatoes is, more or less maple syrup may be added.

Pinto Bean Soup

YIELD 10 SERVINGS

1 CUP/240 MILLILITERS

Starting with cooked beans—whether one purchases them that way or cooks them oneself—is the key to making bean soups quickly. Pinto beans, often used in southwestern cooking, are seasoned in this soup with chili powder in a nod to that tradition.

onions, small dice	$1\frac{1}{2}$ cups	168 grams
carrots, small dice	$1\frac{1}{2}$ cups	189 grams
celery, small dice	$1\frac{1}{2}$ cups	168 grams
olive oil	1 tablespoon	15 milliliters
garlic, chopped	1 tablespoon	15 grams
salt	1 teaspoon	6 grams
ground black pepper	pinch	pinch
chili powder	1 teaspoon	2 grams
oregano	1 teaspoon	2 grams
bay leaf	1	1
vegetable stock, and/or liquid from cooking beans	6 cups	1.44 liter
pinto beans, cooked	3 cups	840 grams
prepared mustard	5 teaspoons	21 grams
tomato paste	5 teaspoons	21 grams
GARNISH		
scallions, thin bias cut	5 teaspoons	21 grams

Sauté the onions, carrots and celery in olive oil over medium heat for 10 minutes. Add the garlic and sauté 5 minutes. Add the salt, pepper, chili powder, oregano, bay leaf and half of the stock or half of the liquid to the pot and half of the cooked beans. Purée the remaining beans and stock in a blender. Add the bean purée along with the mustard and tomato paste to the soup and bring it to a boil. Simmer for 15 to 20 minutes, then taste for seasoning.

GARNISH: Garnish with sliced scallions.

VARIATION: Prepare soup without blending.

SERVE WITH: Grilled or Roast Vegetable Salad (page 170) and Millet Mash with Winter Squash (page 296).

Chick-pea Tomato and Herb Salvatore

YIELD 10 SERVINGS

1 CUP/240 MILLILITERS

This hardy minestra, *the Italian substantial main-course soup, can be used as a menu focal point for a simple peasant-style meal.*

onions, small dice	$1\frac{1}{2}$ cups	168 grams
carrots, small dice	$1\frac{1}{2}$ cups	189 grams
celery, small dice	$1\frac{1}{2}$ cups	168 grams
olive oil	1 tablespoon	15 milliliters
garlic, chopped	1 tablespoon	15 grams
salt	1 teaspoon	6 grams
ground black pepper	pinch	pinch
oregano	1 teaspoon	2 grams
basil	1 teaspoon	2 grams
bay leaf	1	1
vegetable stock and/or bean cooking liquid	6 cups	1.44 liter
chick-peas, cooked	3 cups	567 grams
prepared mustard	5 teaspoons	8.33 grams
tomato sauce or purée	1 cup	240 milliliters
fresh parsley	$\frac{1}{4}$ cup	28 grams
lemon juice	1 tablespoon	15 milliliters
soy sauce	1 tablespoon	15 milliliters

GARNISH

thinly sliced scallions or minced chives	$\frac{1}{4}$ cup	28 grams

Sauté the onions, carrots and celery in olive oil over medium heat for 10 minutes. Add the garlic and sauté 5 minutes. Add the salt, pepper, oregano, basil, bay leaf and half of the stock or half of the liquid to the pot. Purée the remaining beans and stock in a blender. Add whole beans and blended beans along with mustard and tomato sauce to the soup and bring to a boil. Simmer for 15 to 20 minutes. Stir in the parsley, lemon juice, soy sauce and simmer 5 more minutes. Season to taste.

GARNISH: Garnish bowls of soup with scallions or chives.

SERVE WITH: Salad Rouge with Glazed Red Onions and Hazelnuts (page 179), tossed greens with White Balsamic Vinaigrette (page 181), Crostini with Pesto (page 55) or a nice loaf of Italian bread.

Black Bean Soup with Cumin and Garlic

YIELD: 10 SERVINGS
1 CUP/240 MILLILITERS

Black beans have long been popular throughout Latin America. The Brazilian specialty
feojoada was an inspiration for this soup. To further emulate the deep flavors
of the prototype, add a few drops of liquid smoke.

onions, small dice	$1\frac{1}{2}$ cups	168 grams
carrots, small dice	$1\frac{1}{2}$ cups	189 grams
celery, small dice	1cup	112 grams
olive oil	1 tablespoon	15 milliliters
salt	1 teaspoon	6 grams
ground black pepper	pinch	pinch
oregano, dried	1 teaspoon	2 grams
bay leaf	1	1
vegetable stock, and/or bean cooking liquid	6 cups	1.44 liters
black beans, cooked	3 cups	840 grams
prepared mustard	5 teaspoon	21 grams
tomato paste	5 teaspoon	21 grams

FLAVOR BOOSTER

olive oil	1 tablespoon	15 milliliters
garlic, minced	$\frac{1}{4}$ cup	56 grams
coriander seeds	1 teaspoon	2.33 grams
cumin seeds	1 teaspoon	2.33 grams
water	$\frac{1}{2}$ cup	120 milliliters
fresh cilantro, chopped	2 tablespoons	14 grams
lime or lemon juice	2 tablespoons	30 milliliters

GARNISH

scallions or chives, thinly sliced	$\frac{1}{4}$ cup	28 grams
red onions, finely diced	$\frac{1}{4}$ cup	28 grams
lime or lemon slices	10	10
fresh cilantro, chopped	$\frac{1}{4}$ cup	28 grams
fresh tomatoes, seeded and finely diced	1 cup	140 grams

Sauté the onions, carrots and celery in olive oil over medium heat for 10 minutes. Add the salt, pepper, oregano, bay leaf, half of the stock or half of the bean liquid and half of the beans to the pot. Purée the remaining beans and stock. Add the blended beans along with mustard and tomato paste to the soup and bring to a boil. Simmer for 15 to 20 minutes.

For the flavor booster, in a separate small pot or sauté pan, heat the olive oil and sauté the garlic, coriander and cumin seeds until the garlic begins to brown. Add lime juice, the water and chooped cilantro, bring to a boil and pour into the soup. Simmer the soup for a few minutes longer. Remove the bay leaf. Season to taste.

GARNISH: Depending on the occasion, garnish with all or some of the following: chopped chives or thinly sliced scallions, lime or lemon slices, chopped cilantro and/or diced tomatoes. The garnish ingredients may be arranged on small plates and served on the side or arranged in the bottom of soup bowls with the soup ladled in at tableside.

SERVE WITH: Brazilian-Style Greens (page 196), Almond Rice Croquettes (page 310).

Yellow Split Pea Curry

YIELD 10 SERVINGS
1 CUP/240 MILLILITERS

There are many different types of beans and legumes used in Indian cooking. They are referred to collectively as "dal." Other varieties that can be used in place of the yellow split peas are green or red lentils, yellow moong dal and green split peas. The cooking time may be reduced somewhat with the smaller varieties.

yellow split peas	2 cups	450 grams
onions, small dice	$1\frac{1}{2}$ cups	168 grams
carrots, small dice	$1\frac{1}{2}$ cups	189 grams
celery, small dice	1 cup	112 grams
canola oil	1 tablespoon	15 milliliters
garlic, minced	1 tablespoon	14 grams
ginger, minced	1 tablespoon	14 grams
black mustard seeds	pinch	pinch
ground cumin	1 tablespoon	6 grams
ground coriander	1 tablespoon	6 grams
ground cardamom	1 teaspoon	2 grams
ground turmeric	1 teaspoon	2 grams
salt	1 teaspoon	6 grams
ground black pepper	pinch	pinch
vegetable stock or water	9 cups	2.16 liters
lemon juice	1 tablespoon	15 milliliters
kelp (optional)	1 inch piece	2.5 centimeter piece

GARNISH

chopped fresh cilantro	$\frac{1}{4}$ cup	14 grams
thin lemon wedges or slices	10	10

Sort and rinse the split peas, then cover with water and set aside to soak while you prepare the other soup ingredients.

Sauté the onions, carrots and celery in canola oil over medium heat for 10 minutes. Add the garlic, ginger, and mustard seeds and sauté 5 minutes. Stir in the cumin, coriander, cardamom, turmeric, salt and pepper. Add soaked and drained split peas, vegetable stock, lemon juice and kelp. Bring to a boil, then simmer for 1 hour. Season to taste.

GARNISH: Garnish with chopped cilantro and a slice of lemon or serve lemon wedges on the side.

SERVE WITH: India-Style Flatbread (page 353), Basmati Rice (page 315), Spiced Cauliflower Potatoes and Peas (page 236), Greens Sautéed with Ginger (page 195).

Note: Prepared curry powder may be used in place of the Indian spices. Split peas can be cooked without soaking, but they will require more vegetable stock.

Lentil Soup with Soy Sausage and Toasted Cumin and Fennel Seeds

YIELD 10 SERVINGS

1 CUP/240 MILLILITERS

The soy sausage recommended for this soup is available frozen. For best results and easiest handling, cook it while still frozen. Check the Resource Guide for suppliers.

onions, small dice	$1\frac{1}{2}$ cups	168 grams
carrots, small dice	$1\frac{1}{2}$ cups	189 grams
celery, small dice	$1\frac{1}{2}$ cups	168 grams
olive oil	1 tablespoon	15 milliliters
garlic, minced	1 tablespoon	14 grams
gingerroot, minced	1 tablespoon	14 grams
lentils, sorted and washed	2 cups	448 grams
vegetable stock or water	8 cups	1.92 liters
kelp	1 inch piece	2.5 centimeters
bay leaf	1	1
soy sauce	1 tablespoon	15 milliliters
prepared mustard	1 tablespoon	15 milliliters
fresh parsley, chopped	2 tablespoons	7 grams
salt	1 teaspoon	6 grams
ground black pepper	pinch	pinch

GARNISH

frozen soy sausage patties	8 ounces	226 grams
cumin seeds	1 teaspoon	2 grams
fennel seeds	1 teaspoon	2 grams
scallions, thinly sliced	2 tablespoons	7 grams

Sauté the onions, carrots and celery in olive oil over medium heat for 10 minutes. Add the garlic and ginger and sauté 5 minutes. Add all remaining ingredients except the garnish.

Bring the soup to a boil, then simmer with the cover ajar for 1 hour until lentils are tender. Sauté the frozen breakfast soy sausage in a nonstick pan brushed with oil for about 10 minutes or until done. Remove from the pan to cool. Place the cumin and fennel seeds in the pan and dry sauté over medium heat for about a minute or until fragrant. When the soy sausage is cool enough to handle, cut it into a medium dice. Mix the toasted seeds with the soy sausage and add half of the mixture into the soup. Season to taste. Remove the bay leaf.

GARNISH: Ladle the soup into bowls and garnish with scallions and the remaining soy sausage mixture.

SERVE WITH: Braised Red Cabbage with Dried Cranberries (page 192), Garlic Roasted Potatoes with Rosemary (page 208).

Note: Some lentils will require more stock, add more for desired consistency.

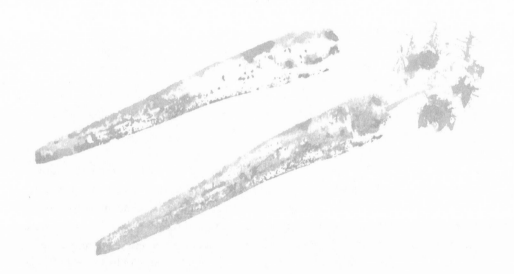

Miso Soup

YIELD 10 SERVINGS

1 CUP/240 MILLILITERS

This traditional Japanese style soup can be made with any of the several styles of miso, the soy paste that gives it its name. The flavors run from mild for white miso to more developed in the longer aged red miso to very intense and unique for the longest aged dark hatcho miso. For more information on miso see Ingredients chapter.

water	10 cups	2.4 liters
kelp, dried sea vegetable	4–inch piece	10–centimeter piece
onions, halved and thinly sliced	1 cup	112 grams
carrots, thinly sliced	$1\frac{1}{2}$ cups	189 grams
ginger root, minced	1 tablespoon	14 grams
white miso paste	$\frac{3}{4}$ cup	168 grams
firm or extra firm tofu, small dice	$2\frac{1}{2}$ cups	450 grams
GARNISH		
scallions, thinly sliced	$\frac{1}{2}$ cup	28 grams
toasted nori, cut to small triangles	2 sheets	2 sheets

Bring water and kombu to a boil. Remove kombu and set aside to cool. Add onions and carrots and simmer for five minutes. Julienne kombu and return to soup with the ginger. Simmer five more minutes or until carrots are tender. Add miso to soup by either holding a strainer into the soup and pressing it through the strainer to disperse it, or by removing some of the miso stock to a small container and dissolving the paste in it, then stirring it into the soup. Reduce the heat to low and add tofu to the soup. Season to taste.

GARNISH: Garnish with scallions and cut toasted nori.

VARIATIONS: Other vegetables that could be added to the soup with or in place of the onions and carrots are broccoli, cabbage, mushrooms, especially shiitake, and celery.

JAPANESE VEGETARIAN STOCK (DASHI): The stock that is made for the Miso Soup recipe, could be strained and used in a recipe that required a vegetarian version of the traditional Japanese stock called dashi.

SERVE WITH: Adzuki Beans with Squash (page 291), Millet Mash with Winter Squash (page 296), Almond Brown Rice Croquettes (page 310), Greens Sautéed with Ginger (page 195), Arame with Carrots and Onions (page 209), Corn on the Cob with Ume Boshi Plum Paste (page 206), Sesame Roasted Butternut Squash (page 204), Maple Glazed Kelp, Carrots, and Onions (page 214).

Vegetable Barley Soup

YIELD 10 SERVINGS
1 CUP/240 MILLILITERS

onions, medium dice	$1\frac{1}{2}$ cups	168 grams
carrots, medium dice	$1\frac{1}{2}$ cups	189 grams
celery, medium dice	$1\frac{1}{2}$ cups	168 grams
rutabagas, medium dice	$1\frac{1}{2}$ cups	168 grams
olive oil	1 tablespoon	15 milliliters
toasted sesame oil	1 teaspoon	5 milliliters
garlic, minced	1 tablespoon	15 grams
mushrooms, coarsely chopped	$1\frac{1}{2}$ cups	154 grams
vegetable stock	8 cups	1.92 liters
soy sauce	2 tablespoons	30 milliliters
pearled barley	$\frac{1}{2}$ cup	98 grams
prepared mustard	$1\frac{1}{2}$ teaspoons	7.5 grams
salt	$\frac{1}{2}$ teaspoon	3 grams
black pepper	pinch	pinch
parsley, chopped	2 tablespoons	7 grams
bay leaves	2	2
lemon juice	1 tablespoon	15 milliliters

Sauté the onions, carrots, celery and rutabagas in olive and sesame oils for 5 minutes over medium heat. Add the garlic and sauté for 5 minutes. Add the mushrooms and sauté for 5 minutes. Add the remaining ingredients and bring to a boil, then simmer for about 1 hour.

GARNISH: For a simple garnish sprinkle bowls of soup with chopped fresh parsley, chives or thinly sliced scallions.

Mushroom Barley Soup

YIELD 10 SERVINGS

1 CUP/240 MILLILITERS

*What seems to be a small amount of barley in this recipe attests to the ability of
this ancient grain to expand when cooked.*

onions, small dice	$1\frac{1}{2}$ cups	168 grams
carrots, small dice	$1\frac{1}{2}$ cups	189 grams
celery, small dice	$1\frac{1}{2}$ cups	168 grams
olive oil	2 teaspoons	10 milliliters
toasted sesame oil	1 teaspoon	5 milliliters
garlic, minced	1 tablespoon	15 grams
mushrooms, coarsely chopped	$4\frac{1}{2}$ cups	448 grams
vegetable stock	8 cups	1.92 liters
soy sauce	2 tablespoons	30 milliliters
pearled barley	$\frac{1}{2}$ cup	98 grams
prepared mustard	$1\frac{1}{2}$ teaspoons	7.5 grams
salt	$\frac{1}{2}$ teaspoon	3 grams
black pepper	pinch	pinch
parsley, chopped (extra for garnish if desired)	2 tablespoons	7 grams
bay leaves	2	2
sherry wine (optional)	1 tablespoon	15 milliliters

Sauté the onions, carrots and celery in olive and sesame oils for 5 minutes over
medium heat. Add the garlic and sauté for 5 minutes. Add the mushrooms and sauté
for 5 minutes. Add the remaining ingredients and bring to a boil, then simmer for
about 1 hour.

GARNISH: For a simple garnish, sprinkle bowls of soup with chopped fresh parsley,
chives or thinly sliced scallions. For special presentations put some of the strained soup
ingredients into the bottom of each bowl and top with some sautéed mushrooms such
as shiitake, portobello or oyster, sprinkle with chopped herbs, then ladle in some
broth tableside.

VARIATION: Different mushroom flavors can be achieved by using one or more of
the various fresh mushrooms available. Add a few rosemary leaves or a small sprig of
thyme for additional flavor.

Note: For more intense mushroom flavor, $\frac{1}{4}$ cup dried mushrooms plus 1 cup of stock or
water may be added to the soup.

Mushroom Cashew Crème Soup

YIELD 10 SERVINGS

1 CUP/240 MILLILITERS

Dried mushrooms added during the simmering of this soup provide concentrated flavor. For more intense mushroom taste, at the end of the cooking add some dried mushrooms, preferably the less gritty domestic white type, which have been pulverized in a blender.

dried mushrooms	$\frac{1}{2}$ cup	28 grams
hot water	1 cup	240 milliliters
onions, small dice	$1\frac{1}{2}$ cups	168 grams
carrots, small dice	$1\frac{1}{2}$ cups	189 grams
celery, small dice	$\frac{3}{4}$ cup	84 grams
olive oil	2 teaspoons	10 milliliters
toasted sesame oil	1 teaspoon	5 milliliters
garlic, minced	2 teaspoons	4 grams
fresh mushrooms, coarsely chopped	6 cups	500 grams
flour, white	$\frac{1}{2}$ cup	70 grams
hot vegetable stock	7 cups	1.72 liters
sherry wine	1 tablespoon	15 milliliters
bay leaf	1	1
salt	1 teaspoon	6 grams
black pepper	pinch	pinch
soy souce	$\frac{1}{3}$ cup	80 milliliters
fresh parsley, minced	$\frac{1}{2}$ cup	28 grams
toasted Cashew Crème (page 157)	$\frac{2}{3}$ cup	160 milliliters

Place the dried mushrooms in hot water to soften and make mushroom liquor set aside. Sauté the onions, carrots and celery in olive and sesame oils over medium heat for 10 minutes. Add the garlic and mushrooms and sauté for 5 minutes. Stir in the flour. Gradually stir in the hot vegetable stock. Into the soup, slowly pour off the mushroom liquor from the rehydrated mushrooms, being careful not to add any sediment that may be in the bottom of the container. Rinse off the re-hydrated mushrooms, chop finely and add to the soup. Add all the remaining ingredients except the toasted cashew crème to soup. Simmer for 20 minutes. Add the toasted cashew crème and simmer for 5 minutes. Season to taste.

GARNISH: For a simple garnish sprinkle bowls of soup with chopped fresh parsley, chives or thinly sliced scallions. For special presentations place some sautéed mushrooms such as shiitake, portobello or oyster in each bowl, then ladle in the soup tableside. Drizzle a little cashew crème over the soup as well.

VARIATION: Different mushroom flavors can be realized by using one or more of the various fresh mushrooms available. Add a few rosemary leaves or a small sprig of thyme for additional zest.

SERVE WITH: Rice Salad Medley with Wild, Japonica, and Wehani (page 168), Carrot and Parsnip Salad with Smoked Dulse (page 171), Golden Mashed Potatoes with Caramelized Onions (page 205), Guiness Barley with Tri-Color Confetti (page 298).

Kale Pumpkin Seed Crème Soup

YIELD 10 SERVINGS

1 CUP/240 MILLILITERS

Kale, like parsley, has long been used as a garnish without regard for either its great flavor or nutritional properties. Here it is paired with pumpkin seed crème, showing one possibility for its enjoyment.

onions, small dice	$1\frac{1}{2}$ cups	168 grams
carrots, small dice	$1\frac{1}{2}$ cups	189 grams
celery, small dice	$1\frac{1}{2}$ cups	168 grams
olive oil	1 tablespoon	15 milliliters
garlic, minced	1 tablespoon	15 milliliters
flour, white all-purpose	$\frac{1}{2}$ cup	70 grams
hot vegetable stock	6 cups	1.44 liters
bay leaf	1	1
oregano, dry	1 teaspoon	2 grams
prepared mustard	1 teaspoon	5 milliliters
lemon juice	2 teaspoons	10 milliliters
salt	1 teaspoon	6 grams
ground black pepper	pinch	pinch
kale, finely chopped, large stems removed	6 cups	504 grams
Pumpkin Seed Crème (page 157)	1 cup	240 milliliters
toasted black sesame seeds	1 tablespoon	15 milliliters

Sauté the onions, carrots and celery in olive oil over medium-low heat for 10 minutes. Add the garlic and sauté 5 minutes. Stir in the flour, then slowly whisk in hot vegetable stock. Add the bay leaf, oregano, mustard, lemon juice, salt and pepper. Bring to a boil, then simmer for 10 minutes. Add the kale and simmer for a few minutes longer until kale is tender. Stir in the pumpkin seed crème and remove from heat. Season to taste.

GARNISH: Garnish soup with toasted black sesame seeds. For special presentations, add a little fresh kale sautéed in garlic to each bowl of soup.

VARIATIONS: Use collard greens in place of kale. Use sunflower seed crème or cashew crème in place of pumpkin seed crème.

SERVE WITH: Oatmeal Herb Scones (page 355), White Bean Cakes (page 289), Almond Brown Rice Croquettes (page 310), Sea Czar Salad with Blackened Tofu (page 175).

Note: Kale stems and peels may be used in the vegetable stock for this soup; however, cook them only for a short time as long cooking can make the stock bitter.

Corn Chowder

YIELD 10 SERVINGS

1 CUP/240 MILLILITERS

Starting the potatoes in cold water and bringing them to a boil before adding them to the soup keeps them from becoming tough on the outside. While the frozen corn kernels are available year-round, you may wish to try the soup with fresh corn when in season, adding the corn cobs to the stock.

onions, small dice	$1\frac{1}{2}$ cups	168 grams
carrots, small dice	$1\frac{1}{2}$ cups	189 grams
celery, small dice	$1\frac{1}{2}$ cups	168 grams
corn or canola oil	1 tablespoon	15 milliliters
garlic, minced	1 teaspoon	5 milliliters
all-purpose white flour	$\frac{1}{2}$ cup	70 grams
hot vegetable stock	6 cups	1.44 liters
bay leaf	1	1
thyme	$\frac{1}{4}$ teaspoon	.5 gram
salt	1 teaspoon	6 grams
ground black pepper	pinch	pinch
corn kernels, frozen	4 cups	560 grams
potatoes, fine dice	$1\frac{1}{2}$ cups	210 grams
water	1 cup	240 milliliters
parsley, finely chopped	$\frac{1}{2}$ cup	28 grams
Cashew Crème, raw (page 157)	$\frac{1}{2}$ cup	120 milliliters

Sauté the onions, carrots and celery in oil over medium–low heat for 10 minutes. Add the garlic and sauté 5 minutes. Stir in the flour, then stir in 4 cups/960 milliliters of hot vegetable stock. Add the bay leaf, thyme, salt and pepper along with half of the corn kernels to the soup. In a separate pot, bring potatoes and water to a boil, then add both to the soup. Put the remaining corn kernels and remaining vegetable stock in a blender and process until smooth. Add the corn purée to soup. Bring the soup to a boil, then simmer for 10 minutes or until potatoes are tender. Add half of the parsley and the cashew crème to the soup. Simmer for 5 minutes. Season to taste. Remove the bay leaf.

GARNISH: Garnish with remaining chopped parsley.

VARIATIONS: Raw sunflower seed crème or raw pumpkin seed crème could be used in place of the cashew crème. Chives or finely sliced scallions could be used for garnish.

SERVE WITH: Irish Soda Bread (page 351) or Peach and Pecan Cornbread (page 352), Black-eyed Pea Salad (page 166), Sesame Roasted Butternut Squash (page 204), Red Swiss Chard Sauté with Garlic (page 194).

Note: Potatoes may be scrubbed and diced with peel on or off as preferred.

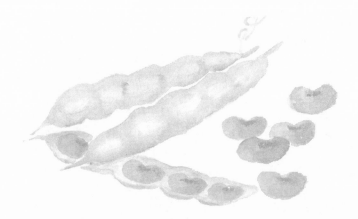

Manhattan Sea Vegetable Chowder

YIELD 10 SERVINGS

1 CUP/240 MILLILITERS

Sea vegetables along with herbs and tomatoes provide the familiar flavor for this vegetarian version of a perennial chowder favorite.

onions, small dice	1 cup	112 grams
carrots, small dice	1 cup	126 grams
celery, small dice	1 cup	112 grams
green pepper, small dice	1 cup	112 grams
garlic, minced	1 tablespoon	7 grams
olive oil	4 teaspoons	20 milliliters
dulse flakes	6 tablespoons	7 grams
nori flakes	1 tablespoon	1.66 grams
oregano leaves, dry	2 teaspoons	4 grams
ground fennel seeds	$\frac{1}{2}$ teaspoon	1.2 grams
thyme	1 teaspoon	2 grams
bay leaves	2	2
vegetable stock	$7\frac{1}{2}$ cups	1.8 grams
crushed tomatoes	$1\frac{1}{2}$ cups	360 milliliters
soy sauce	1 teaspoon	5 milliliters
balsamic vinegar	1 teaspoon	5 milliliters
sea salt	$1\frac{1}{2}$ teaspoons	9 grams
ground black pepper	pinch	pinch
potatoes, fine dice	$1\frac{1}{2}$ cups	210 grams
water	$1\frac{1}{2}$ cups	360 milliliters
freshly chopped parsley (for garnish)		

Sauté the onions, carrots, celery, green peppers and garlic in olive oil over medium heat for 15 minutes or until just beginning to brown. Add all remaining ingredients to pot except potatoes and water. Bring the chowder to a boil, then simmer for 45 minutes. Fifteen minutes before chowder is done put the potatoes and water into a small pot and bring to a boil. Add the hot potatoes and their cooking liquid to the chowder and simmer until the potatoes are tender. Season to taste. Remove the bay leaf.

GARNISH: Garnish with chopped parsley.

VARIATION: A small amount of other sea vegetables, (1 or 2 tablespoons) such as wakame, kelp, hijiki, or arame could be used in addition to the dulse and nori.

Sea Vegetable Bisque

YIELD 10 SERVINGS

1 CUP/240 MILLILITERS

Sea vegetables are pressed into service to achieve the bisque's flavor and the texture is refined by the cashew crème.

onions, small dice	$1\frac{1}{2}$ cups	168 grams
carrots, small dice	$1\frac{1}{2}$ cups	189 grams
celery, small dice	$1\frac{1}{2}$ cups	168 grams
garlic, minced	1 tablespoon	7 grams
olive oil	1 tablespoon	15 milliliters
dulse flakes	6 tablespoons	7 grams
nori flakes	1 tablespoon	1.66 grams
ground fennel seeds	1 teaspoon	2 grams
thyme	1 teaspoon	2 grams
bay leaves	2	2
fresh parsley, chopped (extra for garnish)	$\frac{1}{4}$ cup	14 grams
paprika, mild	1 teaspoon	2 grams
all-purpose white flour	$\frac{1}{4}$ cup	35 grams
sea salt	$1\frac{1}{2}$ teaspoons	9 grams
ground black pepper	pinch	pinch
hot vegetable stock	$7\frac{1}{2}$ cups	1.8 liters
tomato sauce	$\frac{3}{4}$ cup	80 milliliters
sherry wine	1 tablespoon	15 milliliters
Cashew Crème (page 157)	1 cup	240 milliliters

Sauté the onions, carrots, celery and garlic in olive oil over medium heat for 10 to 12 minutes or until just starting to brown. Stir in the dulse, nori, fennel, thyme, bay leaves, parsley and paprika. Stir in the flour, salt and pepper. Then slowly stir in the vegetable stock, two thirds of the tomato sauce and sherry wine. Bring to a boil, then simmer for 25 minutes. Reserve $\frac{1}{4}$ cup strained cashew crème for garnish if desired. Stir in the remaining cashew crème and simmer for 5 more minutes, then remove from heat. Allow the soup to cool for a while, then purée the entire soup in a blender. Heat gently before serving. Season to taste. Remove the bay leaves.

GARNISH: The bisque may be garnished by streaking reserved cashew crème and tomato sauce across the top and sprinkling with parsley.

Gazpacho Andalusia

YIELD 10 SERVINGS
1 CUP/240 MILLILITERS

A creamy version of the chilled Spanish specialty.

fresh tomato, seeded and diced	$2\frac{1}{2}$ cups	350 grams
cucumber, peeled, seeded and diced	$2\frac{1}{2}$ cups	70 grams
chilled vegetable or tomato juice	4 cups	960 milliliters
garlic, crushed	1 teaspoon	5 grams
onion, fine dice	2 tablespoons	14 grams
red wine vinegar	3 tablespoons	45 milliliters
salt	1 teaspoon	6 grams
ground black pepper	pinch	pinch
ground cumin	1 teaspoon	2 grams
chili powder	1 teaspoon	2 grams
Cashew Crème (page 157)	1 cup	240 millliliters

GARNISH

green pepper, finely diced	$\frac{1}{2}$ cup	56 grams
celery, finely diced	$\frac{1}{2}$ cup	56 grams
parsley, finely chopped	$\frac{1}{4}$ cup	14 grams
fresh cilantro, finely chopped	2 tablespoons	7 grams
fresh lime	10 small wedges	10 small wedges

Reserve 1 cup each diced tomatoes and cucumbers for garnish. Put the remaining ingredients for soup into a blender and blend until smooth. Season to taste.

GARNISH: To serve the soup, first arrange some of the reserved tomatoes, cucumbers and other garnish ingredients except lime wedges in bowls, then ladle in the gazpacho purée. Serve the lime wedges on the side.

VARIATION: Mix all ingredients except the parsley, cilantro and lime wedges together in a soup tureen and garnish with reserved chopped parsley and cilantro. Serve chilled with lime wedges on the side.

Note: A little cayene pepper or hot sauce may be added to spice up the soup.

Chilled Cantaloupe Soup with Mint

YIELD 10 SERVINGS
1 CUP/240 MILLILITERS

To select ripe cantaloupes, look for melons that are soft to the touch at the ends, shake to feel if the seeds are loosening and smell them for a ripe aroma.

raw Cashew Crème (page 157)	1 cup	240 milliliters
apple juice	$2\frac{1}{2}$ cups	480 milliliters
ripe cantaloupe, large dice	8 cups	1.125 kilograms
fresh lime juice	2 tablespoons	30 milliliters
fresh mint, minced	3 tablespoons	10.5 grams
salt	pinch	pinch
ground black pepper	pinch	pinch
maple syrup if needed		

GARNISH

fresh strawberries	2 cups	308 grams
balsamic vinegar	a few drops	a few drops
fresh mint sprigs		
reserved strained Cashew Crème or Sunflower Crème (pages 157, 158)		

Strain off $\frac{1}{4}$ cup/60 ml cashew and reserve for garnish. Put remaining cashew crème into blender with $2\frac{1}{4}$ cups/540 ml apple juice and cantaloupe. Purèe until smooth. Remove the purée to a soup tureen or other container and stir in lime juice, mint, salt and pepper. Season to taste using a little maple syrup if needed. Chill the soup until service time.

Rinse, hull and slice about one-third of the strawberries for garnish. Purée the re-maining strawberries with the remaining fruit juice and season with a few drops of balsamic vinegar, a sprinkle of black pepper and a little maple syrup if needed. To serve, pour the cantaloupe purée into a chilled bowl and float some of the strawberry purée on top, along with a drizzle of the reserved strained cashew and a few slices of strawberry.

SERVE WITH: Bow-tie Pasta Salad (page 274), Chilled Vegan Ravioli (page 282), Green Beans with Balsamic Vinegar (page 202), Golden Potato Salad with Olives and Apricots (page 176).

Creole Vegetable Soup

YIELD 10 SERVINGS

1 CUP/240 MILLILITERS

To develop a deep, rich savory quality the mirepoix is added to the pot in 2 stages. The first batch is sautéed and attains a well-cooked, caramelized flavor, and the second batch is added later in the cooking to maintain the bright flavors of less-cooked vegetables. The next step to building flavor comes when the flour is incorporated into this mixture to create a roux and stirred vigilantly, allowing it to brown without burning.

onions, small dice	$1\frac{1}{2}$ cups	168 grams
carrots, small dice	$1\frac{1}{2}$ cups	189 grams
celery, small dice	$1\frac{1}{2}$ cups	168 grams
green pepper, small dice	$1\frac{1}{2}$ cups	168 grams
garlic, minced	1 tablespoon	7 grams
scallions, diagonally sliced	$\frac{1}{2}$ cup	28 grams
olive oil	4 teaspoons	20 milliliters
all-purpose white flour	6 tablespoons	52 grams
salt	1 teaspoon	6 grams
ground black pepper	pinch	pinch
dulse flakes	2 tablespoons	2.3 grams
dried thyme	1 teaspoon	2 grams
dried rosemary	1 teaspoon	2 grams
bay leaves	2	2
cayenne pepper	pinch	pinch
sherry	1 tablespoon	15 milliliters
hot vegetable stock	$7\frac{1}{2}$ cups	1.8 liters
tomato sauce or purée	$\frac{1}{2}$ cup	120 milliliters
soy sauce	3 tablespoons	45 milliliters
fresh parsley, chopped	$\frac{1}{2}$ cup	28 grams

Sauté half of the onions, carrots, celery and green peppers in olive oil over medium-low heat for 15 minutes. Add the remaining mirepoix along with the scallions and garlic and sauté for 5 minutes longer. Raise the heat to medium, stir in the flour and sauté for 3 minutes, stirring constantly. Stir in the salt, pepper, dulse, thyme, rosemary, bay leaves, cayenne and sherry. Stir in vegetable stock, tomato sauce and soy sauce. Bring to a boil and simmer for 20 minutes. Add half of the parsley and simmer 5 minutes. Season to taste. Remove the bay leaves.

GARNISH: Garnish with the remaining parsley.

SERVE WITH: Sea Czar Salad with Blackened Tofu (page 175), Garlic Roasted Potatoes with Rosemary (page 208).

CHAPTER FIVE

Sauces

S auces are an integral part of fine cuisine. Some

possess a crisp, clean taste and provide a splash of

color to a dish. Others are deep and rich,

challenging the taste buds with layers of

complexity. They can provide a finishing touch,

harmonizing all components of a plate

presentation.

While a few of the sauces such as the Salsas and Simple Dipping Sauce are not thickened, I generally prefer lightly thickened sauces for their pleasant texture and the way they linger on the palate, allowing them to be savored longer.

How sauces are thickened is a matter of personal choice and sometimes expediency. Some methods for thickening like reduction, or the evaporation of water, as for the Roast Tomato and Garlic Sauce with Dulse and Lime (page 146) or the Vegetable Juice Reduction Sauces (pages 150–154), require a certain amount of time. Other sauces that use thickening agents such as flour, arrowroot or cornstarch, come together more quickly. Another method of creating texture is to use a vegetable purée as in the Carrot Ginger Sauce (page 133). The Watermelon Catsup (page 135) uses both reduction and purée. The Shiitake Sweet Potato Hazelnut Sauce (page 139) uses a vegetable purée with a nut butter to thicken it.

Vegetable Juice Reduction Sauces

Very intensely flavored sauces can be achieved by reducing fresh extracted vegetable juices or fruit juices to a syrup-like consistency. The result is a pure essence of flavor and color. Because of their high cost reduction sauces are recommended for special occasions or for those operations serving more expensive cuisine. However, the flavors are so intense that only a couple of teaspoons are needed per serving.

The reduction sauces can be made from a single juice or by combining several juices. Adding other flavoring agents such as diced vegetables, herbs or spices further builds the taste.

The wider the bottom of the pan used for reduction or evaporation of the juices, the faster the cooking time. A Windsor-style pan, wide at the top and narrow at the bottom, allows juice to reduce rapidly at first, then as the sauce thickens the volume is confined to a smaller area at the bottom of the pan, protecting it from burning as it turns to a syrup. Wash down any caramelized sauce from the sides of the pan by swirling up the boiling juice with a whip. This gives your reduction sauce part of its distinction from frozen juice concentrates.

These sauces can be drizzled onto a dish with a squeeze bottle or with a teaspoon and used in conjunction with other sauces for heightened flavor and great color combinations. The small serving size of these sauces is due to their concentrated nature and can easily flavor and color a cup of grain such as plain, cooked rice.

Basic Cashew Butter Sauce

YIELD 10 SERVINGS

$\frac{1}{4}$ CUP/60 MILLILITERS

The Basic Cashew Butter Sauce serves as a base that can be flavored with any one or more of the suggested add-ins. Following it are several sauces all made by enhancing the base sauce with highly flavored additions.

onions, fine dice	1 cup	112 grams
olive oil	1 tablespoon	15 milliliters
all-purpose white flour	4 tablespoons	28 grams
hot vegetable stock	3 cups	720 milliliters
cashew butter	2 tablespoons	28 grams
salt	pinch	pinch
pepper	pinch	pinch

Sauté the onions in olive oil over medium heat for 3 minutes until softened. Stir in the flour and continue to cook and stir for about 1 minute. Slowly whisk in the hot vegetable stock, then raise the heat to medium–high. Boil, then simmer for about 5 minutes until lightly thickened. Whisk in the cashew butter. Season to taste with salt and pepper.

VARIATION: If cashew butter is unavailable, add $\frac{1}{4}$ cup/28 grams cashews along with the stock and purée the sauce in a blender.

Note: For a smoother texture, purée the sauce in a blender.

Cashew Butter Sauce with Mustard and Capers

YIELD 10 SERVINGS

$\frac{1}{4}$ CUP/60 MILLILITERS

*Really small capers can be added whole to the sauce if that texture is desired.
The larger capers, however, need to be minced before adding them
to the base sauce in order to spread out their flavor.*

Basic Cashew Butter Sauce (page 125)	$2\frac{1}{2}$ cups	600 milliliters
Dijon style mustard	2 teaspoons	10 milliliters
capers, minced	2 teaspoons	4.66 grams
parsley, minced	2 tablespoons	7 grams

Heat Cashew Butter Sauce and combine well with other mustard capers and parsley. Season to taste.

SERVE WITH: Seasoned Baked Tofu (page 322), Tofu Pecan Cutlets (page 327), Golden Mashed Potatoes with Caramelized Onions (page 205).

Cashew Butter Sauce with Green Peppercorns

YIELD 10 SERVINGS

$\frac{1}{4}$ CUP/60 MILLILITERS

*A pinch each of ground black and white peppercorns will intensify
the heat and round out the flavor of this sauce.*

Basic Cashew Butter Sauce (page 125)	$2\frac{1}{2}$ cups	600 milliliters
brined green peppercorns, minced	1 teaspoon	1 teaspoon
ground black pepper	pinch	pinch
ground white pepper	pinch	pinch
parsley, minced	2 tablespoons	7 grams

Heat Cashew Butter Sauce and combine well with peppercorns and parsley. Season to taste.

Cashew Butter Sauce with Cremini Mushrooms

YIELD 10 SERVINGS

$\frac{1}{3}$ CUP/90 MILLILITERS

The mushrooms in this recipe cook right in the sauce, which receives the benefit of their flavorful juices.

Basic Cashew Butter Sauce (page 125)	2$\frac{1}{2}$ cups	600 milliliters
cremini mushrooms, sliced	8 ounces	225 grams
sherry wine	1 tablespoon	15 milliliters
soy sauce	1 tablespoon	15 milliliters
parsley, minced	2 tablespoons	7 grams

Add mushrooms, sherry and soy sauce to Basic Cashew Butter Sauce. Simmer for 5 minutes until mushrooms are cooked and sauce is again thickened. Stir in parsley and cook one minute longer. Season to taste.

SERVE WITH: Seasoned Baked Tofu (page 322), Tofu Pecan Cutlets (page 327), Golden Mashed Potatoes with Caramelized Onions (page 205).

Cashew Butter Sauce with Fresh Herbs

YIELD 10 SERVINGS

$\frac{1}{4}$ CUP/60 MILLILITERS

Simmer the sauce just long enough to flavor it while maintaining the color of the fresh herbs.

Basic Cashew Butter Sauce (page 125)	2$\frac{1}{2}$ cups	600 milliliters
fresh chives, minced	2 tablespoons	7 grams
fresh basil, minced	2 tablespoons	7 grams

Heat Cashew Butter Sauce and combine well with the chives and basil. Season to taste.

SERVE WITH: Tofu Pecan Cutlets (page 327), over steamed vegetables or cooked grains. Use to dress fresh pasta, as a sauce for the Seasoned Baked Tofu or Tempeh (pages 332, 334).

Note: Use other fresh herbs such as chervil or parsley.

Cashew Butter Sauce with Sundried Tomatoes

YIELD 10 SERVINGS

$\frac{1}{4}$ CUP/60 MILLILITERS

The raw garlic flavor is tempered by cooking it in the sundried tomato juices.

Basic Cashew Butter Sauce (page 125)	$2\frac{1}{2}$ cups	600 milliliters
sundried tomatoes	$\frac{1}{2}$ cup	42 grams
hot water	$\frac{1}{2}$ cup	120 milliliters
garlic, minced	1 teaspoon	5 grams
fresh basil, minced	2 tablespoons	7 grams

Cover the sundried tomatoes with hot water and allow to soften for 15 minutes. Drain the tomato liquid into a saucepan, dice the softened tomatoes and set aside. Add the garlic to the saucepan and bring to a boil. Add the tomatoes along with Basic Cashew Butter Sauce to the pan. Simmer until thickened. Stir in the basil and season to taste.

SERVE WITH: Seasoned Baked Tofu (page 322), Tofu Pecan Cutlets (page 327), Golden Mashed Potatoes with Caramelized Onions (page 205).

Rich Cashew Butter Sauce with Tarragon and Shallots

YIELD 10 SERVINGS

$\frac{1}{4}$ CUP/60 MILLILITERS

This richer version of Cashew Butter Sauce uses only cashew butter as a thickener.

shallots, minced	$\frac{1}{2}$ cup	56 grams
white wine	$\frac{3}{4}$ cup	180 milliliters
fresh tarragon leaves	$\frac{1}{2}$ cup	28 grams
fresh thyme	1 sprig	1 sprig
bay leaf	1	1
soy sauce	3 tablespoons	45 milliliters
black peppercorns	3	3
water	$2\frac{1}{2}$ cups	600 milliliters
fresh tarragon leaves	$\frac{1}{2}$ cup	28 grams
cashew butter	6 tablespoons	84 grams

Combine all ingredients except 2 tablespoons/7 grams tarragon leaves and cashew butter in a saucepan and bring to a boil. Simmer until reduced by one-third. Strain the stock and return to medium heat. Whisk in the cashew butter and simmer until thickened. Mince the reserved tarragon leaves and stir into the sauce. Season to taste.

Peach Chutney

YIELD 10 SERVINGS
$\frac{1}{4}$ CUP/60 MILLILITERS

For the fullest flavored chutney, choose juicy ripe peaches in season.

peaches, peeled and pitted, large dice (1$\frac{1}{2}$ pounds)	3 cups	420 grams
garlic, crushed	$\frac{1}{2}$ teaspoon	.5 gram
gingerroot, minced	2 teaspoons	4 grams
apple cider vinegar	2 tablespoons	30 milliliters
barley malt syrup	$\frac{1}{2}$ cup	120 milliliters
golden raisins	$\frac{1}{2}$ cup	84 grams
lime juice	1 tablespoon	15 milliliters
prepared mustard	1 teaspoon	5 milliliters
salt	pinch	pinch
black pepper	pinch	pinch
cayenne	to taste	to taste

Combine all ingredients in a saucepan and simmer over medium-low heat for 10 to 15 minutes. Stir often to prevent the chutney from burning. Season to taste. Cool before serving.

VARIATION: For Spicy Peach Chutney add one minced hot pepper such as a jalapeño or habanero.

SERVE WITH: Savory Summer Pancakes (page 250) or Savory Winter Vegetable Pancakes (page 251).

Fresh Pear Chutney

YIELD 10 SERVINGS

2 TABLESPOONS/9 GRAMS

*As a suggested accompaniment to Vegetable Walnut Pecan Pâté, this fall fruit
relish provides complimentary sweet and sour tang to its rich taste
and a textural counterpoint to its smooth texture.*

ripe pears, peeled, small dice	$1\frac{1}{2}$ cups	168 grams
sherry vinegar	$1\frac{1}{2}$ teaspoons	7.5 milliliters
ground cloves	pinch	pinch
ginger juice	a few drops	a few drops
salt	pinch	pinch
fresh ground black pepper	pinch	pinch

Combine all ingredients and allow to marinate for at least 15 minutes before using.

SERVE WITH: Vegetable Walnut and Pecan Pâté (page 53).

Tamarind Sauce

YIELD 10 SERVINGS
$\frac{1}{4}$ CUP/60 MILLILITERS

Roshan Lal, owner of Taj of India Restaurant in Middletown, Connecticut
was my culinary collaborator for this sauce.

tamarind paste	1 cup	225 grams
ancho chile, whole	$\frac{1}{2}$ ounce	14 grams
water	4 cups	960 milliliters
cloves	2	2
whole black peppercorns	3	3
whole cumin seed	1 teaspoon	2.33 grams
raisins	$\frac{1}{4}$ cup	28 grams
gingerroot, minced	1 tablespoon	7 grams
maple syrup	3 tablespoons	45 milliliters
ripe banana	$\frac{1}{2}$ cup	98 grams

Combine the tamarind, ancho chile and water in a saucepan. Bring to a boil. Cover, remove from heat and set aside for 1 hour. Place a strainer over a saucepan. Pour the cooking liquid through the strainer, then press tamarind and chile through the strainer with the back of a large spoon. Discard any fiber or seeds.

In a small sauté pan dry roast cloves, peppercorns and cumin seeds until fragrant. Crush seeds with a mortar and pestle or in a spice grinder.

Add the spice mixture and all other ingredients to the pan. Bring to a boil, then simmer for about 20 minutes or until lightly thickened. Cool and then blend until smooth.

SERVE WITH: Vegetable Tempura (page 76), Fried Oyster Mushrooms (page 244), Savory Summer Pancakes (page 250), Savory Winter Vegetable Pancakes (page 251) or any other fried food. Also can accompany India-Style Flat bread (page 353).

Note: Different brands of tamarind paste will require more or less sweetener.

Carrot Beet Sauce

YIELD 10 SERVINGS

$\frac{1}{4}$ CUP/60 MILLILITERS

Along with the flavor of the beets comes the bonus of its amazing color.

red beet, small dice	2 ounces	56 grams
Carrot Ginger Sauce (recipe below)	$2\frac{1}{2}$ cups	600 milliliters

Add diced beet to carrots and ginger and proceed as for Carrot Ginger Sauce.

VARIATION: Replace half of the carrots with parsnips for Carrot Parsnip Ginger Sauce or winter squash for Carrot Squash Ginger Sauce; or use a combination of all three.

Carrot Ginger Sauce

YIELD 10 SERVINGS

$\frac{1}{4}$ CUP/60 MILLILITERS

For a more intense flavor make the sauce with carrot juice in place of the water.

carrots, medium dice	$1\frac{1}{2}$ cups	196 grams
gingerroot, minced	1 tablespoon	7 grams
water	$3\frac{1}{2}$ cups	840 milliliters
salt	$\frac{1}{4}$ teaspoon	1.5 grams
soy sauce	to taste	to taste

Simmer all ingredients except soy sauce for 10 to 15 minutes until the carrots are very tender. Cool enough to blend safely. Blend and season to taste with soy sauce.

VARIATION: For a richer sauce such as Carrot Ginger Tahini Sauce, Carrot Ginger Almond Butter or Carrot Ginger Hazelnut Butter Sauce, add up to 1 ounce/28 grams tahini, almond butter or hazelnut butter while blending sauce.

Note: If the sauce is too thick, add a little carrot, orange or apple juice. If the sauce is too thin, simmer until thickened. Carrots could be sautéed or roasted first.

Dulse Cocktail Sauce

YIELD 10 SERVINGS

3 TABLESPOONS/45 MILLILITERS

This cocktail sauce was developed to carry the built-in flavor of the sea.

natural-style catsup	1 cup	272 grams
prepared horseradish	$\frac{1}{4}$ cup	60 grams
lemon juice	$\frac{1}{2}$ cup	120 milliliters
dulse flakes	2 tablespoons	6 grams
sea salt	1 teaspoon	6 grams
maple syrup	1 tablespoon	15 milliliters

Combine all ingredients and let stand for 15 minutes to allow the flavors to come together.

Note: For a quick version, add dulse flakes to your own cocktail sauce.

Watermelon Catsup

YIELD 10 SERVINGS
3 TABLESPOONS/45 MILLILITERS

Besides being easier to eat, seedless watermelon makes the preparation
time much quicker for this recipe.

seedless watermelon, 1-inch/2.5-centimeter chunks	8 cups	1.125 kilograms
gingerroot, minced	2 teaspoons	5 grams
star anise	2 stars	2 stars
stick cinnamon	1 inch	2.5 centimeters
salt	pinch	pinch
black pepper	pinch	pinch
lime juice	1 tablespoon	15 milliliters
balsamic vinegar	1 tablespoon	15 milliliters

Put watermelon in a wide, heavy-bottom saucepan and press down on it to release some of its juices. Add the remaining ingredients to the pan and bring to a boil. Simmer for 30 minutes. Remove the star anise and cinnamon stick from the sauce and cool long enough to be blended. Blend, then return to the saucepan and reduce to a thick purée or catsup consistency. Season to taste.

SERVE WITH: Fried Oyster Mushrooms (page 244), Fried Breaded Zucchini (page 74), or Oven Roasted Sweet Potatoes (page 203).

Chinese Ginger Garlic Sauce

YIELD 10 SERVINGS

$\frac{1}{4}$ CUP/60 MILLILITERS

Ginger and garlic are used together so often in Chinese cuisine that it is said that they are spoken of in the same breath.

garlic, minced	$1\frac{1}{2}$ tablespoons	10 grams
gingerroot, minced	$1\frac{1}{2}$ tablespoons	10 grams
whole scallions, thin diagonal slices	$\frac{1}{2}$ cup	28 grams
peanut oil	2 teaspoons	10 milliliters
Chinese Five-Spice Cooking Stock (page 87)	2 cups	480 milliliters
soy sauce	$4\frac{1}{2}$ tablespoons	67.5 milliliters
sesame oil	$1\frac{1}{2}$ teaspoon	7.5 milliliters
sherry wine	$1\frac{1}{2}$ tablespoons	22.5 milliliters
arrowroot	3 tablespoons	25 grams
salt	pinch	pinch
fresh black pepper	pinch	pinch

Sauté the garlic, ginger, and three-quarters of the scallions in peanut oil over medium-high heat for about 1 minute or until just beginning to brown. Add the stock and bring to a boil. Use the soy sauce, sesame oil and wine to dissolve the arrowroot, then stir into the boiling stock to thicken. Stir in the remaining scallions. Season to taste.

Note: Add a few drops of rice wine vinegar and/or hot pepper oil to the sauce.

Hollandaze Sauce

YIELD 10 SERVINGS

1½ TABLESPOONS/22.5 MILLILITERS

*Hollandaze is my alternative spelling for this vegan version of the sound-alike classic sauce.
For this rendition, silken tofu replaces the egg yolks and soy margarine the butter.*

soy margarine	5 tablespoons	60 grams
silken tofu, extra firm	½ box	168 grams
fresh lemon juice	5 teaspoons	25 milliliters
turmeric powder	pinch	pinch
salt	⅛ teaspoon	.75 gram
ground cayenne pepper	pinch	pinch
fresh ground black pepper	to taste	to taste
cornstarch	1 teaspoon	2.5 grams

Put the margarine in a pan over low heat to melt. In a blender, combine the remaining ingredients and blend until smooth. Increase heat under the margarine until it is bubbling. Add hot margarine to the blender one-third at a time, blending until smooth. Serve warm.

Note: Use too little turmeric and the color will not come through; too much turmeric and the taste will be dusty.

Bearnaze

YIELD 1⅓ CUP/320 MILLILITERS

10 SERVINGS/30 MILLILITERS

Bearnaze imitates its classic namesake by using the same premise and ingredients as the Hollandaze sauce, flavoring it with a shallot wine reduction and minced tarragon.

shallots, minced	¼ cup	28 grams
white balsamic vinegar	¼ cup	60 milliliters
water	⅓ cup	80 milliliters
soy margarine	5 tablespoons	60 grams
silken tofu, extra-firm	½ box	168 grams
fresh lemon juice	2 teaspoons	10 milliliters
turmeric powder	pinch	pinch
salt	⅛ teaspoon	⅛ teaspoon
fresh ground black pepper	to taste	to taste
cornstarch	1 teaspoon	2.5 grams
fresh tarragon, minced	4 teaspoons	5 grams

Simmer shallots, vinegar and water for 10 to 12 minutes or until most of the liquid is evaporated. Add the margarine to the pan over medium heat to melt. In a blender or food processor, combine all remaining ingredients except the tarragon and blend until smooth. When the margarine and shallot reduction starts to bubble, add to the blender a third at a time, blending until smooth. Add the tarragon to the blender and pulse in. Season to taste. Serve warm.

Note: If fresh tarragon is not available, add some dry tarragon to the shallot vinegar reduction and some minced fresh parsley at the end of the process. White wine, apple cider or another vinegar of choice can be added. Use too little turmeric and the color will not come through; too much turmeric and the taste will be dusty. Over-blending the tarragon will result in a green-tinged sauce.

Shiitake Sweet Potato Hazelnut Sauce

YIELD 10 SERVINGS
$\frac{1}{3}$ CUP/80 MILLILITERS

Puréed sweet potato gives body and texture to this sauce.

onions, fine dice	2 cups	225 grams
olive oil	2 tablespoons	30 milliliters
salt	$\frac{1}{4}$ teaspoon	1.5 grams
fresh rosemary, minced	$\frac{3}{4}$ teaspoon	1 gram
sweet potatoes, peeled, large dice	2 cups	280 grams
water	$1\frac{2}{3}$ cup	400 milliliters
plain rice beverage	1 cup	240 milliliters
hazelnut butter	2 tablespoons	28 grams
fresh shiitake mushrooms, sliced	$1\frac{1}{2}$ cups	140 grams
soy sauce	$1\frac{1}{2}$ tablespoons	22.5 milliliters
fresh ground black pepper	to taste	to taste

Sauté the onions in olive oil over medium heat for 5 minutes or until starting to brown. Remove half the onions from the pan and set aside. To the onions in the pan add salt, rosemary, sweet potatoes and $1\frac{1}{3}$ cups/320 milliliters water. Simmer for about 15 minutes or until the sweet potatoes are tender. Cool to room temperature.

Put the cooled sweet potatoes, rice beverage and hazelnut butter in a blender and blend until smooth. Set aside.

Combine the reserved onions, mushrooms, soy sauce and pepper with the remaining water. Cook for 5 minutes, then add the sweet potato mixture and simmer 5 minutes longer.

SERVE WITH: Hazelnut Squash Ravioli (page 266), pasta (page 259), Making and Cooking Ravioli (page 257), or over other fresh pastas.

Note: Some of the shiitake stems may be woody and should be reserved for stock or soup.

Spinach Pecan Pesto

YIELD ABOUT 4 CUPS
960 MILLILITERS

I sometimes refer to this sauce as winter pesto because of the availability of spinach when basil and other herbs are scarce or higher in price.

fresh spinach, washed	1 pound	450 grams
extra virgin olive oil	½ cup	120 milliliters
pecans, toasted	1 cup	98 grams
white miso	2 tablespoons	28 grams
garlic, minced	½ teaspoon	2.5 grams
salt	pinch	pinch
pepper	pinch	pinch
nutmeg	pinch	pinch
parsley, minced	2 tablespoons	7 grams
basil, minced	2 tablespoons	7 grams

Blanch spinach in boiling salted water for 10 seconds. Drain, cool under running water and squeeze out excess moisture. Put the spinach, two-thirds of the pecans and all the remaining ingredients into a blender and blend with a pulsing action until smooth. With the power off, scrape down the sides of the blender as needed. Season to taste. Use the reserved pecans as a garnish.

Basil Pine Nut Pesto

YIELD 1½ CUPS/308 GRAMS

10 SERVINGS/3 TABLESPOONS/45 MILLILITERS

Basil is easy to grow and great to have on hand to complement tomatoes, zucchini and other produce of summer. Because basil pesto is best when made from plants that haven't yet flowered be sure to pinch off any buds starting at the tops of the plants and also discard from use when purchasing the fresh herb.

basil leaves, washed and spun dry	4 cups	112 grams
pine nuts (pignoli), toasted	½ cup	56 grams
white miso	2 tablespoons	28 grams
garlic, minced	½ teaspoon	2.5 grams
extra virgin olive oil	6 tablespoons	42 grams
salt and pepper	pinch each	pinch each

In a blender or food processor combine half the basil with all the other ingredients except 2 tablespoons/14 grams pine nuts. Blend until smooth, then gradually add the remaining basil. Season to taste. Use the remaining pine nuts for garnish.

Sweet and Sour Sauce

YIELD 10 SERVINGS

$\frac{3}{8}$ CUP/90 MILLILITERS

To create an entrée, pair this sauce with cooked tofu, tempeh or vegetables.

garlic, minced	1½ teaspoon	3.5 grams
gingerroot, minced	1½ teaspoon	3.5 grams
peanut oil	1 teaspoon	5 milliliters
apple juice	3 cups	720 milliliters
maple syrup	¼ cup	60 milliliters
apple cider vinegar	¼ cup	60 milliliters
prepared mustard	1½ tablespoons	22.5 milliliters
tomato paste	3 tablespoons	45 milliliters
soy sauce	3 tablespoons	45 milliliters
toasted sesame oil	1 teaspoon	5 milliliters
arrowroot	¼ cup	36 grams
water	4 tablespoons	60 milliliters

Put the garlic, ginger and peanut oil in a saucepan large enough for all other ingredients. In a bowl combine the apple juice, maple syrup, vinegar, mustard, tomato paste, soy sauce and oil. In a small bowl dissolve the arrowroot with water. Place the saucepan over medium-high heat and sauté ginger and garlic for about a minute or until they start to brown. Quickly add the juice mixture and bring to a boil. Simmer for 5 minutes. Stir the arrowroot mixture, then stir into the sauce to thicken. Immediately remove from heat. Season to taste.

Note: Apple raspberry juice or apple cranberry juice may replace the apple juice. Cornstarch can be used in place of arrowroot and cranberry juice in place of the water.

Simple Dipping Sauce

YIELD 10 SERVINGS

1 ½ TABLESPOONS/24 MILLILITERS

This light Japanese sauce is quick to assemble can be used with any fried food or over roasted vegetables.

soy sauce	$\frac{1}{2}$ cup	120 milliliters
rice vinegar	$\frac{1}{4}$ cup	60 milliliters
water	$\frac{1}{4}$ cup	60 milliliters
gingerroot, minced	1 tablespoon	7 grams
scallions, short thin diagonal slices	1 tablespoon	3.5 grams
red pepper flakes (if desired)	pinch	pinch

Combine all ingredients and allow them to marry for about 20 minutes.

SERVE WITH: Corn and Arame Pancakes (page 71).

Note: Apple juice can be used in place of the water.

Thai Coconut Sauce with Basil

YIELD 2½ CUPS/600 MILLILITERS

When cooking for those who enjoy spicier food, increase the Thai green chile paste to the desired level of heat.

garlic, minced	1 tablespoon	7 grams
gingerroot, minced	1 tablespoon	7 grams
peanut oil	1 tablespoon	5 milliliters
flour	3 tablespoons	28 grams
coconut milk	2 cups	480 milliliters
fresh lime juice	1 tablespoon	15 milliliters
fresh basil leaves, fine julienne	2 tablespoons	7 grams
soy sauce	2 tablespoons	10 milliliters
Thai green chile paste	½ teaspoon	2.5 grams

Sauté garlic and ginger in peanut oil over medium-high heat for about 1 minute or until they begin to brown. Stir in the flour and reduce heat to medium. Slowly stir in the coconut milk. Bring to a boil, then simmer for about 10 minutes or until thickened. Stir in the lime juice, basil and soy sauce. Season to taste.

VARIATION: Thai Coconut Sauce with Cilantro. Replace the basil with cilantro leaves.

SERVE WITH: Corn and Arame Pancakes (page 71), Tofu Pecan Cutlets (page 327), Seasoned Baked Tofu or Tempeh (pages 332, 334).

Note: On the market there is both pure coconut milk and coconut milk made with fruit juices. The latter may be used for a lower fat version of the sauce. Also available is a half-fat version of the pure coconut milk, labeled lite. If the Thai green chile paste is unavailable use a pinch of cayenne to add some heat.

Fresh Tomato Sauce with Basil and Garlic

YIELD 10 SERVINGS

$\frac{1}{2}$ CUP/120 MILLILITERS

A quick sauce full of bright summer flavors.

garlic, minced	4 teaspoons	9 grams
olive oil	4 teaspoons	20 milliliters
fresh tomatoes, medium dice	2 quarts	1.125 kilograms
fresh basil, chopped	$\frac{1}{2}$ cup	14 grams
red wine vinegar	1 tablespoon	15 milliliters
extra virgin olive oil	2 teaspoons	10 milliliters
salt	$\frac{1}{2}$ teaspoon	3 grams
fresh ground black pepper	pinch	pinch
cayenne pepper	to taste	to taste

Sauté garlic in olive oil over medium heat for about 1 minute or until it begins to brown. Quickly add the tomatoes, cover and simmer for 12 minutes. Add the remaining ingredients to pan, cover and simmer for 3 minutes longer. Season to taste.

SERVE WITH: Corn and Arame Pancakes (page 71), White Bean Cakes (page 289), Tomato Herb Pasta (page 260), Butternut Squash Pasta (page 259).

Roast Tomato and Garlic Sauce with Dulse and Lime

YIELD 10 SERVINGS
$\frac{1}{2}$ CUP/120 MILLILITERS

This sauce resonates with a medley of intense flavors. To get the best results be aware that dulse burns easily.

ripe plum tomatoes	$2\frac{1}{2}$ pounds	1.125 kilograms
whole garlic cloves, peeled	16 cloves	42 grams
extra virgin olive oil	1 tablespoon	15 milliliters
salt	pinch	pinch
crushed black pepper	pinch	pinch
fresh lime juice	2 teaspoons	10 milliliters
dulse, whole leaf	$\frac{1}{2}$ cup	10 grams
water	$\frac{1}{2}$ cup	120 milliliters

Preheat oven to 400°F/200°C.

Cut the tomatoes in half lengthwise and place in a roasting pan, skin-side down. Insert a garlic clove halfway into top of each tomato. Drizzle the tomatoes and garlic with olive oil and season with salt and pepper.

Place in the oven and roast for 15 minutes. Drizzle with lime juice, stir and roast for 10 minutes longer. While tomatoes are roasting, put dulse on small baking sheet and oven roast for 30 seconds to a minute and then set aside.

When tomatoes are done remove from oven and place in a blender. Deglaze the pan with water and add to the blender. Crumble toasted dulse into blender and purée the mixture.

Put the purée into a saucepan and simmer over medium heat until reduced to about 6 cups/1.45 liters.

SERVE WITH: Sea Vegetable Ravioli (page 267) and other fresh pasta.

Vegetable Gravy

YIELD 10 SERVINGS
$\frac{1}{4}$ CUP/60 MILLILITERS

This quick brown sauce develops surprisingly good flavor in a short period of time.

onions, small dice	$\frac{1}{2}$ cup	56 grams
carrots, small dice	$\frac{1}{2}$ cup	56 grams
celery, small dice	$\frac{1}{4}$ cup	28 grams
kale, chopped	1 cup	28 grams
garlic, chopped	1 teaspoon	5 grams
olive oil	2 tablespoons	30 milliliters
all–purpose white flour	$\frac{1}{4}$ cup	35 grams
hot vegetable stock	3 cups	720 milliliters
soy sauce	2 tablespoons	30 milliliters
salt	pinch	pinch
pepper	pinch	pinch

Put the onions, carrots, celery, kale and garlic in a saucepan and sauté in olive oil over medium high heat for 10 minutes. Reduce the heat to low, stir in the flour and sauté for 3 minutes. Gradually stir or whisk in the hot vegetable stock. Add the soy sauce, salt and pepper. Simmer for 15 minutes. Season to taste. Purée the gravy for a smoother sauce.

Gravy Flavor Chart

These items could be used to flavor the Vegetable Gravy:

anise or fennel seeds	apple cider vinegar
bay leaf	rutabagas
parsley	mushrooms
tarragon	instant roasted barley beverages
red miso paste	barley malt syrup
tomato paste, or tomato puree	molasses for color
tomato sauce	red wine
puree or sauce	sherry wine
prepared mustard	stock from adzuki beans
maple	chocolate

SERVE WITH: Mashed potatoes, stuffing, Acorn squash, Tofu Pecan Cutlets (page 327), Seasoned Baked Tofu (page 322).

Wild Mushroom Sauce

YIELD 10 SERVINGS
$\frac{1}{4}$ CUP/60 MILLILITERS

This recipe was inspired by the writing and generosity of the monarch of mushroom cookery, Jack Czarnicki, author of Joe's Book of Mushroom Cookery. *Jack's suggested method of making mushroom extracts using dried mushrooms is an important concept for this sauce.*

dried cèpes	$\frac{1}{2}$ cup	10 grams
water	3 cups	720 milliliters
shallots, small dice	$\frac{1}{2}$ cup	56 grams
soy margarine	1 tablespoon	14 grams
soy sauce	1 tablespoon	15 milliliters
salt	$\frac{1}{2}$ teaspoon	3 grams
maple syrup	$\frac{1}{2}$ teaspoon	2.5 milliliters
ground black pepper	pinch	pinch
fresh rosemary	5 leaves	5 leaves
cornstarch	2 tablespoons	15 grams
apple cider	2 tablespoons	30 milliliters

Simmer the dried cèpes in water for 5 minutes. Remove the cèpes from the mushroom extract with a slotted spoon. When the mushrooms are cool enough to handle, squeeze out any liquid into the extract. Rinse off the mushrooms to remove any grit, chop coarsely and set aside. Pass the extract liquid through a paper coffee filter to remove any soil sediment. Set the extract aside.

In a saucepan, sauté the shallots in soy margarine over medium heat for about 5 minutes or until they start to brown. Add the reserved chopped cèpes and mushroom extract to pan. Add the soy sauce, salt, syrup, pepper and rosemary to the pan, bring to a slow boil, 5 minutes.

To thicken, combine the cornstarch with the apple cider and stir into the boiling stock. Season to taste with salt, pepper and soy sauce as needed.

SERVE WITH: Seasoned Baked Tofu (page 322), Tofu Pecan Cutlets (page 327), Golden Mashed Potatoes with Caramelized Onions (page 205).

Note: Cèpe is the French name for a prized member of the *boletus* mushroom family. It is found in other countries by the names *steinpilz* (Germany), *porcini* (Italy), and *borowik* (Poland).

Miso Ginger Tahini Sauce

YIELD 3 CUPS

$\frac{1}{4}$ CUP/60 MILLILITERS

Miso styles range from the lesser aged, mild tasting white to the pronounced deep flavor of red and other darker examples. Try other kinds in this sauce for a variation in flavor.

water	3 cups	720 milliliters
gingerroot, minced	1 tablespoon	7 grams
red miso	3 tablespoons	42 grams
barley malt syrup	1 tablespoon	15 milliliters
cornstarch	3 tablespoons	24 grams
lemon juice	3 tablespoons	45 milliliters
sesame tahini	$\frac{1}{4}$ cup	60 milliliters

Combine the water and ginger in a sauce pot and bring to a boil. Whisk in the miso and the barley malt syrup. Simmer for 5 minutes. Dissolve the cornstarch with the lemon juice and stir into the simmering liquid to thicken. Remove from heat and whisk in the tahini. Season to taste.

SERVE WITH: Millet with Winter Squash (page 296), Basmati Rice with Asparagus and Cashews (page 303).

Note: Reheat the sauce gently as high heat can cause the tahini to separate.

Vegetable Juice Demi-Glaze

YIELD ½ CUP

2 TEASPOONS/10 MILLILITERS

A Windsor-style pan is perfect for the process of creating a vegetable-based demi-glaze.

beets	approx. 5 cups	560 grams
carrots	approx. 5 cups	560 grams
celery	approx. ⅔ cup	56 grams
onions	approx. ⅔ cup	56 grams
kale chopped	approx. 5 cups	560 grams
garlic, halved	1 clove	1 clove
salt	pinch	pinch
pepper	pinch	pinch
olive oil	1 tablespoon	15 milliliters

Put the beets, carrots, celery and onions through a juice extractor. Put the juice in a heavy-bottom saucepan along with the kale, garlic, salt and pepper. Boil slowly for about 15 minutes or until reduced by half. Swirl the pan to wash down the caramelized sauce on the side and/or scrape down the sides with a wet spatula. Strain the sauce and return to heat; reduce to a syrup-like consistency. Whisk in the olive oil. Season to taste.

SERVE WITH: Acorn Squash with Apricot Cashew Stuffing (page 232).

Red Pepper Porcini Reduction Sauce

YIELD $\frac{1}{2}$ CUP

2 TEASPOONS/10 MILLILITERS

This sauce combines the two intense complementary flavors of dried porcini mushrooms and concentrated red pepper juice.

dried porcini	$\frac{1}{2}$ cup	14 grams
water	1 cup	240 milliliters
red peppers	approx. 8 cups	900 grams
salt	pinch	pinch
pepper	pinch	pinch
garlic, minced	$\frac{1}{2}$ teaspoon	2.5 grams
olive oil	1 tablespoon	15 milliliters
fresh oregano, minced	2 teaspoons	2 grams

Simmer the dried porcini in water for 5 minutes. Remove the porcini from the mushroom extract with a slotted spoon. Rinse off the mushrooms to remove any grit, chop finely and set aside. Pass the extract liquid through a paper coffee filter to remove any soil sediment. Set the extract aside.

Juice the peppers. Put juice in a heavy-bottom saucepan along with the porcini extract, salt and pepper. Boil slowly for about 15 minutes or until reduced by half. Swirl the pan to wash down caramelized sauce on the side and or scrape down sides with a wet spatula. In another smaller saucepan, sauté the garlic in olive oil over medium heat until it begins to brown. Add reserved mushrooms and juice reduction. Return to heat and reduce to a syrup-like consistency. Stir in the oregano. Season to taste.

SERVE WITH: Mushroom Duxelles Ravioli (page 265).

Red Swiss Chard Reduction Sauce

YIELD ½ CUP

2 TEASPOONS/10 MILLILITERS

This sauce uses the stems of red Swiss chard. Reserve the leaves for
Red Swiss Chard Sauté with Garlic (page 194).

red Swiss chard stems	approx. 5 cups	560 grams
carrots	approx. 5 cups	560 grams
celery	approx. ⅔ cup	56 grams
onions	approx. ⅔ cup	56 grams
garlic, halved	1 clove	1 clove
salt	pinch	pinch
pepper	pinch	pinch
olive oil	1 tablespoon	15 milliliters

Put the chard stems, carrots, celery and onions through a juice extractor. Put the juice in a heavy-bottom saucepan along with the garlic, salt and pepper. Boil slowly for about 15 minutes or until reduced by half. Swirl the pan to wash down the caramelized sauce on the side and/or scrape down sides with a wet spatula. Strain the sauce and return to heat and reduce to a syrup-like consistency. Whisk in olive oil. Season to taste.

SERVE WITH: Tofu Pecan Cutlets (page 327).

Carrot Juice Cinnamon Reduction Sauce

YIELD ½ CUP

2 TEASPOONS/10 MILLILITERS

The sweet concentrated carrot juice is enhanced by the spicy flavor of the cinnamon.

carrots	approx. 12 cups	1.35 kilograms
cinnamon stick	1	2.5 centimeters
salt	pinch	pinch
pepper	pinch	pinch
soy margarine	1 tablespoon	14 grams

Put the carrots through a juice extractor. Put the juice in a heavy-bottom saucepan along with the cinnamon, salt and pepper. Boil slowly for about 15 minutes or until reduced by half. Swirl the pan to wash down the caramelized sauce on the side and/or scrape down sides with a wet spatula. Continue to reduce to a syrup-like consistency. Whisk in the soy margarine. Season to taste.

SERVE WITH: Hazelnut Squash Ravioli (page 266), or Butternut Squash Pasta (page 259).

Mirepoix Reduction Sauce

YIELD $\frac{1}{2}$ CUP

2 TEASPOONS/10 MILLILITERS

This sauce uses the fresh extracted juices from the traditional mirepoix vegetables, carrots, celery and onion.

carrots	approx. 10 cups	1.125 kilograms
celery	approx. $\frac{2}{3}$ cup	56 grams
onions	approx. $\frac{2}{3}$ cup	56 grams
garlic, halved	1 clove	1 clove
salt pinch	pinch	
pepper	pinch	pinch
soy margarine	1 tablespoon	14 grams

Dice and reserve 2 tablespoons/14 grams each carrots, celery and onion. Put the remaining carrots, celery and onion through a juice extractor. Put the juice in a heavy-bottom saucepan along with the garlic, salt and pepper. Boil slowly for about 15 minutes or until reduced by half. Swirl the pan to wash down the caramelized sauce on the side and/or scrape down the sides with a wet spatula. Remove the garlic from the sauce and add the reserved diced vegetables. Continue to cook to a syrup-like consistency. Whisk in the soy margarine. Season to taste.

SERVE WITH: Sea Vegetable Ravioli (page 267), Blackened Tofu (page 325).

Fusion Tartar Sauce

YIELD 10 SERVINGS

2 TABLESPOONS/28 GRAMS

The coriander chutney is available in East Indian and specialty grocery stores. Sushi ginger is now available from many purveyors, in many large supermarkets, and in Asian grocery stores.

sushi ginger, minced	2 tablespoons	28 grams
coriander chutney	2 tablespoons	28 grams
fresh lime juice	1 tablespoon	15 milliliters
Vegenaise	1 cup	225 grams
salt	pinch	pinch
ground black pepper	pinch	pinch

Combine all ingredients.

SERVE WITH: Serve with any breaded and fried or baked foods such as Fried Oyster Mushrooms (page 244), or Fried Breaded Zucchini (page 74).

Orange Cider Cranberry Sauce

YIELD 3 CUPS

Place a piece of plastic wrap onto the side of a grater before grating the citrus peel. It will catch the grated peel, keeping the grater from getting clogged up and make the cleanup easier.

fresh cranberries, rinsed, stems removed	12 ounces	336 grams
Florida crystals	$1\frac{1}{4}$ cups	245 grams
apple cider	$1\frac{1}{4}$ cups	300 milliliters
orange rind, grated	1 tablespoon	9.33 grams
salt	pinch	pinch
ground black pepper	pinch	pinch

Combine all ingredients in a saucepan and bring to a boil. Simmer for about 10 minutes. Season to taste. Serve warm or chilled.

SERVE WITH: Tofu Pecan Cutlets (page 327).

Note: See ingredients chapter for note on Florida crystals.

Cashew Crème

YIELD ABOUT 1 CUP/240 MILLILITERS

Raw or roasted cashews may be used to make cashew crème as called for in a particular recipe.

cashews, raw	$\frac{1}{2}$ cup	70 grams
water	$\frac{3}{4}$ cup	180 milliliters

Place the cashews in a blender and using a pulsing action, grind as fine as possible. With the blender turned off, loosen the ground nuts from the sides and bottom of the blender. Add water and start pulsing the blender at a low speed. Increase blender speed and blend until very smooth.

If only salted cashews are available, reduce or eliminate salt from recipe the crème is used in. For finer cashew crème pour through a strainer to remove any particles. Strained cashew crème can be placed in a squirt bottle and used to garnish. Cashew crème will thicken a bit when placed in the refrigerator overnight. Add a few drops of water to thin the cashew crème if needed.

Note: For Thick Cashew Crème reduce water to $\frac{1}{2}$ cup/120 milliliters.

Pumpkin Seed Crème

YIELD ABOUT 1 CUP/240 MILLILITERS

Raw or toasted pumpkin seed may be used to make pumpkin seed crème as called for in a particular recipe.

pumpkin seeds, hulled	$\frac{1}{2}$ cup	56 grams
water	$\frac{3}{4}$ cup	180 milliliters
maple syrup or other sweetener	1 tablespoon	15 milliliters
salt	pinch	pinch

Place the pumpkin seeds in a blender and using a pulsing action grind as fine as possible. Turn the blender off and loosen from the sides of the bottom of the blender. Add the water and start pulsing the blender at a low speed. Increase the blender speed and blend until very smooth.

Sunflower Crème

YIELD ABOUT 1 CUP/240 MILLILITERS

This plant-based preparation provides a creamy texture and color to recipes with a similar effect to dairy cream.

sunflower seeds, raw	$\frac{1}{2}$ cup	70 grams
water	$\frac{3}{4}$ cup	180 milliliters

Place the sunflower seeds in a blender and using a pulsing action, grind as fine as possible. With the blender turned off, loosen the ground seeds from the sides and bottom of the blender. A long tined fork works well for this job. Add the water and start pulsing the blender at a low speed. Increase the blender speed and blend until very smooth. For a finer textured crème, pass it through a strainer.

Nori Sesame Seed Condiment

YIELD ABOUT 1 CUP/112 GRAMS

1 TABLESPOON/7 GRAMS

toasted sesame seeds	1 cup	112 grams
sea salt	$\frac{1}{4}$ teaspoon	2 grams
sheet nori	1	1

Grind together in a blender or food processor.

SERVE WITH: This condiment can be sprinkled on any dish that needs a flavor boost. It makes a good garnish for plain cooked rice or other grains.

Soy Sauce Roasted Almonds with Dulse

YIELD ABOUT 1$\frac{1}{2}$ CUPS/200 GRAMS

2 TABLESPOONS/9 GRAMS

whole almonds	1$\frac{1}{4}$ cups	147 grams
maple syrup	2 tablespoons	30 milliliters
soy sauce	2 tablespoons	30 milliliters
dulse flakes	2 tablespoons	6 grams

Preheat oven to 350°F/180°C.

Toast the almonds on a sheet pan for 5 minutes. Remove the almonds from the oven and toss with syrup, soy sauce and dulse flakes. Return to oven for another minute. Allow to cool, then grind coarsely in a food processor.

SERVE WITH: This condiment can be sprinkled on any dish that needs a flavor boost. It makes a good garnish for plain cooked rice or other grains.

Note: Soy sauce roasted almonds are available through natural foods suppliers.

CHAPTER SIX

Salads

*I*n its simplest form a salad might be a single

type of lettuce tossed with oil and vinegar. There

is, however, no limit to the possibilities of salad

compositions.

A salad may be arranged from several components and can be served chilled or hot, or perhaps coated with a warm dressing. A salad can be garnished with more substantial ingredients and be presented as a main course or it can be one of many non-leafy varieties such as potato, pasta or grain salad.

For interesting and attractive salad presentations try to incorporate various flavors and textures and to combine contrasting colors. For example, a variety of lettuces could provide the firmness and crunch of Romaine with the softness of spinach, the pungency of arugula and the color and bitter characteristics of radicchio. Add sautéed mushrooms or roasted vegetables along with some crunchy croutons or toasted nuts for further flavor and texture development.

An important step in salad making is the washing and drying of all the greens and vegetables to be used. For the various types of lettuce, use lukewarm water to remove any grit from your greens, then spin them dry in a salad spinner. (Salad spinners are now available in commercial sizes.) Wrap the cleaned leaves in a paper or lint-free cloth towel, place in a plastic bag or container and store in the refrigerator. The towels will absorb any residual moisture from the greens, which, if not removed, will prevent the dressing from coating the salad. Other vegetables used in salad should be washed and dried before cutting.

The position that salad occupies in a meal has evolved to include tossed greens or other types of salads as components or garnishes for almost any course. Therefore, salads can be combined with appetizers or hot vegetable sides and with main course dishes, as a layer or a complimentary component.

Broccoli Couscous Almond Salad

YIELD 10 SERVINGS

$1\frac{1}{2}$ CUPS/252 GRAMS

There are several varieties of couscous. Some are made from the polished hearts of semolina wheat, while other types of couscous are made from a pasta-like dough cut into various sizes.

water	5 cups	1.2 liter
couscous	$2\frac{1}{2}$ cups	350 grams
salt	$1\frac{1}{4}$ teaspoons	9 grams
bay leaves	2	2
ground black pepper	pinch	pinch
broccoli, 1 inch/2.5 centimeter pieces, cooked	5 cups	364 grams
almonds, sliced, toasted	2 cups	196 grams
chives, minced	4 teaspoons	4.5 grams
mint, minced	4 teaspoons	4.5 grams
Orange Mustard Dressing (page 182)	$1\frac{1}{2}$ cups	360 milliliters

GARNISH

mesclun salad mix	5 cups	150 grams
mint leaves	20	20
whole chives	10	10

Bring the water to a boil. Add the couscous, salt, bay leaves and pepper. Simmer for 5 minutes, then remove from the heat. Fluff with a fork and allow to cool. Remove the bay leaves.

Combine the couscous with broccoli and three-quarters of the almonds, the chives, the mint and half of the dressing. Season to taste, bearing in mind that more dressing will be drizzled over the salad.

GARNISH AND PRESENTATION: Arrange Broccoli Couscous Almond Salad on a base of greens and garnish with mint, chives and remaining toasted almonds. Drizzle with reserved dressing.

SERVE WITH: Brazilian Style Greens (page 196), Black Bean Soup with Cumin and Garlic (page 102).

Note: Couscous can be tossed with any of the juice reduction sauces for a flavor and color boost.

Asparagus with Strawberry Dressing

YIELD 10 SERVINGS

4 TO 5 MEDIUM SPEARS

*After observing that different size asparagus grow at the same time and by trying both the thin
and the thick versions, I've come to the conclusion that the medium to thick sizes are best.
As long as they are fresh, indicated by a smooth compact tip, all sizes are tender.
The large examples may need to have the stems peeled.*

asparagus	3 pounds	1.35 kilograms
Strawberry Dressing (page 185)	$2\frac{1}{2}$ cups	600 milliliters
salt	pinch	pinch
fresh ground black pepper	pinch	pinch
mango, fine dice	1 cup	224 grams
black sesame seeds, toasted	1 tablespoon	7 grams

Trim asparagus by holding each spear firmly and snapping off the bottom end just
where it will allow itself to break to yield the greatest amount of spear possible. For
really large amounts, snap a few and use them as a guide to trim the ends of each bundle with a knife. Reserve the stems for soup or stock. Generally only the largest stalks
need to be peeled.

Cook the asparagus in a generous amount of boiling, lightly salted water.
Medium spears will take 5 to 7 minutes, large spears may take 10 minutes or longer.
The color should be bright green and the asparagus should be fork-tender.

When cooked, drain water and reserve it for soup stock if desired. Shock the asparagus in cold water, drain and dry with paper towels. Sprinkle the asparagus with
salt and pepper.

GARNISH AND PRESENTATION: Drizzle $\frac{1}{4}$ cup/60 milliliters Strawberry Dressing on
each plate. Lay the asparagus across the sauce. Garnish the plates with the diced
mango and sesame seeds.

SERVE WITH: Tofu and Duxelles in Fillo (page 331). Tofu Pecan Cutlets (page
327).

Aztec Sun Salad

YIELD 10 SERVINGS

*Build each salad just off-center of the plate, leaving a space at the bottom right
of the plate to make a sun design with the dressing.*

Oven-Roasted Sweet Potatoes (page 203)	5 cups	840 grams
red leaf lettuce, whole (attractive leaves) (torn for salad)	10 5 cups	10 210 grams
radicchio, whole		140 grams
Orange Mustard Dressing (page 182)	$1\frac{1}{2}$ cups	360 milliliters
fresh cilantro, minced	2 teaspoons	2.5 grams
sundried tomatoes, slivered	$\frac{1}{2}$ cup	42 grams
fresh cilantro leaves	30	30
corn chips, round	20	20

Cut the sweet potatoes for Oven Roasted Sweet Potatoes recipe into half-moon-shaped slices and proceed with the recipe, omitting the garnish. When potatoes are roasted remove from oven and set aside.

Separate ten attractive pieces of lettuce from the red leaf and ten cup-shaped leaves from the radicchio. Tear the remaining red leaf lettuce into bite-size pieces and shred the radicchio. Place a piece of red leaf on each of ten plates.

Combine the Orange Mustard Dressing with the minced cilantro. Toss the torn lettuce with enough of the dressing to coat lightly, reserving the remainder to drizzle on the sweet potatoes and to garnish the plates. Divide the coated lettuce among the ten plates.

Put $\frac{1}{2}$ cup/84 grams roasted sweet potato into each radicchio cup, drizzle with a little dressing and place atop each salad. Decorate with the slivered sundried tomatoes, the cilantro leaves, and the corn chips. Put a little pool of dressing on the bottom right corner of the plate and using the tip of a paring knife, pull points away from the center to give the effect of a sun.

SERVE WITH: Brazilian Style Greens (page 196), Black Bean Soup with Cumin and Garlic (page 102).

Black-eyed Pea Salad

YIELD 10 SERVINGS

1 CUP/196 GRAMS

The recipe for the Black-eyed Pea Salad was developed for a 1992 Culinary Olympics platter. The presentation as a salad follows a concept of Chef Gary Brummett.

black-eyed peas	$2\frac{1}{2}$ cups	450 grams
water	10 cups	2.4 liters
kelp	1 inch piece	2.5 centimeter piece
salt	pinch	pinch

DRESSING

olive oil	$2\frac{1}{2}$ tablespoons	37.5 milliliters
scallions, thin diagonal slices	$1\frac{1}{4}$ cups	70 grams
garlic, crushed	2 teaspoons	5 grams
lemon juice	$2\frac{1}{2}$ tablespoons	37.5 milliliters
Dijon mustard	$2\frac{1}{2}$ tablespoons	37.5 milliliters
apple cider vinegar	$\frac{1}{4}$ cup	60 milliliters
salt	$\frac{1}{2}$ teaspoon	3 grams
ground black pepper	pinch	pinch
grilled red peppers, diced	2 cups	450 grams

GARNISH

dark rye bread	10 slices	10 slices
spring/mesclun mix		336 grams
fresh dill, chopped	$\frac{1}{4}$ cup	28 grams

Put the black-eyed peas in the water with the kelp, bring to a boil, then simmer for 50 minutes or until tender. Drain and reserve liquid for soup if desired; the kelp, if not completely dissolved, can also be saved for soup. Cool the beans under water and rub them together to remove the outer skins, which will float to the top of the water, making them easy to discard. Drain and shake off excess moisture.

Combine the dressing ingredients and toss with the black-eyed peas. Chill, stirring occasionally, for at least 1 hour. Several hours to overnight would bettter develop the flavor. Before serving, allow the salad to come to room temperature and season to taste.

Toast rye bread slices then cut into four triangle-shaped pieces each, or bake triangles as for Croutons (page 187).

Divide mesclun mix among ten plates, top with black-eyed pea salad; garnish with rye triangles and chopped fresh dill.

SERVE WITH: Toasted Spice Hummus (page 51).

Note: Black-eyed peas are also called cow peas. For the rye bread garnish, use large sandwich-size rye bread.

Wild, Japonica and Wehani Rice Medley

10 SERVINGS

¾ CUP/168 GRAMS

The different rice varieties for this salad may be purchased individually or in a blend which includes brown rice as well. Use one part each of the individual rice varieties, including brown rice or a blend. Some blends contain other types of rice and grains such as basmati rice, quinoa and/or wheat berries.

water	5 cups	1.2 liters
bay leaves	2	2
salt	½ teaspoon	3 grams
carrots, 1-inch/2.5-centimeter pieces	2 cups	252 grams
yellow summer squash, 1-inch/2.5-centimeter pieces	2 cups	252 grams
zucchini, 1-inch/2.5-centimeter pieces	2 cups	252 grams
rice blend or ¼ part each rice	2 cups	392 grams
Apple Cider Dressing (page 184)	1½ cups	360 milliliters
fresh basil, minced	2 teaspoons	2.25 grams
fresh herb fennel, minced	2 teaspoons	2.25 grams
lettuce leaves	10	10
fresh basil sprigs	10	10
fresh herb fennel sprigs	10	10

Bring water, bay leaves and salt to a boil. Blanch the carrots first, then yellow squash and zucchini together until bright in color and just tender. Remove from the water, then shock the vegetables in cold water to stop cooking, drain and set aside. Reserve the cooking liquid and bay leaves for rice.

Measure the reserved stock with bay leaves and add water if needed to make 5 cups/1.2 liters. Bring the liquid to a boil, add the rice, return to a boil. Cover and simmer for 45 to 50 minutes or until done. Turn the rice into a bowl, fluff with a fork and allow to cool down. Remove the bay leaves. When cooled a bit, add half of the dressing, the cooked vegetables and the minced herbs. Season to taste.

GARNISH AND PRESENTATION: Place a lettuce leaf on plate, spoon Wild, Japonica and Wehani Rice Medley over lettuce leaf, then drizzle with remaining dressing. Garnish with fresh basil and fennel sprigs.

Broccoli Quinoa Pecan Salad

YIELD 10 SERVINGS

$1\frac{1}{2}$ CUPS/252 GRAMS

To fully enjoy this ancient grain from Peru, wash the quinoa well, rubbing the grains together to remove a bitter flavor that is a natural pest deterrent.

water	$4\frac{1}{2}$ cups	1.08 liters
quinoa	$2\frac{1}{2}$ cups	350 grams
salt	$1\frac{1}{4}$ teaspoons	7.5 grams
bay leaves	3	3
ground black pepper	pinch	pinch
broccoli, 1-inch/2.5-centimeter pieces, blanched	2 cups	147 grams
carrots, 1-inch/2.5-centimeter pieces, blanched	$1\frac{1}{2}$ cups	189 grams
yellow squash, 1-inch/2.5-centimeter pieces blanched	$1\frac{1}{2}$ cups	210 grams
pecans, toasted	2 cups	196 grams
chives, minced	4 teaspoons	4.5 grams
mint, minced	4 teaspoons	4.5 grams
Orange Mustard Dressing (page 182)	$1\frac{1}{2}$ cups	360 milliliters
GARNISH		
mesclun salad mix	5 cups	150 grams
mint leaves	20	20
whole chives	10	10

Bring the water to a boil, add quinoa, salt, bay leaves and pepper. Simmer for 5 minutes, then remove from the heat. Fluff with a fork and allow to cool. Remove the bay leaves.

Combine the quinoa with the broccoli, carrots, yellow squash and three-quarters of the pecans, the minced chives, and mint, along with half of the dressing. Season to taste, bearing in mind that more dressing will be drizzled over the salad.

GARNISH AND PRESENTATION: Arrange Broccoli Quinoa Pecan Salad on a base of greens and garnish with mint, chives and remaining toasted pecans. Drizzle with reserved dressing.

Grilled Vegetable Salad

YIELD 10 SERVINGS

Grilled vegetables are a wonderful salad addition and can be served hot, warm or chilled.

Grilled or Broiled Red Peppers, Zucchini, and Anise (page 212)	5 cups	1.12 kilograms
White Balsamic Miso Vinaigrette (page 181)	1 cup	240 milliliters
mesclun salad mix	$\frac{3}{4}$ pound	336 grams
pine nuts, toasted	$\frac{1}{4}$ cup	28 grams

Cut grilled vegetables to smaller pieces if desired. Dress with some White Balsamic Miso Vinaigrette, using the remainder to dress the salad greens. Plate the salad greens and garnish with grilled vegetables. Sprinkle on toasted pine nuts.

VARIATION: Use broiled or roasted vegetables. In place of mesclun serve a grilled quarter Romaine head per person. To grill the Romaine, leave the core intact to keep the leaves from falling off; brush with olive oil and place on a grill to wilt and become a little charred.

SERVE WITH: Black Bean Soup with Cumin and Garlic (page 102), Millet with Winter Squash (page 296).

Carrot and Parsnip Salad with Smoked Dulse

YIELD 10 SERVINGS
$\frac{1}{2}$ CUP/56 GRAMS

This salad is great used as a garnish for other dishes.

carrots, grated	2 cups	224 grams
parsnips, grated	2 cups	224 grams
celery, fine dice	$\frac{3}{4}$ cup	84 grams
red onion, minced	1 tablespoon	7 grams
smoked dulse, toasted, crumbled	2 tablespoons	2 to 3 grams
apple cider vinegar	2 teaspoons	10 milliliters
prepared mustard	2 teaspoons	10 milliliters
parsley	1 tablespoon	3.5 grams
sunflower seeds	2 tablespoons	14 grams

Combine all ingredients and mix well. Season to taste.

SERVE WITH: Smokey Braised Portobello Mushrooms (page 242).

Note: If you can only find regular whole dulse and wish to give the salad a smoke flavor, add a few drops of liquid smoke to apple cider vinegar. Be aware that liquid smoke is very strong in flavor and may easily overpower a dish. Dulse burns easily.

Cherry Tomatoes with Spinach and Basil Parsley Vinaigrette

YIELD 10 SERVINGS
$\frac{1}{2}$ CUP / 112 GRAMS

When the tomato was still a wild plant before hybridization, the fruit it yielded was about the size of a cherry tomato. The petite modern strains of these fruits come in different shapes and colors. When native and in season, they are packed with flavor and ready to display their heritage as more than just a garnish.

cherry tomatoes	$2\frac{1}{2}$ pints	1.125 kilograms
salt	pinch	pinch
pepper	pinch	pinch
Basil Parsley Vinaigrette (page 180)	5 tablespoons	25 milliliters

GARNISH

fresh basil chiffonade	$\frac{1}{2}$ cup	
fresh spinach, salad ready	$6\frac{3}{4}$ cups	280 grams
toasted pine nuts	3 tablespoons	21 grams

Wash and hull the cherry tomatoes and halve them if they are too large for a single bite. Toss with salt and pepper and Basil Parsley Vinaigrette. Season to taste. Plate and garnish with basil chiffonade, spinach and pine nuts.

SERVE WITH: Mushroom Cashew Crème Soup (page 112), Guiness Barley with Tri-Color Confetti (page 298).

Note: Use cherry tomatoes in a medley of colors and shapes, such as the yellow round and pear-shaped varieties.

Avocado, Orange and Red Onion Salad

YIELD 10 SERVINGS

$1\frac{1}{2}$ CUPS/168 GRAMS

To ease preparation use seedless varieties of oranges.

red onions, thinly sliced	$1\frac{1}{2}$ cups	112 grams
red wine vinegar	3 tablespoons	45 milliliters
oranges	3 pounds	1.35 kilograms
avocados, 8 ounces/ 224 grams each	5	5
Romaine, salad-ready	5 cups	140 grams
chicory, leafy, salad-ready	5 cups	140 grams
Fresh Herb Vinaigrette (page 180)	1 cup	240 milliliters

Toss sliced red onions with red wine vinegar and a sprinkle of salt and pepper. Set aside to marinate tossing occasionally. Peel and break all but two oranges into segments. Cut segments into 3 or 4 pieces each. With a knife, peel the remaining oranges and remove the segments. Set aside for garnish, squeeze out juice from remaining membranes and save to coat avocados.

Slice the avocados in half lengthwise, remove pit and peel. Cut about 20 small slices from the top solid ends of the avocados for garnish, drizzle with some of the reserved orange juice and set aside. Cut the remainder into bite-sized chunks and combine with the cut orange pieces. Toss with the reserved orange juice.

Toss the torn salad greens with about one-third of the dressing. Divide the salad greens among 10 plates. Place the orange and avocado chunks on top of the salad greens, garnish with marinated red onions, the reserved orange segments and sliced avocados. Drizzle each salad with about a teaspoon of the remaining vinaigrette.

SERVE WITH: Penne, Sundried Tomatoes, Calamata Olives, and Capers (page 271).

Note: For a salad dressing option use fresh orange juice in place of apple juice for White Balsamic Miso Vinaigrette (page 181). Use lemon juice or a little of the dressing if there is not enough juice from the oranges to coat avocados. This helps to maintain their color.

Ruby Grapefruit, Pomegranate and Assorted Greens

YIELD 10 SERVINGS

The pomegranate seeds are used in this recipe; in addition to their flavor they supply texture with their considerable crunch.

ruby-red grapefruits	3	448 grams each
pomegranate	1	1
mesclun salad mix	10	336 grams
White Balsamic Miso Vinaigrette (page 181)	$\frac{2}{3}$ cup	160 milliliters

Peel the grapefruits and cut segments into bite-sized pieces. Seed the pomegranate and mix the seeds with the grapefruit segments.

Dress the mesclun salad with White Balsamic Miso Vinaigrette (page 181), season to taste and divide among 10 plates. Garnish with grapefruit and pomegranate.

SERVE WITH: Linguine with Vegetarian Bolognaise Ragu (page 279), Ziti with White Beans, Dulse and Kale (page 280).

Sea Czar Salad with Blackened Tofu

10 SERVINGS

When using Romaine lettuce, be sure to wash well, checking for any sand or grit at the base of the stalks; also, remove the center ribs from the large leaves.

Romaine, salad-ready	10 cups	336 grams
Sea Czar Dressing (page 186)	$\frac{3}{4}$ cup	180 milliliters
Blackened Tofu (page 325)	1 recipe	1 recipe
Garlic Crostini (page 55)	30	30

Toss the Romaine with half of the dressing. Divide among 10 plates. Place the Blackened Tofu on top of the greens. Place the crostini along side of the salad. Drizzle with the remaining salad dressing as desired.

SERVE WITH: Mushroom Barley Soup (page 111), Green Pea and Watercress Soup with Mint (page 95), Chilled Cantaloupe Soup with Mint (page 121), Creole Vegetable Soup (page 122).

Note: Romaine heads can be quartered, brushed with olive oil and placed on a grill to wilt and blacken a little.

Mesclun Mix with Smoked Dulse and Warm Shiitake Dressing

YIELD 10 SERVINGS
ABOUT 84 GRAMS

mesclun or spring mix salad	10	336 grams
smoked dulse, shredded	1 cup	28 grams
Shiitake Dressing (page 183)	2 cups	480 milliliters

Toss the salad with the shredded smoked dulse. Dress lightly with some of the salad dressing. Season to taste with salt and pepper.

Golden Potato Salad with Olives and Apricots

YIELD 10 SERVINGS

$\frac{1}{2}$ CUP/128 GRAMS

The preferred garnish for this dish, sumac (also spelled sumach and shoomak), is, according to Larousse Gastronomique, the dried, ground fresh leaves and berries of a shrub that originated in Turkey. Cultivated in southern Italy and Sicily, its acid taste is very popular in Middle Eastern cooking.

golden potatoes (10 lbs)	$6\frac{1}{2}$ cups	900 grams
imported green olives, pitted, minced	$\frac{2}{3}$ cup	84 grams
pitted dried apricots, minced	6 tablespoons	56 grams
red onion, minced	2 tablespoons	14 grams
white wine vinegar	2 tablespoons	30 milliliters
lime juice	2 tablespoons	30 milliliters
prepared mustard, spicy brown	2 teaspoons	10 milliliters
salt	$\frac{1}{2}$ teaspoon	3 grams
ground black pepper	pinch	pinch
extra virgin olive oil	4 teaspoons	20 milliliters
fresh basil, minced	2 teaspoons	2.5 grams
fresh parsley, minced	2 teaspoons	2.5 grams
GARNISH		
basil and parsley leaves	to garnish	to garnish
radicchio leaves, cup-shaped	10	10
celery, thinly sliced	$\frac{1}{2}$ cup	56 grams
sliced almonds, toasted	$\frac{1}{4}$ cup	28 grams
frisee	10 sprigs	10 sprigs
sumac	1 teaspoon	

Boil the potatoes in their jackets for about 35 minutes for smaller potatoes to 45 minutes for large potatoes, or until tender. Drain and set aside to cool. Be careful not to overcook the potatoes as they will absorb water and become mushy and less flavorful. When potatoes are cool enough to handle, peel them if desired and cut into bite-sized pieces.

Combine the potatoes with the olives, apricots, onion, vinegar, lime juice, mustard, salt and pepper. Toss well to coat and then stir in the extra virgin olive oil and the minced basil and parsley.

Put $\frac{1}{2}$ cup/128 grams potato salad into each of the radicchio cups, place on plates and garnish with the sliced celery, toasted almonds, herbs and frisee. Sprinkle with sumac.

SERVE WITH: Fried Tomato Sandwiches (page xxx), Asparagus and Pecans in Fillo (page 233).

Notes: Use other types of olives, bearing in mind that the tartness contrasts with the sweetness of the apricots. Use pistachios or walnuts for garnish. If the salad is presented buffet-style, still garnish with celery, almonds and some shredded raddichio. For this recipe small potatoes are about 4 ounces/112 grams each and large potatoes are about 6 ounces/168 grams each. Sumac is available in Middle Eastern grocery stores. If there is any concern about possible allergy to this product, omit and use paprika or ground ancho chile.

Exotic Mushroom Salad

YIELD 10 SERVINGS

$1\frac{1}{2}$ CUPS/168 GRAMS

Use a combination of cultivated exotic mushroom varieties such as portobello, cremini, shiitake, oyster and white button. Two dressings are called for in the recipe, Shiitake Dressing to cook the mushrooms and Walnut Sherry Vinaigrette to dress the salad greens.

garlic	1 tablespoon	7 grams
olive oil	1 tablespoon	15 milliliters
exotic mushrooms, sliced	10 cups	900 grams
Mushroom Vegetable Stock (page 88)	$\frac{3}{4}$ cup	180 milliliters
Shiitake Dressing (page 183)	1 cup	240 milliliters
salt	pinch	pinch
ground black pepper	to taste	to taste
Walnut Sherry Vinaigrette (page 182)	$\frac{3}{4}$ cup	180 milliliters
mesclun or spring mix salad	10 cups	336 grams

Sauté the garlic in olive oil over medium-high heat for a few seconds or until it just begins to brown. Add the mushrooms and sauté for two minutes. Add the stock, Shiitake Dressing, and season with salt and pepper. Cover and simmer for 3 to 4 minutes or until tender. Remove the cover and increase the heat until most of the liquid is evaporated. Serve hot, warm or chilled.

Use Walnut Sherry Vinaigrette to dress salad greens, season to taste, plate and garnish with the cooked mushrooms.

SERVE WITH: Winter Squash Afghani Style (page 240).

Salad Rouge with Glazed Red Onions and Toasted Hazelnuts

YIELD 10 SERVINGS

There are many varieties of red lettuce on the market such as baby beet greens or young red Swiss chard, peacock kale, radicchio, Lola Rosa, and red leaf. For this salad use a variety of those available. This recipe was inspired by Chef Patty Queen of the Cottage Restaurant in Plainville, Connecticut.

red onion, thinly sliced	6 cups	675 grams
olive oil	2 tablespoons	30 milliliters
salt	pinch	pinch
pepper	pinch	pinch
red wine vinegar	$\frac{1}{4}$ cup	60 milliliters
maple syrup	3 tablespoons	45 milliliters
water	1 cup	240 milliliters
a variety of red lettuces	10 cups	336 grams
Fresh Herb Vinaigrette (page 180)	1 cup	240 milliliters
hazelnuts, chopped and toasted	$\frac{3}{4}$ cup	76 grams

Sauté the onions in olive oil on medium-high heat for 5 minutes. Season with salt and pepper and pour the vinegar, syrup and water into the pan. Reduce the heat and simmer for 5 minutes or until most of the liquid is evaporated and a glaze has formed. Remove from heat.

Toss the torn lettuce with half of the dressing; season to taste. Divide among ten plates and garnish with glazed onions and toasted nuts. Drizzle some of the remaining dressing over each salad as needed.

SERVE WITH: Exotic Mushroom Tart (page 238), Savory Summer Pancakes (page 250).

Fresh Herb Vinaigrette

YIELD 1 CUP/240 MILLILITERS

SERVING SIZE 2 TEASPOONS/10 MILLILITERS

Because the acid in the dressing will "cook" the fresh herbs and change their color, the base mixture could be made ahead, adding the fresh herbs just before serving.

vegetable stock	$\frac{2}{3}$ cup	160 millilites
red wine vinegar	$\frac{1}{4}$ cup	60 milliliters
shallots, minced	2 tablespoons	14 grams
cornstarch	2 teaspoons	5 grams
salt	$\frac{1}{4}$ teaspoon	1.5 grams
fresh ground black pepper	pinch	pinch
prepared mustard, spicy brown	$1\frac{1}{2}$ teaspoon	7.5 milliliters
extra virgin olive oil	2 tablespoons	30 milliliters
maple syrup	$\frac{1}{2}$ teaspoon	2.5 milliliters

In a small saucepan whisk together the stock, vinegar, shallots, cornstarch, salt and pepper. Place on high heat and whisk continuously until it comes to a boil and thickens. Remove from the heat and whisk in the mustard, then the extra virgin olive oil and maple syrup. Add the fresh herbs just before serving. Season to taste.

VARIATIONS:

BASIL PARSLEY VINAIGRETTE

fresh basil, minced	2 tablespoons	7 grams
fresh parsley, minced	2 tablespoons	7 grams

A touch of crushed garlic could also be incorporated.

CILANTRO AND MINT VINAIGRETTE

red wine vinegar	$\frac{1}{4}$ cup	60 milliliters
fresh cilantro, minced	2 tablespoons	7 grams
fresh mint, minced	2 tablespoons	7 grams

CHERVIL TARRAGON VINAIGRETTE

white wine or tarragon vinegar	$\frac{1}{4}$ cup	60 milliliters
fresh chervil, minced	2 tablespoons	7 grams
fresh tarragon, minced	2 tablespoons	7 grams

White Balsamic Miso Vinaigrette

YIELD 1 CUP

SERVING SIZE 1 TABLESPOON/15 MILLILITERS

prepared mustard, spicy brown	2 teaspoons	10 milliliters
white balsamic vinegar	$\frac{1}{4}$ cup	60 milliliters
white miso	3 tablespoons	42 grams
ground black pepper	pinch	pinch
olive oil	$\frac{1}{4}$ cup	60 milliliters
apple juice	6 tablespoons	90 milliliters
fresh tarragon, minced	1 tablespoon	3.5 grams

Whisk together the mustard, vinegar, miso and pepper. Whisk in olive oil, then the apple juice and tarragon.

VARIATION: Fresh parsley can be substituted for tarragon.

Note: Use fresh orange juice in place of apple juice when serving Avocado Orange and Red Onion Salad (page 173) or fresh grapefruit juice for Ruby Grapefruit, Pomegranate and Assorted Greens (page 174).

Walnut Sherry Vinaigrette

YIELD ABOUT $\frac{3}{4}$ CUP/180 MILLILITERS

prepared spicy brown mustard	1 teaspoon	5 milliliters
sherry vinegar	3 tablespoons	45 milliliters
salt	pinch	pinch
pepper	pinch	pinch
walnut oil	4 tablespoons	60 milliliters
apple juice	6 tablespoons	90 milliliters
fresh parsley, minced	1 tablespoon	3.5 grams
toasted walnuts, finely chopped	$\frac{1}{4}$ cup	28 grams

Whisk together the mustard, vinegar, salt and pepper. Whisk in the walnut oil, then whisk in apple juice and parsley. Add the walnuts.

Note: Fresh tarragon can be used in place of the parsley. Use fresh orange juice in place of apple juice to dress the Avocado Orange and Red Onion Salad (page 173) or fresh grapefruit juice for Ruby Grapefruit, Pomegranate and Assorted Greens (page 174).

Orange Mustard Dressing

YIELD ABOUT $1\frac{1}{2}$ CUPS/360 MILLILITERS

This colorful, pungent dressing can be used with many dishes and can be drizzled on a plate for a stylish presentation.

orange juice	6 cups	1.44 liters
prepared mustard, coarse brown	1 tablespoon	15 milliliters
olive oil	3 tablespoons	45 milliliters
crushed black pepper	to taste	to taste

Put the juice in a heavy, wide-bottom saucepan. Boil slowly for about 15 minutes or until reduced by half. Swirl the pan to wash down the caramelized sauce on the side and/or scrape down sides with a wet spatula. Continue to reduce to a syrup-like consistency. Whisk in the mustard, olive oil and black pepper. Season to taste. Add a little water or fresh orange juice to the dressing if it is too acid-tasting.

SERVE WITH: Aztec Sun Salad (page 165), Broccoli Quinoa Pecan Salad (page 169) and other dishes as a secondary sauce for color.

Note: When time is short or when cooking for a large number of guests use 12 fluid ounces/360 milliliters defrosted, frozen concentrated orange juice, diluted 1 to 1 with a few drops of soy sauce added for depth of flavor. Add a little more water to cut acidity if needed.

Shiitake Dressing

YIELD 10 SERVINGS

3 TABLESPOONS/45 MILLILITERS

dry shiitake mushrooms	$\frac{1}{2}$ cup	14 grams
water	$1\frac{1}{2}$ cups	360 milliliters
ginger, minced	1 teaspoon	2.5 grams
garlic, minced	$\frac{1}{2}$ teaspoon	1.25 grams
soy sauce	3 tablespoons	45 milliliters
ground black pepper	pinch	pinch
cornstarch	1 tablespoon	8 grams
sesame oil	1 tablespoon	15 milliliters
Japanese ume plum vinegar	$2\frac{1}{2}$ tablespoons	37.5 milliliters
maple syrup	$\frac{1}{2}$ teaspoon	2.5 milliliters

Put the mushrooms, water, ginger, garlic, soy sauce and pepper into a small saucepan, bring to a boil, then simmer for 5 minutes. Turn off the heat. Remove the mushrooms from the pan with a slotted spoon. When cool enough to handle remove the stems and discard. Dice the shiitake caps and return to the pan.

Whisk the cornstarch and remaining ingredients in a small bowl. Return the mushrooms and stock to heat and bring to a boil. Stir in the cornstarch mixture to thicken; remove from heat. Season to taste. Serve warm or chilled.

SERVE WITH: Basmati Rice with Asparagus and Cashews (page 303), White Bean Cakes (page 289).

Apple Cider Dressing

YIELD ABOUT 1½ CUPS/360 MILLILITERS

apple cider	6 cups	1.44 liters
apple cider vinegar	5 teaspoons	25 milliliters
prepared mustard, coarse brown	4 teaspoons	20 milliliters
olive oil	3 tablespoons	45 milliliters
crushed black pepper	to taste	to taste

Put the juice in a heavy-bottom saucepan. Boil slowly for about 15 minutes or until reduced by half. Swirl the pan to wash down the caramelized sauce on the side and/or scrape down the sides with a wet spatula. Continue to reduce to a syrup-like consistency. Whisk in the vinegar, mustard, olive oil and black pepper. Season to taste.

Pungent Peach Dressing

YIELD ABOUT 1½ CUPS/360 MILLILITERS

Peach juice is available from natural foods stores and vendors.

peach juice	6 cups	1.44 liters
prepared mustard, coarse brown	4 teaspoons	20 milliliters
olive oil	3 tablespoons	45 milliliters
crushed black pepper	to taste	to taste
ground cinnamon	pinch	pinch
ground cloves	pinch	pinch

Put the juice in a heavy-bottom saucepan. Boil slowly for about 15 minutes or until reduced by half. Swirl pan to wash down the caramelized sauce on the side and/or scrape down sides with a wet spatula. Continue to reduce to a syrup-like consistency. Whisk in the mustard, olive oil, black pepper, cinnamon and cloves. Season to taste.

Lemon Tahini Dressing

YIELD $1\frac{1}{2}$ CUPS/360 MILLILITERS

toasted sesame tahini	$\frac{1}{2}$ cup	120 milliliters
fresh lemon juice	$\frac{1}{3}$ cup	80 milliliters
soy sauce	$2\frac{1}{2}$ teaspoons	12.5 milliliters
garlic, crushed	$\frac{1}{2}$ teaspoon	1.5 grams
ume boshi (Japanese pickled plum paste)	$\frac{1}{2}$ teaspoon	2.5 grams
water	$\frac{3}{4}$ cup	180 milliliters

Whisk together all ingredients but the water. Slowly whisk in the water. Store in the refrigerator. The dressing will thicken after it is chilled. It may be thinned with a little water or orange juice.

Strawberry Dressing

YIELD 10 SERVINGS/$\frac{1}{4}$ CUP/60 MILLILITERS

Use this dressing to accompany mixed greens, fruit, or on raw or cooked vegetables.

strawberries, washed, hulled and sliced	2 cups	308 grams
olive oil	2 tablespoons	30 milliliters
red wine vinegar	2 tablespoons	30 milliliters
vanilla soy milk	$\frac{1}{2}$ cup	120 milliliters
salt	$\frac{1}{4}$ teaspoon	1.5 grams
ground black pepper	pinch	pinch
maple syrup	1 tablespoon	15 milliliters
basil, minced	2 tablespoons	7 grams

Blend all ingredients except the basil. Stir in the basil. Season to taste.

VARIATION: Substitute tarragon vinegar or balsamic vinegar for the red wine vinegar. Parsley, tarragon or cinnamon basil can be substituted for the fresh herb. Try raspberries in place of strawberries. Try a vanilla rice beverage in place of soy milk.

Sea Czar Dressing

YIELD $\frac{3}{4}$ CUP/180 MILLILITERS

10 SERVINGS, ABOUT 1 TABLESPOON/15 MILLILITERS

The dulse supplies the sea flavor and the white miso a cheese-like flavor
for this familiar-sounding dressing.

vegan mayonnaise	$\frac{1}{2}$ cup	112 grams
extra virgin olive oil	3 tablespoons	45 milliliters
lemon juice	1 tablespoon	15 milliliters
prepared mustard	$\frac{1}{2}$ teaspoon	2.5 milliliters
garlic, crushed	$\frac{1}{2}$ teaspoon	1.5 grams
white miso	1 teaspoon	5 grams
dulse flakes	$\frac{1}{2}$ teaspoon	.5 gram
salt	pinch	pinch
water	1 tablespoon	15 milliliters

Whisk all ingredients together. If using a blender, add the dulse flakes after all other ingredients as overmixing can discolor the dressing.

Large Croutons

YIELD 10 SERVINGS

3 CROUTONS PER PERSON

Use a multigrain or bread of choice and cookie cutters to punch out large croutons in shapes like diamonds, hearts, circles or crescents, or whatever shape that would be appropriate to a special menu, like pumpkins for a Harvest theme.

large punched bread shapes	30	30
extra virgin olive oil	about $\frac{1}{4}$ cup	about 60 milliliters
salt and pepper	as desired	as desired

Preheat oven to 375°F/190°C.

Brush both sides of the croutons lightly with olive oil. Place them on a sheet pan, sprinkle with salt and pepper, if desired, and bake them for 5 minutes. Turn over the croutons and bake for another couple of minutes or until browned as desired.

VARIATION: Add 1 teaspoon/2.5 grams crushed garlic to the oil to make Garlic Croutons.

CHAPTER SEVEN

Vegetable Side Dishes

When choosing vegetable side dishes, consider

flavors that contrast or complement the main

course, textures that add a different dimension

to the plate, and colors that supply visual appeal

to the entrée.

When I think about vegetable side dishes, I try to choose flavors that will either complement the main course or provide a contrast to its predominant seasoning. Examples of dishes with complementary flavors are Oven-Roasted Sweet Potatoes with Soy Sauce (page 203) and Tempeh Braised with Sauerkraut (page 340). Examples of dishes with contrasting flavors are Brazilian-Style Greens (page 196) and Almond Brown Rice Croquettes (page 310).

Texture is another area to be considered. To make a meal more enjoyable serve something crunchy like Garlic Roasted Potatoes with Rosemary (page 208) with Tofu Sundried Tomato Saucisse (page 332), or purée or smooth-textured side like Mashed Rutabagas and Parsnips (page 197) with Asparagus and Pecans in Fillo (page 233). Serve chunky-style vegetable sides such as Sesame-Roasted Butternut Squash (page 204) with an entrée like Savory Winter Pancakes (page 251).

The color of the accompanying vegetable side dish should be different from the entrée, especially when the color of the main course is monochromatic such as the Choucroute Garnie (page 344). Serving the deep colored Greens Sautéed with Ginger (page 195) with this dish makes the appearance much more appealing.

A variety of cooking methods adds to the overall dimension of the presentation and can help spread the workload evenly so that, for example, while one item is being sautéed, another can be oven-roasted and a third can be grilled, fried or steamed.

Mushroom and Kale Sauté with Cherry Tomatoes

YIELD 10 SERVINGS

$\frac{1}{2}$ CUP/100 GRAMS

kale	2 pounds	900 grams
garlic and/or ginger	1 tablespoon	7 grams
olive oil	1 tablespoon	15 milliliters
white mushrooms, sliced	$2\frac{1}{2}$ cups	225 grams
water	$\frac{1}{2}$ cup	120 milliliters
soy sauce	2 teaspoons	10 milliliters
cherry tomatoes, halved	$\frac{1}{2}$ pound	225 grams
salt	pinch	pinch
ground black pepper	pinch	pinch

Rinse the kale well, thinly slice the base of thin stalks (large stalks should be discarded as they tend to be tough) and coarsely chop the leaves. Set aside. In a heavy-bottom pan or pot, sauté the garlic and/or ginger in olive oil over medium-high heat until it begins to brown. Quickly add the reserved greens and sauté for about 1 minute. Add the mushrooms and sauté for 1 minute. Add the water, soy sauce, salt and pepper, cover and cook for 3 minutes. Add the cherry tomatoes and cook 2 minutes longer. Season to taste.

SERVE WITH: Butternut Squash Pasta (page 259), Orange Curry Pasta (page 263), White Bean Cakes (page 289), Braised Lentils with Sesame-Roasted Carrots (page 290).

Braised Red Cabbage with Dried Cranberries

YIELD 10 SERVINGS

$\frac{1}{2}$ CUP/100 GRAMS

Using balsamic vinegar in this recipe will add flavor to the dish and
also help maintain the color of the red cabbage.

onions, small dice	1 pound	450 grams
garlic, minced	1 tablespoon	7 grams
olive oil	1 tablespoon	15 milliliters
red cabbage, large dice	3 pounds	1.35 kilograms
dried cranberries (craisins)	$\frac{1}{2}$ cup	70 grams
balsamic or red wine vinegar	2 tablespoons	30 milliliters
salt	$\frac{1}{2}$ teaspoon	3.5 grams
ground black pepper	pinch	pinch
liquid smoke	3 to 4 drops	3 to 4 drops

Sauté the onions and garlic in olive oil over medium heat for 2 minutes. Add the red cabbage and sauté for 5 minutes. Add the cranberries, vinegar, salt, pepper and liquid smoke. Reduce the heat to medium, cover, and simmer for 25 to 30 minutes or until tender. Season to taste.

SERVE WITH: Tofu Sundried Tomato Saucisse (page 332).

Note: A little toasted sesame oil instead of liquid smoke could be used to enhance the flavor.

Sesame-Roasted Carrots

YIELD 10 SERVINGS
$\frac{1}{2}$ CUP/84 GRAMS

Root vegetables and roasting go well together. The firm texture of root vegetables hold up well to roasting and their flavor is enhanced by the way the natural sugars turn to caramel as they cook.

carrots	3 pounds	1.35 kilograms
toasted seasame oil	1 tablespoon	15 milliliters
salt	pinch	pinch
soy sauce	1 tablespoon	15 milliliters
raw sesame seeds	3 tablespoons	14 grams

Preheat oven 425°F/220°C. Peel or scrub carrots, cut 1-inch/2.5-centimeter chunks on the bias, then toss with toasted sesame oil and salt. Put onto a baking sheet; roast for 30 minutes, turning after about 15 minutes. When carrots are fork-tender, toss them with the soy sauce and the sesame seeds, and return to the oven for about 5 minutes longer.

SERVE WITH: Hazelnut Squash Ravioli (page 226), Adzuki Beans with Squash (page 291).

Note: Carrots will cook faster in a convection oven.

Red Swiss Chard Sauté with Garlic

YIELD 10 SERVINGS
$\frac{1}{2}$ CUP/84 GRAMS

The red Swiss chard will deliver great color along with the flavor; however, the green variety would do nicely in the recipe as well.

red Swiss chard	3 pounds	1.35 kilograms
garlic, minced	3 tablespoons	21 grams
olive oil	2 tablespoons	30 milliliters
soy sauce	3 tablespoons	45 milliliters
water	as needed	as needed
salt	pinch	pinch
ground black pepper	pinch	pinch
pine nuts, lightly toasted	$\frac{1}{4}$ cup	28 grams

Rinse the red Swiss chard well, thinly slice the base of the stalks and coarsely chop the leaves. Set aside. In a heavy-bottom pan or pot, sauté the garlic in olive oil over medium-high heat until it begins to brown. Quickly add the reserved red Swiss chard and sauté for about 1 minute. Add the soy sauce and a little water if the pan is so hot that the soy sauce starts to burn. Sauté for about 3 more minutes or until the red Swiss chard is wilted and tender. Add salt and pepper to taste.

GARNISH: Garnish with lightly toasted pine nuts.

VARIATION: For Spinach Sauté with Garlic, use fresh spinach leaves in place of the chard and toasted sesame seeds in place of the pine nuts.

SERVE WITH: Wild Rice with Mushrooms (page 294), Millet Mash with Winter Squash (page 296).

Note: For a brighter colored dish, use less soy sauce, adding a little extra salt instead.

Greens Sautéed with Ginger

YIELD 10 SERVINGS

$\frac{1}{2}$ CUP/84 GRAMS

When preparing this recipe for a large number, it helps to blanch and shock the greens so one has better control over their cooking time.

kale or collards	3 pounds	1.35 kilograms
fresh gingerroot, minced	3 tablespoons	21 grams
olive oil	2 tablespoons	30 milliliters
soy sauce	3 tablespoons	45 milliliters
water	as needed	as needed
salt	pinch	pinch
ground black pepper	pinch	pinch

Rinse the kale or collards well, thinly slice the base of thin stalks (large stalks should be discarded as they tend to be tough) and coarsely chop the leaves. Set aside. In a heavy-bottom pan or pot, sauté the ginger in olive oil over medium-high heat until it begins to brown. Quickly add the reserved greens and sauté for about 1 minute. Add the soy sauce and a little water if the pan is so hot that the soy sauce starts to burn. Sauté for about 3 more minutes or until the greens are wilted and tender. Season to taste.

SERVE WITH: Almond Brown Rice Croquettes (page 310), Basic Vegetable Fried Rice (page 311), Fried Rice with Mushrooms (page 312) or Fried Rice with Tofu or Tempeh (page 313).

Note: Other greens such as turnip greens, mustard greens, bok choy, napa or green cabbage, could be cooked according to this recipe. The stronger flavored greens such as the mustard or turnip greens can be cooked in combination with one or more of the others. Reduce the amount of soy sauce in the recipe and substitute balsamic vinegar if desired.

Brazilian-Style Greens

YIELD 10 SERVINGS

$\frac{1}{2}$ CUP/84 GRAMS

This recipe was inspired by author Jessica Harris, who writes about Brazilian cuisine.

kale or collards	3 pounds	1.35 kilograms
garlic, minced	3 tablespoons	21 grams
habanero or scotch bonnet pepper, minced	1	1
olive oil	2 tablespoons	30 milliliters
soy sauce	2 tablespoons	30 milliliters
fresh lime juice	1 tablespoon	15 milliliters
water	as needed	as needed
salt	pinch	pinch
ground black pepper	pinch	pinch

Rinse kale or collards well and thinly slice the base of thin stalks (large stalks should be discarded as they tend to be tough); coarsely chop the leaves. Set aside. In a heavy-bottom pan or pot, sauté the garlic and minced pepper in olive oil over medium-high heat until the garlic begins to brown. Quickly add the reserved greens and sauté for about 1 minute. Add the soy sauce, lime juice and a little water if the pan is so hot that the soy sauce starts to burn. Sauté for about 3 more minutes or until the greens are wilted and tender. Add salt and pepper to taste.

SERVE WITH: Tempeh Mushroom Vegetable Cobbler (page 338), Savory Summer Pancakes (page 250).

Note: These are some of the hottest types of peppers available and may be too hot for some people, in which case a milder variety could be used.

Mashed Rutabagas and Parsnips

YIELD 10 SERVINGS
$\frac{1}{2}$ CUP/112 GRAMS

The idea of using this combination of root vegetables came from Michele Moelder, Certified Nutritionist and owner of Health Beat Natural Foods, Johnson City, New York. The sweetness of the parsnips balances the bitterness of the rutabagas.

rutabagas, cut in 1-inch/ 2.5-centimeter chunks	2 pounds	900 grams
parsnips, cut in 1-inch/ 2.5-centimeter chunks	1 pound	450 grams
salt	pinch	pinch
ume boshi plum paste	1 teaspoon	7 grams
rice beverage	$\frac{1}{2}$ cup	120 milliliters
soy margarine	1 tablespoon	14 grams
fresh ground black pepper	to taste	to taste

Put the rutabagas in a pot and cover with water. Bring to a boil and add the parsnips and a pinch of salt. Simmer for 20 minutes or until tender. Drain off the water. Return to low heat, add the rice beverage, ume boshi plum paste, soy margarine and black pepper. Mash, then season to taste.

SERVE WITH: Hungarian-Style Braised Mushrooms (page 247), Tofu Pecan Cutlets (page 327), Tofu and Duxelles in Fillo (page 331).

Oven-Braised Acorn Squash

YIELD 10 SERVINGS

2 WEDGES EACH, 112 GRAMS

*Other winter squash such as butternut, hubbard or hokaido pumpkins
could be prepared in the same manner.*

two small Acorn squash	3 pounds	1.35 kilograms
onions, sliced	$1\frac{1}{2}$ cups	170 grams
fresh gingerroot, minced	$1\frac{1}{2}$ teaspoons	3.5 grams
toasted sesame oil	1 teaspoon	5 milliliters
water	$\frac{3}{4}$ cup	180 milliliters
salt	pinch	pinch
soy sauce	1 tablespoon	15 milliliters
maple syrup	1 tablespoon	15 milliliters
scallions or chives, minced	1 tablespoon	15 milliliters
ground black pepper	to taste	to taste

Wash the squash, split in half and remove the seeds. Cut the squash into thin wedges, 10 wedges per squash. Put the onions, ginger, sesame oil, water and salt in the bottom of a roasting pan and spread out evenly. Put the squash in a layer on top of this mixture. Cover the pan and place in a 350°F oven for 45 minutes or until squash are tender. Pour off any cooking juices and add to them the soy sauce, syrup and scallions or chives. Season to taste. Serve the squash with some onions on top and a drizzle of the enhanced cooking juices.

SERVE WITH: White Bean Cakes (page 289), Braised Lentils with Sesame-Roasted Carrots (page 290).

Note: The ground black pepper could be sprinkled on at this point but would not be appropriate for those clients following a macrobiotic diet.

Orange Braised Butternut Squash with Ginger and Garlic

YIELD 10 SERVINGS
$\frac{1}{2}$ CUP/100 GRAMS

The orange juice enhances both the color and the flavor of the squash and complements the ginger and garlic.

garlic, minced	$1\frac{1}{2}$ teaspoons	3.5 grams
fresh gingerroot, minced	1 tablespoon	7 grams
toasted sesame oil	$1\frac{1}{2}$ teaspoons	7.5 milliliters
butternut squash, 1-inch/ 2.5-centimeter cubes	$6\frac{1}{2}$ cups	1.0125 kilograms
soy sauce	1 tablespoon	15 milliliters
orange juice	$1\frac{1}{2}$ cups	360 milliliters
salt	pinch	pinch
ground black pepper	pinch	pinch
toasted black sesame seeds	1 tablespoon	7 grams

Sauté the garlic and ginger in sesame oil over medium-high heat for about 30 seconds. Add the butternut squash and sauté for another minute. Add the soy sauce, orange juice, salt and pepper. Cover and simmer for 10 minutes over medium heat or until the squash is tender. Season to taste. Serve chunky style or mashed, garnished with the toasted black sesame seeds.

SERVE WITH: Hungarian-Style Braised Mushrooms (page 247), Tofu Pecan Cutlets (page 327), Tofu and Duxelles in Fillo (page 331).

Parsnip Purée

YIELD 10 SERVINGS

$\frac{1}{2}$ CUP/100 GRAMS

Parsnips are said to be best when harvested after a frost, which increases their sugar content. They can be served chunky style, and combined with other root vegetables for variety.

onions, small dice	1 cup	112 grams
toasted sesame oil	2 teaspoons	10 milliliters
parsnips, large dice	2.5 pounds	1.125 kilograms
water	$2\frac{1}{2}$ cups	600 milliliters
lemon juice	1 teaspoon	5 milliliters
salt	pinch	pinch
ground black pepper	pinch	pinch
maple syrup	to taste	to taste
chopped parsley	2 tablespoons	7 grams

Sauté the onions in toasted sesame oil over medium heat for about 3 minutes. Add the parsnips to the pan and sauté for another 5 minutes or until the parsnips start to brown. Add the water, bring to a boil and simmer for about 8 minutes or until the parsnips are very tender. Drain and put the parsnips into a food processor and purée. If the purée is too wet at this time, return to the pan and over medium-low heat and evaporate the excess liquid. This step will also intensify the flavor of the parsnips. Mix in the lemon juice, salt and ground black pepper. Add a little maple syrup if desired. Season to taste.

GARNISH: Garnish with chopped parsley.

SERVE WITH: Smoky Braised Portobello Mushrooms (page 242), Blackened Tofu, (page 325).

Note: Parsnips, because of their high sugar content, may burn easily, so it is important to monitor them closely during the sauté and evaporation stages of cooking.

Tomatoes Baked with Herbed Bread Crumbs

YIELD 10 SERVINGS

$\frac{1}{2}$ TOMATO EACH

Tomatoes are often much larger in diameter at the top or stem end. To yield equal-sized halves, cut them across about one-third of the way from the top toward the center rather than across the center.

5 tomatoes, 3 inches/ 7.5 centimeters in diameter	$2\frac{1}{2}$ pounds	1.2 kilograms
fresh multigrain bread crumbs	$2\frac{1}{2}$ cups	140 grams
white miso	$1\frac{1}{2}$ teaspoons	7.5 milliliters
extra virgin olive oil	$1\frac{1}{2}$ teaspoons	7.5 milliliters
garlic, crushed	$\frac{1}{2}$ teaspoon	2.5 grams
fresh basil, minced	$\frac{1}{4}$ cup	28 grams
fresh parsley, minced	$\frac{1}{4}$ cup	28 grams
salt	$\frac{1}{4}$ teaspoon	1.5 grams
ground black pepper	pinch	pinch

Cut the tomatoes in half, and squeeze out the seeds and discard them. Remove a little pulp from each of the tomato halves to make $\frac{1}{3}$ cup/80 milliliters. Lightly salt and pepper the tomato halves and place them on a baking sheet.

Preheat the oven to 400°F/190°C. In a bowl, combine the tomato pulp, bread crumbs, white miso, extra virgin olive oil, basil and parsley. Top the tomato halves with the bread crumb mixture. Bake for 12 minutes or until the tops are browned and the tomatoes are soft but not mushy.

SERVE WITH: Tofu and Duxelles in Fillo (page 331), Broccoli Quinoa Pecan Salad (page 169).

Note: To make fresh bread crumbs, roughly tear up slices of bread and chop in the food processor or blender. Bread could also be cut into small cubes with a knife.

Green Beans with Balsamic Vinegar

YIELD 10 SERVINGS
3 OUNCES/84 GRAMS

The green beans need to be blanched or softened before being sautéed with the ginger and garlic.

fresh green beans, trimmed	2 pounds	900 grams
fresh gingerroot, minced	1 tablespoon	7 grams
garlic, minced	1 tablespoon	7 grams
olive oil	1 tablespoon	15 milliliters
balsamic vinegar	$2\frac{1}{2}$ tablespoons	37.5 milliliters
salt	pinch	pinch
ground black pepper	pinch	pinch

Blanch the green beans in boiling salted water for about 8 minutes or until al dente. Drain in a colander and cool them under cold running water. Sauté the ginger and garlic in olive oil over medium-high heat until they just start to brown. Add the balsamic vinegar and green beans to the pan and sauté until the beans are well-coated and warmed through. Season to taste with salt and pepper. Drizzle with a little extra virgin olive oil and balsamic vinegar if desired.

SERVE WITH: White Bean Chili with Caramelized Onions (page 288), Orange Sesame Udon Noodles (page 276), Chilled Soba Noodles with Spicy Peanut Sesame Sauce (page 277).

Oven-Roasted Sweet Potatoes with Soy Sauce

YIELD 10 SERVINGS

$\frac{1}{2}$ CUP/84 GRAMS

The soy sauce in this recipe contributes to both the browning effect of roasting and the final flavor.

sweet potatoes	3 pounds	1.35 kilograms
peanut oil	1 tablespoon	15 milliliters
salt and pepper	pinch each	pinch each
soy sauce	1 tablespoon	15 milliliters

GARNISH

toasted almond, chopped	3 tablespoons	14 grams
fresh parsley, chopped	1 tablespoon	3.5 grams

Preheat oven 425°F/220°C. Peel the sweet potatoes and cut into rough 1-inch/2.5-centimeter chunks, toss with peanut oil and sprinkle with salt and pepper. Spread out on a baking sheet and roast for about 30 minutes or until just fork-tender. Drizzle with soy sauce and roast for 5 more minutes. Serve topped with toasted almonds and chopped parsley.

SERVE WITH: Aztec Sun Salad (page 165), Tofu Scrambled Colombian Style (page 330).

Note: Place the sweet potatoes in cold water after peeling to keep them from discoloring.

Sesame-Roasted Butternut Squash

YIELD 10 SERVINGS
$\frac{1}{2}$ CUP/84 GRAMS

When treated in the following manner the butternut squash make a great layer for an entrée, adding texture and flavor. If used hot in a salad the squash adds a dimension of different temperature as well.

butternut squash	$2\frac{1}{2}$ pounds	1.125 kilograms
toasted sesame oil	1 tablespoon	15 milliliters
salt	pinch	pinch
pepper	pinch	pinch
soy sauce	1 tablespoon	15 milliliters
GARNISH		
toasted black or white sesame seeds	3 tablespoons	14 grams
fresh parsley, chopped	1 tablespoon	3.5 grams

Preheat the oven to 400°F/200°C. Peel and seed the butternut squash, then cut into rough 1-inch/2.5-centimeter chunks, toss with toasted sesame oil and sprinkle with salt and pepper. Spread out on a baking sheet and roast in the oven for about 30 minutes or until fork-tender. Serve garnished with sesame seeds and chopped parsley.

SERVE WITH: Mesclun Mix with Smoked Dulse and Warm Shiitake Dressing (page 175), Blackened Tofu (page 325), Baby Bella Risotto (page 302).

Golden Mashed Potatoes with Caramelized Onions

YIELD 10 SERVINGS
$\frac{1}{2}$ CUP/112 GRAMS

Two of the most common foods served in a special way take advantage of their taste and comforting nature without breaking the bank.

Yukon Gold or other yellow potato	3 pounds	1.35 kilograms
salt	$1\frac{1}{2}$ teaspoons	9 grams
onions, small dice	4 cups	448 grams
olive oil	1 tablespoon	15 milliliters
rice beverage	$\frac{1}{2}$ cup	120 milliliters
soy margarine	1 tablespoon	14 grams
fresh ground black pepper	to taste	to taste
fresh parsley, minced	2 tablespoons	7 grams

Peel and cube the potatoes. Put the potatoes into a pot, cover with water, add 1 teaspoon/6 grams salt and bring to a boil. Boil the potatoes for about 20 minutes or until tender. While the potatoes cook, sauté the onions in oil over medium heat for about 20 minutes or until they are well caramelized. When the potatoes are tender, drain the water from the pan and add the rice beverage, soy margarine, and remaining salt and pepper. Return the potatoes to low heat and mash well. Stir in three-quarters of the caramelized onions and taste for seasoning.

GARNISH: Use remaining onions and minced parsley to garnish.

SERVE WITH: Tofu and Duxelles in Fillo (page 331), Corn on the Cob with Garlic Herb Spread (page 206), Hungarian-Style Braised Mushrooms (page 247).

Corn on the Cob with Ume Boshi Plum Paste or Garlic Herb Spread

YIELD 10 SERVINGS

2 HALF EARS OF CORN

Look for corn in the husk that is not dried out at the outer leaves and has a tassel that is still loose and silky.

fresh corn on the cob	10 ears	10 ears
water for boiling		
ume boshi plum paste	5 teaspoons	28 grams

Shuck corn, trim the tips of the ears to leave a flat top, cut into halves and boil for 3 to 5 minutes in unsalted water. To serve, place a dab of plum paste on the end of each half ear and serve standing up. Alternately, brush a little plum paste on each portion and serve.

VARIATION: Substitute plum paste with Garlic Herb Spread; recipe on the following page.

Garlic and Herb Spread

YIELD $\frac{1}{4}$ CUP/60 MILLILITERS

Spread on roasted vegetables, bread or corn.

garlic, crushed	1 teaspoon	3.5 grams
extra virgin olive oil	1 tablespoon	15 milliliters
soy margarine	2 tablespoons	28 grams
parsley, minced	1 tablespoon	1.75 grams
basil, minced	1 tablespoon	1.75 grams
lemon juice	1 teaspoon	5 milliliters
ground black pepper	pinch	pinch

In a small pan, stir the garlic into the extra virgin olive oil and cook over medium heat until the garlic shows the first signs of browning (about 30 seconds). Quickly add all remaining ingredients and continue to stir until the margarine is almost melted. Remove from the heat and continue to stir until the soy margarine is completely melted. Brush onto cooked corn on the cob or other vegetables.

SERVE WITH: Sweet and Sour Tempeh (page 336), Red Swiss Chard Sauté with Garlic (page 194).

Garlic Roasted Potatoes with Rosemary

YIELD 10 SERVINGS

ABOUT $\frac{3}{4}$ CUP/140 GRAMS

In one French kitchen that I worked in the potatoes were spread out to dry a few days before using. This process helps to evaporate some of the water content and concentrate the potato flavor when they are cooked.

white russet potatoes	4 pounds	1.8 kilograms
olive oil	1 tablespoon	15 milliliters
salt	to taste	to taste
garlic, crushed	2 teaspoons	7 grams
rosemary leaves, crumbled	1 teaspoon	2 grams
fresh ground black pepper	pinch	pinch

Peel the potatoes and slice into wedges lengthwise, about 1 inch/2.5 centimeters at the base. Toss the potato wedges with 2 teaspoons olive oil and sprinkle with salt. Place in a 400°F oven and roast for 10 minutes. Turn the potatoes and roast for another 10 minutes. Combine crushed garlic, rosemary leaves, a pinch of salt, remaining olive oil and black pepper. Coat roasted potatoes with garlic rosemary mixture and return to the oven for 5 more minutes. Season to taste.

SERVE WITH: Thin slices of Smokey Braised Portobello Mushrooms (page 242), Asparagus with Hollandaze Sauce (page 210).

Arame with Carrots and Onions

YIELD 10 SERVINGS

3 OUNCES/84 GRAMS

This Japanese-style dish would be appropriate as a component of a macrobiotic platter, or it could be served warm as a topping for a simple green salad or to add taste and flavor to any of the salads or main dishes featuring grains.

arame, dry (sea vegetable)	2 ounces	56 grams
carrots, thinly sliced half moons	$\frac{3}{4}$ pound	337.5 grams
onions, halved and sliced	$\frac{3}{4}$ pound	337.5 grams
canola oil	1 tablespoon	15 milliliters
fresh gingerroot, minced	1 tablespoon	7 grams
soy sauce	$\frac{1}{4}$ cup	60 milliliters
toasted sesame oil	1 tablespoon	15 milliliters
maple syrup	2 tablespoons	60 milliliters
water (for cooking)	2 cups	480 milliliters

Rinse the arame, then cover with water and allow to soak for 15 minutes. Sauté the carrots in canola oil over medium–high heat for 5 minutes. Add the onions and ginger and sauté 5 minutes. Drain the arame and discard the water. Add the arame and all remaining ingredients to the pan. Cover and simmer slowly for 15 to 20 minutes, stirring occasionally. Season to taste.

SERVE WITH: Adzuki Beans with Squash (page 291), and Greens Sautéed with Ginger (page 195), or Kamut, Corn and Lima Beans (page 300).

Asparagus with Hollandaze Sauce

YIELD 10 SERVINGS

4 TO 5 MEDIUM SPEARS

If the asparagus is not drained well, the water will dilute the sauce. Dab off water clinging to the asparagus with a napkin or paper towel.

asparagus	3 pounds	1.35 kilograms
Hollandaze Sauce (page 137)	1 cup	240 milliliters
toasted black sesame seeds (optional)	1 tablespoon	7 grams

Trim the asparagus by holding each spear firmly and snapping off the bottom end just where it will allow itself to break, yielding the most amount of spear possible. For large amounts, snap a couple of spears as a guideline, then cut off the ends of each bundle with a knife. Reserve the snapped-off stems for soup or stock. Generally only the largest stalks need to be peeled. Cook the asparagus in a generous amount of boiling water, lightly salted if desired. Thin spears will be done in as little as 2 minutes, medium spears will take 5 to 7 minutes and large spears may take 10 minutes or longer. The color should be bright green and the asparagus should be fork-tender. When cooked, drain water and reserve for soup stock if desired. Salt and pepper to taste.

GARNISH AND PRESENTATION: Serve the asparagus sauced with Hollandaze Sauce and sprinkle with toasted black sesame seeds.

SERVE WITH: Serve with thin slices of Smoky Braised Portobello Mushrooms (page 242), and Garlic Roasted Potatoes with Rosemary (page 208).

Chinese-Style Broccoli

YIELD 10 SERVINGS
$\frac{1}{2}$ CUP/84 GRAMS

When preparing this recipe for large numbers of guests, blanch the broccoli first to ensure speedy assembly of the dish.

Five-Spice Cooking Chinese Stock (page 87)	2 cups	480 milliliters
broccoli	$2\frac{1}{2}$ pounds	1.125 kilograms
garlic, slivered	1 tablespoon	7 grams
fresh gingerroot, minced	1 tablespoon	7 grams
peanut oil	1 tablespoon	15 milliliters
cornstarch	1 tablespoon	8 grams
soy sauce	2 tablespoons	30 milliliters
toasted sesame oil	$\frac{1}{2}$ teaspoon	2.5 milliliters
maple syrup or other sweetener	1 teaspoon	5 milliliters
GARNISH		
toasted sesame seeds	2 tablespoons	14 grams
scallions, thin bias cut	$\frac{1}{2}$ cup	28 grams

Put Five-Spice Seasoned Cooking Stock into a small pan, boil 5 minutes strain and return to the pan. Reduce to $1\frac{1}{2}$ cups.

Trim off the hard bottom sections of the broccoli stems. Peel the stems, split lengthwise and diagonally slice stems into bite-sized pieces. Break or cut the broccoli tops into bite-sized florets and set aside with sliced stems.

In a large sauté pan or wok, sauté the garlic and ginger in peanut oil over medium-high heat for about 30 seconds or until they begin to brown. Add the broccoli to the pan and sauté for another minute. Combine the cornstarch with an equal amount of Five-Spice Cooking Stock and set aside. Add all remaining ingredients. Cover and cook the broccoli for 4 to 5 minutes longer, or until bright green and tender. Stir the cornstarch mixture into the pan to thicken the sauce. Season to taste.

GARNISH: Garnish with toasted sesame seeds and sliced scallions.

SERVE WITH: Guinness Barley with Tri-color Confetti (page 298) or Chick-pea Tomato and Herb Salvatore (page 101).

Grilled or Broiled Red Peppers, Zucchini and Anise

YIELD 10 SERVINGS

4 OUNCES/112 GRAMS

Grilling and broiling impart the flavor of the fire to the foods being cooked and they also use different equipment, leaving stove top burners available for other parts of the meal.

red peppers, 2 large	1 pound	450 grams
olive oil	1 tablespoon	15 milliliters
salt	to taste	to taste
pepper	to taste	to taste
anise bulb	$1\frac{1}{2}$ pounds	675 grams
zucchini	2 pounds	900 grams
GARNISH		
basil, minced	2 tablespoons	7 grams
balsamic vinegar	to taste	to taste
extra virgin olive oil	to taste	to taste

Pre-heat the broiler or start the grill or coals. Cut the red peppers in half, remove the stem and seeds, then slice into $\frac{1}{2}$-inch/1.5-centimeter strips lengthwise. Toss with one-quarter of the olive oil and sprinkle with salt and pepper. Place on one quarter of a baking sheet to broil or later to be transferred to the grill. Trim the anise of tough stalks and cut off base, leaving the core intact. Slice the anise bulb into 10 slices. Toss with one-quarter of the olive oil and sprinkle with salt and pepper. Place them on one-quarter of a baking sheet, next to peppers, to broil or later to be transferred to the grill. Trim the ends from the zucchini and slice into 20 slices. Coat with the remaining olive oil and sprinkle with salt and pepper. Place on one-half of the baking sheet next to anise and peppers to broil or later to be transferred to the grill.

To broil: Place the vegetables under broiler and broil about 5 minutes on each side or until well-browned and tender.

To grill: Place the vegetables on the grill or into a hinged wire grill basket and grill for about 5 minutes on each side or until well-marked by the grill and tender. The zucchini, if placed directly on the grill, could be given a quarter turn before turning over to give them a traditional diamond pattern grill mark. Season to taste.

GARNISH: Garnish grilled or broiled vegetables with fresh basil, a drizzle of balsamic vinegar and extra virgin olive oil.

SERVE WITH: Serve the grilled vegetables as a base or tossed with Orange Curry or Tomato Herb Pasta (pages 260, 263), or Basmati Rice with Asparagus (page 303).

Zucchini or Summer Squash with Fennel Seeds, Lemon Zest

YIELD 10 SERVINGS

$\frac{1}{2}$ **CUP/100 GRAMS**

Cooking the fennel seeds with the garlic brings out the flavor-enhancing qualities of both of these ingredients.

zucchini, small sliced $\frac{1}{2}$ inch/ 1.25 centimeters	3 pounds	1.35 kilograms
olive oil	1 tablespoon	15 milliliters
garlic, minced	1 tablespoon	7 grams
olive oil	1 tablespoon	15 milliliters
fennel seeds	1 teaspoon	3.5 grams
lemon zest, minced	1 teaspoon	3.5 grams
vegetable stock	$\frac{1}{4}$ cup	60 milliliters
fresh basil, oregano or parsley, minced	2 tablespoons	7 grams
salt and pepper	to taste	to taste
toasted pine nuts	2 tablespoons	14 grams

In a large, nonstick sauté pan, sauté the zucchini in olive oil over medium-high heat for about 3 minutes. Push the zucchini to the outside of the pan, making a space in the center. Add the garlic, olive oil, and fennel seeds to the center of the pan and stir for about 10 seconds. Add the lemon zest and toss the zucchini well to coat with the seasonings. Add the vegetable stock. Continue to cook about 3 minutes longer or until just tender. Toss the zucchini with chopped fresh herbs and season to taste with salt and pepper.

GARNISH: Garnish with toasted pine nuts.

SERVE WITH: Linguine with Vegetarian Ragu (page 279), Baby Bella Risotto (page 302).

Maple-Glazed Kelp, Carrots and Onions

YIELD 10 SERVINGS

$\frac{1}{2}$ CUP/84 GRAMS

Try to purchase chopped kelp, which will ease the preparation of this dish.

kelp, dry, chopped	$1\frac{1}{3}$ cups	28 grams
water (for cooking)	$2\frac{1}{2}$ cups	540 milliliters
carrots, $\frac{1}{2}$-inch/1.25-centimeter, bias cut	3 cups	378 grams
onions, $\frac{1}{2}$-inch/1.25-centimeter, bias cut	3 cups	336 grams
toasted sesame oil	1 tablespoon	15 milliliters
ginger, minced	1 tablespoon	15 grams
soy sauce	3 tablespoons	45 milliliters
maple syrup	3 tablespoons	45 milliliters
apple cider vinegar	1 teaspoon	5 milliliters
sea salt	pinch	pinch
ground black pepper	pinch	pinch
toasted sesame seeds	3 tablespoons	21 grams

Soak the kelp in 2 cups/480 milliliters water for 20 minutes or until softened. Remove the kelp and reserve the water. If only large pieces of kelp are available, soak, then cut to small squares or cut the kelp with kitchen shears while dry. Caution: Kelp is slippery when reconstituted and may cause your knife to bounce.

Over medium heat, sauté the carrots and onions in toasted sesame oil for 5 minutes. Add the kelp and ginger and sauté for 5 minutes. Add all remaining ingredients except the sesame seeds and sauté for 10 minutes or until the pan is dry; add $\frac{1}{2}$ cup/120 milliliters of the reserved water and cook until the kelp is tender. Garnish with sesame seeds. Season to taste.

SERVE WITH: White Bean Cakes (page 289), Braised Lentils with Sesame-Roasted Carrots (page 290), Adzuki Beans with Squash (page 291).

Sautéed Mushrooms

YIELD 10 SERVINGS

ABOUT $\frac{1}{3}$ CUP/84 GRAMS

There are 2 basic methods for sautéing mushrooms. One method uses higher heat for the entire cooking time, which browns the outside of the mushrooms and seals in the flavor and moisture. The second method cooks the mushrooms over lower heat, as for Mushroom Duxelles (page 265), so that the moisture forms in the bottom of the pan and is slowly reduced, creating an essence of mushroom flavor. This recipe works with any of the white or exotic mushroom varieties like shiitake or cremini.

olive oil	2 tablespoons	30 milliliters
garlic, coarsely chopped	2 teaspoons	10 grams
mushrooms	2 pounds	896 grams
onions, fine dice	1 cup	112 grams
salt	$\frac{1}{2}$ teaspoon	3 grams
soy sauce	1 tablespoon	15 milliliters
fresh rosemary, minced	$\frac{1}{2}$ teaspoon	.6 gram
maple syrup	$\frac{1}{4}$ teaspoon	1.25 milliliters

In a large, heavy skillet, sauté the garlic in olive oil over medium-high heat about 30 seconds or until it starts to brown. Stir in the mushrooms and onions and sauté for 3 minutes. Add the remaining ingredients and sauté for 5 minutes or until mushrooms are cooked and most of the moisture is evaporated. Season to taste.

SERVE WITH: As a temperature counterpoint to garnish Wild, Japonica and Wehani Rice Medley (page 168) or as a base for the Millet Mash with Winter Squash (page 296).

CHAPTER EIGHT

Vegetable-Based Entrées

Vegetables, especially when prepared with finesse, are a welcome feature for any course in a meal, including the entrée. As has long been the case in the cuisine of many cultures, vegetables are beginning to assume a central role in the American meal.

When the season's best produce appears in the field it is time to celebrate the harvest with a special dish. Religious holidays often correspond with these occasions and are marked by the elevation of humble vegetables to the status of ambrosial sustenance as a manner of giving thanks for the earth's delicious bounty.

As recipes move back and forth across borders, native cooks opportunistically add their own special twists. In this spirit we can serve Ratatouille (page 220) of southern France in flowers made from Greek or Middle Eastern style fillo pastry, or prepare a Mediterranean Stew with Smoked Sea Vegetables (page 222) from the coast of Maine. Cooking in this modern style labeled "fusion" offers the potential to savor Roasted Vegetables (page 228) bearing the stamp of China or Japan, with Asian-Style Seasoning (page 229), to compare the tastes of Winter Squash Afghani Style (page 240) to Thai Vegetable Curry (page 234) which both share a heritage of seasoning with India, and with the Tomato and Potato Torte (page 224), to acknowledge the masterful tradition of Italian vegetable cookery as it evolved after the discovery of the new world.

Roasted Vegetables

When roasting several types of vegetables together, some cook faster than others. To adjust for this, place softer vegetables towards the center of the roasting pan and harder vegetables around the outer section. Remove them when they are done, if needed, or shift them to the center of the pan, where they will cook more slowly. For larger quantities, use a separate pan for each vegetable, then combine them when almost done so they finish cooking together and mingle flavors.

For a shorter cooking time, the oven temperature can be raised to 450°F/230°C. However, watch them more closely to prevent burning or drying out. I have found the lower temperature suggested to be more forgiving during busy periods. Be aware that if the temperature is too low, the vegetables will dry out without caramelizing; it is the carmelizing that develops that great roasted vegetable flavor.

Sweet and Sour Vegetables

YIELD 10 SERVINGS

$1\frac{1}{2}$ CUPS/336 GRAMS

The vegetables in this recipe provide a variety of colors and textures. Use this idea as a guideline to achieve many other seasonal combinations.

carrots, $\frac{1}{2}$-inch/1.25-centimeter slices	2 cups	252 grams
onions, quartered and sliced	1 cup	112 grams
broccoli, 1-inch/2.5-centimeter pieces	5 cups	364 grams
zucchini, $\frac{1}{2}$-inch/1.25-centimeter slices	4 cups	560 grams
sweet red peppers, halved and sliced	2 cups	224 grams
celery, sliced	1 cup	112 grams
canola oil	1 tablespoon	15 milliliters
garlic, minced	1 tablespoon	7 grams
ginger, minced	1 tablespoon	7 grams
Sweet and Sour Sauce (page 142)	1 quart	760 milliliters
salt	pinch	pinch
pepper	pinch	pinch
soy sauce	to taste	to taste
black sesame seeds	1 tablespoon	7 grams

Bring a pot of salted water to a boil. Add the carrots and onions, cook for 3 minutes, then add the broccoli, zucchini and red pepper for 2 minutes. Stir in the celery. Drain the blanched vegetables, saving the fortified water for stock if desired, then shock them under cold running water to preserve the color and stop the cooking process. Shake off the excess water and allow them to drain well.

Return the pot to medium heat and add the canola oil, garlic, and ginger. Sauté for about 1 minute or until just starting to brown. Add the blanched vegetables and toss well to coat, flavor with the ginger and garlic mixture. Add the Sweet and Sour Sauce and cook until heated through. Season to taste with salt, pepper and soy sauce.

GARNISH: Use black sesame seeds to garnish.

SERVE WITH: Serve over cooked noodles, rice or other grain with Brazilian-Style Greens (page 196), Yellow Split Pea Curry (page 104), or Corn Chowder (page 116).

Ratatouille in Fillo Flowers

YIELD 10 SERVINGS
1 CUP/224 GRAMS

Salting and draining the eggplant removes some of its high moisture content, making it easier to sauté. Small eggplant or Japanese-style eggplant are usually less bitter.

eggplant, large dice	2 cups	224 grams
onions, quartered and sliced	4 cups	560 grams
olive oil	2 tablespoons	30 milliliters
garlic	2 tablespoons	14 grams
zucchini, large dice	4 cups	560 grams
sweet red peppers, halved and sliced	4 cups	448 grams
bay leaves	4	4
salt	$\frac{1}{2}$ teaspoon	3 grams
fresh tomatoes, large dice	3 cups	420 grams
fresh parsley, chopped	$\frac{1}{2}$ cup	28 grams
celery, thinly sliced	1 cup	112 grams
fresh basil, chopped	$\frac{1}{2}$ cup	28 grams
fresh thyme, minced	1 teaspoon	1.25 grams
ground black pepper	pinch	pinch
red wine vinegar	1 teaspoon	5 milliliters
Fillo Flowers (recipe follows)	10	10

Place the eggplant in a colander, salt lightly and allow to drain for 30 minutes. Rinse, then remove as much moisture as possible. Set aside.

Sauté the onions in 1 tablespoon of the olive oil over medium-high heat for 3 minutes. Add the garlic, reduce heat to medium and sauté for 2 minutes. Add the zucchini, red peppers, bay leaves and half of the salt, and sauté 5 minutes. Remove from the pan to another pan or platter.

Return the pan to the heat and in the remaining olive oil, sauté the eggplant over medium-high heat for 5 minutes. Add the remaining ingredients to the pan and sauté 5 minutes longer. Add the cooked pepper and squash mixture and simmer for 5 minutes. Season to taste. Serve ratatouille in fillo flowers.

SERVE WITH: On a bed of Jasmine rice garnished with Greens Sautéed with Ginger (page 195).

VARIATION: For Ratatouille Crepes, serve ratatouille wrapped in Dulse or Nori Crepes (page 248).

Note: Chopped olives could be used as a garnish.

Fillo Flowers

YIELD 10 FLOWERS

fillo dough	5 sheets	5 sheets
olive oil	2 tablespoons	30 milliliters
muffin tin		

Preheat oven to 375°F/190°C. Cut each sheet of fillo dough into 6 squares. Brush each square with olive oil. Make flowers by layering 3 squares of fillo each with its corners offset from the previous sheet to form the flower petals.

Using the back side of the muffin tin, press each flower over the back of a single muffin form. Cover about every other muffin form so as not to overlap the fillo flowers.

Bake for about 5 minutes or until golden brown.

Mediterranean Smoked Sea Vegetable Stew

YIELD 10 SERVINGS
1½ CUPS/360 MILLILITERS

The sea flavors of smoked dulse and kelp provide a taste reminiscent of bouillabaise. The fresh anise, added at 2 stages of the cooking, and using 2 parts of the bulbs also contribute great flavor. You can also use the anise tops as sprigs for garnish.

fresh anise stalks, peeled, medium dice	1 cup	112 grams
onions, large dice	4 cups	504 grams
olive oil	2 tablespoons	30 milliliters
garlic, minced	3 tablespoons	21 grams
orange zest	1 tablespoon	10 grams
orange juice	¼ cup	60 milliliters
salt	1½ teaspoons	9 grams
carrots, split and cut diagonally .25 inch/.75 milliliters	4 cups	504 grams
bay leaf	2 large	2 large
fennel seeds	2 teaspoons	5.6 grams
rosemary	2 sprigs	2 sprigs
smoked dulse, whole, cut with shears	1 cup	28 grams
kelp, chopped	½ cup	14 grams
Basic Enriched Vegetable Stock (page 84)	6 cups	1.44 liters
diced tomatoes	5 cups	700 grams
fresh anise bulb, sliced	3 cups	280 grams
sweet red peppers, large dice	2 cups	224 grams
cooked white beans	3 cups	714 grams
parsley, minced	¼ cup	14 grams

GARNISH

Sundried Tomato Pesto Crostini (page 56)	30	30
anise sprigs	30	30

Over medium-high heat, sauté the diced anise and onions for 3 minutes. Stir in garlic and sauté for 2 minutes. Reduce the heat to medium, add the orange zest, juice, salt, carrots, bay leaf, fennel, rosemary, dulse and kelp, and sauté for 5 minutes. Add the stock and tomatoes and bring to a boil. Reduce the heat and simmer covered for 15 minutes. Add the remaining ingredients and simmer covered 5 minutes longer or until the anise and peppers are done to taste. Season to taste.

GARNISH AND PRESENTATION: Mound vegetables in shallow soup bowls, surround with broth and garnish with Crostini and anise sprigs. Some pesto could be spooned right onto the mounded vegetables as well.

VARIATION: In place of rosemary sprigs, use 1 teaspoon/2.3 grams dry leaves. If smoked dulse and kelp are not available, use plain sea vegetables and a few drops of liquid smoke (see notes on liquid smoke, page 82). The Crostini garnish could be spread with other pesto recipes, or for special events, a combination of 3 different pesto could be used, one on each crostini.

SERVE WITH: Broccoli Couscous Almond Salad (page 163).

Tomato and Potato Torte

YIELD 10 SERVINGS
5.5 OUNCES/158 GRAMS

The herbed bread crumb mixture sprinkled between the layers of the torte serves to season the dish and absorb the juices, maintaining flavor and firming the finished product.

HERBED BREAD CRUMB MIXTURE

whole-grain bread, about 6 slices	8 ounces	224 grams
garlic, minced	1 tablespoon	7 grams
fresh Italian parsley, chopped	$\frac{1}{2}$ cup	28 grams
dry oregano	1 teaspoon	2 grams
salt	$\frac{3}{4}$ teaspoon	3.75 grams
ground black pepper	pinch	pinch
cornstarch	2 tablespoons	16 grams

INGREDIENTS FOR TORTE LAYERS

extra virgin olive oil	1 tablespoon	15 milliliters
fresh tomatoes, sliced, $\frac{1}{4}$ inch/ .75 centimeter	2 pounds	896 grams
golden potatoes, peeled and sliced, $\frac{1}{4}$ inch/.75 centimeter	$1\frac{1}{4}$ pounds	560 grams
green olives, fine dice	2 tablespoons	14 grams
pine nuts, toasted	2 tablespoons	14 grams

Preheat oven to 375°F/190°C. Tear the bread slices into quarters and put them into a food processor along with the remaining bread crumb mixture and pulse to make herbed bread crumb mixture.

Brush the inside of a springform pan (nonstick preferable, 10 inches/25 centimeters) with a little of the olive oil, then coat the inside of the pan with some of the herbed bread crumb mixture.

Medium dice enough of the bottom and top tomato slices which have the tomato skin on one side to make 1 cup/240 milliliters and set aside.

Place a layer of potatoes slightly overlapping into the bottom of the springform pan, then sprinkle with one-quarter of the herbed bread crumb mixture. Repeat the process with the sliced tomatoes and one-quarter of the herbed bread crumbs. Repeat the potato bread crumb and tomato bread crumb layers again. Combine the reserved diced tomatoes, remaining olive oil and diced green olives, and sprinkle on top of the torte, leaving a 1-inch/2.5-centimeter border.

Cover the pan and bake the torte for 1 hour, then remove the cover and bake for 25 to 30 minutes longer, until potatoes are very tender when tested with a fork. Sprinkle on the toasted pine nuts and allow the torte about 15 minutes to set up. Slice and serve warm.

SERVE WITH: Avocado Orange and Red Onion Salad (page 173), Sea Czar Salad with Blackened Tofu (page 175).

Note: Baking potatoes don't work in this recipe because they harden as they cook. Be sure to use egg- and dairy-free bread.

Baked Potatoes with Almond Butter Sauce

YIELD 10 SERVINGS

Almond butter is one of several types of nut butters available through natural foods stores and distributors. While it is expensive on its own, using it in this recipe with a low food cost item such as potatoes balances it out.

baking potatoes, 8 ounces/ 224 grams each	10	10
fermented black beans	2 tablespoons	14 grams
carrots, grated	1 cup	112 grams
alfalfa sprouts, 1 package		
scallions, thin diagonal slices	1 cup	112 grams
rice vinegar	2 tablespoons	30 milliliters
toasted sesame oil	1 teaspoon	5 milliliters
Chinese cabbage, shredded	3 cups	252 grams
salt	to taste	to taste
fresh ground black pepper	to taste	to taste
Almond Butter Sauce (recipe follows)	$2\frac{2}{3}$ cups	660 milliliters
toasted sliced almonds	$\frac{1}{2}$ cup	49 grams

Preheat oven to 400°F/200°C. Scrub the potatoes, then bake for about 1 hour or until fork-tender. While the potatoes cook, soak the black beans in enough water to cover them for 10 minutes, rinse under fresh water and set aside.

Combine the carrots, sprouts, scallions, rice vinegar, sesame oil and Chinese cabbage, season with salt and pepper to make the salad garnish and set aside.

When the potatoes are done, cut an X in the top and squeeze the sides to open. Season with salt and pepper. Put a spoonful of Almond Butter Sauce into each potato. Fill each potato with some of the salad mixture, using about half of the total mixture.

GARNISH AND PRESENTATION: Place a spoonful of salad on each plate for a base and top with sauced and salad–filled baked potato. Drizzle on more sauce and garnish with reserved, drained black beans and toasted almonds.

SERVE WITH: Green Pea and Watercress Soup with Mint (page 95), Mushroom and Kale Sauté with Cherry Tomatoes (page 191), for a second sauce drizzle on Carrot Juice Cinnamon Reduction Sauce (page 153).

Almond Butter Sauce

YIELD 2 $\frac{2}{3}$ CUPS

$\frac{1}{4}$ CUP/60 MILLILITERS

Using almond butter for a richer version, this sauce is reminiscent of and prepared in the same manner as peanut sauce.

almond butter	1 $\frac{1}{3}$ cups	294 grams
toasted sesame oil	4 teaspoons	20 milliliters
soy sauce	$\frac{1}{2}$ cup	120 milliliters
succanat	2 tablespoons	24 grams
Shanxi vinegar	2 tablespoons	30 milliliters
fresh ginger, minced	2 tablespoons	28 grams
garlic, minced	4 teaspoons	20 grams
dark brewed tea	about 1 cup	240 milliliters

Combine all the ingredients in a blender or food processor and process until smooth. Thin with a little water as needed.

Note: Add a little hot sauce or cayenne to the recipe. Substitute rice vinegar for Shanxi vinegar.

Roasted Vegetables with Garlic and Fennel Seeds

YIELD 10 SERVINGS
ABOUT 5 OUNCES/140 GRAMS

To use other vegetables in this recipe, maintain the placement of harder vegetables to the outside of the pan and softer vegetable towards the center.

olive oil	$\frac{1}{4}$ cup	60 milliliters
garlic, crushed	1 tablespoon	15 grams
fennel seeds	1 tablespoon	7 grams
salt	$\frac{1}{2}$ teaspoon	3 grams
ground black pepper	pinch	pinch
butternut squash, 1-inch/ 2.5-centimeter chunks	$1\frac{1}{2}$ pounds	672 grams
carrots, 1-inch/2.5-centimeters, bias cut	$1\frac{1}{2}$ pounds	672 grams
parsnips, 1-inch/2.5-centimeters, bias cut	$1\frac{1}{2}$ pounds	672 grams
small red onions, quartered	$1\frac{1}{2}$ pounds	672 grams
fresh parsley, chopped	3 tablespoons	7.5 grams
balsamic vinegar	1 tablespoon	15 milliliters

Preheat oven to 425°F/220°C. Mix 1 tablespoon/15 milliliters of the olive oil with the garlic and fennel seeds and set aside. Toss each vegetable with some of the remaining olive oil and some salt and pepper. Place vegetables on separate baking sheets or on a single large sheet with the softer vegetables in the center and the harder vegetables around the outside. Put the vegetables in the oven and stir the vegetables with a spatula after about 15 minutes, then continue to roast 15 minutes longer or until just fork-tender. Toss the vegetables with reserved crushed garlic and fennel seeds in olive oil and roast 10 minutes longer. Toss with chopped parsley and balsamic vinegar. Season to taste.

SERVE WITH: Baby Bella Risotto (page 302), or Basmati Rice with Asparagus (page 303).

Note: Chopped parsley and balsamic vinegar may be roasted with vegetables for the last couple minutes of cooking. Vegetables will brown and cook faster in a convection oven.

Asian-Style Roast Vegetables

YIELD 10 SERVINGS

ABOUT 5 OUNCES/140 GRAMS

The sesame oil, soy sauce, ginger, and garlic give this recipe its flavor profile.

toasted sesame oil	2 tablespoons	60 milliliters
garlic, crushed	2 teaspoons	10 grams
ginger, crushed	2 teaspoons	10 grams
soy sauce	3 tablespoons	15 milliliters
salt	pinch	pinch
ground black pepper	pinch	pinch
butternut squash, 1-inch/ 2.5-centimeter chunks	$1\frac{1}{2}$ pounds	672 grams
carrots, 1-inch/2.5-centimeter, bias cut	$1\frac{1}{2}$ pounds	672 grams
parsnips, 1-inch/2.5-centimeter, bias cut	$1\frac{1}{2}$ pounds	672 grams
small red onions, quartered	$1\frac{1}{2}$ pounds	672 grams
toasted black or white sesame seeds	3 tablespoons	21 grams
rice vinegar	1 tablespoon	15 milliliters

Preheat oven to 425°F/220°C. Mix 2 teaspoons/10 milliliters of the sesame oil with the garlic, ginger and soy sauce and set aside.

Toss each vegetable with some of the remaining sesame oil and some salt and pepper. Place the vegetables on separate baking sheets or on a single large sheet with the softer vegetables in the center and the harder vegetables around the outside. Put the vegetables in the oven and stir them with a spatula after about 15 minutes, then continue to roast 15 minutes longer or until just fork-tender. Toss the vegetables with reserved sesame oil, garlic, ginger and soy sauce mixture, and roast 5 minutes longer. Toss with sesame seeds and roast 5 minutes longer, then toss with rice vinegar. Season to taste.

SERVE WITH: Chinese Style Broccoli (page 211), Baby Bella Risotto (page 302), or Basmati Rice with Asparagus (page 303).

VARIATION: Substitute one-fourth of the sesame seeds with cumin seeds.

Root vegetables such as rutabagas, turnips and beets do well in this style of cooking as it concentrates their flavor and caramelizes their natural sugars.

Potatoes and sweet potatoes can also be used. Scallions, the white ends cut to julienne lengths and the green ends sliced and added with the other aromatics towards the end of roasting, can also be used.

Carrot Spinach Potato Terrine

YIELD 10 SERVINGS
1 SLICE PER PERSON

An important step in preparing this terrine is to keep all of the vegetable mixtures warm so that they will adhere to each other when layered into the container.

CARROT MIXTURE

carrots, large dice	3 cups	378 grams
orange juice	$1\frac{1}{2}$ cups	360 milliliters
ground cloves	pinch	pinch
salt	$\frac{1}{4}$ teaspoon	1.5 grams
cornstarch	$\frac{1}{4}$ cup	32 grams
parsley, minced	$\frac{1}{4}$ cup	14 grams

POTATO MIXTURE

potatoes, peeled, large dice	3 cups	504 grams
shallots, small dice	$\frac{1}{2}$ cup	56 grams
bay leaf	1	1
salt	$\frac{1}{4}$ teaspoon	1.5 grams
ground black pepper	pinch	pinch
cornstarch	1 tablespoon	8 grams
dill pickles, small dice	$\frac{1}{2}$ cup	28 grams

SPINACH AND PEA MIXTURE

garlic, minced	1 tablespoon	14 grams
olive oil	1 tablespoon	15 milliliters
green peas	$1\frac{1}{2}$ cups	168 grams
spinach, cooked and drained	12 ounces	336 grams
nutmeg	$\frac{1}{4}$ teaspoon	.5 gram
salt	$\frac{1}{4}$ teaspoon	1.5 grams
ground black pepper	pinch	pinch
potato cooking liquid	$\frac{1}{2}$ cup	120 milliliters
cornstarch	6 tablespoons	42 grams

Put the carrots, juice, cloves and salt in a pan and boil 10 minutes or until the carrots are tender. Purée in a food processor, then add the cornstarch. When each mixture is puréed, return to the pan and cook, stirring constantly until thick. Stir in the parsley, season to taste, cover, remove from heat and keep warm.

Put the potatoes, shallots, bay leaf, salt and pepper in a pan and boil 10 minutes or until the potatoes are tender. Over a pan, drain and reserve the cooking liquid. Save $\frac{1}{2}$ cup/120 milliliters for the spinach and pea mixture and set aside. Return $\frac{3}{4}$ cup/180 milliliters cooking liquid to the potatoes and mash well. Stir in the cornstarch and chopped pickle. When each mixture is puréed, return to the pan and cook, stirring constantly until thick.

Sauté the garlic in olive oil half a minute, then stir in the peas, spinach, nutmeg, salt and pepper.

Combine the reserved potato cooking liquid with cornstarch, stir into the hot spinach and pea mixture, then remove from heat. When all mixtures are ready, warm gently.

Line a $2\frac{1}{2}$ quart/2.4 liter terrine first with enough aluminum foil so that it hangs over the sides and can be folded over to cover the top layer completely as it cools. Repeat with a layer of plastic wrap, which will separate the foil from the pâté. Add the warm mixtures to the pan, starting with the carrot followed by the spinach, pea, then potato. Fold over the plastic and foil to seal. Chill in the refrigerator for 4 hours or overnight. Remove the terrine to a cutting board, unwrap and slice into 10 portions with a sharp slicing knife.

To slice, dip the knife into hot water and shake off moisture. Wipe the knife off after each slice and dip and shake off moisture again.

SERVE WITH: Sauce with Fusion Tartar Sauce (page 155), or Basil Pine Nut Pesto (page 141), and Sea Czar Salad with Blackened Tofu (page 175), Mesclun Mix with Arame and Shiitake Dressing (page 175), or Carrot and Parsnip Salad with Smoked Dulse (page 171).

Acorn Squash with Apricot Cashew Stuffing

YIELD 10 SERVINGS

$\frac{1}{2}$ SQUASH EACH

whole grain bread, $\frac{1}{2}$-inch/ 1.25-centimeter cubes	12 cups	662 grams
acorn squash, about 18 ounces/ 504 grams each	5	5
shallots, fine dice	1 cup	112 grams
celery, fine dice	1 cup	112 grams
olive oil	2 tablespoons	30 milliliters
dried pitted apricots, medium dice	6 tablespoons	56 grams
roasted cashews	1 cup	112 grams
ground sage	2 teaspoons	4 grams
rosemary	1 teaspoon	2 grams
celery seed	1 teaspoon	2.33 grams
salt	$\frac{1}{2}$ teaspoon	3 grams
ground black pepper	pinch	pinch
vegetable stock	4 cups	960 milliliters
canola oil to brush on top		

Toast the bread cubes for 10 minutes in a 350°F/180°C oven. Set aside.

Scrub the outsides of the squash. Cut each acorn squash in half and remove the seeds. If desired, remove a thin slice from the outside of each half so that it will lay flat on the plate when served.

Sauté the shallots and celery in olive oil over medium heat for 2 minutes, then reduce heat to medium-low for 2 more minutes. Stir in the remaining ingredients and reserved toasted bread cubes.

Stuff the squash, brush the top with margarine or oil, and bake in 375°F/190°C oven for about 45 minutes or until the squash tests tender with a fork and the stuffing is golden brown.

VARIATION: Vegetable bouillon can be used for stock. Try currants, raisins or dried cranberries. Soy sausage can be added to stuffing. Toast the bread before cutting. Bake the squash halves empty until done, then cool and fill with grain salads or serve hot with a hot grain dish.

SERVE WITH: Oven Roasted Sweet Potatoes (page 203) and Chinese Style Broccoli (page 211). Sauce with Vegetable Gravy (page 147), Tamarind Sauce (page 132), Carrot Ginger Sauce (page 133), or Wild Mushroom Sauce (page 148).

Note: If the squash is getting too dark, cover with foil.

Asparagus and Pecans in Fillo

YIELD 10 SERVINGS

1 PASTRY PER PERSON

The aroma encapsulated by the pastry is savored and followed by the complementary textures and tastes of asparagus and pecans.

asparagus, $\frac{1}{2}$-inch/1.25-centimeter diagonal slices	$1\frac{1}{2}$ pounds	672 grams
white miso	2 tablespoons	28 grams
lemon juice	2 tablespoons	30 milliliters
fresh tarragon, minced	2 tablespoons	7 grams
salt	pinch	pinch
ground black pepper	pinch	pinch
lightly toasted pecans, chopped	$\frac{2}{3}$ cup	70 grams
fillo pastry	10 sheets	10 sheets
soy margarine, melted	2 tablespoons	28 grams
olive oil	3 tablespoons	45 milliliters
lemon wedges	10	10

Blanch asparagus in salted boiling water for a minute or 2, until just tender. Shock them with cold water. Drain them well and dry off excess moisture.

In a large bowl combine white miso, lemon juice, tarragon salt and pepper until smooth. Mix in the asparagus and pecans.

Preheat oven to 350°F/180°C. Combine the melted soy margarine with the olive oil. Lay sheets of fillo pastry on the work surface and cover unused sheets with a dry towel. Brush the fillo lightly with the margarine/oil mixture.

With the narrow side of the sheet facing you, fold the sheet away to create a 3-inch doubled-over portion for the filling. Place about $\frac{1}{2}$ cup/120 milliliters of the asparagus mixture on the doubled fillo and spread it in a strip about 4 inches $\times$ $1\frac{1}{4}$ inches/10 centimeters $\times$ 3.25 centimeters. Fold the long sides of the fillo over toward center to cover the ends of the filling. Starting at the filling end, roll up the fillo into a tube shape. Place the filled pastry on a baking sheet seam side down. Lightly brush the surface with the oil mixture. Repeat the process until all the filling is used up.

Bake for about 12 minutes and check the bottoms for excess browning. If needed, bake a few minutes longer or until golden brown.

SERVE WITH: Lemon wedges and Avocado, Orange and Red Onion Salad (page 173), or Wild, Japonica, and Wehani Rice Medley (page 168).

Thai Vegetable Curry

YIELD 10 SERVINGS

$1\frac{1}{2}$ CUPS/252 GRAMS

Thai green chile paste is available from Asian grocery stores and gourmet suppliers. It adds both hot spice and a unique flavor to this version of curry.

carrots, half-moon slices	6 cups	672 grams
broccoli, peeled and cut to $\frac{1}{2}$ inch/1.25 centimeters	5 cups	364 grams
zucchini, half-moon slices	6 cups	672 grams
onions, sliced	4 cups	448 grams
peanut oil	2 tablespoons	30 milliliters
garlic, minced	4 teaspoons	20 grams
ginger	2 tablespoons	28 grams
(sweet) red pepper, large dice	$1\frac{1}{2}$ cups	168 grams
curry powder	1 tablespoon	6 grams
lemon zest, minced	1 teaspoon	3 grams
lemon juice	1 tablespoon	15 milliliters
Thai green chile paste (very hot)	1 tablespoon	15 grams
salt	1 teaspoon	6 grams
flour	$\frac{1}{3}$ cup	70 grams
non-sweetened grated coconut	1 cup	112 grams
reserved vegetable stock, hot	4 cups	960 milliliters
fresh tomatoes, medium dice	$1\frac{1}{2}$ cups	224 grams

GARNISH

roasted peanuts	1 cup	140 grams
fresh basil chopped	2 tablespoons	7 grams

Blanch the carrots, broccoli and zucchini in salted boiling water by placing the carrots in the pot first for 4 minutes, then adding broccoli and zucchini for 2 minutes or until brightly colored and al dente. Drain off the resulting stock, reserve 4 cups/32 fluid ounces/960 milliliters, and keep it hot. Shock the vegetables under cold running water, drain and set aside.

Sauté the onions in peanut oil over medium heat for about 5 minutes. Add the ginger, garlic and red pepper and sauté 5 minutes. Stir in the curry powder, lemon zest, lemon juice, chile paste and salt, then stir in the flour and coconut.

Stir in the reserved hot stock, the tomatoes and the reserved blanched vegetables. Bring mixture to a boil, then simmer for 5 minutes. Season to taste.

GARNISH: Use peanuts and chopped basil to garnish.

VARIATION: Parsley or cilantro could be used to garnish in place of basil.

SERVE WITH: Jasmine Rice (page 316), and Black Bean Soup with Cumin and Garlic (page 102), or Winter Squash Hazelnut Bisque (page 97), or Yellow Split Pea Curry Soup (page 104).

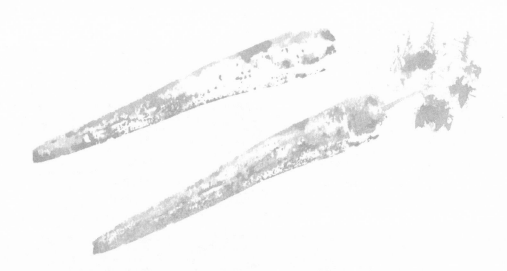

Spiced Cauliflower, Potatoes and Peas

YIELD 10 SERVINGS

1 $\frac{1}{2}$ CUPS/252 GRAMS

This curried dish features the spicing of southern India. An important step in achieving a well-flavored curry is allowing the spices to sauté with the vegetables.

onions, medium dice	4 cups	448 grams
carrots, $\frac{1}{2}$-inch/1.25-centimeters, diagonal slice	4 cups	504 grams
potatoes, 1-inch/2.5-centimeter chunks	4 cups	560 grams
canola oil	2 tablespoons	30 milliliters
ginger, minced	2 tablespoons	30 grams
garlic, minced	2 tablespoons	30 grams
black mustard seeds	1 teaspoon	2.33 grams
ground coriander	2 tablespoons	12 grams
turmeric powder	1 tablespoon	6 grams
ground cumin	3 tablespoons	18 grams
salt	1 $\frac{1}{4}$ teaspoons	7.5 grams
cardamom	1 teaspoon	2 grams
cayenne	pinch	pinch
cauliflower, florets	4 cups	392 grams
lemon juice	3 tablespoons	45 milliliters
raisins	$\frac{1}{2}$ cup	56 grams
dark dry sweetener (succanat)	pinch	pinch
fresh tomatoes, chopped	1 $\frac{1}{3}$ cups	252 grams
Basic Enriched Vegetable Stock (page 84)	4 cups	960 milliliters
green peas, frozen	2 cups	280 grams
Cashew Crème (page 157)	1 cup	240 milliliters
chopped unsalted roasted cashews	$\frac{1}{2}$ cup	70 grams
fresh cilantro, minced	$\frac{1}{4}$ cup	28 grams

Sauté the onions, carrots and potatoes in canola oil over medium-high heat for 5 minutes. Add the ginger, garlic and mustard seeds. Sauté for 3 minutes. Stir the coriander, turmeric, cumin, salt, cardamom and cayenne. Sauté for 1 minute.

Add the cauliflower, lemon juice, raisins and tomatoes. Stir well to mix with spices, then add the stock. Simmer for 20 minutes. When the potatoes are tender, add the peas and Cashew Crème. Bring heat to high and cook for 5 minutes or until the sauce is thick. Season to taste.

GARNISH: Garnish with the cashews and fresh cilantro.

SERVE WITH: Basmati Rice (page 316), India-Style Flat Bread (page 353), Yellow Split Pea Curry Soup (page 104).

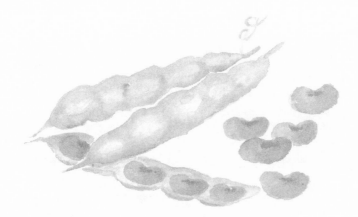

Exotic Mushroom Tart

YIELD 10 SERVINGS
1 TART PER PERSON

There are now several varieties of cultivated mushrooms available on the market. They are often called exotic mushrooms to distinguish them from the truly wild mushroom types. This rustic-style tart is made with a combination of readily available varieties.

Herb Tart Pastry (recipe follows)	about 30 ounces	800 grams raw pastry dough
onions, large dice	$1\frac{1}{2}$ cups	168 grams
carrots, large dice	$1\frac{1}{2}$ cups	196 grams
parsnips, large dice	$1\frac{1}{2}$ cups	168 grams
shallots, minced	$\frac{1}{4}$ cup	28 grams
olive oil	2 tablespoons	30 milliliters
cremini mushrooms, $\frac{1}{4}$-inch/ .75-centimeter slices	5 cups	448 grams
portobello mushrooms, $\frac{1}{4}$-inch/ .75-centimeter slices	$2\frac{1}{2}$ cups	224 grams
shiitake mushrooms, $\frac{1}{4}$-inch/ .75-centimeter slices	$2\frac{1}{2}$ cups	224 grams
fresh thyme, minced	2 tablespoons	2 grams
fresh rosemary, minced	1 teaspoon	1 gram
soy sauce	2 tablespoons	30 milliliters
salt	pinch	pinch
ground black pepper	pinch	pinch

Prepare the Herb Tart Pastry and allow it to chill while the mushroom filling mixture is being prepared.

Sauté the onions, carrots, parsnips and shallots in olive oil over medium-high heat for 2 minutes. Add the mushrooms and sauté 2 minutes. Add the remaining ingredients and sauté 5 minutes longer. If needed, increase the heat and reduce the pan juices until almost completely evaporated.

Preheat oven to 400°F/200°C. Divide the Herb Tart Pastry into 10 parts and roll each piece out to a 6 inch/15.5 centimeter circle. Place about $\frac{1}{2}$ cup/120 milliliters of the mushroom filling onto the center of each tart. Fold up the sides, pleating them as you go around the tart to enclose the filling, leaving the top of the tarts open.

Place the tarts onto a parchment-lined baking sheet and place into the preheated oven for 10 minutes. Reduce heat to 375°F/190°C and bake for about 10 minutes longer or until browned and crisp. If after the first 10 minutes the bottoms are getting too dark, place a second pan underneath the first to add insulation and protect the bottom of the tarts from burning before the tops are done.

VARIATION: Fillo pastry could be used in place of the Herb Tart Pastry. The mushroom filling could be served over rice or noodles.

SERVE WITH: Golden Mashed Potatoes with Caramelized Onions (page 205), Greens Sautéed with Ginger (page 195), and if a sauce is desired use Red Pepper Porcini Reduction Sauce (page 151).

Winter Squash Afghani Style

YIELD 10 SERVINGS

1.2 CUPS/280 GRAMS

The cuisine of Afghanistan boasts some delicious meatless offerings. The basic flavor structure
of this recipe was motivated by the pumpkin purée served at the Shish Kebab House
of Afghanistan, Hartford, Connecticut.

onions, large dice	$4\frac{1}{2}$ cups	504 grams
olive oil	2 tablespoons	30 milliliters
gingerroot, minced	3 tablespoons	21 grams
garlic, minced	3 tablespoons	21 grams
ground coriander	1 tablespoon	7 grams
ground cumin	1 teaspoon	2.33 grams
ground cardamom	1 teaspoon	2.33 grams
salt	1 teaspoon	6 grams
ground black pepper	pinch	pinch
succanat	2 teaspoons	8 grams
butternut squash, $1\frac{1}{2}$-inch/ 3.75-centimeter chunks	16 cups	2.24 kilograms
fresh tomatoes, medium dice	3 cups	420 grams
dried currants	$\frac{1}{2}$ cup	70 grams
toasted sliced almonds	$\frac{1}{2}$ cup	32.5 grams

Sauté the onions in olive oil over medium-high heat for 4 minutes. Add the ginger
and garlic and sauté for 4 minutes. Stir in the spices, salt, pepper and succanat, then
add the squash, tomatoes and currants. Cover and simmer for 30 minutes or until the
squash is very tender. Season to taste. Use toasted almonds to garnish.

SERVE WITH: Basmati Rice (page 316), that is garnished with grated carrots and
chopped cilantro or parsley.

Herb Tart Pastry

YIELD 30 OUNCES/800 GRAMS RAW PASTRY

dry sweetener (succanat)	2 tablespoons	17 grams
lemon zest, minced (optional)	1 teaspoon	3.5 grams
all-purpose white flour	2 cups	280 grams
whole wheat pastry flour	1 cup	140 grams
salt	$\frac{1}{4}$ teaspoon	1.5 grams
fresh parsley, chopped	$\frac{1}{2}$ cup	28 grams
ground black pepper	$\frac{1}{4}$ teaspoon	.5 gram
canola oil	6 tablespoons	90 milliliters
cold soy margarine, large dice	6 tablespoons	84 grams
ice water	$\frac{1}{2}$ cup	120 milliliters

Put the dry sweetener and lemon zest, flours, parsley, pepper and salt into food processor and pulse until well mixed together. Pulse in oil. Pulse in diced chilled margarine. With machine running, add ice water until just mixed.

Turn the dough out on to a work surface and form into a flat disk. Cover with plastic wrap and chill in refrigerator for at least 20 minutes.

Roll out the dough using plastic wrap underneath and over the top. Line tart shell with dough and refrigerate until ready to bake. Fill and bake according to the recipe used.

Smokey Braised Portobello Mushrooms

YIELD 10 SERVINGS

1 CAP PER PERSON

Mushroom varieties, especially the portobello, offer unique textures and flavors to vegetable-based cuisine. When dealing with the whole mushroom, leave about half of the stem connected to the cap for braising and save any useable parts of the remaining stem for soup or stock.

BRAISING LIQUID

apple juice	1 cup	240 milliliters
water	1 cup	240 milliliters
soy sauce	$\frac{1}{4}$ cup	60 milliliters
garlic, crushed	2 teaspoons	4.66 grams
fresh gingerroot, minced	1 teaspoon	2.33 grams
maple syrup	1 teaspoon	5 milliliters
liquid hickory smoke	$\frac{1}{4}$ teaspoon	1.25 milliliters
fresh rosemary leaves	15	15
ground black pepper	pinch	pinch

OTHER INGREDIENTS

portobello mushroom caps, 5 inches/12.5 centimeters	10	10
olive oil	2 tablespoons	30 milliliters

Combine braising liquid ingredients and set aside. Brush a large frying pan with oil and place it over medium-high heat. Place the portobello caps top side down into the pan and brown. Turn the caps over and for each one, add 3 tablespoons/30 milliliters of the braising liquid to the pan, cover and cook for about 5 minutes. Caps are done when they are fork-tender.

Thinly slice the caps and fan them out to serve. Serve with any remaining pan juices. If there seems to be a lot of juice or it is weak in flavor, remove all the cooked mushrooms from the pan and reduce. They may be served hot, at room temperature, lightly chilled but not too cold as they will have less flavor.

VARIATION: Other mushrooms that braise well include shiitake, cremini and white mushrooms of various sizes. All of these mushrooms, including the portobellos, may be sliced before braising to shorten the cooking time. Brush the portobellos or large shiitake caps with White Balsamic Vinaigrette (page 181) and then grill 2 to 3 minutes per side. Whole grilled caps are great for sandwiches.

SERVE WITH: Mesclun Mix with Dulse and Shiitake Dressing (page 175), Parsnip Purée (page 200), Carrot and Parsnip Salad with Smoked Dulse (page 171), Oven-Roasted Sweet Potatoes with Soy Sauce (page 203).

Note: Portobello mushrooms have quite a range in size. Small caps may cook faster and large caps may require a little more cooking time than called for in the recipe. They're also available sliced and can be braised in the same way, or the caps may be sliced ahead for quicker cooking. They can be salty; if the marinade reduces significantly, add water or apple juice if needed.

Fried Oyster Mushrooms

YIELD 10 SERVINGS

ABOUT 6 OUNCES/168 GRAMS

This recipe combines the flavors or mushrooms and sea vegetables in a style that I refer to as "cuisine mirage" for recipes that taste or look like other foods.

The 3-part breading process used in this recipe was developed to build up flavor in each stage and also to spread the color of the sea vegetables so they don't darken the final crumb coating.

STAGE 1—NORI FLOUR MIXTURE

nori flakes/increase nori	$\frac{1}{4}$ cup	12 grams
all-purpose white flour	$1\frac{1}{2}$ cups	196 grams
garlic powder	2 teaspoons	4 grams
salt	$\frac{1}{2}$ teaspoon	3 grams
pepper	pinch	pinch

STAGE 2—LIQUID MIXTURE

Nori Flour Mixture from Stage 1	$\frac{1}{2}$ cup	28 grams
water	2 cups	480 milliliters

STAGE 3—BREAD CRUMB MIXTURE

fresh bread crumbs, unseasoned	7 cups	616 grams
nori flakes	$\frac{1}{4}$ cup	12 grams
garlic, powder	1 teaspoon	2 grams
salt	pinch	pinch
pepper	pinch	pinch
oyster mushrooms	$1\frac{1}{4}$ pounds	560 grams
oil for frying (see note)		

In separate bowls or pans, starting with the first stage, prepare each of the stages for the breading process.

Cut or break up clusters of oyster mushrooms as needed to yield mushrooms of an equal size about 2 inches/5 millimeters long by 1 inch/2.5 centimeters at the wide end. This may mean cutting some of the larger ones in half or leaving 2 of the smaller ones attached together. Just before beginning the breading process, rinse the mushrooms quickly and shake off excess moisture.

Dredge the mushrooms first in the nori flour mixture. Shake off the excess flour and dip into the liquid mixture. Shake off the excess, dredge in the bread crumb mixture and set aside on a sheet pan until all the mushrooms are breaded.

Deep fry at 350°F/180°C for about 1 minute or until golden brown.

VARIATION: Tofu can be cut to "scallop" shapes using a canoli form to punch them out and substituted for the oyster mushrooms. For Shrimp Fried Mushrooms, use dulse in place of the nori. Combine both sea vegetables. Other mushrooms such as sliced white or shiitake could be used.

SERVE WITH: Watermelon Catsup (page 135), Summer or Winter Vegetable Pancakes (page 251), lime wedges. Greens Sautéed with Ginger (page 195), Broccoli Couscous Almond Salad (page 163).

Stewed Oyster Mushrooms

YIELD 10 SERVINGS

1 CUP/7 OUNCES/240 MILLILITERS

This dish is prepared somewhat like oyster stew.

oyster mushrooms	$1\frac{1}{2}$ pounds	450 grams
onions, fine dice	3 cups	336 grams
celery, fine dice	2 cups	224 grams
garlic, minced	1 tablespoon	15 grams
olive oil	2 tablespoons	30 milliliters
sea salt	1 teaspoon	6 grams
ground black pepper	pinch	pinch
dulse flakes	2 tablespoons	6 grams
thyme	$\frac{1}{2}$ teaspoon	1 gram
bay leaves	2	2
all-purpose flour	6 tablespoons	50 grams
rice beverage	7 cups	1.68 liters
soy sauce	$\frac{1}{4}$ cup	60 milliliters
sherry wine	2 teaspoons	10 milliliters
liquid smoke	3 to 4 drops	3 to 4 drops
parsley, finely chopped	$\frac{1}{2}$ cup	28 grams

Cut or break up the clusters of oyster mushrooms as needed to yield mushrooms of an equal size about 2 inches/5 millimeters long by 1 inch/2.5 centimeters at the wide end. This may mean cutting some of the larger ones in half or leaving 2 of the smaller ones attached together. Just before beginning the cooking process, rinse the mushrooms quickly and shake off excess moisture.

Sauté the onions, celery and garlic in olive oil over medium heat for 5 minutes. Add the mushrooms and raise the heat to medium-high. Stir in salt, pepper, dulse, thyme, and bay leaves. Sauté for 4 minutes.

Add the flour, stir well, then slowly stir in the rice beverage. Add the soy sauce, sherry and liquid smoke and bring to a boil. Simmer slowly for 15 minutes, then stir in half of the parsley. Simmer for a couple minutes longer. Season to taste. Remove the bay leaves before serving. Garnish with the remaining chopped parsley.

Variation: Use other specialty mushrooms or white mushrooms.

Note: Liquid smoke has a very powerful flavor and can easily overwhelm a dish. I find it is safer to pour it into a spoon away from the soup and to add less at first until the dish has been tasted.

Hungarian-Style Braised Mushrooms

YIELD 10 SERVINGS

¾ CUP / 6 OUNCES / 168 GRAMS

The paprika, Cashew Crème and the apple cider vinegar together supply the flavor and mouth feel of a typical Hungarian-style dish.

sweet onions, sliced	1 quart	448 grams
olive oil	¼ cup	60 milliliters
garlic, minced	2 tablespoons	14 grams
sweet red peppers, julienne	2 cups	224 grams
baby bella button mushrooms	3 quarts	1.12 kilograms
salt	pinch	pinch
ground black pepper	pinch	pinch
paprika	1 tablespoon	6 grams
cayenne	pinch	pinch
flour	5 tablespoons	42 grams
tomato paste	¼ cup	66 grams
hot vegetable stock	4 cups	960 milliliters
soy sauce	3 tablespoons	45 milliliters
Cashew Crème (page 157)	1 cup	240 milliliters
apple cider vinegar	1 tablespoon	15 milliliters

Sauté the onions in olive oil over medium-high heat for 5 minutes. Add the garlic and red peppers and sauté for 2 minutes. Add the mushrooms and sauté for 5 minutes.

Stir in the salt, pepper, paprika, cayenne and flour. Stir in the tomato paste, then slowly stir in the stock and soy sauce and bring to a boil. Simmer for 5 minutes, then add Cashew Crème and vinegar. Season to taste.

GARNISH: Swirl in Cashew Crème.

VARIATION: White button mushrooms, sliced large white mushrooms.

SERVE WITH: Golden Potato Salad with Olives and Apricots (page 176). Noodles, rice or other grain. As filling for Crepes (page 248).

Basic Crepes

20 CREPES ABOUT 6 INCHES/15 CENTIMETERS

To make light crepes, the batter needs to be thin enough to swirl around the pan, coating the surface as the extra mixture rolls off. Once the first side is browned, the batter needs to hold together without breaking when it is turned over. The tendency of the flour to settle at the bottom of the batter as the pancakes are being made requires it to be stirred before each crepe is ladled out or to be thinned with a little water if the end of the batch is getting thick.

all-purpose white flour	$1\frac{1}{3}$ cups	189 grams
whole wheat bread flour	$\frac{1}{3}$ cup	56 grams
cornstarch	2 tablespoons	16 grams
salt	$\frac{1}{2}$ teaspoon	3 grams
turmeric	$\frac{1}{4}$ teaspoon	.5 gram
canola oil	2 tablespoons	30 milliliters
soy milk	$1\frac{1}{2}$ cups	360 milliliters
water	$\frac{3}{4}$ cups	180 milliliters

In a bowl combine the dry ingredients. With a wire whip add the oil and soy milk and gradually add water to make a smooth batter.

Heat a nonstick or seasoned crepe pan over medium-high heat. Lightly oil the surface with a paper towel dipped in oil. When the oil just begins to smoke, add 3 tablespoons/45 milliliters of batter to the pan. Tilt the pan and swirl out the batter to make a 6-inch/15-centimeter crepe.

After about 15 seconds check for browning. Turn the crepe over when it is golden brown. Cook the second side about 15 to 20 seconds or until covered with brown spots. Lay the cooked crepes spread out on a sheet pan or on parchment paper and repeat the process until batter is used up. Allow crepes time to cool before stacking.

Crepes may be filled at this point or wrapped and held until service time. They can be warmed on a sheet pan in a 350°F/180°C oven for a minute or so, being careful not to dry them out.

VARIATIONS: For Fresh Herb Crepes, crepe batter can be seasoned with 2 tablespoons/.25 ounces/7 grams minced fresh herbs such as parsley, tarragon or basil, or 1 tablespoon/6 grams dried herbs such as oregano.

For Dulse or Nori Crepes start by adding 1 teaspoon/1 gram dried sea vegetables such as dulse flakes or nori flakes.

FILL CREPES WITH: About $\frac{1}{3}$ cup/90 milliliters of various vegetable fillings.

For Ratatouille Crepes, serve Ratatouille wrapped in Dulse or Nori Crepes. Use extra filling as a sauce for crepes.

SERVE WITH: Brown Rice (page 315), Brazilian-Style Greens (page 196), Basmati Rice (page 316), Greens Sautéed with Ginger (page 195).

For Crepes with Hungarian-Style Braised Mushrooms serve Hungarian-Style Braised Mushrooms wrapped in Fresh Herb Crepes. Use extra filling as a sauce for crepes. Jasmine Rice (page 316), Red Swiss Chard Sauté with Garlic (page 194).

For Crepes with Winter Squash Afghani-Style serve Winter Squash Afghani-Style wrapped in Fresh Herb Crepes. Use extra filling as a sauce for crepes.

Note: Once the technique is mastered you can add more pans to the fire depending how many crepes need to be made and how many pans you can handle.

Savory Summer Pancakes

YIELD 10 SERVINGS
30 PANCAKES 2½ INCHES/6.25 CENTIMETERS

*This recipe takes advantage of the abundance of summer vegetables and can be modified to use
other available varieties. When substituting other vegetables, take into consideration the
water content and adjust the amount of flour to maintain the same batter consistency.*

carrots, grated	2½ cups	280 grams
zucchini, grated	2½ cups	280 grams
yellow squash, grated	2½ cups	280 grams
onion, small dice	1 cup	112 grams
red cabbage, shredded	1 cup	84 grams
salt	1 teaspoon	6 grams
ground black pepper	pinch	pinch
ground nutmeg	¼ teaspoon	1 gram
flour	1½ cups	210 grams
lime wedges	10	10
canola oil for frying		

Place the vegetables in a bowl and toss with salt, pepper and nutmeg. Let the mixture
stand for 10 minutes. Stir in flour.

Preheat oven to 300°F/150°C. Heat a lightly oiled nonstick griddle over medium
heat. Spoon enough batter onto the griddle and spread to make pancakes 2½
inches/6.25 centimeters each. When the pancakes are golden-brown turn over. Allow
the second side to brown, then remove to an absorbent paper-lined surface. Place on a
heat-proof platter or pan and place in the oven while cooking the remainder of the
pancakes. Season the cooked pancakes to taste with salt and pepper and serve with
lime wedges.

VARIATION: Season with chopped fresh herbs such as basil, parsley or oregano. Add
a little crushed garlic if desired.

SERVE WITH: Peach Chutney (page 130), Red Swiss Chard Sauté with Garlic
(page 194), and Jasmine or Basmati Rice (page 316).

VEGETABLES THAT COULD BE USED IN THE SAVORY SUMMER PANCAKES

patty-pan squash	Chinese cabbage
green beans, finely sliced	white turnip
bulb fennel or anise	leeks
white cabbage	scallions

Savory Winter Pancakes

YIELD 10 SERVINGS
30 PANCAKES 2½ INCHES/6.25 CENTIMETERS

This is a seasonal variation of the savory summer pancakes.

carrots, grated	2½ cups	280 grams
sweet potato, grated	2½ cups	280 grams
yellow potato, grated	2½ cups	280 grams
onion, small dice	1 cup	112 grams
red cabbage, shredded	1 cup	84 grams
salt	1 teaspoon	6 grams
ground black pepper	pinch	pinch
ground nutmeg	¼ teaspoon	1 gram
flour	1½ cups	210 grams
water	¼ cup	60 milliliters
lime wedges	10	10
canola oil for frying		

Place the vegetables in a bowl and toss with salt, pepper and nutmeg. Let the mixture stand for 10 minutes. Stir in flour and water.

Preheat oven to 300°F/150°C. Heat a lightly oiled nonstick griddle over medium heat. Spoon enough batter onto the griddle and spread to make pancakes 2½ inches/6.25 centimeters each. When the pancakes are golden-brown, turn over. Allow the second side to brown, then remove to an absorbent paper-lined surface. Place on a heat-proof platter or pan and place in the oven while cooking the remainder of the pancakes. Season the cooked pancakes to taste with salt and pepper and serve with lime wedges.

SERVE WITH: Apple butter or Pear Chutney (page 130), Greens Sautéed with Ginger (page 195), and Jasmine or Basmati Rice (page 316).

VEGETABLES THAT COULD BE USED IN THE SAVORY WINTER PANCAKES

parsnips	pumpkin	white turnip
celery root (celeriac)	rutabaga	leeks
butternut squash	white cabbage	scallions
acorn squash	Chinese cabbage	

Note: Fresh herbs, a little crushed garlic and or a little grated horseradish can be added to batter if desired.

Anytime Corn and Chive Pancakes

10 SERVINGS

3 PANCAKES/3 INCHES/7.5 CENTIMETERS EACH

*These savory pancakes can be served as an entrée for lunch or dinner,
or fit just as well into a breakfast or brunch menu.*

DRY INGREDIENTS

flour	3 cups	420 grams
baking powder	1 tablespoon	15.6 grams
salt	$\frac{3}{4}$ teaspoon	4.5 grams
ground black pepper	pinch	pinch
fresh chives, minced	$\frac{1}{2}$ cup	28 grams

WET INGREDIENTS

corn kernels	3 cups	588 grams
rice beverage	3 cups	720 milliliters
corn oil	1 tablespoon	15 milliliters
apple cider vinegar	1 tablespoon	15 milliliters

GARNISH

lemon wedges, small	10	10
chopped chives	1 tablespoon	3.5 grams
warm maple syrup	10 tablespoons	150 milliliters
fresh ground black pepper		

In a large bowl combine the dry ingredients and push to one side of the bowl. Add the wet ingredients to the empty side of the bowl and gradually fold in.

Heat a lightly oiled nonstick griddle over medium heat. Spoon enough batter onto the griddle to make 3-inch/7.5-centimeter pancakes. When bubbles cover the top and the edges begin to brown, turn pancakes over. Allow the second side to brown, then remove to a warm plate, platter or pan.

Garnish with lemon wedges and chives. Serve with warm maple syrup spiked with fresh ground black pepper.

VARIATION: For Anytime Corn and Chive pancakes with Dulse, add 1 tablespoon/.1 ounce/3 grams dulse flakes to the batter. Sauce with Watermelon Catsup (page 135), and/or Spinach Pecan Pesto (page 140).

Note: Fresh corn yields about $\frac{1}{4}$ cup/3.5 ounces/98 grams per medium-size ear. Cobs are good for vegetable stock. When using frozen corn, defrost it first, then weigh. Half each minced onions and parsley in place of chives. Add a little soy margarine to the maple syrup when it is warming.

CHAPTER NINE

Pasta-Based Entrées

One theory of pasta's origin is that long ago,

a cook making flatbread was called away from

the fire and upon returning, found his dough had

dried out. With a meager food supply, he couldn't

afford waste, so he broke it up, tossed it into some

simmering broth and the results were so successful

that people have been doing it ever since.

Both the Chinese and Italians have a long history of pasta- and noodle-making with many innovative recipes. Already a favorite throughout the world, pasta's popularity continues to grow and it is available fresh and dried in an ever-widening array of shapes, colors and flavors.

Some fresh pasta companies offer frozen vegan options such as tofu tortellini, ravioli and other popular shapes. Also available are vegan frozen pasta sheets with flavors such as sweet red pepper.

Pasta as an entrée can be paired with vegetables to add color, taste and texture, then served with a signature sauce. Pasta also can be served with a main sauce with a second or third sauce as garnish, such as Vegan Tortellini with Three Sauces (page 283).

If fresh pasta cooked al dente is first tossed with some sauce, especially one that is on the wet side, it accomplishes several desirable results—first that the sauce has a chance to fully coat the pasta, second, in the case of a moist sauce such as one prepared from fresh tomatoes, it has the chance to be absorbed right into the pasta, increasing its flavor. The sauce also gets thickened and the pasta is moisturized to keep it from sticking together.

To further enhance flavor the addition of a little salt and pepper at this time is also recommended, along with some chopped fresh herbs as appropriate to the recipe. In lieu of using sauce to achieve this end, a little olive oil or soy margarine along with the salt, pepper and herbs will help build a taste foundation to support a layer of sauce to come.

Pasta: Which is Better, Fresh or Dried?

To me, this is like comparing raspberries to mangos (or apple to oranges).

The main difference between fresh and dried pasta is one of texture. Fresh pasta delivers a soft, light, slightly chewy texture that can only be achieved from pasta that hasn't been dried. The dried variety of pasta provides its own unique texture. It is meant to be cooked "al dente," meaning there should still be some firmness left when the boiling process has been stopped.

Fresh and dried pasta can be served in different manners. Fresh pasta is usually cut into noodles or other shapes that may be filled such as tortellini and ravioli. Dried pasta, sometimes referred to as macaroni pasta, is extruded into many shapes such as ziti, mostaciolli, penne, rigatoni and so on, to infinity and beyond.

Fresh Pasta Bases: Handling and Preparation

My approach to fresh pasta uses vegetable purées in the pasta dough and omits the eggs usually associated with this product. Almost any vegetable can be puréed by simply cooking it until soft and puréeing it in a food processor. To save time, some of the pastas can be made with purchased purées such as pumpkin, butternut squash or tomato.

In addition to the above-mentioned vegetable purées, others I have used to make fresh pasta include small yellow summer squash, carrots, sweet potatoes, beets, acorn squash, spinach, kale and fresh green peas. For filled pasta such as the Squash Hazelnut Ravioli (page 266) the purée doubles as both the base for the pasta dough and the filling.

The flavor of these vegetable-based pastas goes from subtle, as with squash or fresh green pea pasta, to bold with tomato or beet pasta. In addition to the unique flavor of these pastas, their colors—often bright—are characteristic of their vegetable base and contribute the element of visual appeal to the finished dish.

The main ingredient of pasta is wheat flour. I generally use an unbleached all-purpose white flour (organic available in bulk), which has a lower protein content than durum semolina. The organic white flour usually available is bread flour with the germ left in, which is high in protein content. The organic white bread flour and the durum semolina can be used to make fresh pasta, but they will absorb more moisture (use a little less flour) and yield a chewier texture. The higher protein wheat flour is generally used for pasta that will be dried before being cooked.

If you want to use whole wheat in the recipes, I have found that using up to 20% whole wheat (bread) flour in the recipe will not hurt the texture of the pasta. The dough may need a little more moisture as the bran in the whole wheat flour seems to absorb it. Add the additional moisture after the mixing of the ingredients, as the moisture of vegetable purées can vary a great deal from batch to batch. Other types of flour may be added; however, the resulting texture and the ability of the pasta to hold together is largely a function of the gluten present in the wheat.

To make fresh pasta simply mix together the flour, vegetable purée, and herbs or spices to form a smooth dough. Cover the dough to keep it from drying out, then allow it to rest for a smoother finished product. The resting stage also helps to tenderize the dough by letting the gluten relax. As you work with the dough you will become familiar with the proper consistency. Consistency is determined by the amount of moisture present in the vegetables for the purée. If the dough is too moist, it will be sticky and difficult to roll out. If it is too dry, it will not hold together well. Either condition is easily remedied by adding a little more flour or water to the recipe as indicated by the consistency of the dough after the initial mixing.

I recommend a stainless steel pasta machine that rolls out the dough and has a couple of cutters to cut the pasta into narrow noodles, called tagliolini, and a wider shape closer to the size of fettucine. I have found that the roller settings are not significantly thinner from one to the next, especially in the lower settings, so it saves time to skip a dial setting when rolling out the pasta dough to its desired thinness.

The pasta machine will roll out the dough to the width of the machine and to a length that is determined by the size of the piece of pasta dough being fed through the rollers. The settings usually are numbered from one to six or seven and may run up or down in sequence from thick to thin. My machine, an Atlas, starts at one being the thickest setting, and going up to seven, the thinnest setting. The number seven setting, however, is so thin that it tears apart the pasta so I usually go up to four, five or six depending on how thick I want the final product and how it will be cut.

To roll out pasta, cut a piece of the dough and flatten it by hand enough so that it will fit into the widest setting of the pasta machine. Lightly flour the dough and feed it through the machine. Usually this step is repeated a couple of times at the widest setting to smooth out the pasta. Also, more flour can be added at this time if the dough is too sticky.

Next, using the dial on the side of the machine, narrow the space between the rollers by 2 settings. The job goes much faster by skipping over a setting, going from setting one to setting three for example, if that is the sequence in which the machine runs. Some pasta machines have the numbers reversed so that the highest number is the widest setting.

For noodles, roll out all pasta dough into several long sheets as wide as the machine starting with widest setting and then rolling again up to the fourth or fifth setting. Starting with the first rolled sheet, cut to the desired noodle length, then run them through the cutter blades of the attachment to the machine. Lightly flour the noodles to keep them from sticking together and spread them out on a sheet pan in a single layer until all the pasta is cut.

Tips for Making Fresh Pasta with Vegetable Purées

- Well-cooked vegetables purée easier.
- Dough can be stored overnight in the refrigerator or frozen and thawed in the refrigerator.
- Keep the portion of dough that is not being worked with covered until ready to use to prevent it from drying out. If the dough becomes a little dry, fold in the dry outside as in kneading dough and allow to rest again. If the outside of the dough becomes very dry, it may need to be cut away and discarded.
- A quick way to flavor and color pasta is to toss it with fresh beet or carrot juice, then add a little extra virgin olive oil or soy margarine and some salt and pepper.

Making and Cooking Ravioli

There are many ways to make ravioli-type filled pasta.

RAVIOLI METHOD 1

The pasta dough can be rolled out into a long strip as wide as the machine will allow and the rollers set on the fifth or sixth, or the narrowest, setting. With the rolled-out pasta running horizontal to you, place teaspoons (half walnut-size) mounds of filling on the half of the sheet closest to you at about 2-inch/5-centimeter intervals in just far enough from the edge to be able to fold over the far side of the sheet of pasta to cover the filling. With a pastry brush or your finger, very lightly moisten the area around the filling with water to help the top layer stick. Gently fold over the top layer of pasta and press down between the mounds of filling to create individual ravioli. Cut between each ravioli to separate them and pinch or press the edges with a fork to seal. Place the filled pasta on a plastic-lined sheet pan and store in the freezer as you work to keep the bottoms from becoming soggy. When thoroughly frozen they may be stored in a plastic bag.

RAVIOLI METHOD 2

Roll out the pasta dough, this time with two separate sheets for the tops and the bottoms of the ravioli. The amount of filling will determine the size of the ravioli you want to make. The filling is again placed at intervals, this time on the center of the sheet of pasta, then moistened and topped by the second sheet. Using a 3-inch/7.5-centimeter round or square ravioli cutter, punch out the ravioli and pinch the edges to seal. Various shaped cookie cutters may be used to make custom ravioli. Cut pasta rounds or squares may be folded over filling to make half-moon or triangle shapes.

For a special presentation inlay whole leaves of parsley or cilantro between two sheets of thinly rolled pasta (about setting five on my machine). Then pass through the rollers again to create a fossil-like pattern. Use a plain sheet of pasta for the bottom and decorated sheets for ravioli covers. Then proceed as for Ravioli Method 2.

Wonton wrappers, sometimes available in an egg-free version, can be used as well.

Cooking Pasta

Use at least four quarts of rapidly boiling water per pound of dried pasta, six quarts for fresh pasta, include a heaping teaspoon of salt for either.

Have a pitcher of water on hand to add to the pot if boiling over occurs. This happens when the starch builds up in water and there is not enough water. Dry pasta cooks according to the package recommendations. Fresh pasta will cook in as little as 15 seconds for very thin noodles up to a minute and a half for thicker and wider cuts.

Drain pasta well so the sauce is not watered down. Do not rinse the pasta unless it will be served chilled.

Butternut Squash Pasta

YIELD 10 SERVINGS
45 OUNCES/1.68 KILOGRAMS TOTAL WEIGHT RAW DOUGH
4.5 OUNCES/136 GRAMS RAW PASTA PER SERVING
5.5 OUNCES/154 GRAMS COOKED PASTA PER SERVING

This basic fresh pasta made with butternut squash resembles egg pasta in color and can be flavored using different herbs and spices.

all-purpose white flour	$4\frac{3}{4}$ cups	665 grams
cooked butternut squash	2 cups	448 grams
ground black pepper	pinch	pinch
garlic powder	pinch	pinch
ground nutmeg	pinch	pinch

Reserve $\frac{1}{2}$ cup/112 grams flour. Combine the remaining flour with all ingredients in a food processor using the knife blade until a dough is formed. Add the reserved flour to the processor as needed. Turn the dough out onto a floured work surface and knead until smooth. Allowing the dough to rest at this point will yield a smoother pasta; however, it is not crucial. Follow the directions for rolling out pasta for noodles or ravioli.

SERVE WITH: Toss freshly cooked pasta with Mushroom and Kale Sauté with Cherry Tomatoes (page 191), Sea Czar Salad with Blackened Tofu (page 175).

Note: For the butternut squash recipe I like to bake enough squash to be able to use some to make the pasta and some to be used in the recipe for Hazelnut Squash Ravioli Filling (page 266). By baking the squash, it will have less moisture, making it better for the filling. Too much moisture in a ravioli filling will cause the bottom of the ravioli to become soggy and break.

Tomato Herb Pasta

YIELD 10 SERVINGS

45 OUNCES/1.68 KILOGRAMS TOTAL WEIGHT RAW DOUGH

4.5 OUNCES/136 GRAMS RAW PASTA PER SERVING

5.5 OUNCES/154 GRAMS COOKED PASTA PER SERVING

This pasta dough makes a great ravioli wrapper when filled with either the Spinach Pecan Pesto (page 140), Mushroom Duxelles (page 265), or the Basil Pine Nut Pesto (page 141).

all-purpose white flour	$4\frac{3}{4}$ cups	665 grams
tomato purée	$1\frac{3}{4}$ cups	392 grams
garlic powder	1 teaspoon	2 grams
fresh basil, coarsely chopped	$\frac{1}{2}$ cup	28 grams

Reserve $\frac{1}{2}$ cup/112 grams flour. Combine the remaining flour with all ingredients in a food processor using the knife blade until a dough is formed. Add the reserved flour to the processor as needed. Turn the dough out onto a floured work surface and knead until smooth. Allowing the dough to rest at this point will yield a smoother pasta; however, it is not crucial. Follow the directions for rolling out pasta for noodles or ravioli.

SERVE WITH: Spinach Pecan Pesto (page 140), Red Pepper Porcini Reduction Sauce (page 151), Red Swiss Chard Reduction Sauce (page 152), Grilled or Roast Vegetable Salad (page 170).

Ruby Beet Pasta

YIELD 10 SERVINGS

45 OUNCES/1.68 KILOGRAMS TOTAL WEIGHT RAW DOUGH

4.5 OUNCES/136 GRAMS RAW PASTA PER SERVING

5.5 OUNCES/154 GRAMS COOKED PASTA PER SERVING

Beets give this pasta its incredible vibrant color.

all-purpose white flour	$4\frac{3}{4}$ cups	665 grams
beets, cooked and puréed	3 cups	672 grams
salt	pinch	pinch
ground black pepper	pinch	pinch

Reserve $\frac{1}{2}$ cup/112 grams flour. Combine the remaining flour with all ingredients in a food processor using the knife blade until a dough is formed. Add the reserved flour to the processor as needed. Turn the dough out onto a floured work surface and knead until smooth. Allowing the dough to rest at this point will yield a smoother pasta; however, it is not crucial. Follow the directions for rolling out pasta for noodles or ravioli.

SERVE WITH: Spinach Pecan Pesto (page 140), Salad Rouge with Glazed Red Onions and Hazelnuts (page 179).

Emerald Green Pea Pasta

YIELD 10 SERVINGS

45 OUNCES/1.68 KILOGRAMS TOTAL WEIGHT RAW DOUGH

4.5 OUNCES/136 GRAMS RAW PASTA PER SERVING

5.5 OUNCES/154 GRAMS COOKED PASTA PER SERVING

This adaptation sprang from the traditional way of serving peas with mint. Be sure to process the peas and mint well before adding the flour.

frozen green peas, defrosted	3 cups	672 grams
fresh mint, chopped	6 tablespoons	21 grams
salt	$\frac{1}{2}$ teaspoon	3 grams
ground black pepper	pinch	pinch
all-purpose white flour	$4\frac{3}{4}$ cups	665 grams

Put the peas, mint, salt and pepper in a food processor and purée. Reserve $\frac{1}{2}$ cup/ 112 grams flour. Combine the remaining flour with other ingredients in the food processor until a dough is formed. Add reserved flour to the processor as needed. Turn the dough out onto a floured work surface and knead until smooth. Allowing the dough to rest at this point will yield a smoother pasta; however, it is not crucial. Follow the directions for rolling out pasta for noodles or ravioli.

SERVE WITH: Mesclun Mix with Dulse and Shiitake Dressing (page 175), Spinach Pecan Pesto (page 140).

Orange Curry Pasta

YIELD 10 SERVINGS

45 OUNCES/1.68 KILOGRAMS TOTAL WEIGHT RAW DOUGH

4.5 OUNCES/136 GRAMS RAW PASTA PER SERVING

5.5 OUNCES/154 GRAMS COOKED PASTA PER SERVING

The hotter the curry powder that's used for the dough recipe, the spicier will be the resulting pasta.

all–purpose white flour	$4\frac{3}{4}$ cups	665 grams
orange juice concentrate	$1\frac{1}{4}$ cups	336 grams
curry powder	3 tablespoons	18 grams
salt	pinch	pinch
ground black pepper	pinch	pinch

Reserve $\frac{1}{2}$ cup/112 grams flour. Combine the remaining flour with all ingredients in a food processor using the knife blade until a dough is formed. Add the reserved flour to the processor as needed. Turn the dough out onto a floured work surface and knead until smooth. Allowing the dough to rest at this point will yield a smoother pasta; however, it is not crucial. Follow the directions for rolling out pasta for noodles or ravioli.

SERVE WITH: Toss cooked pasta with Thai Coconut Sauce with Basil (page 144).

Golden Carrot Pasta

YIELD 10 SERVINGS

45 OUNCES/1.68 KILOGRAMS TOTAL WEIGHT RAW DOUGH

4.5 OUNCES/136 GRAMS RAW PASTA PER SERVING

5.5 OUNCES/154 GRAMS COOKED PASTA PER SERVING

*To ensure a smooth finished product finely purée carrots and ginger
together before starting the recipe.*

all-purpose white flour	$4\frac{3}{4}$ cups	665 grams
cooked puréed carrots	2 cups	448 grams
salt	pinch	pinch
ground black pepper	pinch	pinch
gingerroot, minced	2 tablespoons	28 grams

Reserve $\frac{1}{2}$ cup/112 grams flour. Combine remaining flour with all ingredients in a food processor, using the knife blade until a dough is formed. Add the reserved flour to the processor as needed. Turn the dough out onto a floured work surface and knead until smooth. Allowing the dough to rest at this point will yield a smoother pasta; however, it is not crucial. Follow the directions for rolling out pasta for noodles or ravioli.

SERVE WITH: Toss cooked pasta with Cherry Tomatoes with Garlic, Spinach, Raisins, and Herbs (page 268), or Spinach Pecan Pesto (page 140).

Mushroom Duxelles Ravioli Filling

YIELD 1¼ CUPS/10.75 OUNCES/300 GRAMS

20 LARGE RAVIOLI WITH 1 TABLESPOON/15 GRAMS FILLING

60 SMALL RAVIOLI WITH 1 TEASPOON/5 GRAMS FILLING

The flavor-concentrating effect of this recipe works well with all of the cultivated types
of mushrooms available and can also be prepared with combinations
of varieties for a more complex flavor.

onions, fine dice	1 cup	112 grams
garlic, minced	1 teaspoon	5 grams
olive oil	1 tablespoon	15 milliliters
mushrooms, fine dice	3 cups	273 grams
soy sauce	1 tablespoon	15 milliliters
sherry wine	1 tablespoon	15 milliliters
salt	pinch	pinch
fresh ground black pepper	pinch	pinch

Sauté the onions and garlic in olive oil over medium-high heat for about 3 minutes. Add the mushrooms and sauté for about 5 minutes. Add the remaining ingredients, reduce heat to medium-low and continue to sauté for 15 to 20 minutes or until all the moisture from the mushrooms has evaporated.

You will need 45 ounces/1.68 kilograms raw pasta dough to make 60 small or 30 large ravioli. Double recipe to make 6 large 1½ ounces/42 grams ravioli per person. See instructions on how to make and cook ravioli (page 257).

Note: Use shallots or scallions in place of onions.

Hazelnut Squash Ravioli Filling

YIELD ABOUT 3 CUPS/500 GRAMS

A wet filling causes the bottom of the ravioli to break. By storing the uncooked ravioli in the freezer the moisture will not be able to compromise the bottom layer of pasta.

onions, small dice	1 cup	112 grams
garlic, minced	1 teaspoon	5 grams
olive oil	1 tablespoon	15 milliliters
butternut squash purée	$1\frac{1}{2}$ cups	336 grams
toasted hazelnuts, coarsely chopped	1 cup	98 grams
salt	pinch	pinch
fresh ground black pepper	pinch	pinch

Sauté the onions and garlic in olive oil over medium-high heat until lightly browned. Add the butternut squash purée and sauté for about two minutes. Add half of the hazelnuts and the remaining ingredients. The filling may be puréed in a food processor at this time if desired. Season to taste. Use remaining hazelnuts to garnish cooked ravioli. Follow instructions (page 257) to make ravioli. Also use this filling in manicotti.

SERVE WITH: Shiitake Sweet Potato Hazelnut Sauce (page 139).

Note: If the filling is on the wet side after the allotted cooking time, it can be thickened by adding and cooking in a little flour, cornstarch or arrowroot.

Sea Vegetable Ravioli Filling

YIELD ABOUT 3 CUPS/500 GRAMS

dry hijiki sea vegetable	1 cup	42 grams
shallots, sliced	$\frac{3}{4}$ cup	84 grams
olive oil	1 tablespoon	15 milliliters
garlic, crushed	1 teaspoon	5 grams
red pepper flakes	pinch	pinch
fresh tomatoes, fine dice	1 cup	140 grams
red wine vinegar	2 tablespoons	30 milliliters
soy sauce	1 tablespoon	15 milliliters
fresh oregano, minced	1 tablespoon	3.5 grams
apple juice	$\frac{1}{3}$ cup	80 milliliters

Cover the hijiki with water and soak for 15 minutes, drain, rinse, chop coarsely and set aside. Sauté the shallots in olive oil over medium heat for 1 minute. Add the garlic and sauté for 1 minute. Add all remaining ingredients including hijiki and simmer over low heat for about 30 minutes or until all liquid is evaporated and the hijiki is tender. Season to taste. Chill the mixture. Follow instructions (page 257) to make ravioli.

SERVE WITH: Roast Tomato and Garlic Sauce With Dulse and Lime (page 146).

Cherry Tomatoes with Garlic, Spinach, Raisins and Herbs

YIELD 10 SERVINGS
½ CUP/120 MILLILITERS

This quick sauté of Mediterranean flavors provides a great treatment for fresh pasta, coating it with flavor and color.

garlic, minced	4 teaspoons	9 grams
olive oil	4 teaspoons	20 milliliters
cherry tomatoes, halved	2 quarts	1.125 kilograms
fresh spinach, cleaned and stemmed	1 pound	448 grams
raisins	⅔ cup	76 grams
fresh basil, chopped	½ cup	14 grams
red wine vinegar	1 tablespoon	15 milliliters
extra virgin olive oil	2 teaspoons	10 milliliters
salt	½ teaspoon	3 grams
fresh ground black	pinch	pinch
cayenne pepper	to taste	to taste

Sauté the garlic in olive oil over medium heat for about 1 minute or until it begins to brown. Quickly add the tomatoes and sauté for 2 to 3 minutes. Add the spinach and raisins to the sauce and sauté for about 2 minutes until the spinach is wilted. Add the remaining ingredients to the pan, cover and simmer for 3 minutes longer. The cooked fresh pasta is added to the pan at this point and tossed with the sauce for 1 or 2 minutes. Season to taste.

SERVE WITH: Fresh cooked pasta noodles or ravioli.

Black Plum Sauce with Basil and Garlic

YIELD 10 SERVINGS
$\frac{1}{2}$ CUP/120 MILLILITERS

Plums are usually picked before they are ripe and may need some time to develop their full flavor potential.

garlic, minced	4 teaspoons	9 grams
olive oil	4 teaspoons	20 milliliters
fresh black plums, pitted and thinly sliced	2 quarts	1.125 kilograms
fresh basil, chopped	$\frac{1}{2}$ cup	14 grams
red wine vinegar	1 tablespoon	15 milliliters
extra virgin olive oil	2 teaspoons	10 milliliters
salt	$\frac{1}{2}$ teaspoon	3 grams
fresh ground black pepper	pinch	pinch
cayenne pepper	to taste	to taste

Sauté the garlic in olive oil over medium heat for about 1 minute or until it begins to brown. Quickly add the black plums, cover and simmer for 12 minutes. Add the remaining ingredients to pan, cover and simmer for 3 minutes longer. Season to taste.

VARIATION: Add a little fresh ginger to the garlic.

Potato Gnocchi

YIELD 10 SERVINGS

ABOUT 8 OUNCES/224 GRAMS

The recipes and ideas that are used by professional cooks often begin as traditional home-style offerings. They then become subject to extrapolation and experimentation. This northern Italian recipe was handed down to succeeding generations of my wife's family by observation rather than written recipe. In this manner, I too learned how to prepare these dumplings from my mother-in-law, Grace Garuti Kropf.

boiling potatoes	5 pounds	2.25 kilograms
all-purpose white flour	4 cups	560 grams
fresh parsley, minced	1 cup	56 grams
salt	1 teaspoon	6 grams
ground black pepper	pinch	pinch

Steam or boil potatoes in their jackets for 45 to 50 minutes or until they are fork-tender. Drain the potatoes and allow them to cool enough to handle. Peel the potatoes and put them through a ricer or grate by hand with a coarse grater.

In a bowl combine the riced or grated potatoes, three-quarters of the flour, the parsley and the salt and pepper. Mix into a dough. Turn out onto a floured work surface and add the remaining flour until the dough no longer sticks to your hands or the work surface.

Divide the dough into 8 portions. Roll out each portion into a rope shape about 16 inches/40 centimeters long by $\frac{3}{4}$ inch/2 centimeters in diameter. Cut each length of dough into 16 pieces. At this point the gnocchi can be boiled as they are. Or they can be, as my mother-in-law would do, rolled and pressed with a floured thumb so that they get flattened and rolled up about halfway. Another traditional method rolls the gnocchi across the tines of a dinner fork. Both methods thin the dough so the dumplings cook more evenly.

To cook, bring at least 6 quarts of water to a boil and have extra hot water on hand to add to the pot if it starts to boil over. Cook one-quarter of the gnocchi at a time. Cook until they float, then for 10 to 15 seconds longer. When done, remove from the water with a skimmer or a slotted spoon and place them in a heated casserole. Nap them with a little sauce and keep them warm until the process is complete.

SERVE WITH: Sauce with Spinach Pecan Pesto (page 140), Basil Pine Nut Pesto (page 141), Roast Tomato and Garlic Sauce with Dulse and Lime (page 146).

Penne, Sundried Tomatoes, Kalamata Olives and Capers

10 SERVINGS

1 CUP/140 GRAMS PASTA PLUS

$\frac{1}{3}$ CUP/80 MILLILITERS SAUCE

Kalamata olives are now available with the pits removed, making this dish a possibility for larger numbers.

sundried tomatoes	$2\frac{2}{3}$ cups	140 grams
boiling water	2 cups	480 milliliters
garlic, crushed	2 tablespoons	14 grams
olive oil	1 tablespoon	15 milliliters
fennel seeds	1 teaspoon	2.33 grams
kalamata olives, pitted	1 cup	140 grams
capers	$\frac{1}{4}$ cup	56 grams
balsamic vinegar	4 teaspoons	20 milliliters
red pepper flakes	pinch	pinch
salt	pinch	pinch
ground black pepper	pinch	pinch
fresh parsley, minced	$\frac{1}{2}$ cup	28 grams
extra virgin olive oil	1 tablespoon	15 milliliters
penne pasta	$1\frac{1}{2}$ pounds	672 grams
toasted pine nuts	$\frac{1}{4}$ cup	28 grams

Cover the sundried tomatoes with boiling water and allow them to soften for about 15 minutes. Remove the tomatoes from water and save the stock. Coarsely chop the softened tomatoes and set aside.

Sauté the garlic in olive oil over medium heat for about 1 minute or until just starting to brown. Stir in the fennel seeds, then add the softened tomatoes, their stock, and all remaining ingredients except the parsley and extra virgin olive oil.

Cook penne al dente, drain and return to the pan with half the parsley, extra virgin olive oil, and half of the sauce. Stir over low heat for about a minute. Season to taste. Plate and top with remaining sauce, parsley and the toasted pine nuts.

SERVE WITH: Red Swiss Chard with Garlic (page 194) and Avocado, Orange and Red Onion Salad (page 173).

Note: Chop large capers.

Angel Hair with Roasted Tomato, Garlic and Dulse Sauce

10 SERVINGS

1 CUP/140 GRAMS PASTA PLUS

$\frac{1}{2}$ **CUP/120 MILLILITERS SAUCE**

This recipe has the best flavor and is most economical when zucchini, tomatoes and basil are at peak season.

angel hair pasta	$1\frac{1}{2}$ pounds	672 grams
small zucchini, fine julienne	5 cups	560 grams
Roasted Tomato, Garlic and Dulse Sauce (page 146)	5 cups	1.2 liters
chiffonade of fresh basil	$\frac{3}{4}$ cup	84 grams

Boil angel hair pasta while sauce is cooking or heating. When the pasta is al dente, stir in the zucchini. Drain the pasta, stir in about a third of the sauce and season to taste. Serve the pasta topped with remaining sauce and garnish with basil chiffonnade.

VARIATION: A little extra virgin olive oil or soy margarine could be stirred into the drained pasta along with the sauce.

Rigatoni with Soy Sausage Pizzaiola

YIELD 10 SERVINGS

1 CUP/140 GRAMS PASTA PLUS

$\frac{1}{3}$ CUP/80 MILLILITERS SAUCE

The Soy Sausage Pizzaiola topping for this pasta could be used as filling for lasagna or cannelloni.

soy sausage, 1-ounce/ 28-gram patties	1 pound	448 grams
onions, sliced	4 cups	448 grams
olive oil	1 tablespoon	15 milliliters
garlic	2 tablespoons	28 grams
dulse flakes	2 teaspoons	2 grams
fennel seeds	1 teaspoon	2.33 grams
extra virgin olive oil	1 tablespoon	15 milliliters
green bell pepper, sliced	2 cups	224 grams
white mushrooms, sliced	5 cups	448 grams
salt	1 teaspoon	6 grams
ground black pepper	pinch	pinch
roasted sweet red peppers, chopped	1 cup	224 grams
tomatoes, crushed	$3\frac{1}{4}$ cups	784 grams
white wine	$\frac{1}{4}$ cup	60 milliliters
fresh basil, chopped	$\frac{1}{4}$ cup	14 grams
fresh oregano, chopped	$\frac{1}{4}$ cup	14 grams
rigatoni (dry weight)	$1\frac{1}{2}$ pounds	672 grams

Bake the soy sausage patties in a 350°F/180°C oven for 10 to 12 minutes or until lightly browned and cooked through. Set aside.

Sauté the onions in olive oil over medium heat for 2 minutes, then add the garlic and sauté 2 minutes longer. Stir in the dulse and fennel seeds, then add the extra virgin olive oil, green pepper, mushrooms, salt and pepper. Sauté for 2 or 3 minutes until moisture starts to form in the bottom of the pan, then increase heat to medium-high and cook 5 minutes longer, stirring and scraping any brown bits from the bottom of the pan.

Slice each of the reserved cooked soy sausage patties into 4 or 5 strips and add them to the pan along with the red peppers, tomatoes and wine. Cover and simmer for 10 minutes longer. Add the fresh basil and oregano, cover and simmer 5 more minutes. Season to taste. Serve over al dente rigatoni.

SERVE WITH: Avocado, Orange and Red Onion Salad (page 173).

Bow-tie Pasta Salad

YIELD 10 SERVINGS

$1\frac{1}{4}$ CUP/168 GRAMS

Farfalle, the Italian name for these bow-tie pasta shapes, can be used in either hot or cold dishes.

bow-tie pasta, uncooked	1 pound	448 grams
sundried tomatoes	2 cups	98 grams
boiling water	1 cup	240 milliliters
garlic, crushed	$\frac{1}{2}$ teaspoon	2.5 grams
fresh oregano, chopped	$\frac{1}{4}$ cup	14 grams
fresh basil, chopped	$\frac{1}{4}$ cup	14 grams
marinated hearts of artichoke	1 cup	336 grams
marinade from artichokes	$\frac{3}{4}$ cup	180 milliliters
capers	2 tablespoons	28 grams
green olives, sliced	$\frac{1}{2}$ cup	98 grams
fresh anise, trimmed, thinly sliced	$1\frac{1}{2}$ cups	154 grams
white wine vinegar	1 tablespoon	15 milliliters
extra virgin olive oil	3 tablespoons	45 milliliters
salt	$\frac{1}{2}$ teaspoon	3 grams
ground black pepper	pinch	pinch

Bring the water to boil for pasta. Place the sundried tomatoes in a small bowl. Remove 1 cup of the boiling water and pour over the sundried tomatoes, cover tightly with plastic wrap and allow to soften. Add the pasta to the boiling water and add salt if desired. Combine the remaining ingredients. When the pasta is cooked, drain and cool under running water. Drain well, then mix with all other ingredients, including chopped softened tomatoes and any liquid not absorbed by the sundried tomatoes.

SERVE WITH: Ruby Grapefruit, Pomegranate and Assorted Greens (page 174).

Note: Fresh anise may be called fresh fennel.

Penne with Asparagus and Strawberry Dressing

YIELD 10 SERVINGS

Select asparagus spears about the same diameter as the penne.

penne	1½ pounds	672 grams
olive oil	as needed	as needed
asparagus	3 pounds	1.35 kilograms
Strawberry Dressing (page 185)	5 cups	1.2 liters
salt	pinch	pinch
fresh ground black pepper	pinch	pinch
mango, fine dice	1 cup	224 grams
black sesame seeds, toasted	1 tablespoon	7 grams

Cook, drain and cool penne under cold running water, drain thoroughly, sprinkle with salt and pepper and coat with a little olive oil. Chill the pasta.

Prepare and cook the asparagus as for Asparagus with Hollandaze Sauce (page 210). After cooking slice asparagus on the bias into bite sized pieces, reserve the asparagus tips for garnish.

Toss the penne with two-thirds of the Strawberry Dressing, and cut asparagus. Plate the pasta and drizzle with remaining Strawberry Dressing. Garnish with mango, black sesame seeds and reserved asparagus tips.

SERVE WITH: Green Pea and Watercress Soup with Mint (page 95).

Orange Sesame Udon Noodles

YIELD 10 SERVINGS

ABOUT 8 OUNCES/224 GRAMS WITH SAUCE

These Japanese-Style noodles are reminiscent of linguine, yet possess
their own unique flavor and texture.

DRESSING

orange juice	2 cups	480 milliliters
toasted sesame tahini	1 cup	240 milliliters
fresh ginger, minced	2 tablespoons	28 grams
fresh garlic, minced	2 teaspoons	10 grams
fresh lemon juice	$1\frac{1}{2}$ tablespoons	22.5 milliliters
rice wine vinegar	$1\frac{1}{2}$ tablespoons	22.5 milliliters
soy sauce	3 tablespoons	45 milliliters

GARNISH

red onions, thinly sliced	$1\frac{1}{4}$ cups	189 grams
red wine vinegar	2 tablespoons	30 milliliters
oranges, peeled and sliced into rounds	5	5
black sesame seeds	1 tablespoon	7 grams
scallions, thin diagonal slices	1 tablespoon	7 grams
udon noodles	2 pounds	896 grams
toasted sesame oil	1 tablespoon	15 milliliters

Combine all ingredients for the dressing except 1 tablespoon/15 milliliters soy sauce, then chill the dressing. Combine the red onions and red wine vinegar and allow to marinate. Ready the remaining garnish ingredients.

Cook the udon noodles al dente and cool with cold running water. Toss the noodles with the remaining soy sauce and toasted sesame oil. Coat with half of the dressing, then plate the noodles. Add a little more dressing to each plate, then garnish with the marinated onions, orange slices, black sesame seeds and sliced scallions. Serve any extra sauce on the side as needed.

SERVE WITH: Miso Soup (page 108), Korean-Style Cucumbers (page 70), Garnish with chilled Seasoned Baked Tofu, or Seasoned Baked Tempeh (page 322).

Chilled Soba Noodles with Spicy Peanut Sesame Sauce

YIELD 10 SERVINGS

ABOUT 8 OUNCES/224 GRAMS WITH SAUCE

This type of chilled noodle dish is often served in Chinese restaurants as Cold Sesame Noodles with a red asterisk to indicate "spicy." While toasted sesame oil is used for flavor, the base of the sauce is usually peanut butter.

soba noodles	2 pounds	896 grams
toasted sesame oil	2 teaspoons	10 milliliters
soy sauce	1 tablespoon	30 milliliters
lime juice	1 tablespoon	15 milliliters
Spicy Peanut Sesame Sauce (recipe follows)	$2\frac{2}{3}$ cups	640 milliliters
scallions, thin diagonal slices	1 cup	56 grams
carrots, grated	$3\frac{1}{3}$ cups	420 grams
cucumbers, peeled, seeded and grated	1 pound	448 grams
toasted peanuts	$\frac{1}{4}$ cup	28 grams
toasted sesame seeds	$\frac{1}{4}$ cup	28 grams
Asian hot chili oil	optional	optional

Boil and cool the soba noodles. Toss the cooked soba with the sesame oil, soy sauce and lime juice. Divide the noodles into 10 servings, then sauce each portion.

Sprinkle on the remaining ingredients, either individually or tossed together first and then applied.

SERVE WITH: Miso Soup (page 108), Korean-Style Cucumbers (page 70), Garnish with chilled Seasoned Baked Tofu, or Seasoned Baked Tempeh (page 322).

Spicy Peanut Sesame Sauce

YIELD 2⅔ CUPS

¼ CUP/60 MILLILITERS

peanut butter	1⅓ cup	320 milliliters
toasted sesame oil	4 teaspoons	20 milliliters
soy sauce	½ cup	120 milliliters
succanat	2 tablespoons	24 grams
Shanxi vinegar	2 tablespoons	30 milliliters
dark brewed tea	about 1 cup	240 milliliters
fresh ginger, minced	2 tablespoons	28 grams
garlic, minced	4 teaspoons	20 grams

Combine all sauce ingredients in a blender or food processor and process until smooth.

VARIATION: Rice wine vinegar in place of Shanxi vinegar.

Linguine with Vegetarian Ragu

10 SERVINGS
ABOUT 8 OUNCES/224 GRAMS WITH SAUCE

Using the classic bolognese sauce as a prototype, this recipe was developed to provide the texture and flavors of a meat sauce.

linguine	$1\frac{1}{2}$ pounds	672 grams

FOR THE SAUCE

onions, small dice	2 cups	252 grams
carrots, small dice	1 cup	126 grams
celery, small dice	$\frac{1}{2}$ cup	56 grams
olive oil	2 tablespoons	30 milliliters
garlic, crushed	1 tablespoon	15 grams
white wine	$\frac{1}{4}$ cup	60 milliliters
bay leaves	2	2
rosemary	15 to 20 leaves	15 to 20 leaves
plum tomatoes, chopped	$3\frac{1}{4}$ cups	784 grams
browned soy bits	4 cups	336 grams
salt	$\frac{1}{2}$ teaspoon	3 grams
soy sauce	1 teaspoon	5 milliliters
fresh ground black pepper	pinch	pinch
fresh parsley, chopped	$\frac{1}{4}$ cup	14 grams
vegetable stock	2 cups	480 milliliters

Sauté the onions, carrots and celery in olive oil over medium-high heat for 3 minutes. Reduce the heat to medium, add the garlic, and sauté for 4 minutes. Stir in the white wine, then add all remaining ingredients except the parsley. Simmer for 20 minutes. Add the parsley and cook a few minutes longer. Season to taste. When the sauce is ready, boil linguine, drain and top with Vegetarian Ragu.

SERVE WITH: Mesclun Mix with Dulse and Shiitake Dressing (page 175), or Salad Rouge with Glazed Red Onions and Hazelnuts (page 179).

Ziti with White Beans, Dulse and Kale

YIELD 10 SERVINGS

10 OUNCES/240 GRAMS

This dish is a treasure of flavor and nutrition, with the variety of ingredients providing tastes, textures and nutrients from throughout the vegetable kingdom.

ziti	1 pound	448 grams
butternut squash, large dice	4 cups	560 grams
red onion, medium dice	1 cup	112 grams
garlic, chopped	$\frac{1}{4}$ cup	56 grams
olive oil	2 tablespoons	30 milliliters
Chianti red wine	$\frac{1}{4}$ cup	360 milliliters
kale, coarsely chopped	4 cups	336 grams
cooked cannelloni beans	$3\frac{1}{2}$ cups	980 grams
fresh tomatoes, medium dice	1 cup	140 grams
dried oregano	1 tablespoon	6 grams
prepared mustard	2 teaspoons	10 grams
bay leaves	2	2
salt	$\frac{1}{2}$ teaspoon	3 grams
ground black pepper	pinch	pinch
dulse, toasted and crumbled	$\frac{3}{4}$ cup	14 grams
parsley	$\frac{1}{2}$ cup	28 grams
chopped toasted walnuts	$\frac{1}{2}$ cup	56 grams

In a large pot of boiling salted water, boil the pasta for 6 minutes. Add the butternut squash to the pasta and cook 3 munutes or until the pasta is al dente.

While the pasta is cooking, sauté the onions and garlic with oil in a 6 quart/$5\frac{3}{4}$ liter sauté pan over medium heat for about 2 minutes. Add the red wine. Stir in the chopped kale, beans, tomatoes, oregano, mustard, bay leaves, salt and pepper. Add two-thirds of the dulse and cook a few minutes longer. If pasta is not yet ready remove from heat.

Drain the pasta, saving about 1 cup/240 milliliters of the cooking water. Add the cooked pasta and vegetables to pan and add half of the reserved water to moisten. Heat all the ingredients together, adding more reserved water as needed. Remove the bay leaves and season to taste.

GARNISH: Serve in shallow soup bowls and, garnish with reserved dulse, parsley and walnuts.

SERVE WITH: Tomato Sunflower Crème Soup (page 94), Ruby Grapefruit, Pomegranate and Assorted Greens (page 174).

Orrechiete Sautéed with Broccoli Rabe, Red Onions and Red Peppers

YIELD 10 SERVINGS

$7\frac{1}{2}$ OUNCES/210 GRAMS

broccoli rabe	1 pound	448 grams
garlic, crushed	2 tablespoons	28 grams
olive oil	2 tablespoons	30 milliliters
red onions, halved and thinly sliced	$2\frac{1}{2}$ cups	336 grams
sweet red peppers, halved and thinly sliced	$3\frac{1}{2}$ cups	392 grams
red wine vinegar	1 tablespoon	15 milliliters
soy sauce	1 tablespoon	15 milliliters
extra virgin olive oil	1 tablespoon	15 milliliters
salt	$\frac{1}{2}$ teaspoon	3 grams
ground black pepper	pinch	pinch
red pepper flakes	pinch	pinch
fresh oregano, minced	$\frac{1}{3}$ cup	21 grams
orrechiete	1 pound	448 grams

Trim the broccoli rabe and blanch in salted boiling water for 5 minutes. Drain, cool and squeeze out excess moisture; chop coarsely. Set aside.

Sauté the garlic in olive oil over medium heat for 30 seconds. Stir in the onions and sauté 3 minutes. Add the red peppers and sauté 5 minutes. Turn heat to high, add the remaining ingredients and reserved broccoli rabe except pasta. Sauté for a minute or two. Season to taste. Remove the pan from heat.

Cook the pasta, drain, return to the pot and stir in half of the broccoli rabe mixture. Season to taste. Plate the pasta and garnish with the remaining broccoli rabe.

SERVE WITH: Chick-Pea, Tomato and Herb Salvatore (page 101), Avocado, Orange and Red Onion Salad (page 173).

Chilled Vegan Ravioli with Fresh Anise

YIELD 10 SERVINGS
ABOUT 12 OUNCES/336 GRAMS

vegan ravioli	$2\frac{1}{2}$ pounds	1.12 kilograms
fresh anise, trimmed, split and thinly sliced	1 pound	448 grams
cucumbers, peeled, large dice	4 cups	560 grams
fresh tomatoes, large dice	4 cups	560 grams
SAUCE		
fresh basil, chopped	$\frac{1}{2}$ cup	28 grams
fresh ripe tomatoes, chopped	4 cups	560 grams
fresh garlic, minced	1 teaspoon	5 grams
balsamic vinegar	$\frac{1}{4}$ cup	60 milliliters
fresh lemon juice	2 tablespoons	30 milliliters
lemon zest, minced	1 tablespoon	9 grams
Dijon-style mustard	2 teaspoons	3.33 grams
salt	pinch	pinch
ground black pepper	pinch	pinch

Trim the anise of tough stalks and cut off the base, leaving core intact. Slice the anise bulb into thin slices. Reserve some of the anise herb leaf for garnish. Cook pasta and when it is al dente, stir the anise into the water, then drain and cool the pasta.

Set aside the basil. Blend all remaining sauce ingredients. Stir in the basil. Season to taste. Combine the pasta with two-thirds of the sauce and half of the tomatoes and cucumbers. Season to taste. Top the plated pasta with remaining cucumbers and tomatoes.

SERVE WITH: Ruby Grapefruit, Pomegranate and Assorted Greens (page 174), or Avocado, Orange and Red Onion Salad (page 173).

Vegan Tortellini with Three Sauces

YIELD 10 SERVINGS

ABOUT 10 OUNCES/280 GRAMS

Combining the tortellini with one or more seasonal vegetables presents an opportunity to add flavor and texture to this dish while offsetting the cost.

vegan tofu tortellini	2 pounds	900 grams
Roast Tomato and Garlic Sauce with Dulse and Lime (page 146)	5 cups	1.2 liters
Spinach Pecan Pesto (page 140)	2 cups	480 milliliters
raw Cashew Crème (page 157)	$\frac{1}{2}$ cup	120 milliliters
zucchini, large dice	2 cups	280 grams
yellow squash	2 cups	280 grams
fresh basil, minced	$\frac{1}{4}$ cup	14 grams

In a large pot of boiling salted water, cook the tortellini. While the pasta cooks, heat Roast Tomato and Garlic Sauce, bring Spinach Pecan Pesto to room temperature if it has been chilled and place the strained Cashew Crème in a squirt bottle.

When the tortellini is almost done, add the zucchini and yellow squash to the pot and finish cooking the pasta. When the pasta is done, drain and toss with two thirds of the Roast Tomato and Garlic Sauce. Season to taste with salt and pepper.

Plate pasta and garnish with small spoonfuls of the remaining Roast Tomato and Garlic Sauce, the Spinach Pecan Pesto, drizzle with Cashew Crème and sprinkle with basil.

SERVE WITH: Mesclun Mix with Arame and Shiitake Dressing (page 175).

Note: Try Olive Pesto (page 57), or Basil Pine Nut Pesto (page 141), in place of Spinach Pecan Pesto.

Pasta Sauce Flavor Booster

YIELD ½ CUP/120 MILLILITERS

When a big flavor is called for, add a tablespoon full of this mixture to the top of each dish of pasta just before serving. The reason for using both 100% olive oil and extra virgin is to preserve the subtle flavors of the extra virgin that can be lost when the garlic is sautéed.

garlic, minced	1 tablespoon	15 grams
olive oil	2 teaspoons	10 milliliters
capers	2 tablespoons	14 grams
extra virgin olive oil	2 tablespoons	30 milliliters
fresh parsley	2 tablespoons	7 grams
brine from capers	1 tablespoon	15 milliliters
water	$\frac{1}{4}$ cup	60 milliliters
salt	$\frac{1}{4}$ teaspoon	1.5 grams
hot pepper flakes	pinch	pinch
ground black pepper	pinch	pinch
balsamic vinegar	1 teaspoon	5 milliliters

Over medium-high heat sauté the garlic in olive oil in a small saucepan for 30 seconds or until just starting to brown, then add remaining ingredients and bring to a boil for 1 minute.

VARIATION: For Pasta Sauce Flavor Booster with Dulse, add 1 tablespoon/3 grams dulse flakes to recipe after the garlic is sautéed.

SERVE WITH: Drizzle on any pasta dish that needs a boost in flavor.

Note: Fresh basil or oregano can be used in addition to or in place of the parsley. Add 1 tablespoon/28 grams soy margarine in place of half of the extra virgin olive oil.

CHAPTER TEN

Bean and Grain–Based Entrées

Many chefs conduct an ongoing search for new and interesting ingredients. Grains and beans provide an array of new possibilities that are also attractive from a food-cost standpoint.

After observing the health effects of centuries-old eating practices throughout the world, modern dietitians suggest that our diet should be largely based upon whole unprocessed grains, together with and complemented by beans. Along with their flavors, colors and textures, beans offer an important source of nutrition and dietary fiber.

Grains in one form or another have been staples in most of the indigenous cooking styles throughout the world. Rice, wheat, oats and barley along with corn, rye, buckwheat and millet are the most widely used. Within each category there are other related grains or varieties.

Rice, the world's most popular grain, comes in over 200 strains, such as wehani, black japonica, arborio, basmati, and jasmine to name a few popular types. Brown rice comes in short, medium and long grains. Wheat has relatives such as spelt and kamut that were once popular and are now becoming known again. Other ancient grains such as quinoa from Peru have been used in their native countries until present and are now being discovered by the rest of the world.

Beans have great taste and texture and provide a solid foundation that can be built on with different flavor combinations. Different beans are used in different cultures and treated with the spices of that particular cuisine. In Brazil, black beans might be cooked with garlic, cumin, lime, tomato and cilantro, or in India yellow split peas may be seasoned with coriander, mustard seeds, turmeric, ginger and lemon.

To enhance the flavor of bean dishes

To provide	Add
earthy base flavors	root vegetables such as carrots, burdock, parsnips, turnips, mirepoix
high notes	lemon, lime vinegar, chiles, tomatoes
sweetness	maple, barley malt syrup, caramelized onions
strong pungent flavors	raw onions, raw scallions, raw garlic, ground black peppers, mustard, horseradish, wasabi
tempered pungent flavors	sautéed garlic and other onion family members
salty flavors	sea salt, sea vegetables which also offer a natural softening agent and enhance flavor, (cook all beans with a small piece of kelp to soften and enhance flavor) soy sauce and miso add salty and base flavors
for aroma fresh herbs	fresh herbs such as parsley, tarragon, cilantro, basil, oregano or dill just before serving. Use dried herbs at earlier stages of cooking to provide undercurrent flavors.

Black Bean Chili

YEILD 10 SERVINGS

1 CUP/224 GRAMS

This hearty-style chili uses a traditional Mexican ingredient, chocolate, for a deep, rich taste and also the nontraditional flavors of soy sauce and toasted sesame oil to provide further depth to the seasoning.

onions, medium dice	5 cups	560 grams
green peppers, large dice	3 cups	336 grams
carrots, medium dice	1 cup	112 grams
celery, medium dice	1 cup	112 grams
olive oil	2 tablespoons	30 milliliters
toasted sesame oil	1 teaspoon	5 milliliters
garlic, minced	1 tablespoon	15 grams
ginger, minced	1 tablespoon	15 grams
vegetable stock	3 cups	720 milliliters
crushed tomatoes	$2\frac{1}{3}$ cups	784 grams
textured vegetable protein	1 cup	70 grams
ground ancho chile	1 tablespoon	6 grams
ground cumin	2 teaspoons	4 grams
oregano	1 tablespoon	6 grams
soy sauce	2 teaspoons	10 milliliters
salt	$\frac{1}{2}$ teaspoon	3 grams
cooked black beans	$3\frac{1}{2}$ cups	980 grams
chocolate chips, dairy free	2 tablespoons	7.5 grams

GARNISH

scallions, thin bias cut	2 tablespoons	7 grams
cilantro, chopped	2 tablespoons	7 grams

Sauté the onions, peppers, carrots and celery in olive oil over medium-low heat for about 12 minutes. Add the garlic and ginger and sauté for 3 minutes. Stir in the stock. Stir in all remaining ingredients except the chocolate chips. Bring to a boil, then add chocolate chips and simmer for 20 minutes. Stir to keep bottom from scorching and add extra vegetable stock if the chili becomes too thick. Season to taste. Garnish with scallions and cilantro.

SERVE WITH: Brazilian-Style Greens (page 196), plain rice, corn chips and salsa.

Note: Chili powder may be used in place of the ground ancho chile.

White Bean Chili with Caramelized Onions

YIELD 10 SERVINGS

1 CUP/224 GRAMS

*Texturized vegetable protein (tvp) is employed in this dish and the
Black Bean Chili for a chewy mouth feel.*

onions, thinly sliced	5 cups	560 grams
olive oil	2 tablespoons	30 milliliters
toasted sesame oil	1 teaspoon	5 milliliters
green peppers, large dice	3 cups	336 grams
carrots, small dice	1 cup	112 grams
celery, small dice	1 cup	112 grams
garlic, minced	1 tablespoon	15 grams
vegetable stock	3 cups	720 milliliters
crushed tomatoes	$2\frac{1}{3}$ cups	784 grams
textured vegetable protein	1 cup	70 grams
ground ancho chile	1 tablespoon	6 grams
ground cumin	2 teaspoons	4 grams
soy sauce	2 teaspoons	10 milliliters
salt	$\frac{1}{2}$ teaspoon	3 grams
cooked cannellini beans	$3\frac{1}{2}$ cups	980 grams
chocolate chips, dairy free	2 tablespoons	7.5 grams

GARNISH

fresh cilantro, chopped	$\frac{1}{4}$ cup	14 grams

Sauté the onions in half of the oil over medium heat for about 12 minutes or until
they are well caramelized, increasing heat if needed to caramelize onions. Remove the
onions from the pot and set aside.

Add the remaining oil, peppers, carrots and celery to pot and sauté over medium
heat for 5 minutes. Add the garlic and sauté for 3 minutes. Stir in the stock. Stir in all
remaining ingredients except the chocolate chips. Add one-third caramelized onions
to pot. Bring to a boil, then add chocolate chips and simmer for 20 minutes. Stir to
keep the bottom from scorching and add extra vegetable stock if the chili becomes
too thick. Season to taste. Garnish with reserved caramelized onions and the cilantro.

SERVE WITH: Brazilian-Style Greens (page 196), corn chips or French bread.

Note: Add a hot sauce of choice or hot pepper flakes to taste. A little balsamic vinegar or
lime juice can be added to perk up the flavor.

White Bean Cakes

YIELD 10 SERVINGS

5 OUNCES/140 GRAMS EACH

This recipe can be assembled ahead to the point of cooking, then frozen.
Defrost in the refrigerator and cook as per the recipe.

white kidney beans, cooked and drained	$3\frac{1}{2}$ cups	896 grams
green peppers, small dice	1 cup	112 grams
onions, small dice	1 cup	112 grams
plain dry bread crumbs	2 cups	168 grams
garlic, crushed	1 tablespoon	15 grams
chopped fresh parsley	2 tablespoons	7.5 grams
salt	$\frac{1}{2}$ teaspoon	3 grams
ground black pepper	pinch	pinch
soy sauce	2 teaspoons	10 milliliters
olive oil	for cooking	for cooking

Combine all ingredients. Form into 10 bean cakes. In a heavy-bottom skillet or on a griddle, brown both sides of white bean cakes, then remove to a sheet pan. Place in a 350°F/180°C oven and bake for about 10 minutes.

Note: White kidney beans are also called cannellini beans.

SERVE WITH: Sauce choices are Roast Tomato and Garlic Sauce with Dulse and Lime (page 146), Plum and Tomato Salsa (page 68), Peach and Tomato Salsa (page 66), or Pineapple and Tomato Salsa (page 67). Mesclun Mix with Dulse and Shiitake Dressing (page 175). Brown Rice (page 315), Brazilian-Style Greens (page 196).

Braised Lentils with Sesame-Roasted Carrots

YIELD 10 SERVINGS

$1\frac{1}{2}$ CUPS/336 GRAMS

In this dish the flavor of the lentils is complimented by the sesame and the roasted carrots.

green lentils	4 cups	896 grams
water	12 cups	2.88 liters
onions, small dice	2 cups	224 grams
soy sauce	4 teaspoons	20 milliliters
ginger, minced	1 tablespoon	15 grams
salt	pinch	pinch
kelp	1-inch piece	2.5-centimeter piece

SEASONING

soy sauce	3 tablespoons	45 milliliters
balsamic vinegar	2 tablespoons	30 milliliters
extra virgin olive oil	2 tablespoons	30 milliliters
Sesame-Roasted Carrots (page 193)	5 cups	840 grams

Combine the lentils, water, onions, soy sauce, ginger, salt and kelp in a pan and bring to a boil. Simmer for about 40 minutes until tender. Less time will yield a lentil that is more intact and al dente.

Toss the cooked lentils with soy sauce, balsamic vinegar and olive oil. Season to taste. Serve with carrots and greens below.

SERVE WITH: Mesclun Mix with Dulse and Shiitake Dressing (page 175), Red Swiss Chard Sauté with Garlic (page 194), Greens Sautéed with Ginger (page 195), Brazilian-Style Greens (page 196).

Adzuki Beans with Squash

YIELD 10 SERVINGS

$1\frac{1}{2}$ CUPS/336 GRAMS

The squash for this recipe could be replaced by the Orange Braised Butternut Squash (page 199) for a variation.

adzuki beans	4 cups	616 grams
kelp, 4–inch/10–centimeter piece	1	1
water	12 cups	2.88 liters
salt	1 teaspoon	6 grams
carrots, fine dice	2 cups	252 grams
onions	2 cups	224 grams
olive oil	2 tablespoons	30 milliliters
soy sauce	$\frac{1}{4}$ cup	60 milliliters
Sesame Roasted Butternut Squash (page 204)	5 cups	980 grams
scallions, thinly sliced	$\frac{1}{2}$ cup	28 grams

Check the beans thoroughly for small stones or twigs, then rinse well. Combine the beans with kelp, water, salt and carrots. Bring to a boil then cover and simmer for about 45 minutes until the beans are tender. If kelp has not disolved, remove, chop and return to pot.

While the beans cook, in another pan sauté the onions in the olive oil over medium heat for about 5 minutes or until they are cooked and starting to brown. Add the sautéed onions and soy sauce to the beans when they are tender. Serve over Orange Braised Butternut Squash and garnish with scallions.

SERVE WITH: Rice Salad Medley with Wild, Japonica, and Wehani Rice (page 168) and/or Salad Rouge with Glazed Red Onions and Walnuts (page 179).

VARIATION: Adzuki Beans with Squash and Burdock Root. Add 2 cups/252 grams of cleaned, thinly sliced burdock root to the pan before adding the onions and sauté for 5 minutes, then add onions and continue with the recipe.

Chick-peas Braised with Root Vegetables

YIELD 10 SERVINGS

1 CUP/240 MILLILITERS

onions, large dice	3 cups	336 grams
carrots, large dice	3 cups	378 grams
rutabagas, large dice	3 cups	378 grams
celery, large dice	1 cup	112 grams
olive oil	2 tablespoons	30 milliliters
shallots, small dice	$\frac{1}{2}$ cup	56 grams
cooked chick-peas	4 cups	756 grams
chick-pea stock	6 cups	1.44 liters
bay leaves	4	4
celery leaves, minced	$\frac{1}{4}$ cup	28 grams
fresh thyme sprigs, 4 inches/ 10 centimeters	3	3
salt	1 teaspoon	6 grams
ground black pepper	pinch	pinch
soy sauce	$\frac{1}{4}$ cup	60 milliliters
apple cider vinegar	1 tablespoon	15 milliliters
fresh parsley, minced	$\frac{1}{2}$ cup	56 grams

GARNISH

chopped toasted walnuts, spiced	$\frac{1}{2}$ cup	50 grams

Sauté the onions, carrots, rutabagas, and celery in olive oil over medium-low heat for 10 minutes. Add the shallots and sauté for 3 minutes. Add all remaining ingredients but parsley and simmer for 20 minutes. Add the parsley and simmer 5 minutes longer. Season to taste.

GARNISH: Garnish with chopped toasted walnuts.

VARIATION: A quarter cup/60 milliliters of one or more of the following may be added. White wine, apple cider, tomato puree, dill pickle brine.

SERVE WITH: Sautéed Greens (page 195), over rice, with Peach and Pecan Corn Bread (page 352), Coconut Curry Biscuits (page 360).

Vimla Raja's Gujrati Dal

YIELD 10 SERVINGS

In India, dal refers to both the beans and the gravy or soup made from them. This hearty entree version was inspired by Vimla Raja, an excellent East Indian cook, and daughter Namisha, owner of "Evolving Appetites" from North York, Ontario, Canada. They invited me into their kitchen as Vimla prepared a few dishes from her repertoire destined for an East Indian communal feast.

Yellow Split Pea Curry (page 104)	10 cups	2.4 liters
fresh green beans, trimmed	$1\frac{1}{2}$ pounds	672 grams
potatoes, large dice	5 cups	700 grams
fresh gingerroot, minced	1 tablespoon	15 grams
peanut oil	1 tablespoon	15 milliliters
whole cumin seed	1 tablespoon	7 grams
ground coriander	1 tablespoon	6 grams
ground cardamom	1 teaspoon	2 grams
lemon juice	1 tablespoon	15 milliliters
roasted unsalted peanuts	1 cup	140 grams
succanat	2 tablespoons	8 grams
small, green chile pepper (spicy), minced	1 tablespoon	7 grams
fresh tomatoes, diced	2 cups	280 grams
salt	$\frac{1}{2}$ teaspoon	3 grams
water	1 cup	240 milliliters

GARNISH

chopped fresh cilantro	$\frac{1}{4}$ cup	14 grams
thin lemon wedges	10	10

First prepare the Yellow Split Pea Curry soup, omit garnish. While the soup simmers, sauté the green beans, potatoes and fresh gingerroot in the peanut oil over medium heat for 5 minutes. Add the cumin seeds and sauté for 2 minutes.

Stir in the coriander and cardamom for about 1 minute, then add the remaining ingredients. Mix well, then simmer until the potatoes and green beans are tender. Season to taste.

To serve, place a mound of the bean and potato mixture in the center of a soup plate, then surround with the Yellow Split Pea Curry soup. Garnish with the reserved soup garnish of chopped cilantro and lemon wedges.

SERVE WITH: India-Style Flat Bread (page 353) and Basmati Rice (page 315).

Wild Rice with Shiitake and Cremini Mushrooms

YIELD 10 SERVINGS

1 CUP/224 GRAMS

Wild rice is the slender dark grain of an attractive aquatic grass and considered to be one of the finest gourmet ingredients. The garnish of puffed wild rice provides a texturally elegant version of snap, crackle and pop.

shallots, medium dice	1 cup	112 grams
carrots, medium dice	2 cups	252 grams
celery, medium dice	1 cup	112 grams
olive oil	2 tablespoons	30 milliliters
soy margarine	2 tablespoons	28 grams
cremini mushrooms, $\frac{1}{4}$-inch/.75-centimeter slices	5 cups	448 grams
shiitake mushrooms, $\frac{1}{4}$-inch/.75-centimeter slices	5 cups	448 grams
wild rice	$5\frac{3}{4}$ cups	1036 grams
vegetable stock	12 cups	2.88 liters
bay leaves	2	2
fresh thyme sprigs, 4 inches/10 centimeters	2	2
salt	1 teaspoon	6 grams
ground black pepper	pinch	pinch
soy sauce	$\frac{1}{4}$ cup	60 milliliters
sherry wine	$\frac{1}{4}$ cup	60 milliliters
fresh parsley, minced	$\frac{1}{2}$ cup	56 grams
Cashew Crème (page 157)	1 cup	240 milliliters

GARNISH

wild rice	$\frac{3}{4}$ cup from above	
hot oil, 75°F/190°C	$\frac{1}{2}$ inch deep	

Sauté the shallots, carrots and celery in olive oil over medium heat for 5 minutes. Add the margarine, and cremini and shiitake mushrooms, sauté 5 minutes. Reserve

$\frac{3}{4}$ cup/140 grams of wild rice. Add the remaining rice and stock, bay leaves, thyme, salt, pepper, soy sauce and sherry to the pot, bring to a boil then cover and simmer for 50 minutes.

Check for doneness. The rice should be tender and each grain should be broken at the seam and slightly curled. If rice is not done, continue to cook, adding a little more vegetable stock if needed. Stir in the parsley and cashew crème, cover, and turn off heat. Let set for ten minutes. Season to taste.

Fry the reserved rice in hot (375°F/190°C) oil until puffed, about 5 seconds. Drain on absorbent paper and garnish.

VARIATION: Olive oil can be used instead of soy margarine. When using vegetable bouillon in place of stock, reduce salt in the recipe and check at the end of the cooking time. Use a wild rice blend.

SERVE WITH: Red Swiss Chard Sauté with Garlic (page 194), Sesame Roasted Butternut Squash (page 204).

Millet with Winter Squash

YIELD 10 SERVINGS

1 CUP/224 GRAMS

The dry roasting technique used for the millet enhances the flavor of this dish. In addition to flavor, the butternut squash adds great texture and color.

millet, rinsed	2 cups	392 grams
peeled butternut squash, 1-inch/2.5-centimeter cubes	4 cups	560 grams
water	6 cups	1.44 liters
salt	1 teaspoon	6 grams
ground black pepper	pinch	pinch
bay leaves	2	2

Wash the millet well, rubbing the grains together, then drain in a strainer and shake off excess moisture. In a heavy-bottom pot, dry roast the millet until lightly browned and giving off a nutty aroma, being careful not to burn the millet. When the millet is browned, add the remaining ingredients to the pot. Cover the pot and bring to a boil, then simmer for about 25 minutes or until the millet is done.

VARIATION: Mash the millet and squash together. Pack the cooked millet into a terrine or triangle mold and chill until firm, as for polenta. Slice the chilled millet and place on a lightly oiled baking sheet, cover and warm in a 325°F/160°C oven for 10 minutes or until heated through. For African Foutou use sweet potatoes in place of butternut squash.

SERVE WITH: Spinach Pecan Pesto (page 140), Carrot Ginger Sauce (page 133), Wild Mushroom Sauce (page 148), Salad Rouge (page 179), and Greens Sautéed with Ginger (page 195).

African Foutou

YIELD 10 SERVINGS

2 CUPS/448 GRAMS

Throughout Africa many dishes are based on a starchy root such as sweet potatoes served with millet and a spicy sauce that might include spinach, peanuts, dates and tomatoes flavored with lime.

Brazilian-Style Greens (Spinach) (page 196)	5 cups	840 grams
Millet with Winter Squash (page 296)	10 cups	2.24 kilograms
Roast Tomato Garlic Lime Sauce (page 146)	5 cups	1.2 liters
roasted peanuts	$\frac{1}{2}$ cup	70 grams
chopped dates	$\frac{1}{2}$ cup	56 grams
hot sauce, optional		

Plate this dish by first placing down a portion of the Brazilian Greens, then top with the Millet mixture, sauce with the tomato sauce and sprinkle with the peanuts and dates. Serve hot sauce on the side.

Guinness Barley with Tri-Color Confetti

YIELD 10 SERVINGS

ABOUT 1 CUP/196 GRAMS

This recipe was inspired by my friend and reference resource for Irish food, chef Marc Hussey, CEC.

onions, medium dice	1 cup	122 grams
carrots, medium dice	1 cup	126 grams
celery	1 cup	112 grams
rutabaga	1 cup	140 grams
canola oil	2 tablespoons	30 milliliters
salt	$1\frac{1}{2}$ teaspoons	9 grams
ground black pepper	$\frac{1}{4}$ teaspoon	.75 grams
stout-style dark beer	1 cup	120 milliliters
pearled barley	2 cups	308 grams
vegetable stock	6 cups	1.44 liters
frozen green peas	2 cups	280 grams
parsley, minced	$\frac{1}{2}$ cup	28 grams

GARNISH

savoy cabbage, coarsely chopped	10 cups	448 grams
shallots, small dice	$\frac{1}{2}$ cup	56 grams
canola oil	1 teaspoon	5 milliliters
vegan mayonnaise	$\frac{1}{3}$ cup	70 grams
potatoes, boiled, cooled in their jackets	2 pounds	900 grams
soy margarine	2 tablespoons	28 grams
leeks, fine julienne	$2\frac{1}{2}$ cups	140 grams
cornstarch	$\frac{1}{4}$ cup	32 grams
oil for deep frying		

Sauté the onions, carrots, celery and rutabagas in canola oil over medium heat for 10 minutes. Stir in the salt, pepper and stout beer. Cook for 5 minutes. Add barley and vegetable stock, bring to a boil then cover and simmer for 20 minutes. Add the green peas and parsley for the last 5 minutes of cooking or if prepared in advance, while heating to serve.

Blanch the cabbage in boiling salted water for about 2 minutes. Shock under cold water, squeeze out excess moisture and set aside. In a nonstick pan, sauté the shallots in canola oil over medium heat for 5 minutes or until lightly browned.

Combine the reserved cooked cabbage, shallots, vegan mayonnaise, salt and pepper to taste and set aside.

Peel the cooked potatoes, slice about $\frac{1}{2}$ inch/1.25 centimeters thick, sauté in soy margarine until golden brown. Season with salt and pepper. Keep warm.

Rinse the leeks in a bowl of cold water and remove by lifting them out of the water to allow any grit to fall to the bottom. Shake off the excess moisture and dredge them with cornstarch. Deep fry at 375°F until crisp. Drain on absorbent paper and salt to taste.

To serve, fan 3 slices of potatoes toward the back left center of a large plate and place about $\frac{1}{3}$ cup of the cabbage on the front right center of the plate, leaving a little space between it and the potatoes. Place a scoop of the barley so it straddles both inside edges of the potatoes and cabbage, then garnish with some of the fried leeks.

SERVE WITH: Irish Soda Bread (page 351).

Kamut, Corn and Lima Beans

YIELD 10 SERVINGS
1 CUP/224 GRAMS

*Using the quick-soak method for beans when cooking kamut will
significantly reduce the cooking time.*

kamut	3 cups	1.014 kilograms
water	12 cups	3.36 liters
salt	1 teaspoon	6 grams
ground black pepper	pinch	pinch
bay leaves	2	2
fresh thyme sprigs, 4 inches/ 10 centimeters	2	2
frozen lima beans	2 cups	322 grams
ground cinnamon	pinch	pinch
frozen corn kernels	2 cups	266 grams
soy sauce	1 teaspoon	5 milliliters
Walnut Sherry Vinaigrette (page 182)	$\frac{3}{4}$ cups	180 milliliters
toasted sliced almonds	1 cup	140 grams
parsley	$\frac{1}{2}$ cup	28 grams

Rinse the kamut and combine in a pot with water. Bring to a boil, boil for 5 minutes, then cover and remove the pot from the heat and let it sit covered for 1 hour.

Return the pot to the heat and add salt, pepper, bay leaves and thyme. Simmer covered for about an hour or until almost tender. Remove the bay leaves and thyme sprig from the pot. Add the lima beans and cinnamon, then cook for 10 minutes. Add the corn kernels and cook 5 minutes. Kamut should be tender but still chewy when done. Toss with half of the dressing and the soy sauce. Season to taste.

GARNISH WITH: Toasted almonds, parsley, and drizzle with remaining dressing.

SERVE WITH: Red Swiss Chard Sauté with Garlic (page 194).

Jasmine Rijsttafel

YIELD 10 SERVINGS

1 CUP RICE/224 GRAMS

PLUS GARNISH

The "rijsttafel" is a tradition in Holland that came originally from Indonesia. Rice is served with an array of condiments, sauces and garnishes, and each diner then prepares his meal from the selection. Aromatic Jasmine rice works very well in this presentation.

water	10 cups	2.4 liters
salt	1 teaspoon	6 grams
Jasmine rice	5 cups	1.12 kilograms
sliced scallions	1 cup	112 grams
cucumbers, peeled, large dice	$2\frac{1}{2}$ cups	280 grams
cherry tomatoes	1 pint	448 grams
roasted unsalted peanuts	1 cup	140 grams
raisins	1 cup	112 grams
grated carrots	1 cup	112 grams
grated unsweetened coconut	1 cup	112 grams
slice toasted almonds	1 cup	112 grams
Spicy Peanut Sesame Sauce (page 278)	$2\frac{2}{3}$ cups	640 milliliters
Seasoned Baked Tempeh (page 334)	2 pounds	896 grams
Oven Roasted Sweet Potatoes (page 203)	5 cups	840 grams

Combine the water and salt and bring to a boil. Add rice, boil, then simmer for 20 minutes. While the rice cooks, assemble the scallions, cucumbers, tomatoes, peanuts, raisins, carrots, coconut and almonds in small bowls or serving containers to be served with the rice. Combine and heat the peanut sauce and tempeh. Warm the sweet potatoes.

This dish can be served individually or as a buffet with all the garnish ingredients plated for guests to serve themselves.

Note: Other possibilities may include orange segments, pineapple chunks and tofu in place of tempeh.

Baby Bella Risotto

YIELD 10 SERVINGS

$1\frac{1}{2}$ CUPS/336 GRAMS

Two key factors for achieving a creamy, chewy textured risotto are first, the method of sautéing the rice, generally with a member of the onion family, and the slow incorporation of the cooking liquid. The second is the type of rice that is used, preferably Italian arborio.

olive oil	2 tablespoons	30 milliliters
shallots, small dice	1 cup	112 grams
arborio rice	$2\frac{1}{2}$ cups	560 grams
soy margarine	2 tablespoons	28 grams
baby bella mushrooms	5 cups	448 grams
Enriched Mushroom Vegetable Stock (page 88)	6 cups	1.44 liters
white miso	1 tablespoon	15 grams
dried mushrooms	$\frac{1}{2}$ cup	28 grams
salt	$\frac{1}{2}$ teaspoon	3 grams
pepper	pinch	pinch
bay leaves	2	2
soy sauce	1 teaspoon	5 milliliters
white wine	$\frac{1}{4}$ cup	60 milliliters
rice beverage, hot	2 cups	480 milliliters
Cashew Crème (page 157)	1 cup	240 milliliters
fresh parsley, chopped	$\frac{1}{2}$ cup	28 grams

In a heavy-bottom pot, sauté the shallots in olive oil over medium heat for 2 minutes. Add the rice and margarine and sauté over medium heat for 5 minutes or until rice becomes translucent. Stir in the mushrooms. Pour in 2 cups of the hot stock and add the miso, dried mushrooms, salt, pepper, bay leaves, soy sauce and white wine. Stir often to keep the rice from sticking. When the first 2 cups of stock are absorbed, continue to add 2 cups at a time until it is all incorporated. When the rice is cooked, stir in the rice beverage, Cashew Crème and the parsley. Season to taste.

SERVE WITH: Sesame Roasted Butternut Squash (page 204) and Red Swiss Chard Sauté with Garlic (page 194).

Note: Occasionally the heat may need to be raised to maintain a steady simmer, especially when more liquid is being added to the pan. If the risotto cannot be served immediately, reserve some of the hot stock to restore the creamy texture before serving.

Basmati Rice with Asparagus and Cashews

YIELD 10 SERVINGS
ABOUT 1 CUP/224 GRAMS RICE/PLUS ASPARAGUS GARNI

Basmati, a wonderful aromatic variety of rice, is available in both white and brown versions. Asparagus season is the best time to serve this vegetable in a starring role.

onions, small dice	4 cups	448 grams
olive oil	2 tablespoons	30 milliliters
brown basmati rice, washed	5 cups	980 grams
celery seeds	1 tablespoon	7 grams
fennel seeds	1 tablespoon	7 grams
salt	2 teaspoons	12 grams
ground black pepper	pinch	pinch
water	10 cups	2.4 liters
bay leaves	2	2
sprig of thyme, 4 inches/ 10 centimeters	2	2
asparagus, thinly sliced	$2\frac{1}{2}$ pounds	1.12 kilograms
fresh parsley, chopped	$\frac{1}{2}$ cup	28 grams
roasted chopped unsalted cashews	$2\frac{1}{2}$ cups	350 grams

Sauté the onions in olive oil over medium heat for 5 minutes or until starting to brown. Stir in the rice and sauté for 1 minute. Stir in the celery seeds, fennel seeds, salt and pepper. Add water, bay leaves and thyme. Bring to a boil, cover and simmer for 35 minutes. Add the asparagus and parsley to the pot, and cook 10 minutes longer or until both rice and asparagus are tender. Serve garnished with roasted cashews.

SERVE WITH: Sea Czar Salad with Blackened Tofu (page 175), or Exotic Mushroom Salad (page 178), or Tangy Tempeh Salad (page 335).

Quinoa with Broccoli, Carrots and Summer Squash

YIELD 10 SERVINGS

ABOUT 1 CUP/168 GRAMS

This quick-cooking ancient grain of Peruvian origin can be used much the same as couscous. In South America, quinoa has long been valued for its culinary adaptability and nutritive properties. There is now a black quinoa on the market that is a salt and pepper color.

Remember that to ensure the best-tasting results, wash the quinoa thoroughly to remove a slight "soapy" taste from saponin, which is a natural pest deterrent the plant has developed.

carrots, thinly sliced	2 cups	252 grams
yellow summer squash	2 cups	280 grams
broccoli, small	2 cups	145 grams
vegetable stock	4 cups	690 milliliters
salt	1 teaspoon	6 grams
ground black pepper	pinch	pinch
bay leaves	2	2
fresh thyme	1 sprig	1 sprig
quinoa, rinsed	2 cups	336 grams
toasted sliced almonds	2 cups	210 grams
fresh chives, minced	2 tablespoons	7 grams
fresh mint minced	2 tablespoons	7 grams
Orange Mustard Dressing (page 182)	$1\frac{1}{2}$ cups	360 milliliters

Blanch the vegetables in boiling salted water. Strain off the liquid and save for stock in the recipe. Shock the vegetables and keep them chilled.

Bring the stock and seasonings to a boil, add quinoa and simmer covered for about 15 minutes or until the water is evaporated. Fluff with a fork and allow to cool.

Toss the cooled quinoa with the chilled vegetables, half the toasted almonds, half of the fresh herbs and half of the dressing. Season to taste and add more dressing if needed. Garnish with remaining almonds, herbs and dressing.

VARIATION: Black Quinoa with Broccoli, Carrots and Summer Squash with Apple Cider Dressing (page 184). Toast quinoa before cooking

Broccoli, Black Quinoa, Pecan Salad

YIELD 10 SERVINGS

1 CUP/168 GRAMS

water	5 cups	1. 2 liters
black quinoa	$2\frac{1}{2}$ cups	420 grams
salt	$1\frac{1}{4}$ teaspoons	7.5 grams
bay leaves	3	3
ground black pepper	pinch	pinch
broccoli, 1-inch/2.5-centimeter pieces, blanched	5 cups	370 grams
pecans, toasted	2 cups	196 grams
chives, minced	4 teaspoons	4.5 grams
mint, minced	4 teaspoons	4.5 grams
Orange Mustard Dressing (page 182)	1 recipe	1 recipe

GARNISH

mint leaves, whole chives

Bring water to a boil. While the water heats, wash the quinoa well, rubbing the grains together to remove a natural bitter flavor that helps keep pests away. Drain well and add the quinoa, salt, bay leaves and pepper to boiling water. Simmer for 15 minutes, then remove from the heat. Fluff with a fork and allow to cool. Remove the bay leaves.

Combine the quinoa with broccoli and three-quarters of the pecans, chives and mint and half of the Orange Mustard dressing. Season to taste. Bear in mind that more dressing will be drizzled over the salad. Garnish with remaining pecans and herbs and dressing to taste.

Tabouli

YIELD 10 SERVINGS
$\frac{1}{2}$ CUP / 112 GRAMS

Tabouli prepared in the Middle East is often as much a salad of parsley as it is of cracked wheat,
also known as bulgur wheat. However, the amount of parsley used in
traditional methods may be overwhelming to a western palate.

A typical garnish of tomatoes, cucumbers, and chopped red onions or scallions is best when produce is at its peak in summer. For the cooler months I like to serve it garnished with roasted vegetables.

BASIC TABOULI MIXTURE

YIELD 10 SERVINGS
$\frac{1}{2}$ CUP / 112 GRAMS

bulgur (cracked wheat)	$2\frac{1}{2}$ cups	294 grams
salt	1 teaspoon	6 grams
boiling water	3 cups	720 grams
ground black pepper	pinch	pinch
chopped parsley	1 cup	56 grams
chopped fresh mint	$\frac{1}{2}$ cup	14 grams
red wine vinegar	2 tablespoons	30 milliliters
extra virgin olive oil	$\frac{1}{3}$ cup	80 milliliters
fresh lemon juice	$\frac{1}{2}$ cup	120 milliliters

Combine the bulgur, salt and boiling water in a bowl and let stand for 30 minutes until all water is absorbed. Stir in the remaining ingredients and season to taste. Garnish tabouli as traditional style or with roasted vegetables as follows.

Traditional-Style Tabouli

YIELD 10 SERVINGS

ABOUT 1 CUP/196 GRAMS WITH TABOULI

Traditionally ripe tomatoes would be chopped and added to the tabouli. If one intends to store the salad, whole cherry tomatoes will hold up better.

Basic Tabouli Mixture (see previous recipe)	5 cups	1.2 kilograms
cherry tomatoes	1 pint	448 grams
cucumbers, peeled, large dice	3 cups	420 grams
kalamata olives	1 pint	448 grams
red onions, fine dice	$1\frac{1}{4}$ cups	140 grams

Combine all ingredients and season to taste.

VARIATION: Use cooked and chilled couscous or quinoa in place of bulgur wheat. Try ripe plum tomatoes if you plan to chop the tomatoes. The Toasted Spice mixture used in the recipe for hummus makes a nice flavor booster to this recipe.

SERVE WITH: Toasted Spice Hummus (page 51), India-Style Flat Bread (page 353).

Tabouli with Roasted Vegetables

YIELD 10 SERVINGS
ABOUT 1 CUP/196 GRAMS WITH TABOULI

whole cherry tomatoes	1 pint	448 grams
olive oil	1 teaspoon	5 milliliters
garlic, minced	1 teaspoon	5 grams
Sesame Roasted Butternut Squash (page 204)	5 cups	840 grams
Oven Roasted Sweet Potatoes (page 203)	5 cups	840 grams
Basic Tabouli Mixture (page 306)	5 cups	1.2 kilograms

Toss cherry tomatoes with olive oil and garlic and sauté over medium high heat for about 3 minutes or until they are a little browned and just softened. Combine with all other ingredients.

VARIATION: Tabouli with Grilled or Broiled Red Peppers, Zucchini and Anise (page 212) or other roasted vegetables could be used in the recipe. For a more intensely flavored dish add Toasted Spices Hummus (page 51). Fresh spinach leaves or steamed and cooled kale can be used as a garnish.

SERVE WITH: Red Swiss Chard Sauté (page 194).

Double Corn Polenta with Three Sauces

YIELD 10 SERVINGS

ABOUT 1¼ CUPS/336 GRAMS

This traditional northern Italian dish can be served in as many different ways as the imagination will allow. The two basic ways are soft and hot from the pot or firm polenta which has been poured into a loaf pan or on a sheet pan to cool and then sliced or cut into various shapes, heated and served.

water	6 cups	1.42 liters
white miso	1 tablespoon	14 grams
salt	½ teaspoon	3 grams
pepper	pinch	pinch
yellow cornmeal	2 cups	336 grams
soy margarine	2 tablespoons	28 grams
fresh parsley, minced	½ cup	28 grams
corn kernels	1½ cups	189 grams
Soysage Pizzaiola (page 273)	3⅓ cups	800 milliliters
Spinach Pesto (page 140)	4 cups	820 grams
Cashew Crème (page 157)	1 cup	240 milliliters

Bring water, miso, salt and pepper to a boil. Using a wire whip, gradually stir in cornmeal. Reduce the heat and simmer polenta, stirring constantly for 10 to 15 minutes. The longer cooking time will produce a creamier texture. Stir in soy margarine, parsley and corn kernels. Season to taste. Serve hot and creamy soft-style polenta with sauce, or pour into a lightly oiled springform pan and chill until set.

Slice chilled polenta into 10 to 12 wedges, place on a lightly oiled baking sheet, cover and warm in a 325°F/160°C oven for 8 to 10 minutes. Heat Soysage Pizzaiola, and bring Spinach Pesto and Cashew Crème to room temperature. Sauce heated polenta with Soysage Pizzaiola, and garnish with Spinach Pesto and Cashew Crème.

SERVE WITH: Black-eyed Pea Salad (page 166), Cherry Tomatoes with Fresh Herbs (page 172), Ruby Grapefruit, Pomegranate and Assorted Greens (page 174), Avocado Orange and Red Onions (page 173).

Note: Try white, blue or red cornmeal in place of the yellow. Coarse yellow corn grits can be used for the recipe. Add 1 or 2 bay leaves to the water. Sometimes I find that certain cornmeal varieties are bitter and that 1 tablespoon/15 milliliters of maple syrup will improve the flavor.

For dishes like polenta I find that a heat diffuser or "flame tamer" gives a little extra protection if one is called away from the stove for a few minutes. A steam jacket kettle also can provide that same sort of protection. See also Polenta with Spinach Pesto (page 72). For a firmer polenta that is chilled and cut into shapes add ½ cup/84 grams more cornmeal to the recipe.

Almond Brown Rice Croquettes

YIELD 10 SERVINGS

3 CROQUETTES/252 GRAMS TOTAL WEIGHT

Well cooked rice works best for this recipe.

cooked brown rice	10 cups	2.24 kilograms
carrots, grated	1 cup	112 grams
onions, grated	1 cup	112 grams
toasted sesame oil	1 tablespoon	15 milliliters
almond butter	$\frac{1}{4}$ cup	60 grams
soy sauce	$\frac{1}{4}$ cup	60 milliliters
almond, coarsely ground		

Preheat oven to 350°F/180°C. Combine all ingredients except ground almonds until well mixed. Form into small barrel-shaped croquettes. Mixture should be moist and stick together. Roll croquettes in ground almonds to coat and place on a foil or parchment-lined sheet pan.

Bake for 10 minutes, then turn and bake for another 10 minutes.

VARIATION: Add chopped scallions, parsley or other fresh herbs to mixture. Miso can be used in place of soy sauce. Other nut and nut butters could be used.

SERVE WITH: Carrot Ginger Sauce or Carrot Beet Sauce (page 133).

Basic Vegetable Fried Rice

10 SERVINGS

ABOUT 2 CUPS/392 GRAMS

carrots, large dice	$2\frac{1}{2}$ cups	315 grams
sweet potatoes, large dice	$2\frac{1}{2}$ cups	315 grams
zucchini, large dice	$2\frac{1}{2}$ cups	343 grams
celery, large dice	$1\frac{1}{2}$ cups	280 grams
onions, large dice	1 cup	112 grams
peanut oil	2 tablespoons	30 milliliters
ginger, minced	2 tablespoons	28 grams
garlic, minced	2 tablespoons	28 grams
cooked brown rice	10 cups	2.25 kilograms
toasted sesame oil	2 teaspoons	10 milliliters
soy sauce	3 tablespoons	45 milliliters

GARNISH

chopped scallions	1 cup	56 grams
toasted black sesame seeds	$\frac{1}{4}$ cup	28 grams
dulse flakes (optional)	$\frac{1}{4}$ cup	12 grams

Choice of griddle, nonstick clad pan, wok, tilt skillet, black cast iron pan

Blanch the carrots, potatoes, zucchini and celery in boiling salted water, cool, drain well and set aside. Sauté the onions in peanut oil over medium-high heat for 2 minutes. Add the ginger and garlic and sauté for 1 minute.

Add the reserved blanched vegetables to the pan and sauté for 2 minutes. Add the rice to the pan and sprinkle with toasted sesame oil and soy sauce. Combine the rice and the vegetables, breaking up the rice with the edge of a spoon or spatula to separate the grains. Allow to brown to build flavor. Season to taste.

GARNISH WITH: Scallions, sesame seeds and dulse flakes if desired.

Note: Any combination of vegetables can be used including greens such as kale or collards, mushrooms or sea vegetables. Other types of rice such as brown basmati or a wild rice mixture could be used in the recipe. Other garnish options include toasted nuts and sunflower seeds or toasted nori sheets cut into small triangles.

Fried Rice with Mushrooms

YIELD 10 SERVINGS
ABOUT 2 CUPS/392 GRAMS

Use a variety of exotic mushrooms or just one type as desired.

carrots, large dice	$2\frac{1}{2}$ cups	315 grams
onions, large dice	1 cup	112 grams
peanut oil	2 tablespoons	30 milliliters
ginger, minced	2 tablespoons	28 grams
garlic, minced	2 tablespoons	28 grams
shiitake mushrooms	5 cups	448 grams
oyster mushrooms	5 cups	448 grams
cremini mushrooms	5 cups	448 grams
cooked brown rice	10 cups	2.25 kilograms
toasted sesame oil	2 teaspoons	10 milliliters
soy sauce	$\frac{1}{4}$ cup	60 milliliters

GARNISH
chopped scallions	1 cup	56 grams
toasted black sesame seeds	$\frac{1}{4}$ cup	28 grams
flaked dulse, optional	$\frac{1}{4}$ cup	12 grams

Griddle, nonstick pan, wok, tilt skillet, black cast iron pan

Sauté the carrots and onions in peanut oil over medium–high heat for 5 minutes. Add the ginger and garlic and sauté for one minute.

Add the mushrooms to the pan and sauté for 5 minutes. Add the rice to pan and sprinkle with toasted sesame oil and soy sauce. Combine the rice and the vegetables, breaking up the rice with the edge of a spoon or spatula to separate the grains. Allow to brown to build flavor. Season to taste.

Fried Rice with Tofu or Tempeh

YIELD 10 SERVINGS

ABOUT 2 CUPS/392 GRAMS

Start with the Basic Vegetable Fried Rice (page 311) and add hot Seasoned Baked Tofu (page 322) or Seasoned Baked Tempeh (page 334).

Basic Vegetable Fried Rice	20 cups	3.92 kilograms
Seasoned Baked Tofu (hot)	about 2 pounds	996 grams
or		
Seasoned Baked Tempeh (hot)	about 2 pounds	996 grams

Prepare basic fried rice, adding the hot tofu or tempeh at the point when the vegetables are sautéed with the onions, ginger and garlic. Proceed as for the basic recipe.

Vegetable Nori Maki Sushi

YIELD 10 SERVINGS

Nori sheets come in various grades, with the most expensive sheets being the ones without tears or holes. They are available not toasted, and are a dark green, almost black in color. Toasted sheets are golden green in color. To toast sheets, simply fan them back and forth over a gas or an electric burner until golden green and aromatic. Be careful not to overcook, as they will shrivel, or to let them catch fire.

water	$12\frac{1}{2}$ cups	3 liters
salt	1 teaspoon	6 grams
short-grain brown rice	5 cups	980 grams
brown rice vinegar	1 tablespoon	15 milliliters
scallions, thin diagonal	$\frac{1}{2}$ cup	28 grams
full nori sheets, toasted	10	10
cucumbers, peeled, seeded, julienned	$2\frac{1}{2}$ cups	350 grams
ume boshi pickled plum paste	1 tablespoon	15 grams
toasted black sesame seeds	$\frac{1}{4}$ cup	28 grams
pickled ginger	$\frac{1}{2}$ cup	70 grams
wasabi powder	1 tablespoon	6 grams
soy sauce	$\frac{1}{2}$ cup	120 milliliters

Bring water to a boil. Add salt and rice. Simmer covered for 45 minutes to 1 hour or until rice is tender and water is evaporated. If water is evaporated and rice is not done, add a little more hot water to the pot and continue to cook until done. The rice should be slightly sticky to help it hold together. When the rice is done stir in the brown rice vinegar and the scallions with a fork to fluff the rice. Allow rice to cool enough to handle.

Put about 1 cup/224 grams of the rice mixture on a nori sheet and flatten it down with moistened hands, leaving a 1 inch/2.5 centimeter border on the side farthest from you. Make a horizontal trough down the center of the rice, line the trough with some cucumbers and spread a little of the plum paste next to the cucumbers. Roll up the sushi pinwheel fashion, starting at the end closest to you. Place the roll seam side down on a plastic-wrap-covered pan, then form the rest of the rolls.

Using a very sharp knife, dip the knife in water, shake off excess water and slice the rolls into 6 sections each. Wipe off the knife and dip again to get nice, clean cuts. Sprinkle the tops of the sushi with black sesame seeds. Arrange on plates or a platter. Place pickled sushi ginger on each plate. Mix the wasabi powder with a few drops of water to make a paste and put a dab on each plate. Serve a little soy sauce on the side in a small ramekin or Japanese bowl.

SERVE WITH: Miso Soup (page 108), Arame with Carrots and Onions (page 209).

Brown Rice

YIELD 10 CUPS/SERVINGS
1 CUP/224 GRAMS

water	$12\frac{1}{2}$ cups	3 liters
salt	1 teaspoon	6 grams
short grain brown rice, rinsed	5 cups	980 grams

Bring water to a boil, add salt and rice. Simmer covered for 45 minutes to 1 hour or until rice is tender and water is evaporated. If water is evaporated and rice is not done, add a little more hot water to the pot and continue to cook until done. Fluff rice with a fork for looser grains.

VARIATION: For Brown Rice with Wheat Berries, rinse and soak wheat berries overnight, then cook with rice or use the quick-soak method for beans.

Jasmine or Basmati Rice

YIELD 10 SERVINGS
1 CUP/224 GRAMS

These two Asian rice varieties require less water than many of their western counterparts. Generally 1 cup/182 grams of rice to $1\frac{1}{4}$ cups/320 milliliters of water.

Jasmine or white basmati rice	5 cups	910 grams
water, plus water to rinse	$6\frac{1}{4}$ cups	1.5 liters
salt	1 teaspoon	6 grams

Rinse rice with cold water then drain. Combine rice with measured water and salt then bring to a boil. Cover and simmer for about 20 minutes or until rice is tender. Fluff rice with a fork before serving.

Note: One can sauté rice with $\frac{1}{2}$ cup onion, 2 teaspoons oil, and use vegetable bouillon in place of water for a pilaf-style rice. Brown basmati rice takes about 45 minutes to cook.

Wild Rice

YIELD 10 SERVINGS

1 CUP/224 GRAMS

water	12½ cups	3 liters
salt	1 teaspoon	6 grams
wild rice	5 cups	896 grams

Bring water to a boil, add salt and the rice. Boil for 10 minutes, then simmer covered for 45 minutes to 1 hour, or until the rice is tender and water is evaporated. If water is evaporated and the rice is not done add a little more hot water to the pot and continue to cook until done. Fluff the rice with a fork for looser grains.

After boiling 10 minutes the rice may be placed in a 350°F/170°C oven for 1 hour and 15 minutes.

Note: Couscous, millet, quinoa and plain brown rice can be tossed with any of the juice reduction sauces to boost flavor and color. I would not use the juice reduction sauces with the aromatic rice varieties so as not to lose their natural flavor.

Use a sweep scoop to serve grains, especially the cone-shaped type scoop.

Sunflower Seed and Roasted Kelp Condiment

YIELD 10 SERVINGS

1 TABLESPOON/ 7 GRAMS

toasted sunflower seeds	½ cup	56 grams
dry chopped kelp	⅓ cup	9 grams

Toast kelp in a 350°F/180°C oven for about 1½ minutes. Remove from the oven and allow to cool. Place the kelp in a blender and grind until well chopped, then add seeds and continue to grind until fine. With the machine turned off stir with a long-tined fork to help mixture blend.

Note: Use toasted sesame seeds, toasted hulled pumpkin seeds or soy sauce roasted almonds in place of the sunflower seeds. Use toasted nori sheets, nori flakes or dulse in place of the kelp.

Rutabaga with Spice Soy Sauce Marinade

1 OR 2 SLICES PER SERVING

Lisa Bishop and Peggy Kozinski, two cooks trained in macrobiotic cuisine, taught me these variations for soy sauce brined pickles.

rutabaga, sliced 1 inch $\times$ $1\frac{1}{2}$ inches $\times$ $\frac{1}{4}$ inch or 2.5 centimeters $\times$ 4 centimeters $\times$ .625 centimeter	1 cup	112 grams
star anise	1	1
fresh gingerroot, minced	2 tablespoons	10 grams
soy sauce	$\frac{1}{3}$ cup	80 milliliters
water	$\frac{1}{3}$ cup	80 milliliters

Put the rutabaga, star anise and ginger in a jar, ceramic or plastic container so that the soy sauce covers half of the vegetables and the water added will cover it completely. Place a small lid inside the jar on top of the rutabagas and press down to submerge the contents. Cover the jar with a piece of cheesecloth or a paper towel or napkin and secure with a string or a rubber band. Let set at room temperature for about 48 hours. This process will be hastened in summer and retarded in winter. Check after first day to make sure all the vegetable slices are still covered by the marinade. Rutabagas should be thoroughly marinated. To serve, you may wish to remove the rutabagas from the marinade and rinse them off to take away some of the saltiness if they are going to be served as a garnish on the side. They may also be cut into julienne or finely diced to sprinkle on top of grain dishes.

Note: Onions blanched in boiling water for about 10 seconds can be drained and placed in this marinade for same-day use.

One star of star anise equals about 1 teaspoon/2 grams. Marinade may be used a second time for different vegetables such as carrots.

CHAPTER ELEVEN

Alternative Protein-Based Main Dishes

The recipes in this chapter are made with foods

developed to provide alternative plant-based

sources of protein in the diet. These dishes

sometimes provide the taste or texture of those

non-vegetarian foods being replaced.

From a history that dates back hundreds of years to Asia and the invention of tofu and then later to Indonesia for tempeh, we can observe some basic reasons for the development of these soy-based foods.

One reason for people to develop these protein-rich processed foods was their shortage of fuel. These early soy foods provided a way for people to obtain the nuritional benefits of the soybean without using as much energy as it takes to cook the whole beans.

Another reason for the evolution this type of cooking was religious motivation. Many of the major religions in Asia promoted a vegetarian diet. As the royalty and other leaders adopted these faiths, their chefs developed a cuisine that used soy products to mimic dishes formerly made with flesh foods.

Another group to pioneer the early western varieties of alternative protein foods are the Seventh Day Adventists. They serve vegetarian cuisine in many settings including hospitals and restaurants, and have developed many types of meat analogs that their clients can purchase and use in their own kitchens.

Today we find many reasons for the proliferation of these protein alternatives. Their demand usually corresponds to the many reasons that people adopt a vegetarian diet. Not to be overlooked is the interest in global cooking in general that has culminated in the development of numerous fusion styles of cuisine. The market for vegetarian products has striven to keep pace with these developments.

Modern interpretations of dishes that appeal to the appetites of those raised on traditional western fare have been formulated to satisfy those on a transition diet or for people who want to try something new. By using a combination of ancient ingredients from the Orient and also modern technology, items such as veggie burgers, vegetarian hot dogs, and wheat meat creations have emerged. Also, value-added products such as smoky cajun spice tofu or Thai-style tofu, tofu salad and marinated tempeh, tempeh burgers and tempeh bacon are available.

Be aware, however, that some people follow a vegetarian diet don't care for these meat analogs and that it is important to identify these guests' preferences before you offer them any of these alternatives. For this group of guests, tofu and tempeh and perhaps even seitan, being traditional vegetarian foods, are less likely to offend.

For those who enjoy the meat-analog style preparations there are several frozen products that include burgers, sausage-style links, patties and in unformed bulk, vegetarian ham and even vegetarian shrimp. There are dry mixes that can be turned into burgers, non-meatloaf and non-meatballs, tacos, sloppy Joe sandwiches and chili. The frozen burgers can be defrosted and mixed with bread crumbs and tomato sauce and formed into non-meatloaf and non-meatballs.

TOFU When I stopped cooking meat, fish and poultry I found myself faced with a big gap in the "center of the plate." Traditional and classical training as a chef taught me to think about a protein as the starting point of a dish from which one decided upon a cooking method, a sauce, a starch and vegetables for garnish.

The first alternative vegetable-based protein source I experimented with was tofu. The first time I purchased it, I put it in the refrigerator and left it there until it had swollen up, then threw it into the trash. Having enjoyed bean curd dishes in Asian restaurants I was aware of the potential for this soybean cheese. Reading about tofu further revealed it to have a long and sometimes noble lineage with enough different presentations to impress even Escoffier. So, I had to overcome my fear of tofu and learn how to work with it in a way that would fit my cuisine.

Pressing Tofu: Tofu may need to be pressed in order to remove excess moisture, which will firm the texture and make it easier to work with. To press tofu, place the blocks in a pan, place another pan on top and evenly distribute some weight in the pan. The weight could be a stack of pans or some plastic bottles filled with water, as long as it provides pressure without squashing the bean curd flat. This process can be done for as little as 20 minutes or as long as overnight. Drain off the liquid that is squeezed out. A perforated pan placed under the tofu and over another pan works well because it drains the liquid off and catches it.

The next step in readying the tofu to cook is to season it, which will give it some underlying flavor. I was taught to fry the tofu to get some texture but have since found that by baking cubes of tofu on a sheet pan in the oven, especially a convection oven, that stove-top burners are freed up for other tasks and that the baking can be done with much less fat. The tofu can also be sliced marinated and breaded, if desired, and baked. Without pressing and cooking the tofu before adding to a recipe it can end up as unappealing scrambled tofu.

TEMPEH The Indonesian native specialty tempeh has a long heritage and provides the protein of soy as a cultured whole bean product. The original all-soybean style has been expanded upon by American tempeh makers to include varieties made with three beans and three grains or soy with three grains, vegetable and sea vegetable add-ins and burgers made from their own recipes.

Tempeh benefits from marinating or seasoning much the same as tofu. While tempeh has more texture than tofu it still gains from cooking that will crisp and firm it further.

SEITAN Seitan is the Japanese name for a protein alternative made from wheat gluten. The traditional method involves a lengthy process that first has one prepare a dough from a high-gluten wheat flour. The dough is allowed to rest, then it is washed under cool water to remove all the starch from the dough, retaining only the gluten.

Seasoned Baked Tofu

YIELD 10 SERVINGS

This treatment for tofu adds flavor and texture and renders it recipe-ready. Other complementary seasoning could be added, such as a little curry power when adding the finished tofu to an East Indian-style recipe. The baked tofu pieces can be added to vegetable, pasta or grain-based dishes or as a garnish for salads.

tofu, firm or extra-firm	2 pounds	900 grams
soy sauce	$\frac{1}{3}$ cup	80 milliliters
toasted sesame oil	1 tablespoon	15 milliliters
garlic, crushed	2 teaspoons	10 grams
gingerroot	1 tablespoon	15 grams

Preheat oven to 400°F/200°C. Remove the tofu from the package and rinse. If the tofu crumbles easily, press it to remove excess moisture. Cut each block of tofu into $\frac{3}{4}$-inch/2-centimeter cubes. Toss the tofu with soy sauce, toasted sesame oil, garlic, and ginger. Spread out tofu on a baking sheet and bake for about 15 minutes. Tofu is now recipe-ready or may be served as is, sprinkled on top of salads, grain or vegetable dishes.

Note: Other shapes may be cut and marinated for different presentations. Large slices can be used for sandwiches and triangles or smaller square or rectangular slices work well for plate presentations. Add a few drops of liquid smoke to marinate. For crisper tofu increase temperature or bake longer. To sauce the Seasoned Baked Tofu, use 1 or 2 batches of sauce per batch of baked tofu. The following sauces could be used: Cashew Butter Sauce with Mustard and Capers and other Cashew Butter Sauces (pages 125–128), Thai Coconut Sauce (page 144), Sweet and Sour Sauce (page 142), Vegetable Juice Demi-glaze (page 150).

Tofu Salad Spread

YIELD 10 SERVINGS
$\frac{3}{4}$ CUP/168 GRAMS

Tofu salad spread can be served in any manner which would be appropriate for serving egg salad such as on a bed of salad greens, on a tomato half or in a sandwich.

tofu, extra-firm	2 pounds	900 grams
carrots, grated	1 cup	112 grams
celery, fine dice	1 cup	112 grams
soy-based egg-less mayonnaise	1 cup	224 grams
parsley, minced	$\frac{1}{4}$ cup	14 grams
grated onion	2 tablespoons	14 grams
celery seeds	$\frac{1}{2}$ teaspoon	2 grams
prepared mustard, country style	$2\frac{1}{2}$ teaspoons	12.5 milliliters
salt	$\frac{1}{4}$ teaspoon	1.5 grams
ground black pepper	pinch	pinch
lemon juice	1 teaspoon	5 milliliters

Cut each pound of tofu into 8 cubes. Steam or cook in boiling water for 5 minutes. Drain and chill.

Combine the remaining salad ingredients. Mash the tofu by hand with a potato masher or for larger batches, use the dough hook of a mixing machine. Combine well with the dressing mixture. Season to taste.

SERVE WITH: Plated with lettuce, tomato, sprouts, and/or toasted seeds, with Broccoli Couscous Almond Salad (page 163), or in pita or on other bread for a sandwich.

Savory Tofu Salad

YIELD 10 SERVINGS
$\frac{3}{4}$ CUP/154 GRAMS

This is a chunky-style tofu salad that can be plated as a main course or be used on a cold buffet or salad bar.

Seasoned Baked Tofu (page 322)	2 pounds	900 grams
soy sauce	4 teaspoons	20 milliliters
celery, fine dice	2 cups	224 grams
soy-based egg-less mayonnaise	$1\frac{1}{3}$ cups	280 grams
dill pickles, fine dice	$\frac{1}{2}$ cup	56 grams
parsley, minced	$\frac{1}{4}$ cup	14 grams
prepared mustard, country style	4 teaspoons	20 milliliters
ground black pepper	pinch	pinch
lemon juice	1 teaspoon	5 milliliters
GARNISH		
almonds, sliced and toasted	$\frac{1}{2}$ cup	50 grams
cranberries, dried	$\frac{1}{2}$ cup	56 grams
lettuce, attractive leaves	10	10

Combine all salad ingredients. Season to taste. Serve on a bed of lettuce and garnish with toasted almonds and dried cranberries.

SERVE WITH: Rice Salad Medley with Wild, Japonica, and Wehani (page 168), Asparagus with Strawberry Dressing (page 164).

Note: Toasted sunflower seeds can be used in place of the almond garnish. Add a few drops of liquid smoke to the marinade for tofu or use purchased smoked tofu.

Blackened Tofu

YIELD 10 SERVINGS

A technique made famous by New Orleans chef Paul Prudhomme, it made such an impact that for a time in the 1980s it was hard to find a menu without a "blackened" item on it. The savory effect delivered by this method adapts well to slices of marinated tofu.

tofu, extra-firm, 20 slices	$2\frac{1}{2}$ pounds	1.12 kilograms
MARINADE		
soy sauce	$\frac{1}{4}$ cup	60 milliliters
toasted sesame oil	1 teaspoon	5 milliliters
garlic, crushed	1 teaspoon	5 grams
liquid smoke	4 drops	4 drops
black pepper	pinch	pinch
cornstarch	1 tablespoon	8 grams
BREADING MIXTURE		
fresh bread crumbs	2 cups	168 grams
dried thyme	2 teaspoons	4 grams
garlic powder	2 teaspoons	4 grams
fresh parsley, minced	2 tablespoons	7 grams
paprika	4 teaspoons	8 grams
salt	$\frac{1}{2}$ teaspoon	3 grams
black pepper	$\frac{1}{2}$ teaspoon	1 gram
white pepper	$\frac{1}{4}$ teaspoon	.5 gram
cayenne pepper	$\frac{1}{4}$ teaspoon	.5 gram

Rinse each block of tofu and slice across the narrow width into 10 slices. Place on paper towel to absorb excess moisture.

Combine the marinade ingredients on a sheet pan, then lay the tofu slice into the marinade. Turn the slices once or twice as needed to cover well with the marinade.

Combine the breading mixture and dredge the tofu slices, coating them well. Lightly oil and preheat a griddle over high heat. Place the tofu slices on the griddle and blacken the first side, then turn slices over, reduce heat to medium and allow the second side to brown thoroughly.

SERVE WITH: Tarragon Shallot Cashew Butter Sauce (page 129), Oven-Roasted Sweet Potatoes with Soy Sauce (page 203) and Brazilian-Style Greens (page 196).

Note: A key to the success of the recipe is to get good color quickly without turning the food to charcoal.

Tofu Boursin Style

This treatment of tofu yields a product that can be combined with other ingredients as a filling or shaped into individual portions and served as the main plate component. I have found that for any savory dish for which the tofu is puréed the texture is much improved by cooking and cooling the tofu first. The exception to this rule would be for the use of silken tofu in desserts and sauces.

tofu, extra-firm	2 pounds	896 grams
garlic, crushed	2 teaspoons	10 grams
white miso	2 teaspoons	10 grams
salt	$\frac{1}{2}$ teaspoon	3 grams
ground black pepper	pinch	pinch
extra virgin olive oil	2 teaspoons	10 milliliters
lemon juice	2 teaspoons	10 milliliters
maple syrup	2 teaspoons	10 milliliters
fresh parsley, minced	$\frac{1}{2}$ cup	28 grams

Press the tofu. Cut tofu into 1-inch/25-centimeter cubes. Blanch in boiling water for 3 minutes. Drain and chill. If the tofu seems wet place it on paper towels to absorb excess moisture. Place the chilled tofu in the food processor and process until smooth. Add the garlic, miso, salt, pepper, olive oil, lemon juice and syrup and process until mixed. Pulse in parsley. Season to taste. The boursin-style tofu can be put into small muffin forms that have been individually lined with plastic wrap.

The bottom of the muffin tins could be filled with a choice of (for 10):

sliced or chopped olives	$\frac{1}{2}$ cup	56 grams
softened sundried tomatoes	10	10
crushed black peppercorns	1 tablespoon	7 grams
toasted sesame and cumin seeds	3 tablespoons	21 grams
toasted almonds and a little lemon zest	$\frac{1}{2}$ cup	56 grams
smoked chopped dulse	2 tablespoons	2.5 grams

SERVE WITH: Grilled Vegetable Salad (page 170), Carrot and Parsnip Salad with Smoked Dulse (page 171), Sea Czar Salad with Blackened Tofu (page 175).

Note: The Tofu Boursin Style can be used for lasagna or manicotti in place of ricotta cheese. It is also great served with ripe pears and figs.

Tofu Pecan Cutlets

YIELD 10 SERVINGS

2 SLICES PER SERVING

tofu	$2\frac{1}{2}$ pounds	1.12 kilograms

MARINADE

soy sauce	$\frac{1}{4}$ cup	60 milliliters
sherry wine	2 tablespoons	30 milliliters
black pepper	pinch	pinch

THREE-STAGE BREADING PROCESS

all-purpose flour	1 cup	140 grams
garlic powder	1 teaspoon	2 grams
salt	$\frac{1}{2}$ teaspoon	3 grams
pepper	pinch	pinch
water	$1\frac{1}{2}$ cups	360 milliliters

BREAD CRUMB MIXTURE

fresh bread crumbs, unseasoned	$2\frac{1}{2}$ cups	252 grams
ground pecans	$\frac{1}{2}$ cup	56 grams
fresh parsley, minced	$\frac{1}{4}$ cup	14 grams
dried basil	2 teaspoons	4 grams

Preheat oven to 400°F/200°C. Rinse each block of tofu and slice across the narrow width into 8 slices for 20 slices total. Place on paper towel to absorb excess moisture.

Combine the marinade ingredients on a sheet pan, then lay the tofu slice into the marinade. Turn the slices once or twice as needed to cover well with the marinade.

In a bowl combine the flour, garlic powder, salt and pepper. Remove $\frac{1}{4}$ cup/35 grams flour mixture to another bowl and gradually whisk in water until smooth. In a third bowl combine bread crumb mixture ingredients.

Dredge the tofu slices first in the flour mixture. Shake off the excess flour and dip into the flour and water mixture. Shake off excess and dredge in the bread crumb mixture and set on a lightly oiled baking sheet.

Bake the cutlets for 10 minutes, then turn them over with a spatula and bake for 8 to 10 minutes longer or until golden.

Tofu with Artichokes and Capers

YIELD 10 SERVINGS
3 SLICES EACH

My wife, Heidi, who enjoys dishes prepared "française" style and also loves capers, encouraged me to develop this dish. The egg replacer and turmeric help to create the illusion of egg-batter-dipped scallopini.

extra-firm tofu, 30 slices	3 pounds	1.35 kilograms
soy sauce	$\frac{1}{4}$ cup	60 milliliters
lemon juice	2 tablespoons	30 milliliters
maple syrup	1 tablespoon	15 milliliters
all-purpose white flour	2 cups	280 grams
ground black pepper	pinch	pinch
egg replacer	$\frac{3}{4}$ cup	100 grams
turmeric	$\frac{1}{2}$ teaspoon	1 gram
rice beverage	$2\frac{1}{2}$ cups	600 milliliters

SAUCE

marinated artichoke hearts, large dice	$1\frac{1}{2}$ cups	504 grams
capers	3 tablespoons	21 grams
artichoke marinade	$1\frac{1}{2}$ cups	360 milliliters
vegetable stock	$1\frac{1}{2}$ cups	360 milliliters
white zinfandel wine	$1\frac{1}{2}$ cups	360 milliliters
olive oil	1 tablespoon	15 milliliters
garlic	1 teaspoon	5 grams
soy margarine	1 tablespoon	14 grams
fresh parsley	$\frac{1}{2}$ cup	28 grams
fresh ground black pepper	pinch	pinch
olive oil for frying		

Combine the soy sauce, half of the lemon juice, maple syrup and pinch of ground black pepper on a sheet pan. Place the sliced tofu in marinade and turn a few times to coat. Reserve 2 tablespoons of flour and place the remainder in a bowl. Whisk together the egg replacer, turmeric, rice beverage and half the parsley. Set these aside.

Combine the reserved flour with diced artichoke hearts and capers and set aside. Put artichoke marinade, vegetable stock, and white zinfandel wine in a sauce pan and reduce by about 25 percent. Combine the olive oil, garlic and soy margarine and set aside.

Place slices of marinated tofu into the bowl of flour to coat, then into the egg replacer mixture, back to the flour and through the egg replacer, coating again so that each piece receives a double coating. At the halfway point you may need to sift the flour and add some more to the bowl. Place on a pan until all tofu slices have been done.

Heat a large nonstick skillet or fry pan over medium-high heat. Drizzle in some olive oil and fry the tofu on each side until golden brown. Place the cooked tofu on a platter and keep warm in a low-temperature oven.

When tofu frying is completed, wipe the pan with some paper towels. Add the olive oil, garlic and margarine mixture and sauté until the garlic it starts to brown. Add the reduced wine mixture, the artichokes, capers and the parsley. Simmer until lightly thickened. Season to taste. Serve the sauce over the tofu.

SERVE WITH: Garlic Roasted Potatoes with Rosemary (page 208), Greens Sautéed with Ginger (page 195), and Wild, Japonica, and Wehani Rice Medley (page 168).

Tofu Scrambled Colombian Style

YIELD 10 SERVINGS

$\frac{1}{2}$ CUP/112 GRAMS

This dish is based on a South American breakfast specialty from Colombia. The tofu is crumbled, seasoned and scrambled along with scallions and tomatoes to duplicate the texture of the eggs used in the traditional recipe.

TOFU MIXTURE

extra-firm tofu	2 pounds	896 grams
cornstarch	2 tablespoons	16 grams
curry powder	$\frac{1}{2}$ teaspoon	1 gram
turmeric	$\frac{1}{2}$ teaspoon	1 gram
salt	$\frac{1}{2}$ teaspoon	3 grams
ground black pepper	pinch	pinch
soy sauce	2 teaspoons	10 milliliters
lemon juice	4 teaspoons	20 milliliters
maple syrup	2 teaspoons	10 milliliters

GARNISH

scallions, thin bias cut	1 cup	56 grams
cherry tomatoes	2 cups	448 grams
canola oil	1 tablespoon	15 milliliters
soy margarine	2 teaspoons	10 grams

Crumble the tofu and mix in all other tofu mixture ingredients. Sauté the scallions and tomatoes in the canola oil over medium heat for about 5 minutes or until the scallions are just starting to brown. Pierce the cherry tomatoes to let out the hot liquid inside and prevent burns when biting into them. Season with salt and pepper to taste. Set scallions and tomatoes aside.

In a nonstick skillet sauté the tofu mixture in margarine for about 5 minutes. Add half of the sautéed vegetables and cook a few minutes longer. Season to taste. Garnish with remaining scallions and tomatoes.

SERVE WITH: Muffins (pages 362–366), or Peach and Pecan Corn Bread (page 352).

Note: If the cherry tomatoes are too large to bite into easily, cut them in half and add them to the pan after the scallions have been sautéing for a few minutes.

Tofu and Duxelles in Fillo

YIELD 10 SERVINGS

1 PASTRY ABOUT 6 OUNCES/168 GRAMS

The tofu and the Mushroom Duxelles can be prepared ahead and assembled before baking.
I find it necessary to bake the pastry once it is filled to prevent the bottom
from becoming soggy and falling out.

tofu, firm or extra-firm	2 pounds	900 grams
soy sauce	$\frac{1}{4}$ tablespoon	90 milliliters
toasted sesame oil	2 teaspoons	10 milliliters
garlic, crushed	1 teaspoon	2.33 grams
ground black pepper	pinch	pinch
fillo sheets	10	10
soy margarine	2 tablespoons	28 grams
olive oil	3 tablespoons	45 milliliters
Mushroom Duxelles (page 265)	$1\frac{1}{4}$ cups	300 grams

Preheat oven to 400°F/200°C. Remove the tofu from the container and rinse. If the tofu crumbles easily, press to remove excess moisture. Cut each block of tofu into 10 slices for a total 20 slices of tofu. For a marinade, combine the soy sauce, sesame oil, garlic and black pepper on a baking sheet, then lay the tofu slices into the mixture. Turn the slices once or twice as needed to coat well with the marinade. Bake for about 15 minutes. Allow the tofu to cool before wrapping in fillo.

Preheat oven to 400°F/200°C. In a small pan melt the margarine and oil together. To assemble, lay out a sheet of fillo pastry with a narrow side towards you. Brush each sheet with some of the margarine and oil blend. Fold about one-fifth of the fillo sheet up and away from you to make a double layer of pastry. Place a piece of the baked tofu on the center of the folded fillo and spread about 2 tablespoons/30 grams of the Mushroom Duxelles across the top of the tofu. Place a second piece of tofu over the duxelles. Fold over the sides of the fillo and roll up the pastry. Place the filled pastry seam side down on a baking sheet and brush the top and sides with a little margarine and oil blend. Repeat the process until all 10 are completed. Bake the tofu-wrapped pastries for 5 minutes, then lower the oven temperature to 325°F/170°C and bake for another 8 to 10 minutes.

SERVE WITH: Vegetable Gravy (page 147), or Wild Mushroom Sauce (page 148), and Brazilian Style Greens (page 196) or Red Swiss Chard Sauté with Garlic (page 194), Sesame Roasted Butternut Squash (page 204).

Tofu Sundried Tomato Sauscisse

YIELD 10 SERVINGS

5 OUNCES/140 GRAMS

This style of tofu presentation was inspired by the pioneering work of Chef Ron Pickarski. By working with the idea for the base mixture and changing seasonings, many different types of tofu sauscisse can be achieved.

tofu	$1\frac{1}{2}$ pounds	672 grams
water	$1\frac{1}{2}$ cups	360 milliliters
sundried tomatoes	$1\frac{1}{2}$ cups	136 grams
tvp	$1\frac{1}{2}$ cups	105 grams
agar flakes	1 tablespoon	2.5 grams
extra virgin olive oil	1 tablespoon	15 milliliters
raisins	$\frac{1}{4}$ cup	28 grams
garlic, minced	1 tablespoon	15 grams
fennel seeds	1 tablespoon	7 grams
chili powder	1 teaspoon	2 grams
salt	$\frac{3}{4}$ teaspoon	4.5 grams
ground black pepper	$\frac{1}{4}$ teaspoon	.5 gram
liquid smoke, hickory flavor	5 to 6 drops	5 to 6 drops
cornstarch	$\frac{1}{4}$ cup	32 grams
fresh parsley	$\frac{1}{2}$ cup	28 grams
toasted pine nuts	$\frac{1}{4}$ cup	28 grams

Rinse and drain the tofu, cut into a very large dice and set aside.

Bring water to a boil, add the sundried tomatoes, cover, remove from heat and allow tomatoes to soften for 10 minutes. Reserving the liquid, strain the tomatoes, slice them into strips and set aside.

Return the pan with the tomato liquid back to the heat and bring to a boil. Add the diced tofu to the pan, cover and cook for 2 minutes. Add the tvp, agar, oil, raisins, garlic, fennel, chili powder, salt, pepper, and liquid smoke to the pan, stir well, cover and remove from the heat. When all moisture has been absorbed put the mixture into a food processor. Add the cornstarch and half of the reserved sundried tomatoes and pulse until smooth. Season to taste, then add the remaining tomatoes, parsley and the pine nuts to the food processor and pulse a couple of times to incorporate these ingredients, leaving their size intact to add texture to the sauscisse. To form a sauscisse you will need:

plastic wrap
wire twist ties
aluminum foil
a wet towel or a French bread loaf pan

Preheat oven to 400°F/200°C. To make the sauscisse, put about 2 cups/504 grams onto a sheet of plastic wrap, forming a rough 8-inch/20-centimeter shape, then cover and roll up with the plastic wrap. Twist one end shut and secure with half of a twist tie. Twist the other end of the plastic wrap to condense the filling, making a firm, solid sauscisse. Rolling the sauscisse will also help to form an even product. Secure second end of plastic wrap with a twist tie. Roll up the sauscisse in a piece of aluminum foil and tighten the ends to further shape, firm and secure the filling. Repeat 2 more times to make 3 sauscisses.

Line the French loaf pan with a wet towel and place the sauscisses onto the towel to provide a cushion while it bakes. If this type of pan is unavailable, wrap the wet towel with aluminum foil, place it on a baking pan and form it to provide cushion and shape to the sauscisse as it bakes. Without these precautions the sauscisse will bake flat on the bottom. Bake for about 50 minutes or until the internal temperature reads 165°F/75°C.

Allow the sauscisse 15 minutes at room temperature to set up. Slice with a knife that has been dipped in hot water and shaken off. Wipe clean and dip between slices. Serve three slices per serving.

SERVE WITH: Sauce with either Roast Tomato and Garlic Sauce with Dulse and Lime (page 146), or Spinach Pecan Pesto (page 140), or both. Serve with Golden Mashed Potatoes with Caramelized Onions (page 205), Greens Sautéed with Ginger (page 195), Orange Braised Butternut Squash with Ginger and Garlic (page 199), Mesclun Mix with Smoked Dulce and Warm Shiitake Dressing (page 175).

Seasoned Baked Tempeh

YIELD 10 SERVINGS
ABOUT 3 OUNCES/84 GRAMS

This treatment for tempeh adds flavor and texture and renders it recipe-ready. Other complimentary seasoning could be added, such as a little curry power when adding the finished tofu to an East Indian-style recipe. The baked tempeh pieces can be added to vegetable, pasta or grain-based dishes or used as a garnish for salads.

tempeh	2 pounds	900 grams
soy sauce	6 tablespoons	90 milliliters
toasted sesame oil	4 teaspoons	20 milliliters
garlic, crushed	1 teaspoon	5 grams
gingerroot	1 tablespoon	7 grams

Preheat oven to 375°F/190°C. Cut, the tempeh lengthwise into strips, then cut across the strips to yield $\frac{3}{4}$-inch/2-centimeter pieces. Toss the tempeh with soy sauce, oil, garlic and ginger. Spread out the tempeh on a baking sheet and bake 10 to 12 minutes. Tempeh is now recipe-ready or may be used as is sprinkled on top of salads, grain or vegetable dishes.

VARIATION: To sauce the Seasoned Baked Tempeh, use 1 or 2 batches of sauce per batch of baked tempeh. Also, one can add some extra seasoning to the tempeh before baking to match the sauce flavor profile.

To serve tempeh with Thai Coconut Sauce (page 144), add the following seasoning to tempeh before baking

ground coriander	1 tablespoon	7 grams
ground cumin	1 tablespoon	7 grams
ground cardamom	1 teaspoon	2.33 grams

Tempeh may be placed on skewers after it is baked and heated on a grill.

Other sauces to serve over the seasoned tempeh include but are not limited to:

Cashew Butter Sauce with Mustard and Capers (page 126)
Tarragon Shallot Cashew Butter Sauce (page 129)
Sweet and Sour Sauce (page 142)
Vegetable Juice Demi-glaze (page 152).

Note: Other shapes may be cut and marinated for different presentations. Large slices can be used for sandwiches, triangles or smaller square or rectangular slices work well for plate presentations. Tempeh makes a great kebob item.

Tangy Tempeh Salad

YIELD 10 SERVINGS

$\frac{3}{4}$ CUP/154 GRAMS

*This is a chunky-style tempeh salad that can be plated as a main course or
be used on a cold buffet or salad bar.*

Seasoned Baked Tempeh (page 334)	2 pounds	900 grams
soy sauce	4 teaspoons	20 milliliters
celery, fine dice	2 cups	224 grams
soy-based egg-less mayonnaise	$1\frac{1}{3}$ cup	280 grams
dill pickles, fine dice	$\frac{1}{2}$ cup	56 grams
dill pickle juice	2 tablespoons	30 milliliters
black olives, sliced	$\frac{2}{3}$ cup	84 grams
carrot, grated	1 cup	112 grams
parsley, minced	$\frac{1}{4}$ cup	14 grams
prepared mustard, country style	4 teaspoons	20 milliliters
ground black pepper	pinch	pinch

Combine all salad ingredients. Season to taste. Serve on a bed of greens or use to fill pita pockets.

SERVE WITH: Broccoli Couscous Almond Salad (page 163).

Sweet and Sour Tempeh

YIELD 10 SERVINGS

$1\frac{1}{2}$ CUPS/210 GRAMS

All the components for this dish can be assembled in advance and then brought up to temperature when the items are sautéed with the ginger and garlic.

carrots, $\frac{1}{2}$-inch/1.25-centimeter slices	2 cups	252 grams
onions, quartered and sliced	1 cup	112 grams
broccoli, 1-inch/2.5-centimeter pieces	2 cups	147 grams
sweet red peppers, halved and sliced	1 cup	112 grams
celery, sliced	1 cup	112 grams
canola oil	1 tablespoon	15 milliliters
garlic, minced	1 tablespoon	7 grams
ginger, minced	1 tablespoon	7 grams
Seasoned Baked Tempeh (page 334), 2 recipes	2 pounds	896 grams
Sweet and Sour Sauce (page 142), 1 recipe	1 quart	760 milliliters
black sesame seeds	1 tablespoon	7 grams

Bring a pot of salted water to a boil. Add the carrots and onions, cook for 3 minutes, add the broccoli and red peppers for 2 minutes, then stir in the celery. Drain the blanched vegetables, saving the fortified water if desired, and shock them under cold running water to preserve the color and stop the cooking process. Shake off the excess water and allow to drain well.

Return the pot to a medium heat and add the canola oil, garlic and ginger. Sauté for about 1 minute or until just starting to brown. Add the blanched vegetables and tempeh and toss well to coat and flavor with the ginger and garlic mixture. Add the Sweet and Sour Sauce and cook until heated through. Season to taste with salt, pepper and soy sauce.

GARNISH: Use black sesame seeds to garnish.

VARIATION: For Sweet and Sour Tofu use Seasoned Baked Tofu (page 322), in place of the tempeh.

SERVE WITH: Serve over cooked noodles, rice or other grain, along with Mesclun Mix with Smoked Dulse and Warm Shiitake Dressing (page 175).

Tempeh with Clementines and Cabernet Citrus Sauce

YIELD 10 SERVINGS

3 TRIANGLES/91 GRAMS

For an attractive presentation cut the tempeh into 32 triangles about $\frac{1}{3}$ inch/.8 centimeters thick and then put into marinade. Clementines are cousins to tangerines, which could be used in their place in the recipe.

tempeh, 32 triangles, $\frac{1}{3}$ inch/ .8 centimeters thick	2 pounds	896 grams
soy sauce	5 tablespoons	75 milliliters
maple syrup	1 teaspoon	5 milliliters
ground coriander	4 teaspoons	8 grams
ground black pepper	pinch	pinch
cabernet sauvignon red wine	2 cups	480 milliliters
lime juice	1 tablespoon	15 milliliters
orange juice	1 cup	240 milliliters
olive oil	2 tablespoons	30 milliliters
garlic	1 tablespoon	15 grams
soy margarine	1 tablespoon	14 grams
fresh tarragon, minced	$\frac{1}{4}$ cup	28 grams
clementine, segments, 30	16 ounces	448 grams

Toss the tempeh triangles with soy sauce, maple syrup, coriander and black pepper and set aside to marinate. Put the cabernet wine, lime juice and orange juice in a saucepan and reduce by one-half.

In a large skillet, sauté the marinated tempeh in some of the olive oil over medium-high heat until brown on both sides, then remove to a warm platter. Continue to sauté the tempeh with olive oil until all are browned. Keep the tempeh warm.

Wipe the pan out with a paper towel, add garlic and margarine and sauté until garlic is just starting to brown. Add the reduced wine and juice mixture and cook until it is slightly thickened. Stir in tarragon and clementine segments. Simmer about a minute, then season to taste.

Heat the tempeh and serve 3 triangles, 3 clementine segments and sauce.

SERVE WITH: Mashed Rutabagas and Parsnips (page 197), Red Swiss Chard Sauté with Garlic (page 194).

Tempeh Mushroom Vegetable Cobbler

YIELD 10 SERVINGS

tempeh, large dice	6 cups	675 grams
button mushrooms	5 cups	450 grams
onions, large dice	2 cups	224 grams
carrots, large dice	2 cups	252 grams
soy sauce	3 tablespoons	45 milliliters
olive oil	3 tablespoons	45 milliliters
sherry wine	3 tablespoons	45 milliliters
fresh thyme, 4–inch/ 10–centimeter sprig	1	1
bay leaves	2	2
salt	pinch	pinch
ground black pepper	pinch	pinch
all-purpose white flour	3 tablespoons	25 grams
vegetable stock	4 cups	960 milliliters
fresh parsley, minced	$\frac{1}{2}$ cup	28 grams

Preheat oven to 400°F/200°C. Put the tempeh, mushrooms, onions, carrots, soy sauce, oil, sherry, thyme, bay leaves, salt and pepper in a roasting pan, toss well together and roast for 20 minutes, stirring occasionally. Stir in the flour, then the stock and half of the parsley; reserve the parsley for cobbler topping. Return to the oven for an additional 10 minutes. Remove from the oven, take out the thyme sprig and bay leaves and season to taste. Set aside and prepare the cobbler topping.

SAVORY COBBLER TOPPING

DRY INGREDIENTS:

all purpose white flour	2 cups	280 grams
whole wheat pastry flour	1 cup	140 grams
baking powder	1 tablespoon	15.5 grams
reserved fresh parsley, chopped	$\frac{1}{4}$ cup	14 grams
salt	$\frac{1}{2}$ teaspoon	3 grams
ground black pepper	pinch	pinch

WET INGREDIENTS:

maple syrup	$\frac{1}{4}$ cup	60 milliliters
water	$1\frac{1}{2}$ cups	360 milliliters
olive oil	$\frac{1}{4}$ cup	60 milliliters
apple sauce	$\frac{3}{4}$ cup	180 milliliters
soy sauce	1 tablespoon	15 milliliters
red wine vinegar	1 teaspoon	5 milliliters

Lower oven to 375°F/190°C. In a bowl combine the dry ingredients and push to one side. In the empty side of bowl combine the wet ingredients and then fold them into the dry mixture to make a thick batter.

Spoon clumps of batter over the top of the tempeh mixture. If the top is covered with the mounds of batter and there is still a little space between them, the spaces will fill in as the cobbler cooks.

Bake for 35 minutes on the top shelf of the oven, then check for doneness with a toothpick. The top should be golden brown and the toothpick should come out clean from any raw batter. The batter close to the filling will still be moist even when the cobbler is cooked through.

VARIATION: Make individual cobblers in small soufflé cups or ceramic baking dishes.

SERVE WITH: Avocado Orange and Red Onion Salad (page 173), Chinese-Style Broccoli (page 211), Oven Roasted Sweet Potatoes with Soy Sauce (page 203).

Tempeh Braised with Sauerkraut

YIELD 10 SERVINGS
ABOUT 8 OUNCES/224 GRAMS

The intense flavor of the sauerkraut works well with the unique taste of the tempeh.

onions, sliced	$2\frac{1}{2}$ cups	280 grams
carrots, thin bias cut	$2\frac{1}{2}$ cups	322 grams
canola oil	1 tablespoon	15 milliliters
toasted sesame oil	1 tablespoon	15 milliliters
fresh gingerroot, minced	1 tablespoon	15 grams
sauerkraut, drained	2 pounds	896 grams
Seasoned Baked Tempeh (page 334)	2 pounds	896 grams
soy sauce	2 tablespoons	30 milliliters
apple juice	1 cup	240 milliliters
fresh parsley, minced	$\frac{1}{4}$ cup	14 grams
ground toasted sesame seeds	$\frac{1}{4}$ cup	28 grams

In a large frying pan, sauté the onions and carrots over medium-high heat for 3 minutes. Push the vegetables to the outside edge of the pan and put the toasted sesame oil and ginger in the middle. Sauté until ginger starts to brown then mix with the onions and carrots. Add the sauerkraut, tempeh, soy sauce and apple juice to the pan and simmer covered for about 20 minutes. Stir in the parsley. Season to taste with a little prepared mustard, if desired. Serve garnished with a sprinkling of ground toasted sesame seeds.

SERVE WITH: Greens Sautéed with Ginger (page 195), and Millet Mash with Winter Squash (page 296).

Note: For large carrots split them lengthwise before slicing. Rinse sauerkraut if it is too strong for your taste.

Indonesian Tempeh with Spicy Peanut Sauce

YIELD 10 SERVINGS

ABOUT 11 OUNCES/308 GRAMS INCLUDING RICE

By adding some extra spices to the basic Seasoned Baked Tempeh recipe (page 334), it lends itself to a different cuisine, in this case its own native Indonesian style of cooking.

Seasoned Baked Tempeh (page 334)	2 pounds	900 kilograms
ground coriander	1 tablespoon	7 grams
ground cumin	1 tablespoon	7 grams
Spicy Peanut Sesame Sauce (page 278)	$2\frac{1}{2}$ cups	600 milliliters
sambal chile paste	$\frac{1}{2}$ teaspoon	1 gram
cooked Jasmine Rice (page 315)	10 cups	2.24 kilograms

GARNISH

roasted peanuts, chopped	$\frac{1}{2}$ cup	84 grams
non-sweetened shredded coconut, toasted	$\frac{1}{2}$ cup	56 grams
fresh cilantro, chopped	$\frac{1}{4}$ cup	14 grams

Prepare the Seasoned Baked Tempeh with the ground cumin and coriander before baking. Add the sambal chile paste to the Spicy Peanut Sesame Sauce, then combine with the tempeh. Season to taste. Serve over jasmine rice and garnish with peanuts, shredded coconut and cilantro.

SERVE WITH: Greens Sautéed with Ginger (page 195), and Sesame Roasted Butternut Squash (page 204).

Note: Toast the shredded coconut on a baking sheet for a few minutes in a 350°F/180°C oven.

Basic Seitan Quick Method (raw gluten)

YIELD RAW, 26 OUNCES/760 GRAMS

COOKED, 52 OUNCES/1.52 KILOGRAMS

gluten flour	2 cups	280 grams
all–purpose white flour	$\frac{1}{2}$ cup	56 grams
soy sauce	2 tablespoons	30 milliliters
vegetable juice cocktail	$\frac{3}{4}$ cup	180 milliliters
water	$\frac{1}{2}$ cup	90 milliliters
liquid smoke (optional)	4 drops	4 drops

Combine the flours and liquid ingredients separately, then mix together as quickly as possible. Knead until ingredients are well mixed, then allow the dough to rest for at least 15 minutes. Proceed as indicated in the recipe for the finished dish.

VARIATION: For Corned Seitan, beet juice may be used in place of half of the vegetable juice for a more authentic color.

Corned Seitan

YIELD 10 SERVINGS

In earlier times the word "corn" was used in the British Isles to describe grains in general. The process of curing which used salt granules the size of grain or "corn" gave rise to the term "corned," which today refers to a method of brining with salt and spices. In this rendition flavoring agents are added to the raw gluten wet and dry mixes as well as flavoring the brining/braising marinade.

DRY INGREDIENTS
raw wheat gluten/pure gluten flour	2 cups	280 grams
all–purpose white flour	$\frac{2}{3}$ cup	75 grams
garlic powder	2 teaspoons	4 grams
ground coriander	2 teaspoons	4 grams

WET MIXTURE
beet juice	1 cup	240 milliliters
soy sauce	$\frac{1}{4}$ cup	60 milliliters
tomato juice	$\frac{1}{4}$ cup	60 milliliters
red wine vinegar	$\frac{1}{4}$ cup	60 milliliters

MARINADE AND BRAISING STOCK

pickling spice	$\frac{1}{4}$ cup	28 grams
carrots, large dice	1 cup	126 grams
onions, large dice	1 cup	112 grams
garlic cloves, bruised	4	4
gingerroot, minced	2 tablespoons	30 grams
soy sauce	$\frac{1}{4}$ cup	60 milliliters
red wine vinegar	$\frac{1}{4}$ cup	60 milliliters
water	10 cups	2.4 liters

In a bowl, mix together the dry ingredients. Combine the wet ingredients and quickly mix with the dry ingredients to form a dough. Knead the dough right in the bowl for a minute, then cover and set aside.

Combine all ingredients for the marinade/braising stock, then flatten the gluten dough to make a rough disk shape, place it into a container and cover with marinade. Cover and refrigerate overnight.

Preheat oven to 375°F/190°C. Put the corned gluten into an oven-proof casserole, bring to a boil and boil for 10 minutes. Cover, place in oven and braise for 30 minutes. Carefully remove the lid to avoid steam burns and turn over the corned seitan. Return to the oven and cook for 30 minutes longer or until fork-tender. Remove from the pan to a platter and allow to cool. Strain the vegetables and spices from braising liquid and reserve the stock to reheat corned seitan.

At this point the corned seitan will need to be sliced and cooked a little longer in order to be tender enough to serve.

Thinly slice the corned seitan on the bias. Arrange portioned slices in a pan and cover with braising liquid. Cover the pan and place over a heat source or in an oven and simmer until corned seitan is hot and tender.

SERVE WITH: Cabbage and potato garnish from Guinness Barley with Tri-Color Confetti (page 298). Serve prepared mustard and grated horseradish on the side.

Note: For a New England or Irish-style Boiled Dinner, dilute the reserved braising liquid to half strength and use to boil accompanying vegetables such as cabbage, carrots and potatoes. Braise the seitan New England style, then slice seitan and coat with barbeque sauce and bake to glaze.

Choucroute Garnie

YIELD 10 SERVINGS

This name of this popular French dish from the Alsace region translates to "garnished sauerkraut."
The beer used as the braising liquid along with the sauerkraut shows influence
from across the border in Germany.

For this vegetarian version baked tofu, baked tempeh, vegetarian hot dogs, cooked seiten and soysages are used as the "garnie." To create a mellow flavor fresh cabbage is used along with the sauerkraut.

onions, medium dice	2 cups	224 grams
olive oil	2 tablespoons	30 milliliters
green cabbage, large dice	8 cups	672 grams
carrots, split and diagonally sliced	$1\frac{1}{2}$ cups	189 grams
garlic, chopped	2 tablespoons	28 grams
ginger, chopped	1 tablespoon	14 grams
cold baeer	$4\frac{1}{2}$ cups	1.8 liters
sauerkraut	2 pounds	896 grams
soy sauce	2 tablespoons	30 milliliters
Dijon mustard	1 tablespoon	15 grams
potatoes, large dice	4 cups	560 grams
bay leaves	2	2
salt	pinch	pinch
ground black pepper	pinch	pinch
fresh thyme	1 sprig	1 sprig
fresh parsley, chopped	1 cup	56 grams
vegetarian style hot dogs, diagonally sliced	8	336 grams
seasoned baked tofu (page 322)	1 pound	448 grams
seasoned baked tempeh (page 334)	1 pound	448 grams

In a large casserole, sauté the onions in olive oil over medium heat for 2 minutes, then add the cabbage, carrots, garlic and ginger and sauté 10 minutes longer or until starting to brown.

Turn off the heat and add the beer, sauerkraut, soy sauce, mustard, potatoes, bay leaves, salt, pepper, thyme and parsley. Bring the mixture to a boil, then simmer for 15 minutes or until the potatoes are almost tender. Add vegetarian hot dogs, tofu and tempeh, and simmer 15 minutes longer.

Seitan with Mushrooms and Red Wine

YIELD 10 SERVINGS

For this recipe the raw seitan is cut into a large dice before being browned and braised.

Basic Seitan Quick Method (raw gluten) (page 342)	26 ounces	760 grams
olive oil	2 tablespoons	30 milliliters
salt	$\frac{1}{2}$ teaspoon	3 grams
ground black pepper	pinch	pinch
garlic, minced	2 tablespoons	14 grams
pinot noir red wine	2 cups	480 milliliters
vegetable stock	4 cups	960 milliliters
soy sauce	$\frac{1}{4}$ cup	60 milliliters
bay leaves	2	2
Hungarian-Style Braised Mushrooms (page 247)	$7\frac{1}{2}$ cups	1.68 kilograms

Cut the raw gluten into a large dice and toss with the olive oil, salt and pepper. Heat a large nonstick casserole over medium-high heat. Brown seitan and remove from the pot until all seitan is done. Return all seitan to the pot along with garlic and sauté until garlic is fragrant. Add wine, stock, soy sauce and bay leaves to pot. Bring to a boil, then simmer 45 minutes or until cubes are tender. Add more stock to pan if needed.

When tender combine and heat with Hungarian-Style Braised Mushrooms. Season to taste.

SERVE WITH: Sesame Roasted Butternut Squash (page 204), Golden Mashed Potatoes with Caramelized Onions (page 205), Greens Sautéed with Ginger (page 195).

CHAPTER TWELVE

Breads and Quick Breads

Quick breads refers to the group of breads

including muffins, biscuits, corn breads and scones

leavened by baking powder, baking soda or both.

Generally some type of acid ingredient is present

in the recipe to help activate the leavening agent.

Successful baking relies upon several factors: good formulas, accurate measurements, how ingredients are measured, the integrity and behavior of the ingredients, the weather as it affects temperature and humidity while mixing the dough or batter, the different heating zones inside the oven, and the experience to know what the products look like at various stages of preparation. This is especially important when baking with organic and less refined ingredients. Whole wheat flour may have more or less bran, germ, gluten and starch from batch to batch, which make a batter heavier or lighter and may require more or less moisture to achieve the same results as an earlier batch. Other factors are the size of the oven and the material it is constructed from, how it is heated, if it is convection and the pans used for baking.

Heat rises and collects above baked goods at the top of an oven, which may brown them too quickly. The heating element at the bottom of the oven can create high heat that gets trapped by pans on the lower shelves, browning the bottoms of baked goods too quickly. Some strategies to avoid overbaked products are: the use of baking parchment and doubling pans for insulation when the base is browning too fast; rotating the baked goods by moving them to the opposite part of the oven with attention to browning patterns at the sides of the pans, which indicate that the pans themselves should be turned 180°; cover tops that are browning too fast with aluminum foil. The effect of weather on the way baked goods behave could be observed in the example of a yeasted bread dough, which rises much faster on a hot moist summer day than in the winter, when the kitchen is significantly cooler and dry. If flour has been stored in a refrigerator, allow it to come to room temperature before starting the recipe. The incorporation of whole-grain flour into recipes in place of white flour may sometimes create a need for extra liquid as the bran in these flours tends to absorb more moisture. Add 2 tablespoons/30 milliliters more liquid for each cup/4.75 ounces/133 grams of whole wheat flour.

Flours and Other Common Grains

WHEAT FLOUR

There are different types of wheat flour available. This is determined by the type of wheat berry, which could be hard or soft and tells about the amount of protein in the flour. Hard wheat generally has more protein than soft wheat. Also the amount of milling that the wheat has gone through affects the finished product.

Whole wheat flour affects the taste, texture and color of baked goods, making them more chewy, creating a darker dough and adding more earth tones to the color of the finished products.

The types of flour called for in the recipes are all-purpose unbleached white, white bread flour, organic whole wheat bread, organic whole wheat pastry and organic white wheat pastry available in bulk.

Knowing some of the terminology of the flours available is a major help.

- Whole wheat flour usually means that the outer hull or bran and the germ have been left in during the milling process.
- Whole wheat bread flour and white bread flour are high in gluten, higher in protein.
- High gluten content will increase elasticity which is great for making bread but will toughen pastry.
- Whole wheat pastry flour and white pastry flour are low in gluten, lower in protein.
- Organic white flour is often a bread flour unless otherwise noted.
- All-purpose flour is usually a mixture of half each bread and pastry flours.

The method of measuring the flour greatly affects the weight. I use the following process: stir to lighten the flour, dip in the measuring cup, then level off with the back of a knife. This will be about 4.25 ounces per cup of all-purpose white flour. When spooned into the measure, or when it is dipped from a bucket or sack in which the flour has settled or when the flour is tapped down while measuring can further alter the weight. If flour has been stored in a refrigerator, allow it to come to room temperature before starting the recipe.

Because whole grain flour has different properties than its refined white version I urge you to make subtle changes to your existing recipes until the desired results are achieved.

The fat in recipes for baked goods helps to tenderize the dough and different types of fats such as oil or margarine will have different effects on the result. For cake and muffin recipes, some items that can be used in place of fat are purée of softened dried fruit such as prune, cooked fruit purées such as apple sauce or apple or pear butter, and cooked vegetable purée made from carrots, pumpkin, butternut and other winter squash. When moisture is added to a dough or batter the gluten starts to develop, so because of the water content of these purées more care is needed to not overmix the batter, which would make the finished product tough.

Another way to incorporate the texture and moisturizing qualities of fruit or vegetables is to add them grated raw into a batter. These batters will be much thicker because they depend on the release of the fruit or vegetable juices during the cooking process. This technique can be seen in the formulas for the Chocolate Zucchini "Nanny" Cake (page xxx) and the Garnet Yam Cake (page xxx) and some of the muffin recipes.

The Beet Cake with Dried Cranberries (page xxx) uses grated cooked beets because of their long cooking time.

OTHER COMMON GRAINS

Oats

Rolled oats are graded by how finely they are crushed during the process. Natural foods distributors generally sell a very coarse grind; the conventional variety of rolled oats would be finer and those labeled quick-cooking or instant oats would be ground even finer. The coarser the grind the greater the moisture absorption. A slight adjustment to the liquid in a recipe may be needed. Since this is usually only apparent after the recipe has been mixed I sprinkle the additional moisture over the top of the batter and either poke it down with a spatula for cakes, or for muffins, simply scoop off a layer of batter and sprinkle again.

Cornmeal

Milled in various degrees of fineness, it comes in white, yellow, red and blue colors that also have subtle but unique flavor differences as well.

I use the stir, scoop and level method to measure, which means to first stir the flour to lighten it up, scoop the flour up into a measuring cup so that it is overflowing, then level off the top of the measure with the back of a knife or spatula. The ingredients for the recipes were then weighed after being measured in this way.

Irish Soda Bread

YIELD 10 SERVINGS

2 LOAVES

With maple product prices rising you may wish to use another sweetener.

DRY INGREDIENTS

flour, all-purpose white	4 cups	560 grams
maple sugar★	1 tablespoon	9 grams
baking soda	$1\frac{1}{4}$ teaspoons	6.5 grams
salt	1 teaspoon	6 grams
raisins	$\frac{2}{3}$ cup	76 grams
orange zest, finely minced	1 tablespoon	10 grams

WET INGREDIENTS

rice beverage	1 cup	240 milliliters
fresh orange juice	$\frac{1}{4}$ cup	60 milliliters
canola oil	$2\frac{1}{2}$ tablespoons	37.5 milliliters

In a bowl, thoroughly combine the dry ingredients, then push to one side of the bowl. Pour the wet ingredients into the other side of bowl and combine with the dry ingredients to form a dough. Turn the dough out onto a lightly floured work surface and knead lightly for about 1 minute. Divide dough in half and form two round loaves. Cut a large X on top of each loaf. Place loaves on a baking sheet and bake at 375°F/190°C for 35 to 40 minutes.

VARIATION: Use up to one-quarter whole wheat pastry flour and increase liquid slightly.

★Other dry sweeteners may be used.

Peach and Pecan Corn Bread

YIELD 10 SERVINGS
2 INCHES × 3 INCHES/7.5 CENTIMETERS × 5 CENTIMETERS

The cornmeal is included with the wet ingredients, allowing it to soften before being combined with the dry mixture. The applesauce and the whole-grain flour contribute to the moist, dense texture of this bread.

WET INGREDIENTS

peach juice	2 cups	480 milliliters
yellow cornmeal	1 cup	170 grams
apple sauce	1 cup	240 milliliters
corn oil	$\frac{1}{4}$ cup	60 milliliters
maple syrup	$\frac{1}{2}$ cup	120 milliliters

DRY INGREDIENTS

white all-purpose flour	$2\frac{1}{2}$ cups	330 grams
whole wheat pastry flour	1 cup	140 grams
pecans, lightly toasted and chopped	1 cup	100 grams
baking powder	2 tablespoons	28 grams
salt	$\frac{1}{2}$ teaspoon	3 grams

Preheat oven to 375°F/190°C. Lightly oil or line with parchment a 10-inch × 15-inch or 25-centimeter × 38-centimeter baking sheet pan.

In a small saucepan, warm peach juice to lukewarm (about 100°F/38°C), whisk in cornmeal and the remaining wet ingredients and then set aside in a warm place.

In a bowl combine all dry ingredients and push to one side of the bowl. Add wet ingredients to the other side of the bowl. Gently fold wet ingredients into the dry ones until just mixed.

Gently spread the batter out onto the baking sheet pan. Bake 25 to 30 minutes, starting on top shelf of the oven. Move the corn bread down to a lower shelf if it appears to be browning too quickly. The corn bread should be golden and beginning to crack slightly on top when done. Cool in pan for about 5 minutes and then turn out onto a cooling rack.

VARIATION: For Orange and Pecan Corn Bread use orange juice in place of the peach juice. For Apple-Raspberry and Pecan Red Corn Bread, use apple raspberry juice in place of the peach juice and red cornmeal in place of the yellow.

India-Style Flatbread

YIELD 10 SERVINGS
$\frac{1}{2}$ FLATBREAD EACH

Featuring East Indian-style spices, this tasty flatbread can be cooked on a griddle, under the broiler or on a gas or charcoal grill.

DRY INGREDIENTS

white all-purpose flour	3 cups	375 grams
whole wheat bread flour	1 cup	140 grams
baking powder	2 teaspoons	10.4 grams
fennel seeds	1 tablespoon	7 grams
cumin seeds	1 tablespoon	7 grams
salt	$\frac{1}{4}$ teaspoon	1.5 grams
ground black pepper	pinch	pinch
onions, fine dice	$\frac{2}{3}$ cup	70 grams

WET INGREDIENTS

rice beverage	$1\frac{1}{2}$ cups	360 milliliters
canola oil	2 tablespoons	30 milliliters

In a bowl combine the dry ingredients and mix well. Add the wet ingredients and mix until a soft dough is formed. Turn the dough out onto a well-floured surface and knead for a minute until smooth. Cover the dough with a towel or plastic wrap and let it rest for about 15 minutes.

Divide dough into 5 portions, then on a floured surface flatten and shape them by hand or with a rolling pin into a circle 6 inches/15 centimeters in diameter.

Preheat oven to 375°F/190°C. Preheat a griddle or heavy frying pan over medium heat. Lightly brush the pan with oil, then cook the flatbreads for about 1 minute on the first side or until golden brown. Then turn and cook on the other side for about a minute or until lightly browned. Put the flat breads on a baking sheet and into the oven at this point for another few minutes to cook through and to keep them warm while the others are browned. Serve hot, brushed with a little soy margarine or olive oil.

SERVE WITH: Carrot Hazelnut Spread (page 49), Vegetable Walnut and Pecan Pâté (page 52), Garlic Herb Spread (page 207), with extra virgin olive oil or soy margarine or as a garnish on the side of salads.

Note: While preparing a special dinner at Shiriats of Louisville, Kentucky, chef-owner Anoosh Shiriat suggested that we put the flatbreads on a preheated grill which worked well. Using a hot broiler also works to cook the flatbreads. Turn them as they brown and finish in the oven if needed.

Lemon Prune Scones

YIELD 12 LARGE SCONES OR
24 SMALL SCONES

Some of the dry ingredients, in this case the oats and chopped prunes, are combined first with the wet ingredients, allowing them to soften before joining the remaining dry mixture.

WET INGREDIENTS		
rolled oats	$1\frac{1}{2}$ cups	150 grams
rice beverage	1 cup	240 milliliters
maple syrup	3 tablespoons	45 milliliters
pitted prunes, small dice	$\frac{3}{4}$ cup	126 grams
lemon juice	3 tablespoons	45 milliliters

DRY INGREDIENTS		
white all-purpose flour	$4\frac{1}{2}$ cups	504 grams
cream of tartar	1 tablespoon	14 grams
baking soda	$2\frac{1}{4}$ teaspoons	10 grams
lemon zest	3 tablespoons	28 grams
ground cardamom	$\frac{3}{4}$ teaspoon	.75 gram
salt	$\frac{1}{2}$ teaspoon	3 grams
canola oil	6 tablespoons	90 milliliters

Preheat oven to 375°F/190°C. Combine all wet ingredients in a bowl and set aside. Combine all dry ingredients except the oil and mix well. Add the oil to the dry mixture and mix until well distributed. Add the wet mixture to the dry mixture and mix gently until a soft dough is formed.

Turn the dough onto a well-floured work surface and shape the dough into a long, narrow rectangle about 5 inches/12.5 centimeters wide. Cut the dough into 12 wedges. Place the scones on a dry baking sheet and bake, preferably on the upper shelf of the oven if possible, for about 15 minutes. For small scones, cut the dough lengthwise in half before cutting to wedges, and reduce cooking time to about 10 minutes.

SERVE WITH: Jam, fruit butter, soy margarine.

Oatmeal Herb Scones

YIELD 12 LARGE SCONES OR
24 SMALL SCONES

Some of the dry ingredients, in this case the oats, are combined first with the wet ingredients, allowing them to soften before joining the remaining dry mixture.

WET INGREDIENTS

rolled oats	$1\frac{1}{2}$ cups	150 grams
rice beverage, plus extra to brush on	$1\frac{1}{2}$ cups	360 milliliters
maple syrup	3 tablespoons	45 milliliters

DRY INGREDIENTS

white all-purpose flour	$4\frac{1}{4}$ cups	504 grams
baking soda	$2\frac{1}{4}$ teaspoons	10 grams
cream of tartar	1 tablespoon	14 grams
garlic powder	1 teaspoon	2 grams
salt	$\frac{1}{2}$ teaspoon	3 grams
ground black pepper	$\frac{1}{4}$ teaspoon	.5 gram
fresh parsley, minced	6 tablespoons	21 grams
canola oil	6 tablespoons	90 milliliters

Preheat oven to 375°F/190°C. Combine all wet ingredients in a bowl and set aside. Combine all dry ingredients except oil and mix well. Add the oil to the dry mixture and mix until well distributed. Add the wet mixture to the dry mixture and mix gently until a soft dough is formed.

Turn the dough onto a well-floured work surface and shape the dough into a rectangle about 5 inches/12.5 centimeters wide by 14 inches/35 centimeters long. Cut the dough into 12 wedges. Place the scones on a dry baking sheet and brush with a little of the rice beverage.

Bake on the upper shelf of the oven for about 15 minutes. They should be light golden brown.

VARIATION: For small scones, cut the dough lengthwise in half before cutting into wedges and reduce cooking time to about 10 minutes. Other fresh herbs such as dill or basil can be used in place of the parsley. Soy milk can be used in place of the rice beverage.

SERVE WITH: Sautéed Oyster Mushrooms (page 60), Mushroom and Kale Sauté with Cherry Tomatoes (page 191), or for the bread basket with soy margarine or Carrot Hazelnut Spread (page 49).

Sesame, Sunflower and Poppy Seed Bread

YIELD 2 LOAVES

This recipe originated at It's Only Natural Restaurant and has been handed off from bakers David Mandel to Bo Celotto to Dave Muckle to musician-turned-chef-turned-bread-baker Bobby Gotta. Their combined efforts have produced more than 50,000 loaves.

DRY INGREDIENTS

organic white bread flour	3 cups	420 grams
whole wheat bread flour	2 cups	280 grams
sesame seeds	$\frac{1}{4}$ cup	28 grams
sunflower seeds	$\frac{1}{4}$ cup	28 grams
poppy seeds	1 tablespoon	7 grams
salt	1 teaspoon	6 grams

WET INGREDIENTS

warm water, 110°F/44°C	2 cups	480 milliliters
barley malt syrup	$\frac{1}{4}$ cup	60 milliliters
active dry yeast granules	1 tablespoon	9 grams
canola oil	1 tablespoon	15 milliliters

Combine all dry ingredients except one cup of white bread flour. In a large bowl combine the wet ingredients and gradually incorporate the dry mixture. Add the reserved flour a little at a time until dough is no longer sticky.

Turn the dough onto a floured work surface and knead for about 10 minutes or until smooth and elastic. Put the dough into a lightly oiled bowl, cover with a towel and allow the dough to rise in a warm place until doubled in bulk. Punch down the dough and allow a second rise.

After the second rise, preheat the oven to 350°F/170°C. Punch the dough down again and then form into 2 loaves. Place them seam side down onto a baking sheet or into loaf pans that have been lightly oiled. Allow the loaves to rise again until doubled.

Brush the tops of the loaves with oil and bake for about 35 minutes or until bread is golden brown and sounds hollow when tapped on the bottom.

SERVE WITH: Toasted Spice Hummus (page 51), or Carrot Hazelnut Spread (page 49).

Biali-Style Rolls

YIELD 12 ROLLS

Sesame, Sunflower and Poppy Seed Bread dough (page 356)	1 recipe	1 recipe
onions, fine dice	$1\frac{1}{3}$ cups	140 grams
canola oil	2 tablespoons	30 milliliters
salt and pepper	to taste	to taste

Prepare Sesame, Sunflower and Poppy Seed bread dough through the second rise. Divide the dough into 12 portions. Flatten each piece of dough into about a 5-inch/13-centimeter round. With fingertips, press several dimples into the top of each round, brush with oil and sprinkle with one-twelfth of the diced onions and salt and pepper.

Preheat oven to 400°F/200°C. Place the Biali on a lightly oiled baking sheet and allow it to rise to about double. Bake for about 14 minutes.

SERVE WITH: Toasted Spice Hummus (page 51), Carrot Hazelnut Spread (page 49).

Olive and Red Onion Foccacia with Rosemary and Garlic

YIELD 12 SERVINGS

warm water, 120°F /48°C	$1\frac{1}{4}$ cups	300 milliliters
applesauce	2 tablespoons	30 milliliters
maple syrup	1 tablespoon	15 milliliters
yeast, rapid rise (SAF)	$2\frac{1}{2}$ teaspoons	7 grams
all-purpose white flour	3 cups	420 grams
whole wheat flour	1 cup	140 grams
salt	1 teaspoon	6 grams
extra virgin olive oil (plus extra for pan)	1 tablespoon	15 milliliters
red onions, fine dice	$\frac{1}{4}$ cup	28 grams
olives	$\frac{1}{4}$ cup	28 grams
garlic, crushed	1 teaspoon	5 grams
fresh rosemary, minced	1 teaspoon	1.3 grams
black pepper	pinch	pinch

In a bowl combine the water, applesauce, maple syrup, yeast, and flours with half the salt and one-third of the olive oil. Mix until a ball forms, then cover the bowl and let the dough rest for about 20 minutes.

Preheat the oven to 375°F/195°C. Brush a 7 inch × 15 inch (17.5 centimeter × 37.5 centimeter) baking sheet lightly with olive oil. Roll out the dough into a rectangle and press it into the prepared baking sheet, make indentations in the top of the bread with finger tips and brush with the remaining olive oil. Sprinkle with the remaining salt and then all the other ingredients. Bake for 15 minutes and check for browning and doneness.

SERVE WITH: Spinach Pesto (page 140), Black Olive Pesto (page 57), or Sundried Tomato Pesto (page 56).

Braided Sweet Bread

YIELD 2 LOAVES

For special occasions this dough can be braided in the style of Challah bread.

white bread flour	4 cups	560 grams
whole wheat pastry flour	1 cup	140 grams
succanat	6 tablespoons	70 grams
rapid-rise yeast	$2\frac{1}{4}$ teaspoons	7 grams
salt	1 teaspoon	6 grams
ground turmeric	$\frac{1}{4}$ teaspoon	.5 gram

WET INGREDIENTS

warm water, 130°F/54°C	2 cups	480 milliliters
canola oil	2 tablespoons	30 milliliters

Combine the dry ingredients in a large bowl. Heat the water and the oil and stir into the dry mixture to form a soft dough. Turn the dough out onto a lightly floured work surface and knead for about 5 minutes or until smooth, using only enough flour to keep dough from sticking to the hands and work surface. Cover the dough and allow it to rest for about 10 minutes.

Preheat the oven to 375°F/190°C. Divide the dough in half. Divide each half into 3 strips and roll the strips on the work surface to lengthen them for braiding. Braid 3 strips together for each of the loaves. Place the braided loaves on a baking sheet. Turn the ends under and pinch them to keep them secure as they rise during baking.

Bake the loaves for 15 minutes, then check for browning. Because of the high sugar content of the dough, the temperature may need to be lowered and another sheet pan could be placed under the first one to protect the bottom of the bread. The loaves should be golden and ready after about 25 minutes. Remove to a wire rack to cool. Serve with soy margarine, jam, preserves or Carrot Hazelnut Spread (page 49).

VARIATION: To braid the loaves Challah style, divide the dough into thirds. Take 2 of the thirds, divide and proceed to braid as for 2 loaves above. Take the remaining third piece of dough and divide it into 6 strips. Proceed to braid as for 2 small loaves with 3 strips each. Brush the tops of the larger loaves lightly with water and top each one with a small braided loaf.

At this point you may wish to brush the tops of the loaves with liquid rice beverage or soy milk and sprinkle with poppy seeds. Bake with the same precautions as for single braided loaves.

Coconut Curry Biscuits

YIELD 10 BISCUITS

The coconut in this recipe is coconut milk, which contributes to both taste and texture.
Preheat oven to 400°F/200°C.

DRY INGREDIENTS

flour, all-purpose white	$2\frac{1}{2}$ cups	350 grams
baking powder	1 tablespoon	15 grams
salt	$\frac{1}{2}$ teaspoon	3 grams
curry powder	1 teaspoon	6 grams

SHORTENING

soy margarine	3 tablespoons	42 grams

WET INGREDIENTS

coconut milk	1 cup	240 milliliters
maple syrup	1 teaspoon	5 milliliters
water	2 tablespoons	30 milliliters

Thoroughly combine the dry ingredients. Cut in the shortening. Stir in the wet ingredients until a dough is formed. Turn the dough onto a work surface and knead for about 30 seconds. Dough can be patted or rolled out to $\frac{3}{4}$ inch/2 centimeters thick and cut with a $2\frac{3}{4}$-inch/7-centimeter biscuit cutter using up all the dough to make 10 biscuits.

Place the biscuits on a baking sheet and bake for 12 to 14 minutes.

SERVE WITH: Serve warm with jam or Carrot Hazelnut Spread (page 49). Can be used as shortcake biscuit with fruit.

Flaky Dinner Rolls

YIELD 20 ROLLS

This recipe requires rolling out the shortening between the layers of yeast dough, using the same technique employed when making croissants or Danish pastry.

DRY INGREDIENTS

all-purpose white flour	4 cups	500 grams
rapid rise yeast (SAF)	1 package	7 grams
dry sweetener	2 teaspoons	7 grams
salt	1 teaspoon	6 grams

WET INGREDIENTS

warm water (130°F/54°C)	10 ounces	300 milliliters
canola oil	2 tablespoons	60 milliliters

SHORTENING

soy margarine, chilled	4 tablespoons	56 grams

In a bowl or in a food processor combine all the dry ingredients. Add water and oil and mix until a soft dough forms. Turn the dough out onto a floured work surface and knead for about 2 minutes until smooth. Put dough back into bowl, cover and allow to rest for 10 minutes.

Remove the soy margarine from refrigerator. On a lightly floured surface roll the dough out to a rectangle roughly 12 inches × 16 inches/30 centimeters × 40 centimeters. Spread the soy margarine to cover the rectangle to about 1 inch/2.5 centimeters from all outer edges. Starting at the narrow end, roll up the dough tightly, then fold it in half. Cover with a towel or plastic wrap and refrigerate for 30 minutes to an hour.

Divide the dough in half. Roll the dough out to make two 8-inch/20-centimeter circles. Divide the circles into 6 wedges each. Starting from the wide end, roll up each wedge and place onto a baking sheet.

Bake at 400°F/200°C for 10 minutes. Reduce the heat to 350°F/180°C and bake for 10 minutes longer or until done.

SERVE WITH: Serve warm with jam, soy margarine or Carrot Hazelnut Spread (page 49).

Note: To substitute one-quarter of the flour with whole wheat pastry flour, increase the water by about 10 percent. Rapid rise yeast is also marketed by the name SAF yeast. Regular yeast can be used in the recipe, allowing for longer rising times; see package directions.

Apple Walnut Muffins

YIELD 10 TO 12 MUFFINS

The grated apples add flavor and texture.

DRY INGREDIENTS

all-purpose white flour	$1\frac{1}{2}$ cups	190 grams
whole wheat pastry flour	$1\frac{1}{2}$ cups	210 grams
rolled oats	1 cup	98 grams
succanat	$\frac{1}{2}$ cup	84 grams
walnuts, chopped	$\frac{1}{3}$ cup	35 grams
raisins	$\frac{1}{3}$ cup	38 grams
baking powder	4 teaspoons	20 grams
ground cinnamon	$\frac{1}{2}$ teaspoon	3 grams

WET INGREDIENTS

apple, grated	1 cup	112 grams
maple syrup	$\frac{1}{2}$ cup	120 milliliters
apple juice	$1\frac{1}{2}$ cups	360 milliliters
apple sauce	$\frac{1}{4}$ cup	60 milliliters
canola oil	2 tablespoons	30 milliliters
apple cider vinegar	1 teaspoon	5 milliliters

In a large bowl combine all dry ingredients and push to one side of bowl. In the empty side of the bowl combine all the wet ingredients, then gently fold them into the dry until just mixed. Let the batter rest for about 10 minutes to allow the oats to soften.

Preheat the oven to 350°F/180°C. Scoop the batter out into a lightly oiled muffin tin to make 10 or 12 muffins. Bake for about 25 minutes starting out on the upper shelf of the oven, then moving down to the lower shelves if the muffins are browning too quickly.

SERVE WITH: Jam or soy margarine.

Carrot Orange Sunflower Muffins

YIELD 10 TO 12 MUFFINS

For more orange flavor add a teaspoon/3 grams of grated orange zest.

DRY INGREDIENTS

all-purpose white flour	$1\frac{1}{2}$ cups	190 grams
whole wheat pastry flour	$1\frac{1}{2}$ cups	210 grams
rolled oats	1 cup	98 grams
succanat	$\frac{1}{2}$ cup	84 grams
sunflower seeds	$\frac{1}{3}$ cup	35 grams
prunes, small dice	$\frac{1}{3}$ cup	38 grams
baking powder	4 teaspoons	20 grams
ground cinnamon	$\frac{1}{2}$ teaspoon	3 grams
ground ginger	$\frac{1}{4}$ teaspoon	1.5 grams

WET INGREDIENTS

carrot, grated	1 cup	112 grams
maple syrup	$\frac{1}{2}$ cup	120 milliliters
orange juice	$1\frac{1}{2}$ cups	360 milliliters
apple sauce	$\frac{1}{4}$ cup	60 milliliters
canola oil	2 tablespoons	30 milliliters

In a large bowl combine all the dry ingredients and push to one side of bowl. In the empty side of the bowl combine all the wet ingredients, then gently fold them into the dry ingredients until just mixed. Let the batter rest for about 10 minutes to allow the oats to soften.

Preheat the oven to 350°F/180°C. Scoop the batter out into a lightly oiled muffin tin to make 10 or 12 muffins. Bake for about 25 minutes starting out on the upper shelf of the oven, then moving down to the lower shelves if the muffins are browning too quickly.

SERVE WITH: Jam or soy margarine.

Blueberry Muffins

YIELD 10 TO 12 MUFFINS

The balsamic vinegar used here will help activate the baking powder and also add to the flavor of the muffins.

DRY INGREDIENTS

all-purpose white flour	$1\frac{1}{2}$ cups	190 grams
whole wheat pastry flour	$1\frac{1}{2}$ cups	210 grams
rolled oats	1 cup	98 grams
succanat	$\frac{1}{2}$ cup	84 grams
walnuts, chopped	$\frac{1}{3}$ cup	35 grams
baking powder	4 teaspoons	20 grams
ground cardamom	$\frac{1}{2}$ teaspoon	1 gram

WET INGREDIENTS

blueberries	$1\frac{1}{4}$ cups	140 grams
maple syrup	$\frac{1}{2}$ cup	120 milliliters
rice beverage	$1\frac{1}{2}$ cups	360 milliliters
apple sauce	$\frac{1}{4}$ cup	60 milliliters
canola oil	2 tablespoons	30 milliliters
balsamic vinegar	1 teaspoon	5 milliliters

In a large bowl combine all dry ingredients and push to one side of the bowl. In the empty side of the bowl combine all the wet ingredients, then gently fold them into the dry ones until just mixed. Let the batter rest for about 10 minutes to allow the oats to soften.

Preheat the oven to 350°F/180°C. Scoop the batter out into a lightly oiled muffin tin to make 10 or 12 muffins. Bake for about 25 minutes starting out on the upper shelf of the oven, then moving down to the lower shelves if the muffins are browning too quickly.

SERVE WITH: Jam or soy margarine.

Butternut Squash Almond Muffins

YIELD 10 TO 12 MUFFINS

*A potato or vegetable peeler is one of the best tools to remove the hard
outer layer of skin from the butternut squash.*

DRY INGREDIENTS

all-purpose white flour	$1\frac{1}{2}$ cups	190 grams
whole wheat pastry flour	$1\frac{1}{2}$ cups	210 grams
rolled oats	1 cup	98 grams
succanat	$\frac{1}{2}$ cup	84 grams
almonds, chopped or sliced	$\frac{1}{3}$ cup	35 grams
currants	$\frac{1}{3}$ cup	38 grams
baking powder	4 teaspoons	20 grams
ground cinnamon	$\frac{1}{2}$ teaspoon	3 grams
ground nutmeg	$\frac{1}{4}$ teaspoon	1.5 grams

WET INGREDIENTS

butternut squash, grated	1 cup	112 grams
maple syrup	$\frac{1}{2}$ cup	120 milliliters
apple juice	$1\frac{1}{2}$ cups	360 milliliters
apple sauce	$\frac{1}{4}$ cup	60 milliliters
canola oil	2 tablespoons	30 milliliters
apple cider vinegar	1 teaspoon	5 milliliters

In a large bowl combine all the dry ingredients and push to one side of bowl. In the empty side of the bowl combine all the wet ingredients, then gently fold them into the dry ones until just mixed. Let the batter rest for about 10 minutes to allow oats to soften.

Preheat the oven to 350°F/180°C. Scoop the batter out into a lightly oiled muffin tin to make 10 or 12 muffins. Bake for about 25 minutes starting out on the upper shelf of the oven then moving down to the lower shelves if the muffins are browning too quickly.

SERVE WITH: Jam or soy margarine.

Zucchini Pecan Muffins

YIELD 10 TO 12 MUFFINS

The zucchini will contribute to taste and texture. Use small zucchini if possible.

DRY INGREDIENTS

all–purpose white flour	$1\frac{1}{2}$ cups	190 grams
whole wheat pastry flour	$1\frac{1}{2}$ cups	210 grams
succanat	$\frac{1}{2}$ cup	84 grams
rolled oats	1 cup	100 grams
pecans, chopped	$\frac{1}{3}$ cup	35 grams
raisins	$\frac{1}{3}$ cup	38 grams
baking powder	4 teaspoons	20 grams
ground cinnamon	$\frac{1}{2}$ teaspoon	3 grams

WET INGREDIENTS

zucchini, grated	1 cup	112 grams
maple syrup	$\frac{1}{2}$ cup	120 milliliters
apple juice	$1\frac{1}{2}$ cups	360 milliliters
apple sauce	$\frac{1}{4}$ cup	60 milliliters
canola oil	2 tablespoons	30 milliliters
apple cider vinegar	1 teaspoon	5 milliliters

In a large bowl combine all the dry ingredients and push to one side of bowl. In the empty side of the bowl combine all the wet ingredients, then gently fold them into the dry until just mixed. Let the batter rest for about 10 minutes to allow the oats to soften.

Preheat the oven to 350°F/180°C. Scoop the batter out into a lightly oiled muffin tin to make 10 or 12 muffins. Bake for about 25 minutes starting out on the upper shelf of the oven, then moving down to the lower shelves if the muffins are browning too quickly.

SERVE WITH: Jam or soy margarine.

Banana Kiwi Bread

YIELD 4 SMALL LOAVES ABOUT 10.5 OUNCES/294 GRAMS

Mike Stella, a former baker at the Garden of Light Natural Foods Market in Glastonbury, Connecticut, developed this excellent recipe.

WET INGREDIENTS

bananas	2 cups	392 grams
kiwi fruit, peeled (about 2)	$\frac{1}{2}$ cup	112 grams
canola oil	$\frac{1}{4}$ cup	60 milliliters
orange juice	2 tablespoons	30 milliliters
vanilla extract	1 teaspoon	5 milliliters

DRY INGREDIENTS

whole wheat pastry flour	$3\frac{1}{2}$ cups	462 grams
unrefined cane sugar (crystals)	$\frac{7}{8}$ cup	196 grams
baking soda	$1\frac{1}{2}$ teaspoons	6 grams
baking powder	1 tablespoon	15.5 grams
salt	1 teaspoon	6 grams
ground cinnamon	1 teaspoon	6 grams
ground nutmeg	$\frac{1}{2}$ teaspoon	3 grams

Preheat oven to 350°F/180°C. In a food processor or blender purée the wet ingredients. Combine the dry ingredients in a bowl. Fold the wet ingredients into the dry mixture to make a very thick batter. Divide the batter into 4 lightly oiled demi-loaf pans. Bake for 25 minutes and check for doneness with a toothpick. Continue baking a few minutes longer as needed. Remove from the oven and cool in pans for a few minutes, then remove from pans to a cooling rack.

Note: The demi-loaf pans I use measure 5 inches × $2\frac{1}{2}$ inches × 2 inches and hold 2 cups or 12.5 centimeters × 6.25 centimeters × 5 centimeters and hold 480 milliliters.

CHAPTER THIRTEEN

Desserts

Desserts have been the greatest challenge of

creating an all-vegan menu because the staples of

mainstream pastry cookery—eggs, white sugar,

butter, milk, cream and cream cheese—are not

used.

Our guests still want the qualities of good-tasting desserts. Moist cake, tender pastry or tart crust, and different textures like the crunch of toasted nuts and smoothness of frostings are all still desirable for this course.

Through trial and error and with the help of others, I have learned what types of recipes will work in this medium and how to use the available ingredients to the best advantage. Items like silken tofu can be used for its creamy texture, regular and whole wheat fillo for crisp pastry wrappers, and soy margarine alone or with canola oil to tenderize dough or batters. Grated fresh fruits and vegetables, cooked fruit like applesauce, apple or pear butters or prune purée can also be added for moisture and texture. Various types of sweeteners, wet or dry, add their own flavor; in addition, dairy-free, grain-sweetened chocolate chips, various nut butters, and even corn kernels used to create a custard-style sauce are all documented in this chapter.

NOTES ON TESTING DONENESS AND TIPS FOR FROSTING CAKES:

- The arrowroot or cornstarch helps lighten the batter.
- Done means the cake will be pulling slightly away from the sides of the pan; it may have slight cracks in the top and should feel firm to the touch at the center, which can further be tested with a toothpick which should come out dry when inserted into the center.
- When frosting a cake, apply a crumb coat, a very thin coating of icing that helps keep any loose bits of cake from being spread around with the frosting. This affects the smoothness and appearance, especially of a cake with a light-colored frosting. Once the crumb coat is applied, then proceed with the final coat of icing.
- Cakes should be firm in the center and when a skewer or toothpick is inserted into the center of the cake, it should come out clean.
- Prepared pans for cakes are lined with baking parchment or oiled and coated with flour.
- Vinegar is added to quick breads and cakes to activate the baking powder, which gives more rise to the batter as it bakes.
- Pass baking soda through a strainer to make sure it is well distributed with the dry ingredients of a recipe.
- When scaling up recipes double check the quantities of salt, baking powder and baking soda as these may need to be adjusted down; too much of these ingredients adversely affects the taste of baked goods.

Almond Rice Pudding

YIELD 10 SERVINGS

$\frac{1}{2}$ CUP/120 MILLILITERS

This "homey," comfort food dessert is appropriate for less formal occasions and for a snack.

cooked brown rice	5 cups	630 grams
water	6 cups	1.44 liters
maple syrup	$\frac{1}{2}$ cup	120 milliliters
raisins	$\frac{1}{2}$ cup	56 grams
almond extract	$\frac{3}{4}$ teaspoon	3.75 milliliters
cinnamon	$\frac{1}{4}$ teaspoon	.5 gram
nutmeg	pinch	pinch
allspice	pinch	pinch
almond butter	$\frac{1}{4}$ cup	60 grams

GARNISH

sliced toasted almonds	$\frac{1}{2}$ cup	32.5 grams
fresh raspberries	1 cup	140 grams

In a blender liquefy $\frac{3}{4}$ cup/95 grams cooked rice with 1 cup/240 milliliters water, then combine with the remaining rice and water and syrup, raisins, almond extract, cinnamon, nutmeg and allspice. Bring to a boil, then simmer for about 30 minutes, stirring often. When the rice is tender and creamy, stir in the almond butter. Taste for sweetness and flavor. For a creamier pudding, blend one-third and mix back in. Use the toasted almonds and fresh berries for garnish.

Butternut Squash Mousse

YIELD 10 SERVINGS
$\frac{1}{2}$ CUP/112 GRAMS

Baking the squash will concentrate and develop the flavor.

butternut squash, cooked	$3\frac{1}{2}$ cups	784 grams
firm silken tofu, 1 package	12.3 ounces	345 grams
maple syrup	$\frac{1}{2}$ cup	120 milliliters
vanilla extract	2 teaspoons	10 milliliters
ground cinnamon	1 teaspoon	2 grams
ground nutmeg	$\frac{1}{4}$ teaspoon	.5 gram
ground allspice	$\frac{1}{4}$ teaspoon	.5 gram
ground ginger	$\frac{1}{4}$ teaspoon	.5 gram
chopped toasted walnuts	3 tablespoons	21 grams

Combine the squash, tofu, syrup and spices in a food processor and process until smooth. Chill the mixture and serve garnished with toasted chopped walnuts.

SERVE WITH: Cranberry Dessert Sauce and Orange or Hazelnut Silken Crème topping (page 394), Almond Coconut Cookies (page 399).

Chocolate Coconut Pudding

YIELD 12 SERVINGS

$\frac{1}{2}$ CUP/148 MILLILITERS

For a low-fat version purée or slice 2 or 3 ripe bananas and fold them into the pudding.

non-sweetened shredded coconut	1 cup	112 grams
carob-flavored soy milk	1 cup	240 milliliters
chocolate chips, dairy-free	$2\frac{1}{2}$ cups	420 grams
silken tofu, 2 packages	24.5 ounces	686 grams
maple syrup	$\frac{1}{4}$ cup	60 milliliters
vanilla extract	2 teaspoons	10 milliliters
almond extract	1 teaspoon	5 milliliters

In a heavy-bottom pan, toast the coconut over medium heat for 2 or 3 minutes or until lightly browned. Remove 2 tablespoons/7 grams toasted coconut and set aside for garnish. Add the carob soy milk to the pan and bring to a simmer. Stir in the chocolate chips and remove from heat. Continue to stir until all the chocolate chips are melted.

Put the silken tofu, maple syrup, vanilla and almond extract into a food processor and process, scraping down the sides of the work bowl with a spatula a couple of times, until smooth. Add the coconut chocolate mixture to the food processor and combine well.

GARNISH AND PRESENTATION: Turn out pudding into individual serving containers and garnish with the reserved toasted coconut.

Chocolate Hazelnut Cake

YIELD 10 SERVINGS

My variation of a cake that has been influenced by former It's Only Natural Restaurant pastry personnel David Mandel, Bo Celotto and Dave Muckel. Makes two 9-inch/22.5-centimeter round layers.

DRY INGREDIENTS

all-purpose flour	2 cups	280 grams
cornstarch	$\frac{1}{4}$ cup	32 grams
cocoa powder	$\frac{1}{2}$ cup	40 grams
baking powder	4 teaspoons	21 grams
succanat	$\frac{1}{2}$ cup	61 grams
Florida crystals	$\frac{1}{2}$ cup	84 grams

WET INGREDIENTS

canola oil	$\frac{1}{4}$ cup	60 milliliters
apple butter	$\frac{1}{4}$ cup	63 grams
pure vanilla extract	2 teaspoons	10 milliliters
almond extract	$\frac{1}{2}$ teaspoon	2.5 milliliters
rice beverage	$1\frac{3}{4}$ cups	420 milliliters
balsamic vinegar	1 teaspoon	5 milliliters

FROSTING

seedless all-fruit raspberry jam	$\frac{1}{2}$ cup	136 grams
chopped toasted hazelnuts	$\frac{1}{2}$ cup	49 grams
Chocolate Almond Tart Filling ($\frac{1}{2}$ recipe★) (page 388)	3 cups	630 grams

Preheat the oven to 325°F/160°C. Grease and flour two 9-inch/22.5-centimeter cake pans.

Sift together the dry ingredients into a bowl. In a separate bowl combine the wet ingredients with a whisk. Add the wet mixture to dry ingredients and fold together.

Divide the cake batter into prepared pans and bake for 18 to 20 minutes or until done. Remove the cake to the cooling rack. After 5 minutes remove the cake layers from the pans.

★ One-half of the recipe, Chocolate Almond Tart Filling, will frost the top and between the center layer, plus a little on sides to coat with toasted nuts. A full recipe will generously coat the entire cake.

When the cake is cooled, slice each layer in half horizontally with a slicing knife or a long chef's knife. To do this, line up the blade of the knife horizontally to the side of a layer and slice into the cake to the width of the blade, then begin to rotate the cake and continue slicing the same distance in until a complete circle around the cake has been completed. This will allow an even cut across and through the cake and may need just a little slicing to free the center of the top from bottom.

Spread a little of the tart filling on a cake plate, then place down the first layer. The bit of filling at the bottom will act like glue and keep the first layer in place. Spread raspberry jam onto the first layer and sprinkle with some hazelnuts. Place the next layer of cake on top of the first and spread with filling. Then repeat the process until all four layers are attached and the top receives a light coat of filling. Crumb-coat the cake, then frost it with a spatula and decorate it with a piping bag if desired. Sprinkle on any remaining toasted hazelnuts.

Note: The beginning of this chapter has tips on baking and frosting.

Chocolate Icebox Cake

YIELD 12 SERVINGS

Using the carob soy beverage enhances the chocolate with another layer of flavor. For a deeper chocolate flavor use chocolate soy milk.

carob soy milk	4 cups	960 milliliters
cornstarch	6 tablespoons	49 grams
maple syrup	$\frac{1}{4}$ cup	60 milliliters
vanilla extract	1 teaspoon	5 milliliters
almond extract	$\frac{1}{4}$ teaspoon	1.25 milliliters
chocolate chips, malt-sweetened, dairy-free	1 cup	168 grams
chopped toasted walnuts	$\frac{1}{2}$ cup	49 grams
vegan cookies	12 ounces	336 grams

one 10-inch/22.5-centimeter baking dish, 6-cup/1.44-liter capacity

Mix $\frac{1}{2}$ cup/120 milliliters soy milk and cornstarch and set aside. Put the remaining soy milk, maple syrup, vanilla extract and almond extract into a pot and bring to a boil.

Whisk in the reserved soy milk and cornstarch to thicken. Turn off the heat and stir in the chocolate chips. When the chips are melted stir in half of the toasted walnuts.

In baking dish layer the hot pudding mixture and graham crackers until all are used up. Sprinkle the top with remaining walnuts. Chill the dessert for about an hour and a half.

SERVE WITH: Any of the Silken Crème (page 395) recipes as a topping.

Note: If only plain or vanilla soy milk is available, add a little carob or cocoa powder to deepen the chocolate flavor.

Chocolate Zucchini "Nanny" Cake

YIELD 12 SERVINGS

This rich dark chocolate confection was adapted by my culinary colleague, Jondahl Mott Meotti, from her grandmother's recipe. In addition to making the recipe vegan she was also able to reduce the amount of fat by two-thirds, using apple butter and canola oil in place of the solid shortening.

WET MIXTURE

canola oil	$\frac{1}{2}$ cup	120 milliliters
apple butter	$\frac{1}{4}$ cup	32 grams
dry sweetener	$1\frac{1}{2}$ cups	287 grams
vanilla extract	1 tablespoon	15 milliliters
rice beverage	6 tablespoons	90 milliliters
balsamic vinegar	1 tablespoon	15 milliliters
grated orange zest	1 teaspoon	2 grams
fresh orange juice	$\frac{1}{4}$ cup	60 milliliters
grated zucchini	2 cups	224 grams

DRY INGREDIENTS

all-purpose flour	$2\frac{1}{2}$ cups	350 grams
cocoa powder	$\frac{1}{2}$ cup	40 grams
baking powder	1 tablespoon	15.6 grams
baking soda	1 teaspoon	4 grams
cinnamon	1 teaspoon	2 grams
chopped walnuts	$\frac{3}{4}$ cup	75 grams
dairy-free chocolate chips	$\frac{3}{4}$ cup	128 grams

Preheat the oven to 350°F/180°C. Oil and flour an 11-inch/27.5-centimeter tart pan and set aside.

In a food processor cream together all wet ingredients except the zucchini. In a bowl combine all dry ingredients and push to one side of the bowl. Combine the wet mixture and zucchini in the empty side of the bowl, then quickly incorporate it with the dry mixture to make a thick batter. Spread batter evenly in pan and bake for about 35 minutes or until it tests done. Allow the cake to cool to room temperature before cutting.

SERVE WITH: A pool of Corn Crème Anglaze (page 396), and drizzled with Chocolate Sauce (page 378), or any of the Silken Dessert Crèmes (page 395).

Chocolate Sauce

YIELD 1 CUP/240 MILLILITERS

soy milk	$\frac{1}{2}$ cup	120 milliliters
maple syrup	$\frac{1}{4}$ cup	60 milliliters
soy margarine	1 teaspoon	5 grams
chocolate chips, dairy-free	1 cup	168 grams
vanilla extract	$\frac{1}{2}$ teaspoon	2.5 milliliters

Bring the soy milk, maple syrup, and soy margarine to a boil. Remove from heat and add the chocolate chips. Stir until chocolate is melted and smooth. Stir in the vanilla.

Note: You can use rice beverage in place of soy milk. For a thinner sauce, add a little more soy milk or rice beverage.

Easy Apple Cake Ewa

When my wife came home with a colleague's original version for this recipe I commented that it wouldn't work. After I admitted that I was wrong, I realized that the cake's dry top mixture is moistened by the steam given off by the fruit as it cooks and the bottom is moistened by the juices as they soak downward. The name honors my wife's coworker.

DRY MIXTURE

Florida crystals	$1\frac{1}{2}$ cups	315 grams
cream of wheat cereal	$1\frac{1}{2}$ cups	264 grams
all–purpose flour	$1\frac{1}{2}$ cups	210 grams
baking powder	1 tablespoon	15.6 grams
soy margarine	$\frac{3}{4}$ cup	168 grams
sliced almonds	$\frac{1}{2}$ cup	45.5 grams

FILLING

grated Granny Smith apples	6 cups	672 grams
dried pitted cherries	$\frac{1}{2}$ cup	56 grams

Preheat oven to 375°F/190°C. Oil and coat a 10-inch/25-centimeter springform pan with plain bread crumbs or flour.

In a bowl combine the Florida crystals, cream of wheat, flour and baking powder. Cut in the soy margarine, then use half of the mixture to evenly coat the bottom of the springform pan. Mix the sliced almonds with the remaining dry mixture and set aside.

Add the grated apples and the dried cherries to the springform pan in an even layer. Cover the fruit layer with the remaining dry cake mixture with almonds.

Bake for 30 minutes and check for browning. If needed, cover the pan with foil. Continue to bake for another 25 to 30 minutes. Allow the dessert a little time to cool and set before cutting. It's best when eaten warm or at room temperature.

SERVE WITH: Silken Dessert Nut Crème (page 395) or Cranberry Raspberry Sauce (page 394).

Note: A little sweetener may be added to the fruit as needed. Other fruit such as pears, blueberries and peaches work well in the recipe. Also, other dried fruit such as raisins, currants or blueberries could be used. The soy margarine can be replaced in part or in full with a light oil. Other dry sweeteners such as succanat, maple sugar, white or brown sugar can be used. Cream of wheat is also called by the brand name Farina. There is also a whole wheat version available (called Bear Mush).

Craisin Beet Cake

YIELD 12 SERVINGS

Craisins is another name for dried cranberries. The balsamic vinegar in the recipe adds flavor and activates the baking powder, allowing the cake to rise better.

DRY INGREDIENTS

all-purpose flour	$1\frac{1}{2}$ cups	210 grams
whole wheat pastry flour	$1\frac{1}{2}$ cups	210 grams
Florida crystals	$1\frac{1}{2}$ cups	315 grams
dried cranberries	$\frac{1}{2}$ cup	56 grams
chopped walnuts	$\frac{1}{2}$ cup	49 grams
baking powder	4 teaspoons	21 grams
ground cinnamon	$\frac{1}{2}$ teaspoon	1 gram
ground ginger	$\frac{1}{2}$ teaspoon	1 gram
ground nutmeg	$\frac{1}{4}$ teaspoon	.5 gram

WET INGREDIENTS

grated cooked beets	2 cups	448 grams
rice beverage	$1\frac{3}{4}$ cups	420 milliliters
canola oil	$\frac{1}{4}$ cup	60 milliliters
prune purée	$\frac{1}{4}$ cup	63 grams
balsamic vinegar	1 teaspoon	5 milliliters

FROSTING

Caramel Vegan Icing (page 398)	$3\frac{1}{4}$ cups	882 grams

Preheat oven to 350°F/180°C. Line a shallow 10-inch × $14\frac{1}{2}$-inch/25-centimeter × 36.25-centimeter sheet with baking parchment paper.

In a large bowl combine all the dry ingredients and push to one side of the bowl. In the empty side of the bowl combine the wet ingredients, then quickly fold into the dry mixture until moistened to form a thick batter.

Spread the mixture over a parchment-lined pan to form an even layer. Bake for 20 minutes and then check for doneness with a toothpick.

When the cake is done, cool it in the pan for 5 minutes, then turn it over onto a wire cake cooling rack. Remove the parchment paper and allow the cake to cool thoroughly before frosting.

To frost, place the Caramel Vegan Icing into a pastry bag fitted with a star tip and cover the top of the cake with a zigzag pattern.

Garnet Yam Cake

YIELD 12 SERVINGS

In this recipe the apple cider vinegar works the same as the balsamic vinegar in Craisin Beet Cake, adding flavor and activating the baking powder, allowing the cake to rise better.

DRY INGREDIENTS

all-purpose flour	$1\frac{1}{2}$ cups	210 grams
whole wheat pastry flour	$1\frac{1}{2}$ cups	210 grams
Florida crystals	$1\frac{1}{2}$ cups	315 grams
currants	$\frac{1}{2}$ cup	56 grams
chopped walnuts	$\frac{1}{2}$ cup	49 grams
baking powder	4 teaspoons	21 grams
ground cinnamon	$\frac{1}{2}$ teaspoon	1 gram
ground ginger	$\frac{1}{2}$ teaspoon	1 gram
ground nutmeg	$\frac{1}{4}$ teaspoon	.5 gram

WET INGREDIENTS

grated raw red garnet yams	2 cups	448 grams
rice beverage	$1\frac{3}{4}$ cups	420 milliliters
canola oil	$\frac{1}{4}$ cup	60 milliliters
apple butter	$\frac{1}{4}$ cup	63 grams
apple cider vinegar	1 teaspoon	5 milliliters
Caramel Vegan Icing (page 398)	$3\frac{1}{4}$ cups	882 grams

Preheat oven to 350°F/180°C. Line a shallow 10-inch × $14\frac{1}{2}$-inch/25-centimeter × 36.25-centimeter sheet pan with baking parchment paper. In a large bowl combine all the dry ingredients and push them to one side of the bowl. In the empty side of the bowl combine the wet ingredients, then quickly fold into the dry mixture until moistened to form a thick batter.

Spread the mixture over a parchment-lined pan to form an even layer. Bake for 20 minutes and then check for doneness with a toothpick.

When the cake is done, cool it in the pan for 5 minutes, then turn it over onto a wire cake cooling rack. Remove the parchment paper and allow the cake to cool thoroughly before frosting.

To frost, place the Caramel Vegan Icing into a pastry bag fitted with a star tip and cover the top of the cake with a zigzag pattern.

Apple Streusel Cake

YIELD 12 SERVINGS

After many tests I discovered that this cake works best when the fruit is pressed into the top of the batter rather than mixed in. The fruit on top method results in a moist rather than a very wet cake.

DRY INGREDIENTS

all-purpose white flour	2 cups	280 grams
whole wheat pastry flour	2 cups	252 grams
succanat	1 cup	168 grams
Florida crystals	1 cup	210 grams
baking powder	4 teaspoons	20 grams
cinnamon	2 teaspoons	4 grams

WET INGREDIENTS

canola oil	$\frac{1}{4}$ cup	60 milliliters
apple butter	$\frac{1}{4}$ cup	60 milliliters
rice beverage	$1\frac{3}{4}$ cups	420 milliliters
apple cider vinegar	1 teaspoon	5 milliliters

FRUIT

apples, peeled, cored and sliced	2 cups	336 grams

STREUSEL TOPPING

chopped almonds	$\frac{1}{2}$ cup	49 grams
whole wheat pastry flour	$\frac{1}{2}$ cup	70 grams
succanat	$\frac{1}{2}$ cup	84 grams
soy margarine	3 tablespoons	42 grams

Preheat over to 350°F/180°C. Line a 10-inch × 14$\frac{1}{2}$-inch/25-centimeter × 36.25-centimeter baking sheet with baking parchment.

Combine the dry ingredients. Combine the wet ingredients, then mix them into the dry mixture. Pour the batter out onto a lined baking sheet. Lightly press the apple slices into the top of the batter, making 4 lengthwise rows.

Place the cake in the oven and bake for 10 minutes. While the cake bakes, combine the streusel topping mixture in a food processor and pulse to a coarsely chopped mixture. After the first 10 minutes of baking, sprinkle streusel over the top of the apples and batter. Bake 8 minutes longer or until cake tests done when a skewer is inserted into the thickest part and comes out dry.

VARIATIONS: Make individual streusel cakes in small soufflé cups or ceramic baking dishes.

Blueberry Streusel Cake

YIELD 12 SERVINGS

DRY INGREDIENTS

all-purpose white flour	2 cups	280 grams
whole wheat pastry flour	2 cups	252 grams
succanat	1 cup	168 grams
Florida crystals	1 cup	210 grams
baking powder	4 teaspoons	20 grams
cinnamon	2 teaspoons	4 grams

WET INGREDIENTS

canola oil	$\frac{1}{4}$ cup	60 milliliters
apple butter	$\frac{1}{4}$ cup	60 milliliters
rice beverage	$1\frac{3}{4}$ cups	420 milliliters
apple cider vinegar	1 teaspoon	5 milliliters

FRUIT

blueberries	2 cups	308 grams

STREUSEL TOPPING

chopped almonds	$\frac{1}{2}$ cup	49 grams
whole wheat pastry flour	$\frac{1}{2}$ cup	70 grams
succanat	$\frac{1}{2}$ cup	84 grams
soy margarine	3 tablespoons	42 grams

Preheat oven to 350°F/180°C. Line a shallow 10-inch × 14$\frac{1}{2}$-inch/25-centimeter × 36.25-centimeter sheet pan with baking parchment paper.

Combine the dry ingredients. Combine the wet ingredients, then mix them into the dry mixture. Pour the batter out onto a lined baking sheet. Lightly press the blueberries into the top of the batter.

Place the cake in the oven and bake for 10 minutes. While the cake bakes, combine the streusel topping mixture in a food processor and pulse to a coarsely chopped mixture. After the first 10 minutes of baking, sprinkle the streusel over the top of the blueberries and batter. Bake 8 minutes longer or until cake tests done when a skewer is inserted into the thickest part and comes out dry.

VARIATIONS: Make individual streusel cakes in small soufflé cups or ceramic baking dishes.

Peach Streusel Cake

YIELD 12 SERVINGS

DRY INGREDIENTS

all-purpose white flour	2 cups	280 grams
whole wheat pastry flour	2 cups	252 grams
succanat	1 cup	168 grams
Florida crystals	1 cup	210 grams
baking powder	4 teaspoons	20 grams
cinnamon	2 teaspoons	4 grams

WET INGREDIENTS

canola oil	$\frac{1}{4}$ cup	60 milliliters
apple butter	$\frac{1}{4}$ cup	60 milliliters
rice beverage	$1\frac{3}{4}$ cups	420 milliliters
apple cider vinegar	1 teaspoon	5 milliliters

FRUIT

peaches, peeled, pitted and sliced	2 cups	280 grams

STREUSEL TOPPING

chopped almonds	$\frac{1}{2}$ cup	49 grams
whole wheat pastry flour	$\frac{1}{2}$ cup	70 grams
succanat	$\frac{1}{2}$ cup	84 grams
soy margarine	3 tablespoons	42 grams

Preheat oven to 350°F/180°C. Line a shallow 10-inch × 14$\frac{1}{2}$-inch/25-centimeter × 36.25-centimeter sheet pan with baking parchment paper.

Combine the dry ingredients. Combine the wet ingredients and then mix them into the dry mixture. Pour the batter out onto a lined baking sheet. Lightly press peach slices into the top of the batter, making 4 lengthwise rows.

Place the cake in the oven and bake for 10 minutes. While the cake bakes, combine the streusel topping mixture in a food processor and pulse to a coarsely chopped mixture. After the first 10 minutes of baking, sprinkle the streusel over the top of the peaches and batter. Bake 8 minutes longer or until cake tests done when a skewer is inserted into the thickest part and comes out dry.

VARIATIONS: Make individual streusel cakes in small soufflé cups or ceramic baking dishes.

Apple Blueberry Strudel

Use a sweet eating apple for this dessert such as a red or Golden Delicious. These types of apples work best because of the short baking time.

canola oil	3 tablespoons	45 milliliters
soy margarine	2 tablespoons	28 grams
dry sweetener	4 teaspoons	14 grams
cinnamon	$\frac{1}{2}$ teaspoon	1 gram
FILLING		
Delicious apples, peeled, cored, thinly sliced	3 cups	336 grams
maple syrup	1 tablespoon	15 milliliters
cornstarch	1 tablespoon	8 grams
blueberries, frozen	$\frac{1}{2}$ cup	140 grams
WRAPPERS		
whole wheat fillo	10 sheets	10 sheets

Preheat oven to 375°F/190°C. Put the oil and margarine in a small pan over low heat until the margarine is melted, then set aside and keep warm. Combine the dry sweetener with half of the cinnamon and set aside.

In a bowl, combine the remaining cinnamon with all of the other filling ingredients. Brush a sheet of fillo with some of the warmed oil and soy margarine and sprinkle with some of the sugar cinnamon mixture. Fold over one-third of the fillo sheet from each side toward the center lengthwise into a strip one-third as wide as a full sheet. Place $\frac{1}{3}$ cup/37 grams at the end of the strip closest to you and fold it up into a triangle-shaped pastry. Place each triangle on a baking sheet and brush the top with the oil/margarine mix. Continue to make triangles until filling and fillo sheets are used up. Bake triangles for 13 to 15 minutes until golden brown and the apples are cooked.

VARIATION: For Peach Almond Strudel, use peaches in place of the apples and chopped toasted almonds.

For Peach Raspberry Strudel, use peaches in place of the apples and raspberries in place of the blueberries.

SERVE WITH: Corn Crème Anglaze (page 396).

Note: Some of the peel could be left on the apples for added color and fiber. Expect a 33% loss from the purchased weight when removing the peel and core. Whole wheat fillo is available from Athens Fillo (see Appendix C).

Fruit Cobbler

YIELD 10 SERVINGS

In olden times this dessert's bumpy pastry topping reminded people of their cobblestone streets, providing one explanation for its name. Another possibility is that it came from the term "cobble up" which meant to make something quickly.

COBBLER TOPPING DRY INGREDIENTS

all-purpose white flour	2 cups	280 grams
whole wheat pastry flour	1 cup	140 grams
baking powder	1 tablespoon	15.5 grams
cinnamon	$\frac{1}{2}$ teaspoon	1 gram
salt	pinch	pinch

WET INGREDIENTS

maple syrup	$\frac{3}{4}$ cup	180 milliliters
vanilla rice beverage	$1\frac{1}{2}$ cups	360 milliliters
canola oil	$\frac{1}{4}$ cup	60 milliliters
apple sauce	$\frac{1}{4}$ cup	60 milliliters
vanilla extract	1 teaspoon	5 milliliters

COBBLER FILLING

apples, peeled and thinly sliced	10 cups	1.68 kilograms
ground allspice	1 teaspoon	2 grams

GARNISH

chopped pecans	$\frac{1}{2}$ cup	52.5 grams

a 2-inch/5-centimeter half hotel pan or a 13-inch × 9-inch × 2-inch/32.5-centimeter × 22.5-centimeter × 5-centimeter baking dish

Preheat oven to 375°F/190°C. Combine the dry ingredients. Reserve $\frac{1}{4}$ cup/2 fluid ounces/60 milliliters maple syrup. Combine the wet ingredients, then fold them into the dry mixture to make a thick batter.

Toss the sliced apples with the allspice and the reserved maple syrup. Put the seasoned apple slices into the baking dish.

Spoon clumps of batter over the top of the apple slices. If the top is covered with the mounds of batter and there is still a little space between them, the spaces will fill in as the cobbler cooks. Sprinkle on chopped pecans.

Bake for 35 minutes on the top shelf of the oven then check for doneness with a toothpick. The top should be golden brown and the toothpick should come out free from any raw batter. The batter close to the fruit will still be moist even when the cobbler is cooked through. Bake longer if needed.

SERVE WITH: Silken Nut Crème (page 395) and/or Cranberry Raspberry Sauce (page 394).

Note: Make individual cobblers in small soufflé cups or ceramic baking dishes.

Chocolate Almond Tart

YIELD 12 TO 16 SERVINGS

This recipe can be formed in an 8-inch/20-centimeter or 9-inch/22.5-centimeter springform pan; the smaller pan will produce a taller dessert.

CRUST

toasted almonds	1 cup	98 grams
dairy-free granola	$1\frac{1}{2}$ cups	120 grams
maple syrup	1 tablespoon	15 milliliters
soy margarine	1 tablespoon	14 grams
apple juice	2 tablespoons	30 milliliters
almond extract	$\frac{1}{4}$ teaspoon	.625 milliliter

CHOCOLATE ALMOND TART FILLING

chocolate chips, semi-sweet, dairy-free	3 cups	504 grams
extra-firm silken tofu	$3\frac{1}{2}$ cups	700 grams
maple syrup	4 tablespoons	60 milliliters
vanilla extract	2 teaspoons	10 milliliters
almond extract	1 teaspoon	5 milliliters

For the crust, reserve a few almonds for garnish, then put all the remaining crust ingredients into a food processor and process to a coarse mixture that sticks together. Turn out the crust mixture into the springform pan and evenly coat the bottom, making it slightly higher at the edges.

For the filling, melt the chocolate chips over barely simmering water. As chocolate melts put all other filling ingredients into the food processor and process until smooth. Add the melted chocolate and process until completely incorporated. Taste the mixture and adjust if needed.

Reserve about 1 cup/240 milliliters of the filling and chill. Turn the mixture into the crust-lined springform pan. Smooth the top, cover the pan and chill for 2 hours. Put the reserved chilled chocolate filling into a pastry bag fitted with a star tip and pipe decorations around the top edge of the tart. Chop the reserved toasted almonds and sprinkle on top. Chill to firm up the piping work. Using a sharp pointed knife, wipe with a damp towel between each slice, and cut and serve. The point of the knife will help loosen the slices from the pan.

VARIATION: The soy margarine could be omitted from the crust and replaced with a little more juice to bind it. It will, however, be a little more crumbly. Other juice flavors could be used. Use hazelnuts in place of the almonds. The filling can be used as a frosting.

Tart Pastry

YIELD 1 TART SHELL 11 INCHES/27.5 CENTIMETERS

ABOUT 20 OUNCES/560 GRAMS RAW PASTRY DOUGH

For tart or pie pastry, keys to success are to keep the pastry cold as you work with it even if it means returning it to the refrigerator during the process and then to bake it in a hot oven to start out, lowering the temperature once the tart is set.

dry sweetener	$\frac{1}{4}$ cup	52.5 grams
lemon zest, minced	1 teaspoon	3.5 grams
all-purpose white flour	2 cups	280 grams
salt	pinch	pinch
canola oil	$\frac{1}{4}$ cup	60 milliliters
cold soy margarine, large dice	$\frac{1}{4}$ cup	56 grams
ice water	5 tablespoons	75 milliliters

Put dry sweetener and lemon zest into the food processor and pulse until well ground together. Pulse in the flour and salt. Pulse in the oil. Pulse in the diced chilled margarine. With the machine running, add ice water until just mixed.

Turn the dough out onto a work surface and form it into a flat disk. Cover with plastic wrap and chill in refrigerator for at least 20 minutes.

Roll out the dough using plastic wrap underneath and over the top. Line the tart shell with dough and refrigerate until ready to bake. Fill and bake according to the recipe used.

Maple Walnut Pecan Tart

YIELD 12 SERVINGS

This pecan pie variation uses a dry egg replacer product in place of eggs.

11-inch/27.5-centimeter tart pan

Tart Pastry (page 389)	20 ounces	560 grams
cashews	$\frac{1}{2}$ cup	70 grams
egg replacer	2 tablespoons	16.8 grams
cornstarch	1 tablespoon	8 grams
water	$\frac{3}{4}$ cup	180 milliliters
maple syrup	$\frac{3}{4}$ cup	180 milliliters
barley malt syrup	$\frac{1}{4}$ cup	60 milliliters
vanilla extract	1 teaspoon	5 milliliters
almond extract	$\frac{1}{2}$ teaspoon	2.5 milliliters
whole walnuts	1 cup	100 grams
whole pecans	1 cup	100 grams

Preheat oven to 400°F/200°C. Line the tart pan with crust and refrigerate.

Put the cashews, egg replacer, and cornstarch in a blender and pulse until the cashews are ground fine. Slowly pulse in water. With the blender turned off, scrape down the sides of the blender with a stiff spatula as needed to free stuck ground cashews. Add the syrups, vanilla and almond extracts and blend well.

Sprinkle the walnuts and pecans into the chilled tart shell so they are evenly mixed. Pour the syrup mixture into the tart shell and push the nuts down so they are coated. Place the filled tart shell onto a thin baking sheet and place into the oven.

Bake for 15 minutes at 400°F/200°C, then lower the heat to 325°F/160°C for another 15 minutes or until the tart is browned, firm, and slightly cracked on top. Remove the tart from the oven and allow it to cool and settle before serving.

Serve tart warm or at room temperature.

SERVE WITH: Praline Crème (page 397), or Silken Dessert Nut Crème (page 395).

Note: EnerG egg replacer is available through natural foods vendors. If unavailable, use $2\frac{1}{2}$ teaspoons/6 grams constarch and $\frac{1}{2}$ teaspoon/3.6 grams baking powder in place of 1 tablespoon/8.4 grams egg replacer.

Pear Tart with Dried Cranberries, Almond and Lime

10 SERVINGS

11-inch/27.5-centimeter tart pan		
Tart Pastry, recipe (page 389)	20 ounces	560 grams
apricot jam	1 tablespoon	17 grams

FILLING

ripe pears	$2\frac{1}{2}$ pounds	1.12 kilograms
lime juice	2 teaspoons	10 milliliters
dry sweetener	3 tablespoons	14 grams
cornstarch	4 teaspoons	10.6 grams
cinnamon	$\frac{1}{4}$ teaspoon	.5 gram
cardamom	pinch	pinch

TOPPING

dried cranberries (craisins)	$\frac{1}{3}$ cup	35 grams
dry sweetener	3 tablespoons	14 grams
grated lime rind	1 teaspoon	3.5 grams
flour	2 tablespoons	17 grams
almonds	$\frac{1}{4}$ cup	25 grams
rum extract	$\frac{1}{4}$ teaspoon	1.25 milliliters
canola oil	1 tablespoon	14 grams

Preheat oven to 400°F/200°C. Prepare the tart shell, spread jam across bottom of shell and refrigerate. Peel, core, halve and slice the pears thinly. Toss them with the remaining filling ingredients. Arrange the pear slices by first making a circle of pear slices around the outer edge of the tart shell so that the skin-side edge of each slice touches the tart shell. Next, make a circle of pear slices that point toward the edge and the center of the tart. Make a second smaller circle of slices inside the first, then fill in the center with remaining slices.

Bake the tart for 20 minutes. While tart bakes, combine the topping ingredients in a food processor and pulse the machine several times to form a coarse crumb topping. After the tart has baked 20 minutes, reduce the oven temperature to 375°F/190°C, remove the tart from the oven and sprinkle the topping on thicker at the outer edge, the center and just lightly over the space in between, allowing the pear slices to show through. Bake the tart for about 5 minutes longer. Remove the tart from the oven and cool on a wire rack.

VARIATION: Rum or almond extract can be used in place of rum extract.

Spiced Summer Berries

YIELD 10 SERVINGS

From different traditions we learn different ways to enhance flavor. To perk up the flavor of strawberries in Italy, balsamic vinegar is used; in France, a sprinkle of fresh ground black pepper; and in New England the traditional taste and sweetness of maple syrup is utilized. Raspberries, other berries or ripe sliced peaches can be used in place of or in combination with the strawberries.

strawberries, rinsed, hulled, and sliced	5 cups	770 grams
balsamic vinegar	$1\frac{1}{2}$ teaspoons	7.5 milliliters
maple syrup, grade A medium amber	1 tablespoon	15 milliliters
fresh ground black pepper	a sprinkle	a sprinkle

Gently toss all ingredients, then season to taste.

SERVE WITH: For shortcake, the berries could be served over Coconut Curry Biscuits (page 360) or Lemon Prune Scones (page 354) with Strawberry or Raspberry Dessert Sauce (page 393) and a Silken Dessert Nut Crèmes (page 395) topping. The peaches would go well over the Peach and Pecan Corn Bread (page 352) with the Peach Dessert Sauce (variation of Strawberry Sauce) (page 393) and Silken Dessert Nut Crèmes topping (page 395) made with almond butter.

Raspberry Dessert Sauce

YIELD 12 SERVINGS

2 TABLESPOONS/30 MILLILITERS

fresh raspberries	$\frac{1}{2}$ cup	70 grams
all-fruit seedless raspberry jam	$\frac{1}{2}$ cup	136 grams
apple-raspberry juice	$\frac{1}{2}$ cup	120 milliliters

Blend all ingredients until smooth. Chill before serving. Strain to remove the seeds if desired.

VARIATION: Plain apple juice could be used in the recipe. Frozen raspberries (measured frozen) work well. A grind or two of black pepper from a pepper grinder and a drizzle of balsamic vinegar can be used to enhance flavor.

Note: Many flavors of juices are available through natural foods purveyors and stores.

Strawberry Dessert Sauce

YIELD 12 SERVINGS

2 TABLESPOONS/30 MILLILITERS

fresh strawberries	$\frac{1}{2}$ cup	77 grams
all-fruit strawberry jam	$\frac{1}{2}$ cup	136 grams
apple-strawberry juice	$\frac{1}{2}$ cup	120 milliliters

Blend all ingredients until smooth. Chill before serving.

VARIATION: Plain apple juice could be used in the recipe. Peach and/or raspberry jam work well with the strawberries. A grind or two of black pepper from a pepper grinder and a drizzle of balsamic vinegar can be used to enhance flavor.

Cranberry Raspberry Dessert Sauce

YIELD 12 SERVINGS

2 TABLESPOONS/30 MILLILITERS

fresh cranberries	$\frac{1}{2}$ cup	56 grams
all-fruit seedless raspberry jam	$\frac{1}{2}$ cup	136 grams
apple cider	$\frac{1}{2}$ cup	120 milliliters

Blend all ingredients until smooth. Chill before serving. Strain to remove seeds if desired.

Note: A touch of fresh ground black pepper and a drizzle of balsamic vinegar can be used to enhance the flavor.

Orange Silken Crème

YIELD 10 SERVINGS

$\frac{1}{4}$ CUP/60 MILLILITERS

silken tofu	12.3 ounces	345 grams
orange juice concentrate	6 tablespoons	90 milliliters
maple syrup	6 tablespoons	90 milliliters
vanilla rice beverage	3 tablespoons	45 milliliters
vanilla extract	1 teaspoon	5 milliliters
almond extract	$\frac{1}{2}$ teaspoon	2.5 milliliters

Combine all ingredients in a blender or food processor and blend until smooth.

VARIATION: For a richer crème, add a little almond oil. For a low-fat version use 1% fat silken tofu. Add a little cinnamon when serving with Butternut Mousse (page 372).

Silken Dessert Nut Crème

YIELD 10 SERVINGS

$\frac{1}{4}$ CUP/60 MILLILITERS

Chef Ron Pickarski introduced me to this style of dessert crème during one of our Culinary Olympic practice sessions.

firm silken tofu	12.3 ounces	345 grams
hazelnut butter	3 tablespoons	48 grams
maple syrup	6 tablespoons	90 milliliters
vanilla rice beverage	3 tablespoons	45 milliliters
vanilla extract	1 teaspoon	5 milliliters
almond extract	$\frac{1}{2}$ teaspoon	2.5 milliliters

Combine all ingredients in a blender or food processor and blend until smooth.

VARIATION: Almond butter, peanut butter or other nut butter of choice can be used in place of the hazelnut butter. For a richer crème topping, use oil in place of the rice beverage. Another variation is to add a little ginger powder or touch of ginger brandy.

Note: Hazelnuts are also called filberts. The oil at the top of a jar of hazelnut butter is an excellent source of flavor for these silken nut crèmes. By removing the oil, the remaining nut butter is lower in fat. Use the hazelnut oil in place of the hazelnut butter.

Corn Crème Anglaze

YIELD 10 SERVINGS

3 TABLESPOONS/45 MILLILITERS

A vegan custard-style sauce perfumed with the flavor of fresh vanilla bean that may be served warm or chilled.

rice beverage	1 cup	240 milliliters
cornstarch	1 tablespoon	8 grams
frozen corn kernels	2 cups	350 grams
maple syrup	$\frac{1}{4}$ cup	60 milliliters
vanilla bean	$\frac{1}{2}$ bean	$\frac{1}{2}$ bean
salt	pinch	pinch
soy margarine	1 tablespoon	14 grams

Combine 1 tablespoon/15 milliliters rice beverage with the cornstarch and set aside. Place all the remaining ingredients except soy margarine into a saucepan. Bring to a boil and simmer for 5 minutes. Remove the vanilla bean and set aside.

Pour the mixture into a blender and process until smooth. Pass the mixture through a strainer back into the saucepan. Split the vanilla bean lengthwise, scrape out the seeds and add the seeds to the corn crème mixture. Discard the pod. Add the soy margarine to the pan.

Bring the mixture to a simmer and stir in the dissolved cornstarch. As soon as the sauce thickens, remove the mixture from the heat, pour into another container if desired, cover and chill.

Praline Crème

YIELD 10 SERVINGS
$\frac{1}{4}$ CUP/60 MILLILITERS

Florida crystals	$\frac{1}{2}$ cup	91 grams
water	3 tablespoons	45 milliliters
silken tofu	(1) 12.3 ounce box	349 grams
vanilla extract	1 teaspoon	5 milliliters
cinnamon	$\frac{1}{4}$ teaspoon	.5 gram
canola oil	2 teaspoons	10 milliliters
toasted pecans, chopped	$\frac{1}{4}$ cup	24.5 grams

Combine the sugar and water in a small, heavy-bottom saucepan and place on medium heat. Place the remaining ingredients in a blender and blend until smooth, turning the blender off and scraping down the sides as needed.

Boil the sugar syrup until it starts to turn a caramel color. When it is a medium-dark and fragrant caramel, carefully pour the syrup into the blender and blend until smooth.

Caution: The caramel syrup burns easily and also can cause burns if it comes in contact with the skin.

VARIATION: Use maple syrup in place of the sugar, omit the water and skip the caramel cooking step. Flavor with some rum extract.

Caramel Vegan Icing

YIELD 3¼ CUPS/882 GRAMS

Use either plain or vanilla rice beverage for the liquid in the recipe.

rice dream rice beverage	2 cups	480 milliliters
succanat	2 cups	336 grams
vanilla extract	2 teaspoons	10 milliliters
white miso paste	2 teaspoons	10 grams
apple cider vinegar	1 teaspoon	5 milliliters
lemon juice	1 teaspoon	5 milliliters
almond extract	⅛ teaspoon	.65 milliters
all-purpose white flour	½ cup	56 grams
canola oil	¼ cup	60 milliliters
cornstarch	⅓ cup	42 grams
soy margarine	2 cups	450 grams

Combine 1¾ cup/420 milliliters rice dream with the succanat, vanilla, miso, vinegar, lemon juice and almond extract and bring to a boil. While the mixture heats combine flour and canola oil. Stir the flour-oil mixture into the boiling liquid, then simmer for 2 minutes. Combine the cornstarch with the remaining rice beverage and whisk into simmering liquid. While continuing to stir, bring to a boil and then remove from the heat. Chill the mixture thoroughly.

When the mixture is cold place into a food processor. Cut the chilled soy margarine into pieces and process 1 stick at a time until a smooth icing is achieved. It may appear separated at first but will come together by the time the last stick is added. Also, scrape down the mixture to mix thoroughly. If at this point it still appears separated, add 1 teaspoon/5 milliliters lemon juice and continue to process until smooth. More sweetener such as Florida crystals can also help bring together the frosting. Sometimes the base mixture builds up moisture from condensation during the cooling process. If this happens, pour off or absorb any moisture with a paper towel.

Almond Coconut Cookies

YIELD 20 TO 22 COOKIES

2 COOKIES AS A GARNISH

These almond-based cookies can be used as a garnish for another dessert or be served after the last course as the final note of a meal.

whole almonds, skin on	1 cup	126 grams
Florida crystals	$\frac{1}{2}$ cup	105 grams
non-sweetened shredded coconut	$\frac{1}{2}$ cup	56 grams
cornstarch	2 tablespoons	16 grams
baking powder	1 teaspoon	5.2 grams
water	$\frac{1}{4}$ cup	60 milliliters
vanilla extract	$\frac{1}{2}$ teaspoon	2.5 milliliters
almond extract	$\frac{1}{4}$ teaspoon	1.25 milliliters
chopped almonds	$\frac{1}{2}$ cup	63 grams

Preheat oven to 325°F/170°C. In a food processor grind the almonds, Florida crystals, and coconut for 1 minute or until very fine. Add the cornstarch and baking powder and pulse a few times. Add the water and extracts and pulse a few times until combined. Using a tablespoon or $\frac{1}{2}$ ounce/14 gram scoop, place mounds of mixture onto chopped almonds and press down to coat the tops of cookies with nuts. Place cookies, nut side up, on a parchment-lined or nonstick cookie sheet. Bake for about 12 minutes. Remove the cookies to a cooling rack.

VARIATION: Use chopped hazelnuts or whole pine nuts to coat the tops of the cookies.

Chocolate Chip Cookies

YIELD 32 LARGE COOKIES
64 SMALL COOKIES

Flatten out the scooped cookie dough well for crisper cookies.

DRY MIXTURE

all-purpose white flour	4 cups	500 grams
rolled oats	2 cups	196 grams
succanat	$1\frac{1}{2}$ cups	252 grams
baking powder	2 tablespoons	31 grams
salt	$\frac{1}{2}$ teaspoon	3 grams
chocolate chips, semi-sweet, dairy-free	$1\frac{1}{2}$ cups	250 grams
walnuts, chopped	1 cup	100 grams

WET INGREDIENTS

firm silken tofu	5 ounces	140 grams
canola oil	$\frac{3}{4}$ cup	180 milliliters
maple syrup	$1\frac{1}{2}$ cups	360 milliliters
vanilla extract	1 tablespoon	15 milliliters

In a large bowl combine the dry ingredients and push to one side of the bowl. In a food processor purée the silken tofu until very smooth, then add the remaining wet ingredients to the processor and process until smooth. Pour the wet mixture into the bowl with the dry ingredients and mix quickly and thoroughly. Chill the dough for at least 1 hour.

Preheat oven to 350°F/180°C. On a baking sheet lined with parchment paper, place $\frac{1}{4}$-cup/56-gram pieces of cookie dough. Cover the sheet with plastic wrap and flatten each cookie to about 3 inches/7.5 centimeters, carefully remove plastic wrap and save to use again.

Bake for about 11 minutes, or make smaller cookies and bake for about 7 minutes. If the bottoms of the cookies seem to be browning too fast try doubling the sheet pans.

Note: For a lower fat version replace up to one-half of the oil with apple butter, prune purée, or pear butter. The dry sweetener could also be creamed together with the wet mixture.

Oatmeal Raisin Cookies with Pecans

YIELD 32 COOKIES OR

64 SMALL COOKIES

The search for traditional-tasting yet egg- and dairy-free cookies resulted in this recipe.

DRY INGREDIENTS

all-purpose white flour	4 cups	500 grams
rolled oats	2 cups	196 grams
succanat	$1\frac{1}{2}$ cups	252 grams
baking powder	2 tablespoons	31 grams
salt	$\frac{1}{2}$ teaspoon	3 grams
raisins	$1\frac{1}{2}$ cups	168 grams
pecans, chopped	1 cup	100 grams

WET INGREDIENTS

firm silken tofu	5 ounces	140 grams
canola oil	$\frac{3}{4}$ cup	180 milliliters
maple syrup	$1\frac{1}{2}$ cups	360 milliliters
vanilla extract	1 tablespoon	15 milliliters

In a large bowl combine the dry ingredients and push to one side of the bowl. In a food processor purée silken tofu until very smooth, then add the remaining wet ingredients to the processor and process until smooth. Pour the wet mixture into the bowl with the dry ingredients and mix quickly and thoroughly. Chill the dough for at least 1 hour.

Preheat the oven to 350°F/180°C. On a baking sheet lined with parchment paper place $\frac{1}{4}$-cup/56-gram pieces of cookie dough. Cover dough with plastic wrap and flatten each cookie to about 3 inches/7.5 centimeters, carefully remove plastic wrap and save to use again.

Bake for about 11 minutes, about 7 minutes for the $\frac{1}{2}$-size cookies. If the bottoms of the cookies seem to be browning too fast, try doubling the sheet pans.

Note: For a lower fat version, replace up to one-half of the oil with apple butter, prune purée, or pear butter. The dry sweetener could also be creamed together with the wet mixture.

Sesame Sunburst Cookies

rolled oats	$1\frac{1}{2}$ cups	150 grams
sunflower seeds	$\frac{1}{2}$ cup	63 grams
sesame tahini	6 tablespoons	90 milliliters
maple syrup	$\frac{1}{2}$ cup	120 milliliters
salt	pinch	pinch

Combine all ingredients in a bowl and chill for a least 1 hour. This resting period allows the oats to soften and helps the cookies stick together.

Preheat oven to 325°F/160°C. Place heaping tablespoons on parchment-lined baking sheet and bake for about 10 minutes.

VARIATION: Combine all ingredients in a food processor and pulse a few times to mix.

APPENDIX A

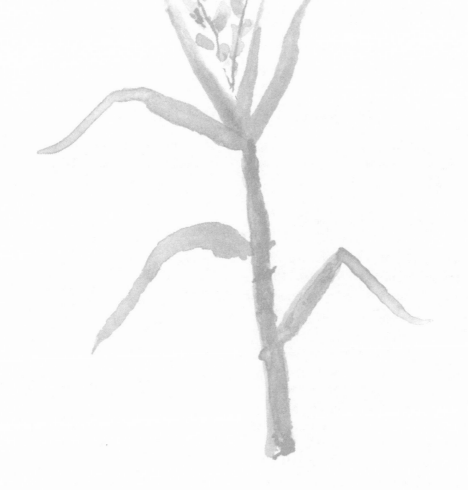

*M*enus

Holiday Themes: Year's End Holiday Menu

Sundried Tomato and Black Olive Pesto (pages 56, 57)
  with French Bread and Extra Virgin Olive Oil
Salad of Mixed Greens with Cajun Roasted Tofu and Sea Czar Dressing
  (page 186)
Sesame Roasted Butternut Squash (page 204)
Oven-Roasted Sweet Potatoes with Soy Sauce (page 203)
Roasted Garlic Potatoes with Rosemary (page 208)
Baby Bella Mushroom Risotto (page 302)
Rigatoni Pizziaola (page 273)
Maple Nut Tart (page 390)
Chocolate Coconut Pudding (page 373)

Gold Medal Menu Dishes

All of these dishes have been part of Gold Medal-winning presentations either at an American Culinary Federation Culinary Arts Salon or at the Culinary Olympics in Germany.

Carrot Hazelnut Spread (page 49)
Winter Squash Hazelnut Bisque (page 97)
Carrot Ginger Almond Bisque (page 96)
Corn and Arame Pancakes (page 71)
Smokey Braised Portobello Mushrooms (page 242)
Mushroom Duxelles, Ravioli (page 265)
Wild Mushroom Sauce (page 148)
Fried Oyster Mushrooms (page 244)
Carrot Juice Cinnamon Reduction Sauce (page 153)
Roast Tomato and Garlic Sauce with Dulse and Lime (page 146)
Red Pepper Porcini Reduction Sauce (page 151)
Aztec Sun Salad, Orange Mustard Dressing (pages 165, 182)
Black-eyed Pea Salad (page 166)
Savory Winter Pancakes (page 251)
Almond Brown Rice Croquettes (page 310)
Tofu Sundried Tomato Saucisse (page 332)

Chocolate Almond Tart (page 388)

Raspberry Dessert Sauce (page 393)

Hors d'oeuvres Menu

Vegetable Walnut and Pecan Pâté (page 52)

Artichoke Hearts in Fillo (page 64)

Smokey Braised Portobello Mushrooms (page 242)

Crostini with Three Types of Pesto

   Sundried Tomato, Black Olive and Spinach Pesto (pages 355, 56, 140)

Korean-Style Cucumbers with Spicy Miso Sauce (page 70)

Dates Stuffed with Almonds (page 77)

Fried Oyster Mushrooms (page 244)

Everyday Menus

MACROBIOTIC MENU

As there are a wide variety of vegetarian diets there are also a number of ways that people follow a macrobiotic diet depending on their personal health.

Please note that in general, macrobiotic cooking relies much less on spices and is often seasoned very mildly. In this regard it is important to know your guests' needs; they can tell you what they would enjoy for their meal.

Generally, a macrobiotic meal is composed of a soup, especially miso soup, and a platter that contains food from the following categories; grain, beans, leafy greens, sea vegetables, root vegetables, a pickle and a ground nut or seed condiment. I find this menu method works well for almost any occasion to be sure of balance.

SOUPS FOR A MACROBIOTIC MENU

Miso Soup (page 108)

Broccoli Tahini Soup (page 92)

Green Pea and Watercress Soup with Mint (page 95)

Carrot Ginger Almond Bisque (page 96)

Winter Squash Hazelnut Bisque (page 97)

Mushroom Barley Soup (page 111)

Kale Pumpkin Seed Crème Soup (page 114)

BEANS, GRAINS AND OTHER COMPONENTS FOR A MACROBIOTIC MENU

Adzuki Beans with Squash (page 291)
Millet Mash with Winter Squash (page 296)
Almond Brown Rice Croquettes (page 310)
Greens Sautéed with Ginger (page 195)
Corn on the Cob with Ume Boshi Plum Paste (page 206)
Sesame Roasted Butternut Squash (page 204)
Maple Glazed Kelp, Carrots, and Onions (page 214)
Arame with Carrots and Onions (page 209)

Breakfast Foods

SOME ITEMS THAT WOULD FIT ON A BREAKFAST MENU

Muffins (pages 362, 364–366)
Peach and Pecan Corn Bread (page 352)
Coconut Curry Biscuits (page 360)
Lemon Prune Scones (page 354)
Banana Kiwi Bread (page 367)
Plain Crepes with jam or maple syrup (page 248)
Corn and Chive Pancakes (page 252)
Scrambled Tofu (page 330)

Special Occasion Lunch

Green Pea and Watercress Mint Soup (page 95)
Sea Czar Salad with Orange Sun Dried Tomato Crostini (pages 175, 55)
Oyster Fried Mushrooms, Watermelon Catsup (pages 244, 135)
Chocolate Almond Tart, Raspberry Sauce (pages 388, 393)

Lunch Menu

Yellow Dal (page 293)
Basmati Rice (page 315)
Vegetable Curry (page 234)
Golden Potato Salad with Olives and Apricots (page 176)
Oatmeal Raisin Cookies (page 401)

Dinner Menu

Winter Squash Hazelnut Bisque (page 97)

Peach Pecan Corn Bread (page 352)

Wild, Japonica, and Wehani Rice Medley (page 168) with Apple Cider Dressing (page 184)

Mesclun Salad Sea Czar (page 175)

Rigatoni with Pizziola Sauce (page 273)

Chocolate Zucchini "Nanny" Cake (page 377) with Corn Crème Anglaze (page 396)

Wedding Buffet Menu

Vegetable Walnut and Pecan Pâté (page 52)

Wild, Japonica, and Wehani Rice Medley (page 168)

Mesclun Salad Sea Czar Dressing (page 175)

Smokey Braised Portobello Mushrooms (page 242)

Winter Squash Afghani Style (page 240)

Tortellini with Cherry Tomatoes, Spinach and Raisins (page 268)

Roasted Potatoes and Vegetables with Garlic and Rosemary (page 208)

Chocolate Almond Tart (page 388)

Summer Fruit Cobbler (page 386)

Guide for Waitstaff and Kitchen Personnel

In order to implement vegetarian menu changes that successfully attract and keep new diners, the following ideas should be considered.

A courteous and informed dining room staff is a key element in the continuing success of any foodservice establishment. The same level of attitude, competence and awareness is just as important in the kitchen. Both groups need to work together to serve guests' needs.

An awareness of special vegetarian diets such as healthy heart, vegan, macrobiotic and so forth will do much to assure the new vegetarian client that they have made the right choice in coming to your establishment.

Providing your clients with what they are seeking sometimes requires a little detective work. Diners, regardless of dietary habits, have one common denominator that provides the basis for them to seek out your food service operation: a certain level of hunger combined with the desire to eat. This may also be accompanied by many other possible physiological and psychological factors such as fatigue, focus on a business associate or the nervousness that might accompany a first date. The key to success for these situations is the service person's attention with details to the guest's requests, noting especially any clue that can lead to a further line of questioning that will ensure that their meal is a satisfactory experience.

The following notes, questions and answers can help a waitstaff in dealing appropriately with guests to ensure a great vegetarian dining experience.

When a diner asks about vegetarian options from the menu the waitperson could ask:

Are you following a special vegetarian diet?

Do you wish to avoid eggs, and dairy products? (vegan)

Are refined sugars or honey a part of your diet? (vegan, macrobiotic)

Are you allergic to or do you avoid members of the nightshade family such as peppers, potatoes or mushrooms? (macrobiotic)

Does the kitchen need to be aware of any food allergies? This is an especially important question because many of the recipes contain or are garnished with nuts which can cause certain individuals with allergies to go into shock.

Is spicy food preferred or not?

Are there any foods that fit your diet that you don't like the taste of such as beets or radish or any spice that you don't care for?

Do you like or dislike products that have the taste, texture or appearance of meat?

This inquiry will let the diner know that the staff is well informed and put them at ease. The waitperson could then point out those items on the menu that best suit the client or be able to make recommendations that the kitchen can fulfill.

Requests or questions about any of the above items should also spur the server on to inquire about the other items on the list.

Often, when talking to people in foodservice who are trying to improve their vegetarian menu offerings, they mention the fact that not all of their clients who follow a vegetarian diet approve of meat analogs. When dealing with this situation I often mention to the clients several reasons for the preparation of such foods, especially that these products can help to increase the number of people following a meatless diet. Also, these meat substitutes seem to be a very good alternative for people who have recently adopted a vegetarian diet and did not have an aversion to the taste of meat; sometimes they provide an attractive alternative for those wishing to reduce their meat consumption.

All this is done, however, with respect for those people who never liked the sight, smell or taste of meat or those who have followed a vegetarian diet for their entire lives and have no desire for such items. For these diners as for any client who wants food that they can enjoy, I would try to provide something for them.

If a large percentage of the meals you serve are vegetarian you may wish to purchase and reserve pots and pans especially for this cooking. This would certainly be appreciated by your guests and further show your commitment to their dining needs. (See Vegetarian Diets Defined pages 9–11.)

Marketing Vegetarian Options

When seeking a way to showcase new culinary skills and to give guests a chance to partake of a special menu, I found that extra effort paid off. By serving a multicourse special *prix fixe* menu at my former restaurant on Thursday evenings, culinary expression could be satisfied, guests could be pleased and overall sales during slow period could be improved and not at the expense of the usually busy weekend nights.

Menu Location for Meatless
Dining Options

INTEGRATED MENU APPROACH

By placing meatless dining options on the menu next to and in between other choices, a statement is being made that these dishes are of the same quality and value as any item prepared by the establishment.

THE SPECIAL SECTION MENU APPROACH

By establishing a special section for vegan and vegetarian options, one may have more room to elaborate on their preparation and to mention options or variations that may also be available. This approach can also provide space to let the clients know that you are aware of the many ways that people choose to dine and that you can meet their needs. A special section is good also for those who do not wish to spend time reading about food they will not choose to order.

VEGETARIAN CROSS-CONTAMINATION CONSCIOUSNESS

A key element for the kitchen staff is to know what food items need to be avoided when serving vegetarian meals. One chef related a story of how he took special care to prepare a vegan meal for a customer, only to have it ruined by one of his assistants who innocently added the house vegetable stock which contained chicken broth.

Sometimes the ingredients that are excluded from a vegetarian diet go beyond the obvious meat, fish and poultry. Vegetarian cuisine should never include the following: gelatin from animal bones, meat, poultry or fish stock. Also be aware of lard and beef fat as a shortening ingredient in prepared baking mixes. Vegan diets avoid all dairy and egg products with some of the less obvious ones being in prepared mixes and foods. Dried milk products, dried buttermilk, whey, lactose and casein are all dairy products or byproducts that show up in many different foods: breads, packaged cereals, even granola, other baked goods and so on.

𝒫urveyor Guide/ Mail Order Source

Purveyors

Ahimsa Brand Vegan Meat analogs, distributed by
Good Taste Vegetarian Foods Import
77 Columbia Street, Suite 17L
New York, NY 10002
Warehouse: 204 Delancey St., New York, NY 10002
E-Mail: Vegetarian Food @MCI2000.com
Tel: 212.353.9779 or 228.1803
Fax: 212.673.7260

Especially good are the vegetarian ham and the vegetarian big prawn

Arrowhead Mills
Box 2059
Hereford, Texas 79045-2059
Tel: 806.364.0730
Fax: 806.364.8242

Many different quality grains, beans and flours, and prepared products. Instant seitan mix. Products available in bulk sizes and custom-made blends available.

Archer Daniel Midland Company
Box 1470
Decatur, Illinois 62525
Clare Morganthaler
Tel: 217.362.8103 or 1.800.637.5824
Fax: 217.362.3959

Offers a variety of ready-to-cook vegan soy-based products under the ADM and Green Giant labels. Their line includes frozen soy burgers in several flavors, frozen sausage patties and links, and frozen ready-to-use browned burger bits for sauces and other preparations. Also available are dry mixes for burgers and loaf, chili, tacos, and sloppy Joes.

Athens Fillo
3600 Snow Road
Brook Park, OH 44142
Tel: 1.800.837.5683

Makers of traditional white fillo sheets and wheat fillo sheets by direct order. Premade fillo pastry cups available ready to fill and serve.

Aux Fines Herbes
301 East Street
New Britain, CT 06051
Tel: 860.224.3724

A specialty certified organic farming business, unique herbs, lettuces and vegetables.

The Bridge
Washington Street (Route 66)
Middletown, CT 06457
Tel: 860.346.3663

Traditional Japanese-style foods, including the best tofu I have ever tasted, along with seitan, amaske and some of their own salads and prepared products.

Carla's Pasta
275A Progress Drive
Manchester, CT 06040
Tel: 860.647.8647
Fax: 860.647.8572

Carla's offers a line of vegan and low-fat filled pasta products called Buona Salute which includes tofu-filled ravioli, tortellini, manicotti, and shells, and vegan basil pesto.

Certified Masters Corporation
Helmut Holtzer C.M.C.
6825 Shiloh Road East
Suite B6
Alpharetta, GA 30005
Tel: 1.800.261.5261

Specialty foods like truffle oil, organic grains and spices, custom-blended spice mixes to order, Stubai Cutlery and new-to-market items such as China's Secret Shanxi Vinegar.

Chieftain Wild Rice Company
1210 Basswood Avenue, P.O. Box 550
Spooner, WI 54801
Tel: 1.800.262.6368

Specialty grains including Red Corn Meal and Black Quinoa.

Ener-G

P.O. Box 84487

Seattle, WA 98124-5787

Tel: 1.800.331.5222

www.ener-g.com

Source for Ener-G egg replacer.

Future Foods

Andy Patterson

Tel: 1.773.561.0207

Fax: 1.773.561.0307

Full line of natural foods specializing in food service.

Krystyna's Pierogis

88 Commerce

East Berlin, CT

Tel: 1.860.829.6658

Krystyna's offers a line of pierogis made without added fat that include vegan-filled varieties such as the mushroom and cabbage or potato.

Mediterranean Delight

1.800.795.1734

Hummus, tabouli, baba ganouj, fresh falafel available; in institutional sized packages.

More than Gourmet

115 Bartges St.

Akron, OH 44311

Tel: 1.800.860.9385

Source for Veggie-Glace Gold, a vegetarian Meatless Demi-Glace Substitute

Cricklewood Soyfoods

Mertztown, PA 19539

Tel: 610.682.4109

Specialties: Three-Grain, Three-Bean, Balance (tempeh burger)
Soy Tempeh, Rice and Soy Tempeh

Florida Crystals

Distribution Center

8501 U. S. Highway 27

South Bay, FL 33493

Tel: 1.800.443.2767

http://www.floridacrystals.com

Evaporated cane juice. Organic available.

Franklin Farms

Franklin, CT

Tel: 1.860.642.3000

White, portobello, shiitake, cremini, and oyster mushrooms.

Lite Life Foods

P.O. Box 870

Greenfield, MA 01302

Tel: 1.800.451.4520

or 1.800.274.6001

Manufacturers of several varieties of tempeh with the three-grain and the soy with brown rice being my favorites. Lite Life also has developed many soy products such as their Tofu Pups and Smart Dogs, which are hot dog-like creations. Also available through Lite Life are burgers and soysage links and bulk-style mixtures in burger and sausage flavors.

Maine Coast Sea Vegetable

RR1 Box 78

Franklin, ME 04634

Tel: 207.565.2907

Fax: 207.565.2144

Source for dulse, kelp, nori, alaria certified organic (OCIA), various sizes from granulated, flaked or chopped to whole-leaf products depending on the type of sea vegetable. Also toasted sushi nori from China, smoked sea vegetables, sea vegetable pickles, and corn sea vegetable chips. Seasoning blends with ground spices and sea vegetables.

Philips Mushroom Farm

909 East Baltimore Pike

Kennet Square, PA 19348

Tel: 1.800.243.8644

Cultivated mushroom exotics such as portobello, shiitake, oyster and cremini.

Smoke & Fire
P.O. Box 743
Great Barrington, MA 01230
Tel: 413.528.6891
Fax: 413.528.1877

Naturally smoked and spiced ready to serve tofu and tempeh. Flavors such as Barbecue Lemon Garlic, Thai, and Savory Herb.

Stowe Mills, Chesterfield, NH
United Natural Foods Distributors
Tel: 1.800.451.5420

Full line of natural foods.

Succanat
Wholesome Foods
Tel: 904.258.4708

Sugar Cane Natural, dry sweetener with a brown sugar to molasses flavor.

Sunspire Chocolates
2114 Adams Avenue
San Leandro, CA 94577
Tel: 510.569.9763
Fax: 510.568.4948

Dairy-free grain malt-sweetened chocolate chips, cane syrup sweetened chocolate chips, both styles available in regular and dark chocolate.

Shedd Willow Run, Soy Margarine
1.800.735.3554

Available from natural foods distributors, has a better flavor than the commercial varieties and doesn't contain all the additives.

St. Maries Wild Rice
Tel: 1.800.225.9453
Fax: 1.208.245.9453

St. Maries, Idaho, offers a State Certified Organic wild rice that has three times been selected for a Chefs in America Gold Medal Award. Their wild rice is ecologically grown with environment enhancing techniques that respect and aid native wildlife inhabitants.

Equipment

All-Clad Metalcrafters
Kathy Fisher
Cannonsburg, PA
Tel: 1.800.All.Clad

Makers of excellent-quality clad cookware, available in a choice of outside finishes including aluminum, a stick-free bonded Ltd. Line, stainless steel, or copper. Inside of pans is available in either stainless steel or nonstick surface.

Hamilton Beach Blender

I use a blender as the best way to purée soups and sauces because of the gravity feed effect. Hamilton Beach offers a commercial-sized machine through its distributors.

Kitchen Aid
Att. Brian Maynard
2000 M 63 North
M. D. 4402
N. Benton Harbor, MI 49022
Tel: 616.923.4600

Manufacturer of many varieties of kitchen equipment. The excellent five-quart stand mixer is a great mixer with a power take off that can be attached to many other tools like a rotary slicer and a grain mill. The fairly new-to-market food processor is great on its own and as a bonus, it has a small workbowl that fits inside the larger bowl for small chopping jobs for which the regular bowl would be too big. Both of these machines were used for this book.

Recommended Reading

Cherie Soria, *Angel Foods*, California: Heartstar Productions, 1996.

Vesanto Melina, R.D., Brenda Davis, R.D., and Victoria Harrison R.D., *Becoming Vegetarian*, Tennessee: Book Publishing Company, 1995.

William Shurtleff and Akiko Aoyagi, *The Book of Tofu*, New York: Ballantine Books, 1975.

Rynn Berry, *Famous Vegetarians* and *Food for the Gods*, New York: Pythagorean Publishers.

Brother Ron Pickarski, O.F.M., *Friendly Foods* and *Eco-Cuisine*, California: Ten Speed Press, 1991.

Jack Czarnicki, *Joe's Book of Mushroom Cookery*, New York: Atheneum Publishers, 1986.

Nettie Cronish, *Nettie's Vegetarian Kitchen*, Toronto: Second Story Press, 1996.

Bryanna Clark Grogan, *Nonna's Italian Kitchen/Delicious Homestyle Vegan Cuisine*, Tennessee: Book Publishing Company, 1998.

Fran Costigan, *Vegan Baking 101*, self-published, 58 Hudson St. 10A, NYC, NY 10013.

Jackson F. Blackman, *Working Chef's Cookbook for Natural Foods*, Vermont: Central Vermont Publishers, 1989.

The following books are available through NAVS:

Jennifer Raymond, *The Peaceful Palate Cookbook*, also "Tips for introducing vegetarian food into institutions," guides for offering vegan menu items.

Joanne Stepaniak, *The Uncheese Cookbook*, dairy-free cheese substitutes and classic dishes made with them. Plus other titles.

Resources

Earth Save
600 Distillery Commons
Suite 200
Louisville, KY
40206-1922

Natural Hygiene (Society) Institute
P.O. Box 2132, Huntington, CT, 06484

The North American Vegetarian Society/NAVS
Box 72, Dolgeville, NY 13329
Tel: 518.568.7970
Resource with many books, guides and publications

People for the Ethical Treatment of Animals/PETA
501 Front St., Norfolk, VA 23510
Tel: 757.622.PETA
www.petaonline.org

Vegedine
George Eisman
3835 Route 414,
Burdett, NY 14818
Tel. 1.607.546.7171
Fax: 1.607.546.4091
Vegetarian and Vegan Home Study Nutrition Certificate Course.

VegeScan, database produced by
Soyfoods Center
PO Box 234, Lafayette, CA 94546-0234
Tel: 510.283.2991
Information on vegetarianism and commercial vegetarian products.
Depending on the amount of information requested there may be a fee.

Vegetarian Resource Group
P.O. Box 1463, Baltimore, MD 21203

Recipe Index

Subject Index